JEFFERSON DAVIS: THE ESSENTIAL WRITINGS

JEFFERSON DAVIS: THE ESSENTIAL WRITINGS

Edited, with an Introduction and Notes,

by William J. Cooper, Jr.

THE MODERN LIBRARY

NEW YORK

LIBRARY OF CONGRESS CATALOGING-IN-PUBLICATION DATA
Davis, Jefferson, 1808–1889.
[Selections 2003]
Jefferson Davis: the essential writings / edited, with an introduction and notes, by
William J. Cooper, Jr.—2003 Modern Library ed.
p.   cm.
Includes bibliographical references and index.
ISBN 0-8129-7208-2
1. Confederate States of America—History. 2. United States—Politics and
government—1815–1861. I. Cooper, William J. (William James). II. Title.

E467.1.D26 A25 2003
973.7'13'092—dc21   2002038017

Modern Library website address: www.modernlibrary.com
Printed in the United States of America

2 4 6 8 9 7 5 3 1

Acknowledgments

Several people have contributed notably to the making of this volume. Dr. Lynda L. Crist, editor of the ongoing letterpress edition of Jefferson Davis's papers, has once again been stalwart for me, unstintingly giving of her time and counsel. My departmental chair, Paul F. Paskoff, was as always most accommodating. M. J. Devaney of the Modern Library suggested this project and supported me throughout my work. My wife, Patricia Cooper, willingly extended Jefferson Davis's stay in her home. Three Louisiana State University (LSU) students—two undergraduates, Wayne Edmondson and Amanda Gustavson, and a graduate student, Marie Therese Champagne—provided indispensable assistance. In addition, Ms. Champagne furnished the translations from Latin.

For permission to publish documents I am grateful to individuals and institutions. The LSU Press generously agreed to permit the use of any material in *The Papers of Jefferson Davis*, which it publishes. Dr. William Richter of Kansas State University authorized the publication of one of the two earliest known Davis letters, which he owns. Librarians at the University of Alabama (Jefferson Davis Papers), Duke University (Jefferson Davis Papers), Seaver Center for Western History Research, Los Angeles County Museum of Natural History,

Pierpont Morgan Library (Gilder-Lehrman Collection on Deposit, GLC 5344.01), North Carolina Division of Historical Resources (Jefferson Davis Papers), and Transylvania University (Jefferson Davis Papers) all granted me permission to publish one or more letters from their collections. Likewise, the editors of the *Journal of American History, Journal of Mississippi History,* and *Journal of Southern History* allowed me to reproduce letters that had initially appeared in their pages, although the first of these was known as the *Mississippi Valley Historical Review* when the item I used was printed. Specifically, my reproductions came from: herein pages 430–31, *Journal of Mississippi History* (XXXI, 1969, 124–25); herein pages 9–11, 418–20, *Journal of Southern History* (XLI, 1975, 519–22, and X, 1944, 209–11); herein pages 407–9, *Mississippi Valley Historical Review* (XXV, 1931, 540-42).

All named in these acknowledgments helped make this book possible, but it is mine, and I accept full responsibility for it.

Contents

DOCUMENTS

INTRODUCTION

JEFFERSON DAVIS: HIS LIFE AND RECORD

William J. Cooper, Jr.

I

Jefferson Davis is a major figure in American history whose principal importance stems from his role in the central event in the country's history, the Civil War.* As president of the Confederate States of America, Davis directed the new nation's mighty struggle for independence. That massive effort failed. In four years of bloody warfare that claimed more than 600,000 American lives, the United States smashed the Confederate States. Even though Davis and his cause failed, the vastness of the war and the profound consequences resulting from it ensure its primacy and his prominence.

Yet Davis's notability does not come solely from his crucial role in the Civil War. Born on the Kentucky frontier in the first decade of the nineteenth century, he witnessed and participated in the epochal transformation of the United States from a fledgling country to a strong nation spanning the continent. In his earliest years his father moved farther south and west to Mississippi. As a young army officer just out of West Point, he served on the northwestern and southwestern frontiers in an army whose chief mission was to protect settlers surging

---

* For a full biography see William J. Cooper, Jr., *Jefferson Davis, American* (New York: Alfred A. Knopf, 2000).

westward. Then, in 1846 and 1847, as colonel of the First Mississippi Regiment, he fought in the Mexican War, which resulted in 1848 in the Mexican Cession, a massive addition to the United States of some 500,000 square miles, including California and the modern Southwest. As secretary of war and U.S. senator in the 1850s, he advocated government support for the building of a transcontinental railroad that he believed essential to bind the nation from ocean to ocean.

Davis cherished a vibrant United States. Not only did he participate in events that charted the country's growth, he shared in the sense of inevitable growth and progress that dominated the national outlook. The agricultural and industrial boom of the 1850s, along with the Mexican Cession, exemplified the inexorable march toward greater wealth and power in the United States.

Certain about America, Davis also had confidence in himself and in his ability to overcome any obstacle. Moreover, his own ambition matched the ambition he had for his country. From young manhood he struggled with a wide range of serious physical illnesses, but he never let their assaults on his body deter him from his course. He also knew deep sadness in his personal life, yet he never permitted that heavy veil to smother him with self-pity. He wanted to succeed, and he did. He became a successful planter, a war hero, and an influential politician whose career carried him into the highest councils of his country. Men spoke seriously about his becoming president.

As Davis witnessed the physical and economic development of his country, he envisioned no conflict between this progress and racial slavery. Growing up in a slave society, he accepted servitude as normal, as moral, and as American. His father was a small slaveholder who worked in the fields alongside his bondspeople. With the aid of his oldest brother Joseph, Jefferson Davis attained a social and economic status his father never did—great planter. Beginning with the one slave he inherited from his father, Davis in 1860 owned 113 slaves, who toiled on his cotton plantation, Brierfield, in Warren County, Mississippi. His personal history paralleled that of his country and state. In the United States between 1800 and 1860 the slave population more than quadrupled to over four million. In Davis's Mississippi cotton raised chiefly with slave labor brought wealth to both Davis and his state. The crop more than doubled in the last antebellum decade, with its value increasing to more than five million dollars.

In his public life Davis defended slavery as moral and as American while maintaining that the institution helped civilize and Christianize an inferior race. Although not all Americans joined his embrace of slavery, few dissented from his belief in the supremacy of the white race, an outlook shared in the nineteenth century by almost all white Americans and Western Europeans. Slave labor, he believed, could flourish in many venues, such as factories and mines, not just in cotton fields. As an owner of slaves, he wanted protection of slavery in his own interest. As a politician representing tens of thousands of slave owners and tens of thousands of aspiring slave owners, he deemed guarding slavery his duty.

When geographic expansion led to conflict over slavery in the territories, he insisted on the rights of slave owners as Americans to participate equally in the national bounty. He also feared where the energy of antislavery might lead, for he defined it chiefly as a political force—the North striving to wrest power from the South. Yet he was willing to compromise; he even advocated a division of the western territories following the example of the Missouri Compromise of 1820, which divided the Louisiana Purchase into an area where slavery would be prohibited and another where the institution would be permitted. Still, he refused to accept a complete prohibition. He was convinced that a substantial segment of northern opinion was prepared to honor what he considered the constitutional rights of the South.

In Davis's judgment the Constitution absolutely guaranteed protection and equal rights for the South and slavery. He always identified himself as a constitutional patriot and a biological as well as an ideological son of the American Revolution and the Founding Fathers. He was especially proud that his own father had fought for the patriot cause against England. Professing the United States a nation created by the sovereign states that upheld it, he looked to Thomas Jefferson, James Madison, and John C. Calhoun as the great explicators of states' rights and strict construction, of the proper understanding of the nation and the Constitution. In Davis's mind a continuum stretching over the decades connected these constitutional statesmen with their disciples of his time.

Davis rejected any notion of a contradiction between slavery and America. So many of the great national heroes who had won and preserved the independence of the nation and led its battalions against foreign foes were slaveholders—men such as George Washington, Thomas Jefferson, James Madison, Andrew Jackson, and Zachary Taylor. Furthermore, his view that the Constitution protected slavery was not at all unique. Most white Americans, Northerners included, shared that interpretation, and the U.S. Supreme Court emphatically sustained it. Davis dismissed as un-American the proposition propounded in the 1850s by the Republican party that the United States could not persist, in Abraham Lincoln's words, "permanently half *slave* and half *free*." A solid majority of Davis's fellow citizens concurred with his belief that slavery and freedom could continue to coexist, as they had since the birth of the nation. In the 1860 presidential election 60 percent of the voters cast their ballots for candidates who found no fundamental problem with slavery in America. The Republican Lincoln captured barely 40 percent of the popular vote, though, of course, he had an indisputable majority in the Electoral College.

Lincoln's election as president brought on the crisis of the Union, a Union Davis still prized. Although he had always preached the constitutionality of secession, he never advocated its implementation, not even in 1860. He still believed that significant Northern support for Southern rights remained, and he had no doubts about the guarantees in the Constitution. But powerful political currents gripped all— Northerners, Southerners, Democrats, Republicans. Compromise proved impossible. For Davis there was no question about his course. Secession was constitutional, and his loyalty to Mississippi underlay his allegiance to the United States. He left the Union with his state.

For Davis the Confederate States provided a way to save the America he had cherished. For him the Confederacy became the true descendant of the American Revolution and the Constitution. Preserving that sacred heritage made the Confederacy a holy cause. It must prevail, and Davis would adopt whatever measures he thought necessary to achieve victory, including the first national conscription law in American history. He contended that the Confederacy alone defended liberty. That guarding this precious liberty also involved sanctioning slavery posed him no problem. To Davis, as to most white southerners, their liberty had since the American Revolution always included their right to own slaves and their right to decide about the institution without outside interference. White liberty and black slavery were inextricably intertwined.

Davis committed himself utterly to the Confederacy and directed a titanic war on its behalf. His commitment to his cause was as total as that of his great antagonist on the other side. Neither he nor Lincoln would relent. To save the Confederacy, Davis even led his fellow Confederates toward an abandonment of slavery, chiefly by supporting the use of slaves as soldiers. Despite a mighty effort, the Confederacy was overwhelmed. Davis lost the war, but he clung to his cause.

Defeated, he could no longer wield a sword, yet he retained influence in the postwar years. His imprisonment between 1865 and 1867 endeared him to former Confederates, who saw him as suffering for their sake. In a fundamental sense he became the embodiment of the Lost Cause, an essential theme in the history of the South after 1865. Even more important, Davis articulated the outlook of the white South that shaped southern and national history from the 1870s to well into the twentieth century.

Although Davis accepted that the war had ended slavery, he did not alter his basic position on race relations. And he cheered the collapse of Reconstruction, which meant in part that northern whites came to the position southern whites had never relinquished: blacks remained inferior to whites, and their fortunes should be controlled by the superior race. Because more than 90 percent of black Americans still lived in the former slave states, those in control would be southern whites.

Davis also never backed away from his contention that secession was constitutional, and he insisted in the 1870s and 1880s that the Civil War was solely about states' rights and the Constitution, not about slavery. In addition, he preached the nobility of the Confederate cause. His views, which he never recanted, were enshrined in his *Rise and Fall of the Confederate Government,* which was published in 1881.

But Jefferson Davis was not mired in the past. Although he continued to maintain the constitutionality of secession, he said that it had now become part of history. According to him, it had been tried, had failed, and would not be attempted again; he certainly would not advocate it. In the last decade of his life he became more positive about the future. He spoke proudly about the grandeur of the United States, its growing wealth and power. He saw the future of his beloved South in its young people. He urged them to hold dear their Confederate heritage but not let the past entrap them. As for himself, Davis looked back with pride on the past and on his part in what had been. At the same time, he looked ahead with the anticipation of his youth. At the end he gloried in what he saw as a permanently reunited United States.

II

Although letters and papers of Jefferson Davis have appeared in print before, this book marks the first time that both the private and public spheres of his life have been covered in a single volume. There are two major multivolume editions of Davis documents. The older— Dunbar Rowland, ed., *Jefferson Davis, Constitutionalist: His Letters, Papers and Speeches,* 10 vols. (Jackson: Mississippi Department of Archives and History, 1923)—retains great value. Rowland was a scrupulous editor, and he included many items, especially speeches, not in the ongoing modern edition. Lynda L. Crist et al., eds., *The Papers of Jefferson Davis,* 11 vols. (Baton Rouge: Louisiana State University Press, 1971–), which to date has reached May 1865, constitutes an impressive achievement. Splendidly edited and thoroughly annotated, these volumes are paragons of the scholarly publications devoted to the papers of major American public figures, even though from the third volume the editors have been forced to be increasingly selective in what they print because there is so much material. For the Confederacy, both James D. Richardson, comp., *A Compilation of the Messages and Papers of the Confederacy . . . ,* 2 vols. (Nashville: United States Publishing Company, 1906; a second edition came out in 1966 and a third in 2001, both from Chelsea House Publishers), which contains Davis's messages to Congress and his proclamations, and *War of the Rebellion: A Compilation of the Official Records of the Union and Confederate Armies,* 70 vols. in 128 (Washington: Government Printing Office, 1880–1901, generally known as the *Official Records*), which has a massive amount of Davis's official wartime correspondence, are invaluable. Finally, there has been one prior effort to put some of Davis's private correspondence between two covers—Hudson Strode, ed., *Jefferson Davis: Private Letters, 1823–1889* (New York: Harcourt, Brace & World, 1966). This volume is most unsatisfactory because Strode was not a scrupulous editor. He apparently had little respect for the integrity of a document, for he repeatedly omitted substantive portions of letters without using ellipses or in any other way indicating the omissions.

The documents printed here have been chosen to span Davis's lifetime, from youth to old age, and also to illustrate his public career as political leader, defender of the South, and Confederate president. They are arranged chronologically so that a reader can sense the life Davis led as he led it. The massive amount of material, literally tens of thousands of documents, has forced me as editor to be harshly selective. Out of that immense trove I selected 216 documents for this edition. As part of that selectivity I decided to use only documents that Davis produced, letters as well as public papers. Thus this book includes no incoming correspondence. The first two documents, bearing the same date, are the earliest known Davis letters, and the last contains the final words he wrote.

The selection includes private letters, public letters, speeches, and official reports and messages. These documents portray an ambitious, albeit unsure, young man maturing into a successful planter and politician. The record, unfortunately, is much more extensive on the latter than the former, a fact apparent in these pages. During the Civil War the capture of Davis lands by Union forces resulted in the destruction of substantial material dealing with Davis as a slave-owning planter, rendering it impossible to treat fully that important part of his life. In contrast, a much richer corpus illustrates Davis's embrace of a political career—his rise from a novice Mississippi politician to congressman and ultimately to a powerful cabinet officer and U.S. senator, with a critical stint in the Mexican War along the way. The records make absolutely clear his sense of the Constitution and his vision of America.

He emphasized the rights of Southerners as Americans, rights he found guaranteed by the Constitution. He did not shy away from speaking about slavery, which he saw as central both to the South and to the sectional conflict. With all his strength he defended Southern institutions, chiefly slavery, against what he perceived as a Northern assault on the South. By the mid-1850s Davis identified this attack with the Republican party and defined it as a struggle for power.

While these documents denote Davis's prominence, they also record his private life. Throughout his life his family was immensely important to him. Even though the surviving documentation is frustratingly thin, it is clear that he adored his first love, Sarah Knox Taylor, who became his first wife but tragically died after only three months of marriage. Then, after almost a decade of seclusion as a planter, he ventured out personally as well as politically. Letters show an older man captivated by a younger woman, Varina Banks Howell. The thirty-six-year-old Davis fell in love with the eighteen-year-old Varina in 1844. They married the next year and shared the subsequent four and a half decades, until Davis's death in 1889. The correspondence charts the history of a relationship that moved from mutual adoration through turbulence to become a strong, enduring partnership forged during the crisis of war.

Davis's distress over disunion is readily apparent. He neither advocated nor desired secession, though he believed it constitutional. In his mind he was correctly convinced that he did all he possibly could to save the Union with his sense of Southern rights intact. But he also contributed to the political maelstrom that made meaningful compromise impossible in the winter of 1860–61.

A considerable number of the documents herein detail Davis's tenure as president of the Confederate States. They depict a different Davis from the leader usually described by historians. He surely understood the fragile nationalism within his new country, and he absolutely comprehended the political dimensions of the war. He made strenuous and generally effective efforts to define his cause and then convey that definition to his fellow Confederates. These records do not reveal Commander in Chief Davis as a micromanager who constantly interfered with his generals. Rather, they show a commander in chief who gave his generals significant latitude and discretion, undoubtedly too much too often. Public and private papers underscore his utter devotion to his cause. He gave total commitment and demanded the same from others. He would not and could not countenance normal human characteristics such as ambition and pride. Too often he based his judgments about people on his perceptions of whether their loyalty and dedication matched his own.

In the postwar years Davis's conviction about the rectitude of his actions and his cause never wavered. Yet he was also a man struggling to make a living for himself and his family while coping with incredibly vexing difficulties and profound heartbreak, including the deaths of two sons. Still, in the last decade of his life he evinced an optimism about the future, glorying in the growing wealth and power of a reunited United States.

III

Most of the documents presented in this volume have been previously published, chiefly in *Jefferson Davis, Constitutionalist* and *The Papers of Jefferson Davis*. Four have been printed in scholarly journals and one in an autograph catalog. The remainder—twelve from manuscript collections and one in private hands—have never before appeared in a modern scholarly edition. The location of each document is specified in parentheses at the end of the document title. The documents that have appeared elsewhere are exactly reproduced here, including such errors as misspellings and missed punctuation, as well as editorial insertions, except where specified.* The addressee—or in the case of a speech, report, or message, the identity and site—and the date are

---

* The documents reproduced from *PJD* contain a number of editorial symbols. Those most frequently used, with their definitions, follow:

    [text] editorial insertions, usually because manuscript was damaged

    <text> deviation from lineal presentation

    <-text-> strikeouts

    /text/ interlined words

    ~~text~~ struck-through word.

placed below the document title. Inside addresses are not included. In the heretofore unpublished documents the spelling and punctuation in the originals have been retained. When the entire document has not been printed, ellipses indicate where material has been omitted. Overwhelmingly, the letters are complete, but many of the public documents have been edited to emphasize the most critical portions. In order not to detract from the papers themselves, I have kept annotation to a minimum, identifying only the most important people, places, and events.

———

WILLIAM J. COOPER, JR., is Boyd Professor of History at Louisiana State University. His most recent book is *Jefferson Davis, American,* winner of the 2001 *Los Angeles Times* Book Prize in Biography and the Jefferson Davis Award. He lives in Baton Rouge.

CHRONOLOGY

1808   June 3, born in Christian (now Todd) County, Kentucky

1810   Family moved to Wilkinson County, Mississippi, after a brief stay in the Bayou Teche country of southern Louisiana

1816–18   Student at St. Thomas College near Springfield, Kentucky

1818–23   Student at Jefferson College near Natchez, Mississippi, and at Wilkinson County Academy in Woodville, Mississippi

1823–24   Student at Transylvania University in Lexington, Kentucky

1824   July 4, death of father, Samuel Emory Davis

1824–28   Cadet at U.S. Military Academy, West Point, New York; July 1, 1828, graduated and was commissioned second lieutenant

1829–35   Active duty on various assignments and posts in the current states of Illinois, Iowa, Missouri, Oklahoma, and Wisconsin; May 1834, promoted to first lieutenant; May 1835, resigned commission

1835   Began career as planter (his plantation known as Brierfield), Davis Bend, Warren County, Mississippi (initially lived with oldest brother, Joseph, on his plantation, Hurricane, which adjoined Brierfield); June 17, married Sarah Knox Taylor near Louisville, Kentucky; September 15, death of Sarah Knox Taylor Davis near St. Francisville, Louisiana; late summer and fall, seriously ill with malaria

1835–36   Winter, traveled to Cuba

1837–38   Winter–spring, traveled to Northeast, especially New York City and Washington

1843   Unsuccessful candidate for Mississippi legislature

1844   Presidential elector for Democratic ticket in Mississippi

1845   February 26, married Varina Banks Howell in Natchez; spring, completed first residence at Brierfield; October 3, death of mother, Jane Cook Davis; November 4, elected to U.S. House of Representatives; December 8, sworn in as congressman

1846   June 18, elected colonel of the First Mississippi Regiment; July 29 or 30, arrived in Rio Grande Valley; September 21–23, Battle of Monterrey; October 17, resigned from House; October 18, granted sixty-day furlough and visited Mississippi

1847   February 23, wounded at Battle of Buena Vista; June, returned to Mississippi; August 10, appointed to U.S. Senate; December 6, sworn in as senator

1848   January 11, elected to U.S. Senate

1850   Fall, completed second residence at Brierfield

1851   September 16, nominated as State Rights Democratic candidate for governor; September 23, resigned from U.S. Senate; mid-September–mid-October, seriously ill with eye disease; November 3–4, defeated for governor of Mississippi

1852   July 30, birth of son, Samuel Emory Davis

1853   March 5, appointed secretary of war by President Franklin Pierce; March 7, sworn in as secretary of war; July 11–September 9 (intermittently), traveled in Northeast, including New England

1854   June 13, death of son, Samuel Emory Davis

1855   February 25, birth of daughter, Margaret Howell Davis

1856   January 16, elected to U.S. Senate (to take seat on March 4, 1857)

1857   January 16, birth of son, Jefferson Davis, Jr.; March 4, sworn in as senator

1858   February 11–May 9, seriously ill with eye disease; July 3–October 22, traveled to Boston, Maine, and New York City

1859   April 18, birth of son, Joseph Evan Davis; late May–early June, underwent eye surgery

1860   November, Republican candidate Abraham Lincoln elected president of the United States; December 20, South Carolina seceded; December 21–28, served on Senate's special Committee of Thirteen

1861   January 9, Mississippi seceded; January 21, delivered farewell speech in Senate; February, returned to Mississippi; February 4, delegates from Deep South states met in Montgomery, Alabama, to create the Confederate States of America; February 9, elected provisional president of the Confederate States; February 16, arrived in Montgomery; February 18, inaugurated provisional president; April 12, firing on Fort Sumter, South Carolina, beginning of Civil War; May 29, arrived in Richmond, Virginia, new capital of Confederate States; July 21–23, visited battlefield at Manassas, Virginia, site of first great battle of war; November 6, elected, without opposition, president of Confederate States; December 6, birth of son, William Howell Davis

1862   February 22, inaugurated president of Confederate States; December 9, 1862–January 4, 1863, first western trip (North and South Carolina, Georgia, Tennessee, Alabama, Mississippi)

1863   January 4, returned from first western trip; July 1–3, Battle of Gettysburg; July 4, fall of Vicksburg; October 6–November 7, second western trip (North and South Carolina, Georgia, Tennessee, Alabama, Mississippi)

1864   April 30, death of son, Joseph Evan Davis; June 27, birth of daughter, Varina Anne Davis; September 20–October 6, third western trip (North and South Carolina, Georgia, Alabama)

1865   April 2, evacuation of Richmond; April 3–10, in Danville, Virginia, temporary seat of government; April 9, surrender of Robert E. Lee and his army at Appomattox Court House, Virginia; April 10–May 10, flight south and west; April 26, surrender of Joseph E. Johnston and his army near Durham, North Carolina; May 10, captured near Irwinville, Georgia; May 22, imprisoned at Fortress Monroe, Virginia

1867   May 13, released on bail; May, in Canada (Montreal and Lennoxville) with family; November 1867–March 1868, traveled to United States, especially Richmond and Mississippi

1868 March, returned to Lennoxville; July, departed for Europe (with family); August 1868–October 1869, in Europe (England, France, Scotland, Switzerland)

1869 February 26, U.S. government dropped all charges against Davis; October, returned to United States (alone); November, named president of Carolina Life Insurance Company (headquartered in Memphis, Tennessee, where Davis resided)

1870 August, second European trip (England, Ireland, Scotland); September 18, death of brother, Joseph E. Davis; November, returned to Memphis (accompanied by wife)

1872 October 16, death of son, William Howell Davis

1873 August, resigned as president of Carolina Life; company dissolved

1874 January, third European trip (England, France, Scotland; unaccompanied by wife); June, returned to Memphis

1875 June–August, traveled to Colorado, Missouri, and Kentucky; August, returned to Memphis

1876 January 1, marriage of Margaret Howell Davis to J. Addison Hayes in Memphis; January, named president of U.S. branch of Mississippi Valley Society (headquartered in New Orleans, where Davis resided); May–November, fourth European trip (England, France, Germany; accompanied by wife); November, returned to New Orleans (unaccompanied by wife); December, employment disappeared along with Mississippi Valley Society

1877 January, moved to Beauvoir, near Biloxi, Mississippi (home of his benefactress, Sarah E. Dorsey)

1878 May, regained ownership of Brierfield; May, joined at Beauvoir by wife; October 16, death of son, Jefferson Davis, Jr.

1879 July 4, death of Sarah E. Dorsey, who bequeathed Beauvoir to Davis; Beauvoir remained his residence for the rest of his life

1881 June, publication of *The Rise and Fall of the Confederate Government*; August, fifth European trip (England and France; accompanied by wife); December, returned to Mississippi

1886   April–May, traveled to Montgomery, Alabama, and Atlanta, Georgia, for celebrations of the Confederacy and to Savannah, Georgia, for patriotic celebration; November, traveled to his birth site in Kentucky

1887   October, traveled to Macon, Georgia, for celebration of the Confederacy

1889   December 6, died in New Orleans, Louisiana

Abbreviations

DU   Duke University, Durham, North Carolina, William R. Perkins Library

JD   Jefferson Davis

JDC   Dunbar Rowland, ed., *Jefferson Davis, Constitutionalist: His Letters, Papers and Speeches,* 10 vols. (Jackson: Mississippi Department of Archives and History, 1923)

JMH   *Journal of Mississippi History*

JSH   *Journal of Southern History*

LAM   Seaver Center for Western History Research, Los Angeles County Museum of Natural History, Los Angeles, California

MVHR *Mississippi Valley Historical Review*

NC   North Carolina Division of Historical Resources, Raleigh, North Carolina

PJD   Lynda L. Crist et al., eds. *The Papers of Jefferson Davis,* 11 vols. (Baton Rouge: Louisiana State University Press, 1971–)

PM   The Pierpont Morgan Library, New York, New York

TR   Transylvania University, Lexington, Kentucky

UA   University of Alabama, Tuscaloosa, Alabama, W. Stanley Hoole Special Collections Library

JEFFERSON DAVIS: THE ESSENTIAL WRITINGS

To Amanda Davis Bradford (*William L. Richter*)*

LEXINGTON, KENTUCKY, AUGUST 2, 1824

DEAR SISTER,

A few days since I received the *sad* intelligence that our *Father was no more.*† Separated as I am from every friend on earth, save some that I have *made since* I have been here, I have been doomed twice to receive the lamentable news, of the Death of that friend. You must conceive, I cannot describe, the anguish I felt at the news of the Death of my Father: he was a parent ever dear to me, but rendered more so (if possible,) by the disasterous storms that attended the winter of his old age.

When I saw him last, he told it was probable we should never meet again. I then hoped to see him again, but his fears have been but too true, and much do I fear the list of misfortunes to be greatly increased, as I leave here for West Point, where I will probably remain four years, in about a week: and where I shall expect to hear from you. It was no desire of mine to go on, but as Brother Joseph evinced some anxiety for me to do so, I was not disposed to object. Excuse the brevity of my letter. Kiss Benn and little Davy for Uncle Jeff. Present me affectionately to Brother David.‡ And accept to yourself the

SINCERE REGARD
OF YOUR BROTHER,
JEFFERSON

---

* JD's sister, who married David Bradford.
† JD's father, Samuel Emory Davis, died on July 4, 1824.
‡ JD's nephews, Benjamin and David Bradford, and his brother-in-law.

To Susannah Gartley Davis (PJD)*

LEXINGTON, KENTUCKY, AUGUST 2, 1824

DEAR SISTER,

It is gratifying to hear from a friend, especially one from whom I had not so long as yourself, but the intelligence contained in yours, was more than <sufficient to mar> the satisfaction of hearing from anyone. You must imagine, I cannot describe the shock my feeling sustained, at that sad intelligence. In my Father I lost a parent ever dear to me, but rendered more so (if possible), by the disasters that attended his dclining years.

When I saw him last, he told we would probably never see each other again, but I still hoped to meet him once more But Heaven has refused my wish. This is the second time, I have <been> doomed to receive the heart rending intelligence of the *Death* of a *friend*. God only knows, whether or not it will be the last. If all the dear friends of my childhood are to be torn from earth, I care not how soon I may follow. I leave in a short time for West-Point, State of New York, where <-I-> it will always give me pleasure to hear from you. Kiss the Children for Uncle Jeff. Present me affectionately to Brother Isaac, tell him I would be happy to hear from him. And to yourself the sincere regard of Your Brother,

JEFFERSON

To Joseph Emory Davis (PJD)†

WEST POINT, NEW YORK, JANUARY 12, 1825

DEAR BROTHER,

Yours of the 13th was gratefully received last night, was supprised that you had not received a letter from me for the time specified, on

---

* JD's sister-in-law, married to his brother Isaac D.

† JD's eldest brother. Twenty-four years older than JD, his youngest sibling, Joseph became JD's surrogate father.

opening a letter from Sister L, Stamps & finding the same complaint, when I recollected having <written> to both her and yourself at the sametime concluded, (what you least expected to be the cause of not having heard from me,) that something had happened to the mail.*

As for your fear that I might be confined in the guard-house I trust ever to have enough prudence to keep from being confined.

You mentioned Brother Isaac had some intention of moving to Kentucky. I hope this only a romantic notion of his, which will die away as soon as it arose. Kentucky being the last <place> I would go to for the purpose of making a subsistence.

The long silence of both Brothers Isaac, & Saml has not a little surprised me.† I opened a communication and finished it, so let it rest.

Say to Florida‡ I received her letter and answered, addressing at St Francisville the place whence she wrote me. If you bring her on with you I have no doubt but the trip will be improving and interesting to her, it would besides give me great pleasure to see her.

I have to make a request of you which having made so often before, I feel a delicacy in making again, indeed I had not expected it would be necessary again, but it is that you would if convenient in your next remit me some Cash, I expect my pay generally to satisfy every demand, hope entirely, which however depends entirely upon the company I keep. *The Yankee part of the corps find their pay entirely sufficient some even more, but these are* <not> *such as I formed an acquaintance with on* my arrival, it having originated in the introductory letters I brought on with me; *nor are they such associates as I would* <-illegible-> *at present select,* enough of this as you have never been connected with them, you cannot know *how pitiful they generally* are.

Am happy to hear of the restoration of your health, I hope after your visit to the North you will entirely <feel> free from the effects of the ill health you have lately experienced.

Let me hear from you. Your Brother,

JEFFERSON

---

* JD's sister, who married William Stamps.
† Samuel A. Davis.
‡ Florida Ann Davis, Joseph's daughter.

Record of Delinquencies of the Corps of Cadets (PJD)*

WEST POINT, NEW YORK, JUNE 5, 1828

DAVIS. J

Absent from G[uar]d Mounting	16 Oct 1824
Dis[obedience] of ord[ers]	17
Absent from g[uar]d mounting	17
Visiting in Study Hours	3 Nov
Dis[obedience] of ord[ers]	18
Violation of 93. Par. Reg.	28. "
" " " " "	13 Feb 1825
" " " " "	5 March
Fender insecurely placed	19
Door not Closed	28.
Visiting in Study Hours	31.
Ab[sent] from qrs.	"
" " "	6. April
" " Class parade	6.
Late at " "	6.
Absent from qrs.	12 April
Bad police	13.
Ab[sent] from qrs.	14.
" " marching to French	18.
Cot down after reveille.	23.
Ab[sent] from qrs. from 7 'til 11. P.M.	23.
Ab[sent] from Reveille	23.
Ab[sent] from qrs. from 8 untill 9 P.M.	23.
Long hair at Inspection.	24.
Dis[obedience] of B[attalion] O[rder] No 40.	17. May.
Ab[sent] from drill	8 June
Bed not strapped 30' after rev[eille]	17.
Room not policed	24.
Not Marching from Mess Hall	5 July

---

* JD was not a model cadet. This record specifies the range of violations that brought him many demerits. In his senior year JD amassed 137 demerits, which in the corps as a whole ranked him 163 of 208.

Orderly paper not posted	17
Ab[sent] from 12 O Clock Drill	29
" " Eve[ning] Parade	31
In rear rank at Ev[ening] Parade	4 Augt.
Candlestick out of Place	10 Sepr.
Carrying his musket improperly on Drill	12
Dis[obedience] of Post order No 117	26
Bed not strapped 30' after rev[eille]	29
Candlesticks out of order	3 Oct

Excused

Name not Posted as orderly	"
Bad Police. (Foul clothes not in Clothes Bag)	2 Novr
Ab[sent] from Art[iller]y drill	9
Dis[obedience] of Special order and not to be found for drill	9
Ab[sent] from Inf[antr]y drill	11
Making unnecessary noise in S[tudy] H[ours]	27
Ab[sent] from Church	27
" " Qrs. in S[tudy] H[ours]	4 23 Decr.
Visiting in S[tudy] H[ours]	3 31.
" " " "	3 31.
Ab[sent] from Reveille	5 9 March
" " Parade	5 11
" " Reveille	5 20
" " "	5 28
Leaving the Academy during the first hour of recitation	6 28
Neglect of Fender	3 4 April
Bed not strapped 30' after Reveille	7 11
Ab[sent] from qrs. between 7 & 8 PM	3. 11
" " Parade	5 24
Improper conduct firing his musket from the window of his room	2 2 May
In bed after reveille	7 14
Late at reveille	7 June
Bed not strapped	23
Neglect of duty as Compy Police Officer	21 *July*
Neglect of Police	1 25 Nov
Us[in]g Sp[iri]t[ou]s Liquors	8 25 Decr

Disord[erl]y conduct in B[arrac]ks	4 " "
Ab[sent] from Qrs after taps	8 24 "
Ab[sent] from church	8 April 1827
Dis[o]b[edienc]e of special order in not going to Church when ordered	" "
Allowing noise on his post	13 "
Ab[sent] from Philosophy	14 "
In Bed after Rev[eille]	27 "
Absent from Qrs (12 & 1) A.M.	29 "
Inattention on drill	7 June
Ab[sent] from Qrs. (8 & 9) P.M.	12
" " Drill	28 July
In bed 30 min after Rev[eille]	12 [illegible] 1827
Leaving the mess hall without permission	6 Aug
Ab[sent] from B[arrac]ks (8.9) P.M	2 Sept
In rear rank at parade	5 "
Ab[sent] from Laboratory	6 "
" " parade	20 "
Out of uniform in mess sq[ua]d	" "
Going to mess-Hall without Marching	18 "
Spitting on the floor	4 Oct
Inattention on p[ara]d[e]	21 Nov
Bed not strapped 30' after Rev[eille]	2 Decb'
In mess hall after the Batt[alion]s [Rise?]	25
Bed not made 30' after Rev[eille]	31 " 1828
Vis[itin]g (10 & 11) A.M.	5 Jany
Cooking in Qrs. (7 & 8) P. M	18 "
Abs[ent] from Church	19 Feby
Not n[oting?] ch[angin]g[?] off[icer] G[uar]d	" "
In bed 30' after Reve[ille]	15 March
Visiting 11 & 12	2 Apl
Going to Engineering before the proper time	12 "
Visiting 3 & 4	16 "
Ab[sent] from Reve[ille]	27 "
" " "	11 May
" " "	13 May
In bed 30' after Reve[ille]	13 "
Abs[ent] from Qrs. after Taps	5 June

To Lucinda Davis Stamps (JSH)

Fort Winnebago, Ouisconsin Portage, Michigan Territory,
June 3, 1829

Dear Sister

Shortly after my arrival here I wrote to you giving you some account of my trip and will now give you some account of my situation which is one of the most elevated in the country by which I do not mean that I am near the highest station of the nation but that the Portage is the summit level of the western and Eastern wateres the ouisconsin running into the Mississippi and the Fox into Green Bay which communicates with the lakes the Fort is on the Fox the country around being prairie is now beautiful and being studded by islands of woods possesses by a variety in the scene an advantage over most Prairies the Fox is a sluggish and very crooked river its banks low and the grass grows to the waters edge which makes it look beautiful at a distance the water so clear that you see the fish swimming all through it and affording a fine opportunity for gigging, the officers of the Post are like those of the army generally men of light habits both of thinking and acting having little to care about and less to anticipate, promotion does not depend on merit at all and the duties being plain there is but small inducement to study and as you readily suppose they like other men will not labour for the love of it. Their manners are genteel and as far as morality is deemed necessary in the intercourse of men of the world it is strictly observed dissipation less common than among the citizens of Mississippi and drunkards not to be found in the army at this time and as fast as young ones grow up they are dismissed from the service.

Yours of March 17th arrived yesterday forwarded from Jefferson Bks.[*] You cannot Dear Sister regret more than myself our more distant seperation but perhaps next year I may be stationed near you perhaps I may be sent further from you perhaps remain stationary but I think the first perhaps most probable. I cannot say that I like the army

---

[*] Jefferson Barracks was an army post near St. Louis.

but I know of nothing else that I could do which I would like better your partiality for me has caused you to anticipate too much from me I believe that if I had returned home from Lexington I might have made a tolerably respectable citizen but now I do not believe I could get along well with citizens for the four years I remained at west Point made me a different creature from that which nature had designed me to be I shall however endeavour to improve myself as much as circumstances will permit I have sent on to New York for some books among others some law Books which I intend to make when I can procure such a considerable part of my reading my means and situation in life prevent me from buying any thing like a course of professional books but I shall be stationed at some place when I leave this where they can probably be hired and returned if I should be suddenly ordered to another post. I was ordered to join the troops at Jefferson Barracks because that was the head-Quarters of the Infantry I was retained there because it was the school of Infantry practice and I did not belong to any Regiment I was afterwards assigned to the first Regiment of Infantry and ordered to report to it's head Quarters which was at Prairie Du Chien on my arrival at head Quarters I was ordered to this post because it was thought my services were most required here.

I Know you feel an anxiety to Know what I expect to do and if I had any definite plan I would most willingly unfold it to you but as I have not I will give you a sort of composition the chief ingredient of which I am afraid you will say is nothing I intend to read with a view to acquire general information & to mix with general, legal reading if at anytime I should determine on a civil course of life I think I would prefer the practice of law to any other profession and [if] I should remain in the army a Knowledge of law [will qualify me?] the better for the duties of Judge Advocate whic[h] [is?] an honorable and frequently pleasing and profita[ble] duty. To day I am 22 years old when I was a boy and dreamed with my eyes open as most do I thought of ripening fame at this age of wealth and power as I grew older I saw the folly of this but still thought that at the age of 22 I should be on the high way to all ambition desired and lo: I am 22 and the same obscure poor being that I was at fifteen with the exception of a petty appointment which may long remain as small as it is at present—and yet I am not dissatisfied for I behold myself a member though an humble one of an honorable profession one in which sychophancy though it may be beneficial is not necessary to success and the close of which will be a mere stoppage of the current, not attended by the maledictions which so often hang round the closing scene of the politician whose struggles begun in folly are closed in disgrace.

I fulfilled Mr. Stamps's expectations in writing to him the second letter before I left Missouri and hope to hear from him shortly.[*] Miss Hooke's marriage was regretted by some of the officers here who were acquainted with her as they said because she had married a man unworthy of her. Tell William he must not forget me though I am far from him and that I hope to see him before he gets married unless he should be in a hurry in which case I do not wish him to wait for my arrival. When you write to me give me all the news of the family and do not believe any thing which con[c]erns you too small to interest me.

The diamond breast pin you gave me was universally admired by the Missouri girls and drew an attention in ball rooms which if I had been about four years younger might have made me vain but as it was I was disposed to believe they viewed it as the index of a Cotton plantation and if so the poor creatures would have been wofully dissappointed if enticed by the index they had examined the contents but I did not of course put myself to the trouble of telling them this. Remember me affectionately to Mother and tell her I will [write] to her shortly

I hope some day to be permanently settled near you but if I never should if the distance between us should increase with time of separation still will my affections remain unchanged and unchangeable my reflections will often be about you and my greatest happiness consist in the Knowledge of your welfare and those who are to us an object of common anxiety. I feel something like the pain of leaving you but letters like meetings must have an end. You will doubtless think this one long enough.

FAREWELL YOUR BROTHER

J. F. DAVIS[†]

---

[*] William Stamps, JD's brother-in-law.

[†] JD did have a middle name, but only the initial *F.* survived. He used it at West Point but dropped it completely in early manhood.

To Sarah Knox Taylor (PJD)*

FORT GIBSON [UNORGANIZED TERRITORY], DECEMBER 16, 1834†
Tis strange how superstitious intense feeling renders us. but stranger
still what aids chance sometimes brings to support our superstition,
dreams my dear Sarah we will agree are our weakest thoughts, and yet
by *dreams* have I been latly almost crazed, for they were of you and the
sleeping immagination painted you not such as I left you, not such as I
could like and see you, for you seemed a sacrifice to your parents desire the bride of a wretch that your pride and sense equally compelled
you to despise, and a <-illegible-> creature here, telling the on dits
of the day at St Louis said you were "about to be married to a Doctor Mc[Laraine?]" a poor devil who served with the Battalion of
Rangers possibly you may have seen him—but last night the vision
was changed you were at the house of an Uncle in Kentucky, Capt
McCree was walking with you when I met you he left you and you
told me of your Father and of yourself almost the same that I have
read in your letter to night. Kind, dear letter, I have kissed it often
and it has driven many mad notions from my brain. Sarah whatever I
may be hereafter I will ascribe to you. Neglected by you I should be
worse than nothing and if the few good qualities I possess shall under
your smiles yield a fruit it will be your's as the grain is the husband-
man's.

It has been a source productive of regret with me that our union
must seperate you from your earliest and best friends, a test to which
the firmness of very few are equal, though giddy with passion or
bouant by the hope of reconciliation there be many who brave it, from
you I am prepared to expect all that intellect and dignified pride
brings, the question as it has occured to you is truly startling Your own
answer is the most grattifying to me, is that which I should expected
from you, for as you are the first with whom I ever ought to have one
fortune so you would be the last from whom, I would expect desertion.

---

* JD's fiancée, daughter of Zachary Taylor. They were married on June 17, 1835; she died on
September 15, 1835.
† In Oklahoma.

When I wrote to you I supposed you did not intend soon to return to Kentucky. I approve entirely of your preference to a meeting elsewhere than at Prarie-du-Chien and your desire to avoid any embarrassment might widen the breach made already cannot be greater than my own, did I know when you would be at St Louis I could meet you there. At all events we meet in Kentucky. Shall we not soon meet Sarah to part no more? oh! how I long to lay my head upon that breast which beats in unison with my own, to turn from the sickening sights of worldly duplicity and look in those eyes so eloquent of purity and love. Do you remember the "hearts ease" you gave me, it is bright as ever—how very gravely you ask leave to ask me a question. My dear girl I have I no secrets from you, have a right to ask me any question without an apology. Miss Bullitt did not give me a guard for a watch but if she had do you supose I would have given it to *Capt* Mccree. But Ill tell you what she did give me, [torn] most beautifell and lengthy lecture on my and your charms, the which combined, once upon an evening at a "fair" in Louisville, as she was one of the few subjects of conversation we had apart from ourselves on that evening you can & I have left you to guess what beside a sensibility to your charms constituted my offence. the reporters were absent and the speech I made is lost.

<Pray what manner of messages could la belle Elvin have sent you concerning me? I supose no attempt to destroy harmony. I laughed at her demonstrations against the attachment existing between myself a subaltern of Dragoons but that between you and I is not fair, gains it is robbing to make another poor, but No! She is too discerning to attempt a thing so difficult and in which sucess would be valueless. "Miss Elizabeth one very handsome; lady" Ah; Knox what did you put that semicolon between handsome and lady for? I hope you find in the society of the Prarie enough to amuse if not to please The griefs over which we weep are not those to be dreaded. It is the little pains the constant falling of thy drops of care which wear away the heart, I join you in rejoicing that Mrs McCree is added to your society. I admire her more than anyone else you could have had Since I wrote to you we have abandoned the position in the Creek Nation and are constructing quarters at Ft Gibson

My lines like the beggars days are dwindling to the shortest span. Write to me immediately My dear Sarah My betrothed No formality is proper between us. Adieu Ma chere tres chere amie adieu au Recrire

JEFFN.>

To *Joseph Emory Davis* (PJD)

WASHINGTON, D.C., JANUARY 2, 1838

DEAR BROTHER,

You have probably learned through the correspondence of Mr. Van Benthuysen of my arrival at and departure from New York˙—when I reached Baltimore I was too unwell to proceed, a Surgeon of the Army who was travelling from Philad. with me stopped and attended to me the next day was much better, went a few miles into the country to see some late importations of the "Short Horned Durhams" very superior to any I had seen before, & on the following morning continued my journey to this place. I arrived here <Dec. 26th> with a severe cough and considerable fever, which latter became intermittent and has confined me to my room until yesterday, I believe I am now free of disease but the unfavorable weather renders me fearful of exposure and I am to day a prisoner. I have therefore as you will suppose little news. Yesterday the President's rooms were thrown open to "all the world" I went up the house was closely crowded and being weak of body and luke warm of spirit I hung like a poor boy at a frolick about the empty corners for a short time and left the House without being presented.

I have been disappointed at not hearing from you at this place and if you had been in time past a punctual correspondent should be very anxious on account of silence.

It is expected that three Regiments of Infantry will be added to the Army this year—tomorrow I hope I shall be able to call on such persons as I know in public life here and adding the Missi. delegation to whom I must become known, review the whole & then endeavor to estimate what influence I can bring to bear on my purpose.

˙ Watson Van Benthuysen, Joseph Davis's brother-in-law.

The Mississippi Election is before the house of Rep. the committee to whom the question was referred will probably report to day—it is said that courtesy required the reference &c but that no change can be anticipated, to-morrow Mr. Calhoun will introduce his resolution denying the right of the abolitionists to petition the senate as they have done and Mr. Morris will follow with his counter resolutions which you will probably see in the paper of last week—the Vermont Senators also on the part of the Vermont Legislature will present memorials of like character, they are said to be unfavorably disposed to the documents themselves—and altogether it is hoped that the discussion will be calmly conducted at least more so than heretofore.*

My love to all the family. Remember me to James.† Write to me when you can affectionately your Brother

JEFFN

To William Allen (PJD)‡

WARREN COUNTY, MISSISSIPPI, JULY 24, 1840

"I long hae thought my honored friend

A something to hae sent ye," and though I have nothing now more than my thanks for your kind recollection of me and these in my heart I have often returned to you. I take the occasion of your return from the sphere of your public duties—to break perhaps you will say the only repose which those duties leave you to enjoy—well, I bring my offering of thanks, the sacrifice of a pure spirit would always burn, I am willing that mine should be adjudged by that test.

I received your speech of Feby. eleventh on the assumption of state debts and could but illy express to you the gratification it gave me as your friend and as such I candidly tell you, I consider it the best English sample of the Demosthenean style. I recollect you saw in Mr.

---

* John C. Calhoun, U.S. senator from South Carolina, and Thomas Morris, U.S. senator from Ohio.

† James Pemberton, JD's first slave, an inheritance from his father. Pemberton was JD's overseer at Brierfield until his death in 1850.

‡ U.S. senator from Ohio; JD met him in Washington in 1838.

Calhoun's speech on the independent Treasy, an especial likeness to the grecian orator I thought he was too sententious, nor indeed could anyone opening a question of expediency or dwelling on details of finance speak as Demosthenes did when he addressed men nearly as well informed as himself on the subject of which he spoke and addressed them not to argue but to lay bare before them the true issue and excite them to action—but perhaps like the Vicar of Wakefield said to the lecturer on Cosmogony you may say to me—however with this difference that instead of once you may have heard all this a dozen times before and that instead of the second it is the first time you have heard it from me.

Before I quit the subject of speeches I must tell you of an old democratic friend of mine who lives some distance back in the hills and who notwithstanding the great increase of Post Offices is quite out of striking distance of a mail line—he came to see me in the spring of '38 I handed him your speech on the independent Treasy. Bill after reading it, he asked me to let him take it home and show it to some of his neighbors. I have seen him frequently since but his "neighbors" have not yet gotten through with it—when Lord Byron saw an American edition of his works he said it seemed like to posthumous fame—recurring to my old friend of the hills, he states it as a political maxim that "no honest sensible whig can read Allen's and Benton's speeches without turning their politics'"

I am living as retired as a man on the great thoroughfare of the Mississippi can be, and just now the little society which exists here—about has been driven away by the presence of the summer's heat and the fear of the summer's disease.

Our Staple, Cotton, is distressingly low and I fear likely to remain so until there is a diminished production of it, an event which the embarassed condition of cotton planters in this section will not allow them to consider—if our Yankee friends and their coadjutors should get up a scheme for bounties to particular branches of industry I think the cotton growers may come in with the old plea of the manufacturers "not able at present to progress without it."

˙ Thomas Hart Benton, U.S. senator from Missouri.

With assurances of sincere regard of the pleasure it will always give me to hear from you and to mark your success I am yr. friend

JEFFN. DAVIS

To Varina Banks Howell (PJD)*

HURRICANE, WARREN COUNTY, MISSISSIPPI, MARCH 8, 1844†
MY OWN DEAREST VARINA,

I cannot express to you my gratitude for your kind letter; when the "Concordia" put out the letters and I looked in vain in the package for one from you by which I might hear *of you* for I did not expect you would write *to me*, my heart sunk within me, my fears painted you sick, unable to write, Some hours afterwards Sister Eliza handed me your letter, it was more than I had hoped for, it was what I wished, it came to dispel my gloomy apprehensions, to answer the longings of a love so selfish that it wished you to overcome your unwillingness to write to me, in other words to struggle against your own opinions to gratify my feelings.‡

When the weak cord is stretched it breaks, the strength of the strong one is proved by the trial. Ephemeral passion or accidental preference is withered by seperation; sincere affection is sufficient for it's own support, by absence it is not cast down, neither is it heightened, the latter will, however, often seem to be the effect because in losing that which is essential to our happiness we are brought most actively to realize it's value. Your letter is proof that absence has thus acted on you, when we parted you did not (I believe) intend to write to me. You are always such as I wish you.

I am truly obliged by the defence put in for me by my friend the Judge, yet it is no more than I expected from him, his discretion keeps him so free from error, that he can give his charity to the errors of others, and it is but in Keeping with his discriminating analyzing mind to

---

* JD's fiancée; they were married on February 26, 1845.

† Hurricane was the name of Joseph Davis's plantation; it adjoined JD's plantation, Brierfield. JD lived at Hurricane until his marriage.

‡ Eliza Van Benthuysen Davis, JD's sister-in-law, Joseph's wife.

pass immediately from the statement of such a case to the consideration of the character & motives of the parties.* He would have a poor
opinion I doubt not of any man who having an opportunity to know
you would not love you, and this narrows my case down to the circumstances under which the avowal was made, "quand on commence
a raisonner, on cesse a sentir, I take the converse of the proposition,
and here rest the case for the judgement of all except yourself, to you
are known all the circumstances, how they led me from my design of
visiting you after you had returned home, to make my declaration
there, you whose good opinion I would have forfeited had I attempted
to draw you into an engagement to me to be fulfilled despite a parental
opposition, can judge me be<s>t<-er than-> an<d> if to you I am
justified then am I more content than if deprived of this I had the justification of the world beside

But why shall I not come to see you in addition to the desire I have
to be with you every day and all day, it seems to me but proper and
necessary, to justify my writing to you that I should announce to your
parents my wish to marry you, if you had not interdicted me, I should
have answered your letter in person, and let me ask [you] to recon-
sider your position I am willing in this matter to be guided by you, although your reason may if you so wish not be given. How did you
happen to call your Father by [my] name? Was it a mistake of lan-
gua[ge] if it so may be called to think of one thing and speak of another, or have you, my dear child, been sick again?

I wished myself so earnestly on the Boat that was bearing you off
that had you called me when you were on the "guard" or could I have
found any other excuse for going back I should have substituted your
feeling of desolation with either surprise, annoyance or confusion. In
you[r] next letter which make as long as you can, please make the period of my prohibition as short as you ca[n.]

Since you <-have-> left I have found the house particularily dull I
believe every body thinks of you as soon as they see me, or may be
only that when I enter any of the rooms in which we have been together I think of you, and thus suspect in others what <alone> exists

---

* Judge George Winchester, Varina's tutor and a close friend of the Howell family.

in myself. I saw my friend Walter since his trip to Natches, could any effort of mine cure the evil of which you spoke I would most cheerfully make it. If I have time I will write this better i.e. with less scratching. Pray don't read at night, nor punish your angel eyes by Keeping a light in your chamber all night. In all things be careful of your health, otherwise what pain shall I not suffer to Know that you are sick, suffering, and that I cannot be with you, then since you are always so good as to think last of yourself, for my sake take care of your health. Bon soir, mon cher ange, Je suis votre—

JEFFN. DAVIS

To Varina Banks Howell (PJD)

HURRICANE, WARREN COUNTY, MISSISSIPPI, MARCH 15, 1844
MY DEAREST, MY OWN ONE,

I have just returned from the performance of a most painful and meloncholy duty. My Brother-in-law David Bradford was assassinated day before yesterday. I went over to his late residence yesterday and returned to-day bringing with me my sister and her Children.

In such gloom nothing could give me pleasure unless it were a part of you, your letter all that I could have of you was waiting my arrival, and deeply do I thank you for it

It had been my intention if you did not further interdict me, to have gone down to night by the "Concordia" to be seen of you, not to see you, because I do that notwithstanding the space that divides us; but your own heart will tell you of reasons enough to prevent my going away under the existing circumstances.

Two things in your letter are very gratifying to me, that your Mother has ceased from opposing the course of your love, and that *you are in good health*, the latter which is to me the cause of constant hopes and fears you seem almost to have forgotten to tell me, again I entreat you take care of my wife.

You surely did not think how much it would cost me when you asked me to burn your letters, if the house was on fire those letters with the flowers you have made sacred by wearing and the lock of your hair, would be the first thing I should think of saving. I have not the ability to comply with that request without more pain than I can believe you would willingly inflict upon [me]. I therefore hope you will recal it indeed I expect you will do so—you need not fear that any body will see them unless my death should justify the opening of their present place of deposit, now as that is a contingency which I have no reason to expect for many years, and as it would debar the discoverer from making any light use of the discovery, so do I think your request as far as it is founded on that fear, should be withdrawn.

You were equally wrong to blame and scold me for having neglected to write to you and then when you went to the other extreme, and concluded I must have the small-pox as I had not written. If after the unlimited declarations I have made to you of my love I could neglect you, it would not become you to give me another thought, at least not to confess that you did, and on the other hand a sprained wrist, a hurt eye, a severe headache, many other things greatly short of small pox might prevent even your own Jeff. from writing to his dearest Varina. Since you have given your consent and I do "wish to see" you face to face I will visit you as soon as I can possibly do so. until then be assured my spirit is always with you.

I will ask Mr. V. Benthuysen to deliver this to you and though generally I would expect his visits to [be] somewhat dull to you, I suppose his ability to answer questions about us here may render him tolerable, and if he bear an answer from you his coming will be to me most agreeable.

Adieu, au revoir, ma chere, tres chère, plus chère Varina Dieu te benisse. I commenced with no expectation of being able to [write] one page, I have nearly filled three with what I know not and have't time [to] examine. Ever and entirely I am your

JEFFN. DAVIS

To William Allen (PJD)

HURRICANE, WARREN COUNTY, MISSISSIPPI, MARCH 25, 1844

DR. SIR,

"The sick man knows the Physician's step", but I assure you that if breaking a long silence to ask a favor of you should expose me to the suspicion of remembering you only because of my trouble, the fact is nevertheless quite otherwise. I am one of the <Presidential> "Electors" for the State of Mississippi and though I do not doubt the democratic character of our people I fear false statements and false issues in the approaching canvass and expect the Whigs to make great exertions,

I wish you aid me with any statements which can be made available against the charge of *defalcation* and extravagance under Mr. Van Buren's administration—against the present Tariff as productive of Revenue—against the U.S. Bank—against the charge of improper removals of officers and if there be such statement the removals in the first year of the Harrison & Tyler's administration. Further I should be glad to have the evidence of Mr. Clay's refusal to divide the resolution of censure upon President Jackson for the removal of the deposites and the rule of the senate in relation to the division of questions—Secretary Taney's report on the removal of the deposites from the U.S. Bank—Secretary Poinsett's annual report recommending reorgan<i>zation of the Militia and answer to call of the house on the same subject. Was not President V. Buren one of the first to point out the unconstitutionality of the military districts as projected in that answer? I had but cannot now find a speech of yours showing that the U.S. Bank loaned at a time which indicated the purpose, more money to members of Congress than the amount of their pay—can you send me a copy of that speech?*

---

* Martin Van Buren, president of the United States 1837–41 and in 1844 candidate for the Democratic party's nomination for president; William Henry Harrison, president of the United States in 1841 (he died after only one month in office); John Tyler, sitting president of the United States; Henry Clay, U.S. senator from Kentucky; Andrew Jackson, president of the United States 1829–37; Roger B. Taney, cabinet officer under Jackson and chief justice of the U.S. Supreme Court 1835–64; Joel R. Poinsett, cabinet officer under Van Buren.

I have mingled but little in politics and as you perceive by this letter have an arsenal poorly supplied for a campaign. Labor is expected of me and I am willing to render it. I believe much depends on this presidential election, and that every man who loves the union and the constitution as it is should be active.

You will understand what I want or should want better than myself, so far as you can conveniently send such you will greatly oblige me; and any suggestions you may find leisure to make to me will be highly appreciated. Vy. Respectfly. and truly yours—

JEFFN. DAVIS

To Martin Van Buren (PJD)

WARREN COUNTY, MISSISSIPPI, MARCH 25, 1844

SIR,

You will oblige me and many other Democrats of this section of the country by giving your opinion on the following questions—

First,   The annexation of "Texas" to the Territory of United States

Second,   The constitutional power of Congress over slavery in the District of Columbia

Third,   The Tariff of 1828 and whether your vote on that bill was entirely the result of the instructions you received.

With great consideration   I am very truly yrs.

JEFFN. DAVIS

To Varina Banks Howell (PJD)

HURRICANE, WARREN COUNTY, MISSISSIPPI, SEPTEMBER 6, 1844

MY DEAREST VARINA,

after writing to you yesterday I had the good and unexpected fortune to receive your kind letter of the 1st Inst. which whilst it relieved a portion of the anxiety I felt concerning [you] increased if possible the desire I had previously to see you. Circumstances which to be understood would have to be related at wearisome length prevented me from visiting you as I intended when I wrote to you at "Ripley," some day I hope it will be mine always to be with you and then that I shall possess increased power to allay nervous excitement, until then may God and your good sense preserve you. Pray never again allow a whig report to affect you. Genl. Fox was sick, but when I saw him was rapidly recovering—and I hope his death is far distant.

You find me changed in the matter of "speaking to Ladies," but remember you were not among them, and further that as public speaking was a new thing to me a change was to be expected and in more particulars than one has no doubt occurred. "How little do we know that which we are," but it is as far from being agreeable or desirable to me as ever.

If I were half as good as you believe me surely such little faults as you suppose you may commit could never disturb the harmony of our lives, and if I be no worse than I believe myself they could not, there is but one species of error of which an honorable woman is capable that could distress me if committed by my wife—e.g. such love of admiration, or excess of politeness as might induce one to fear that ridicule, or even detractive remarks were secretly made, but of this as a morbid feeling in its extent I have long since informed you as one of my many weaknesses,

Eliza sends you "The Rose of Thistle Island." I send you my deepest truest purest love, and hope soon in person to give you renewed assurances of that which you cannot doubt, the reluctance with which I am ever apart from you. Farewell my dearest and may all that your husband wishes for you still be yours—once more my dearest

<-Yrs->Farewell
Jeffn. Davis

To Varina Banks Howell (PJD)

DEAREST VARINA,

The first wish of my heart is my first though[t] my first prayer this morning need I say that wish is for your welfare

Mon ange, I beseech you if not for your own sake, yet for mine, that you will be more careful of your health, and as a part of the sanitary cordon with which you should invest yourself let me remind you of the easy approach to the gate of feeling, and urge upon you gr[e]at caution in the selection of your guards for that gate, do not understand as wishing you to barricade it but only that it should not be opened too hastily nor too violently, to the end that you may not endan[ger] the citadel.

Be prudent and be resolved to preserve yourself, which is to ensure happiness [to] your own

JEFF.

To Varina Banks Howell (PJD)

MY OWN VARINA,

His is truly a sad fate who is doomed to inflict pain where he is most anxious to confer happiness. I hope it will not often be mine as it concerns you, and that the time will soon arrive when you can speak as you feel, and when I can unrestrained make those efforts to which my heart so eagerly [com?]pels me to increase your happiness—vous la meritez.

I have felt as I have acknowledged to you my unworthiness of the love you bear me, yet never so deeply as when reading your kind, generous expressions towards me; and feeling [as] candor compels me to own I felt that you viewed me through the medium of your own noble nature, and ascribed to the object a brightness not it's own.

When circumstances shall give you greater opportunities to instil into me goodness and purity I believe I shall be more worthy of [the] opinion you now have of me, incorrigible indeed would he be that could constantly drink at so sweet [a] fountain and not become fond of its properties

Don't cry out against prosing this time, and I will try to be less dull for the future.

I pray you never let any fears of my censuring you keep you awake again. nothing could make me doubt your heart and I hope you will not believe that I could treasure up heedless expressions and elaborate from their harmlessness the poisons of suspicion and discontent.

Your spirit is with me I feel it's presence, my heart is yours, my dreams are of our union, they are not dreams, for I will not wake from them.

Your own Jeff

To Margaret K. Howell (PJD)*

Brierfield, Warren County, Mississippi, April 25, 1845

My Dear Mamma,

Varina showed me this morning a portion of your letter in which you speak affectionately of me and request that I should write to you, playfully alluding to my former reluctance for your perusal of the letters written to Varina. Did you ever write a love letter? or has it been so long that you have forgotten the feeling with which you sent it forth? as for myself though past the age of boyish fondness before I wrote the letters to which you referred, my reason had not yet gained the control of my sensibility, and my practice in that species of composition had been so small that I was nodoubt sometimes obscure, without the obscurity being an ingredient of the sublime, and this alone might have justied in wishing those letters restricted to her who had the key for their construction. But being now the head of a family I can better appreciate the necessity for the caution used in supervising your daughter's correspondence & will be willing for you to read

* JD's mother-in-law.

all the letters I write to Sister Maggy.* Varina has not been entirely well for many days together, though she says her health has been better heretofore, she is much thinner than when she left you and appears sometimes very languid, which latter effect might be well ascribed to the company she habitually keeps, being your corresponding son and a mongrel puppy in both of whom by a power of vision peculiarily her own she sees highly valuable and loveable qualities, but un<less> (which you will hardly believe to be possible) she is inclined to coquetry, your son has the honor of being first among her present visitors whilst she avows the Puppy to be second.

We are living so humbly that we may well expect happiness if it be true that it springs from a condition which exchanges for the better, in the mean time Varina seems as much occupied with the flowers and vines she is raising as though our situation was permanent, and we should not probably be more happy if the walls of a castle sheltered us, than we are beneath the protection of our rugged hut. Varina has written to you fully and I should probably repeat what she has said if I were to say much about her and as time presses will only add, that I think she grows calmer discreeter happier & lovelier with each passing day, that my relations hereabouts have been quite as attentive as I expected and they harmonize together better than I had hoped. With my best wishes for yourself, with my sympathies for the late accident of Mr. Howell and my kindest regards for him always, and with my love to the young folks, I am vy. truly &c&c†

JEFFN. DAVIS

Speech in U.S. House of Representatives (PJD)

DECEMBER 18, 1845

Mr. DAVIS, of Mississippi, was opposed to the reference of these resolutions to a select committee on two grounds: and the first was, that, in his opinion, they deserved at the hands of this House no reference anywhere. They called upon Congress to purify the ballot-box. If the

* Varina's younger sister, Margaret.
† William B. Howell, JD's father-in-law.

ballot-box was impure in Massachusetts, let her legislature look at home. Massachusetts had no right to inquire into its condition in other States. So far as the modification of laws for regulating elections went, it was no concern of Congress.

And why did Massachusetts ask for an alteration in our naturalization laws—laws which had existed since the formation of the Constitution? When this country had declared that a man was not the natural and perpetual subject of the Government under which he was born, and had maintained and established the right of foreigners to expatriate themselves, it contended, of course, in that very act, for their right of admission here. And, if so, why did the gentleman from Pennsylvania demand a select committee? Such a request proceeded on the presumption that the Judiciary Committee was wanting either in patriotism, fidelity, or legal learning; neither of which allegations Mr. D[avis] had ever heard advanced in any quarter. And, if that committee was possessed of these qualifications, to that, as the law committee of this House, let the resolutions go. This was a question which deeply interested the people of his district. They, too, wanted a modification of our naturalization laws; but it was that they might be simplified, and that the process of naturalization might be more easily accomplished. So far as his own wishes, therefore, were concerned, he should rather be inclined to ask a select committee on the other side of the question.

Much had been introduced in this discussion which was not referred to in these resolutions. A broad field had been thrown open, but here the ancient maxim, *"Media tutissimus ibis,"** would not hold. We must either make naturalization easy, or we must withhold it entirely; for if we admitted foreigners, and yet denied them the enjoyment of all political rights among us, we did but create enemies to our Government, and fill our country with discontented men. Let the principles of Native Americanism prevail, and the foreigner would look in vain for happiness and liberty on the American shore. He detested that party, above all others, for its sordid character and its arrogant assumption.

Mr. D[avis] here referred to a speech which had been made by a

---

* *Media tutissimus ibis:* You are safest in the middle of the road.

gentleman from Massachusetts [Mr. ROCKWELL] some days since, in which he had maintained that wherever slavery existed there the high moral character and perfectability of man was not to be found. Had the gentleman forgotten that both the Adamses, and Otis, and Gerry, and Hancock, had all sprung from a State which tolerated slavery?* Would he deny to these men a high moral character? He had heard it maintained that the way to elevate the character and increase the prosperity of these States was to adopt the policy of excluding foreigners. As a commentary on that doctrine he would refer its advocates to the ancient empire of China, which had for centuries shut out all the world by her great wall and her exclusive laws. And what had been the result? She had been falling back behind all the other nations of the world in commerce and in power, until at last a little British squadron had been able to dictate terms to the most ancient and populous nation on the earth. He stigmatized this doctrine of exclusion as the doctrine of barbarism. Among savage nations a stranger was counted an enemy, and the same word designated both; but as civilization and every humanizing influence advanced and prevailed, the gates of admission were gradually thrown open. Like another celebrated system which had prevailed in this country, this barbarian doctrine of exclusion had been called "the American system." It was no such thing; it was the European system; but even there it was melting away before the dictates of common sense and a more enlightened policy. Even in France, that stronghold of the feudal system, foreigners were now permitted to hold real estate—England alone retained this blot on her national escutcheon. And should we imitate her in that which was her disgrace? Mr. D[avis] here referred to the services of foreigners in our modern revolution; but though he would not affirm that without it we could not have achieved our freedom, still it furnished a strong reason why we should not shut our gates against those who came to us from abroad. Such a doctrine was never heard among the patriots of the Revolution, and never had he been more surprised than when he heard the name of Washington quoted in their support. Washington was born for no age and for no land; he stood out alone in his native

---

* John Adams, John Quincy Adams, Harrison Gray Otis, Elbridge Gerry, and John Hancock were all political leaders from Massachusetts.

grandeur, and was the boast and the property of the world. His correspondence was still extant in which he referred to his native land as an asylum for the oppressed; and in a letter to Mr. Jefferson had expressed his wonder that those who were oppressed in the Old World did not more frequently take refuge in the New. Was this the man whom Native Americans claimed as the bulwark of their exclusive policy? Much had been said about the Declaration of Independence. Did gentlemen forget that among its signers were to be found eight actual foreigners, and nine who were the immediate descendants of foreign parents? Mr. D[avis] here made a reference, not distinctly heard by the reporter, to the adoption of Washington by the Irish as a son of St. Patrick, although he had no Irish blood in his veins. He concluded by expressing his hope that the resolutions would not be referred to a committee who were professedly inimical to our foreign population.

Speech in U.S. House of Representatives (PJD)

FEBRUARY 6, 1846

. . .

In the Annual Message of the Executive to this Congress, we are recommended to pass a law for the termination of the Oregon convention; but we are told in the same communication, "beyond all question, the protection of our laws and our jurisdiction, civil and criminal, ought to be immediately extended over our citizens in Oregon."

We are further recommended to establish agencies among the Indian tribes west of the "Rocky mountains," and to protect the route from our Missouri settlements to Oregon by a sufficient force of mounted riflemen. Now, sir, I wish these recommendations to be carried out in the order which circumstances indicate. The laws, the agencies, and the riflemen first; the notice afterwards.

The emigrant from the United States to Oregon passes over a prairie desert, infested by roving bands of predatory savages, and emigration is retarded by the hazard of the trip. To keep the country "open" to our people, we need riflemen to watch the gate.

The Hudson Bay Company, by its unrivalled trade among the tribes of Oregon, has acquired an influence which it is important to counteract—for this, Indian agents are required.

British laws have long since been extended into Oregon for the benefit of British subjects. Shall we refuse to do as much for the citizens of the United States? No, sir. Nor will the recently manifested spirit of emigration admit of delay. Our people have removed the "Far West" into Oregon. American hearts have gone over the mountain, and American laws should follow.

Sir, we have been asked why our citizens have left the repose of civil government to plunge into the haunts of savage beast and savage man. For an answer, I point to the energy and restless spirit of adventure which is characteristic of our people, and has contributed much to illustrate our history in peace and in war. They have exchanged repose for forest danger and privation; they have gone to the school of the wilderness, from which came forth the moral dignity of Daniel Boone,* the giant greatness of Andrew Jackson.

What obligation—whose right—have our emigrants violated? They have gone into territory indisputably our own: into the valley of the Columbia, to Astoria and its dependencies. If to hold for the common benefit the common property—to tame the wilderness and render it productive—incur sentence of excommunication,

"Methinks the punishment surpasses the offence." But the peaceful agricultural character of the emigration is denied, if, with the axe and plough, they also take the rifle. Sir, the rifle is part and parcel of the frontier man. It contributes both to his food and his defence. You might as well divide the man and horse of the fabled Centaur, as take his rifle from the western pioneer. The tide of emigration bears them westward; westward let it flow, until, to use the idea of the lamented Linn, our people shall sit down on the shores of the Pacific, and weep that there are no more forests to subdue. The purpose with which our citizens have emigrated into Oregon is agricultural; that of the Hudson's Bay Company, to keep the country in its wilderness condition for the advantages of fur trade. The distinction well expresses the differ-

* Noted American frontiersman.

ence between the Governments they represent. One popular, and seeking to enlarge the circle of its benefits; the other restrictive, confines its favors to a few, (in the strong language of an English writer, noticing this subject,) "like a harsh stepmother, pets the favorite, and plunders the family."

Whatever interests Great Britain had were conferred upon the Hudson Bay Company, with power to exclude the British subjects from the territory; and notwithstanding much has been said about colonization by that company, I believe the practice has been to require discharged servants to leave the country. Fur-trading is the antagonist of colonization; and I doubt not, if the Hudson Bay Company could control the destiny of Oregon, with a very small exception, it would remain the field of hunters and the home of fur-bearing beasts.

Sir, both in the legislative halls of the States and in primary assemblies of the people, a general determination has been shown against permitting a policy so narrow and so sordid to control a territory we believe to be our own. This wish of the people meets no opposition here. Then, sir, waiving the consideration of any sinister motive or sectional hate which may have brought allies to the support of the resolution now before us, I will treat it as singly aiming at the object which in common we desire—to secure the whole of Oregon to the United States.

. . .

Speech in U.S. House of Representatives (PJD)

March 16, 1846

From the formation of our Constitution, by which these States became united, the question of strict or latitudinous construction of the compact has divided, as it still divides, our countrymen into the two great political classes of which they are composed.

The people have recently entrusted the Government to the hands of those who always have avowed the faith of strict construction. They have a right, sir, to require that we will thus administer it—that we will restrict appropriations to objects which are clearly constitutional.

To this ancient limit of our creed, I hold each Democrat is bound; and, first, I will address myself to them, in answer to the arguments by which it has been attempted to justify the appropriations of this bill, under the specific grants of the Constitution.

From the grant of power "to provide and maintain a navy," it has been asserted, flows the right to construct harbors and improve rivers, as a mean to promote the extension of our commercial marine for a nursery of seamen. This is to appropriate money, not to execute a granted power, but to effect an object, because it may favorably react upon the grant; to substitute the discretion of this Government for the specific enumeration of objects for which, by the Constitution, appropriations are permitted.

Some who have preceded me in this discussion have defended these appropriations, as ensuing from the power "to regulate commerce." Regulate is not synonymous with facilitate or create—the verb is derived from the substantive *regula,* a rule. To make and enforce rules for commerce, is "to regulate commerce." Nor did the Constitution convey this rule, making power absolutely; but imposed important restrictions upon its exercise; such as—there shall be no duty upon articles of export; no preference, "by any regulation of commerce," to one port over another; and that there shall be free trade among the several States of our Union.

Whether we confine ourselves to the text of the Constitution or turn to its cotemporaneous history, it is impossible to resist the conclusion, that the grant was conferred to secure harmony, uniformity, equality; to give efficiency, and nationalize our regulations of commerce. Ingenuity was severely taxed, when from this grant—the power to make rules for commerce—it was attempted to draw authority to create harbors, as tending to increase our commerce. With equal propriety, and more directly, might be claimed the power to construct merchant ships, to transport the commerce upon which these regulations were to operate.

There is such an apparent want of just relation between the objects to which these appropriations are directed and these grants of the Constitution, that it is little less than mockery to cite them for such application. If the Federal Government should be permitted to take power from a connexion so remote and indirect, it will be no longer limited by the terms of its specific grants; the barriers of the Constitution will be levelled to the ground, the agent will have destroyed his letter of authority, and gone forth upon the illimitable field of usurpation.

The gentleman from Pennsylvania [Mr. STEWART] asserts the constitutional power to make the appropriations in this bill, not because of any particular grant, but by a sort of floating right which he asserts this Federal Government possesses to select the means necessary and proper. A right wholly irreconcilable to the very idea of specific grants, or the existence of reserved and sovereign powers within the States. When the States entered into a union, and established this Government as the agent of their league, they gave to it certain carefully enumerated powers, with authority to make all *laws* which should be *necessary and proper* for carrying those powers into execution.

This, sir, was but authority to legislate upon particular subjects, not to use all means, but to make all laws which should be both necessary and proper.

The gentleman from Tennessee [Mr. EWING] took a position, if possible, less tangible than that of the gentleman from Pennsylvania. He placed the power to make the appropriations asked for in this bill on the broad basis of faith. Faith, sir, is the belief in things not understood. [Mr. E. explained.] The gentleman then only desires that others should have faith, and cares not from what clause in the Constitution it may be derived; his own, he says, is drawn from the power to provide for the common defence and general welfare. There is no such power granted by the Constitution; a power which would have drawn in its train all the specific grants, and rendered their enumeration a superfluous act. The gentleman must refer to the grant which gives power "to lay and collect taxes, duties, imposts, and excises, to pay the debts and provide for the common defence and general welfare of the United States." The power conferred was to raise money, and among other purposes for which it might be exercised were the "common defence and general welfare." This is the plain interpretation, this the

}construction which Mr. Madison and other most eminent commentators have placed upon the language of the grant.* The power claimed by the gentleman would have carried with it, as a necessary means, not only the taxing power, to which it is attached, as declaratory of a purpose; not only the specific grants to borrow money, to raise armies, to provide a navy, to constitute judicial tribunals, but all others—the powers of absolute sovereignty itself.

Sir, there is a just medium, between the claim of unrestrained discretion for this Government, and its restriction to the mere letter of the bond. The grants of power are general, and therefore many things must attach as incidents. If the States deny the means necessary to the existence of this Government, nothing is more sure than that it will usurp them, and then a contest will arise between the rival powers, injurious to both. If, on the other hand, the Federal Government, by indirection, seeks more than is proper to its functions or necessary to their exercise, an indiscriminate opposition may be generated, and the liberality of patriotism be lost in the conflict. The harmony, the efficiency, the perpetuity of our Union require the States, whenever the grants of the Constitution are inadequate to the purposes for which it was ordained, to add from their sovereignty whatever may be needed, and the same motives urge us to seek no power by other means than application to the States.

To all which has been said of the inherent powers of this Government, I answer, it is the creature of the States; as such it could have no inherent power, all it possesses was delegated by the States, and it is therefore that our Constitution is not an instrument of limitations, but of grants. Whatever was then deemed necessary was specifically conveyed; beyond the power so granted, nothing can now be claimed except those incidents which are indispensable to its existence; not merely convenient or conducive, but subordinate and necessary to the exercise of the grants.

. . .

---

* James Madison, Founding Father and president of the United States 1809–17.

"*To a Gentleman in Vicksburg*" (PJD)*

WASHINGTON, D.C., MAY 12, 1846

The Oregon controversy will scarcely be settled, by negotiation, and when the joint convention shall be abrogated, conflict with England will probably ensue. Before that time we ought to close all questions with Mexico, and have the ship overhauled for action on a larger scale. Let the treaty of peace be made at the city of Mexico, and by an Ambassador who cannot be refused a hearing—but who will speak with that which levels walls and opens gates—American cannon.

I signified to our friend Jno. Willis that in the event of war I should like to command a Warren regiment. My position here forces upon me the recollection of all which is due to those who sent me here. Yet I look to the movements of our forces on our Mexican border with a strong desire to be a part of them. My education and former practice would, I think, enable me to be of service to Mississippians who take the field. If they wish it, I will join them as soon as possible, wherever they may be.

JEFFERSON DAVIS

Speech in U.S. House of Representatives (PJD)

MAY 28, 1846

MR. CHAIRMAN:

The gentleman from Ohio says, an education such as may be acquired at West Point, qualifies for the duties of a representative in this hall. If so, that institution surely, sir, should be continued. It should be extended, and the country blessed in all its districts with men suited to the important duties which devolve upon this House. If, sir, the gentleman designed the remark for me, I have to say to him, the hypothesis and the conclusion are his own, not mine. I do not claim to possess all the qualifications necessary for a representative; but know

---

* Originally printed in the *Vicksburg Sentinel and Expositor* and then in other newspapers.

there are very many in which I am deficient. But I will say for that gentleman, that I do not believe the legislator *nascitur non fit;* and therefore hold that any education, of whatever kind, or however imperfect, is still better than none at all. I cannot understand the reasoning which has led him to boast of his blacksmith acquirements as fitting him for the duties of a legislator, though I should have been content if he had forborne from allusions to myself—to have left untouched the cloak of self-sufficiency in which he wraps himself. But the gentleman assumes, and attributes to me the assertion, that a blacksmith is, because of his trade, unfit for a soldier. Now, I venture that no other person understood me to have said so. If the gentleman chooses to draw forced and most unjustifiable inferences, I cannot permit him to attribute them to me; if he stul[ti]fies himself, I must object to his attempting, at my expense, to spread the contagion among others who did not hear me. Who but himself could ever have supposed the army filled by graduates from the military academy. Yet this he would ascribe to me, a supposition so opposed to fact, it was for his brighter imagination to create. With like propriety, he cites instances of mechanics who became distinguished soldiers, and offers this an answer to me. I never denied the radical qualities, never supposed there was any inability in any portion of my countrymen to become soldiers. I claimed, as still I claim, that war was a science of which no man was born possessed, and that the knowledge of it was to be acquired as any other profession or pursuit. To construct a fort, to attack a fort by regular approaches, military pyrotecting, military evolutions, military strategy, can neither be learned on the anvil or in the law book, no more than the trade of the smith or the profession of the lawyer could be acquired by the camp duties of the soldier.

The will to do, the soul to dare, the patriotism which will bear every sacrifice for our country belongs to the American people; is bounded by no class or geographical section; and I glory in the confidence that it is so; I hold in equal respect all which equally contributes to sustain and dignify our national character, and, in the few remarks I made, no particular class was selected as the object of my praise. But

---

* *Nascitur non fit:* born, not created.

because I pointed out the fact, that military science had enabled our few troops to hold their posts at Point Isabel, and on the Rio Grande, because I referred to what skill in the preparation of ammunition and in the use of field artillery had done in the battles of the 8th and 9th, the gentleman called for an instance of a distinguished officer, educated at the military academy; then declined to receive an answer. I will give it to him now: McComb, McCree, the gifted engineer of the sortie at Fort Erie; Wood, who fell on the field, and over whose remains a monument has been raised to commemorate his gallantry. Every Indian campaign has added to the list though the conspicuous positions were occupied by officers whose rank, from long service, gave them the right to command. The gentleman has made one statement which cannot be gainsayed, that Generals Washington and Jackson were not educated at West Point; but he forgot to add to his statement that Gen. Washington recommended the establishment of the school, and General Jackson always treated with contempt the idea that it was useless to teach the science of war.* It was not for their minds to entertain the opinion that ignorance gave military power; though so richly endowed by nature as to overcome the wants of elementary training, none have manifested a more high appreciation of its use. I am asked, if Captain May was an educated soldier? he was not an elevé of the military academy, but I have been informed had received a liberal education before he was commissioned, and has had some ten years' service to teach him his profession, and would, I presume, be little thankful to any one who should cite him as an instance of the advantage of ignorance, or who should seek to heighten his well-earned fame by ungracious reflections on the misfortunes of his brother soldier, Captain Thornton. Sir, I feel as much gratification at his brilliant charge as any can: mine is not the hand that would ruffle a feather of the plume he has so nobly won, and which I hope may wave as haughtily on other fields as this. It was a display of that impetuous daring essential for the cavalry soldier, and soon I hope to see him promoted in that service to a higher grade.

If the gentleman supposed I would wish to detract anything from

* George Washington, Founding Father, commanding general of the Continental army during the American Revolution, and president of the United States 1789–97.

this feat of gallantry, he was most egregiously mistaken. It is not necessary for the friends of a military academy to disparage all who have been educated elsewhere; and well may they leave the value of that institution to be measured by the services of those who have emanated from it, whose merit stands on a foundation too broad and permanent to require such support. But why did he cite the capture of Capt. Thornton, and point him out to injurious animadversion? Had he examined the circumstances of the case he hardly would have done so; or had he known that Capt. Thornton was not educated at West Point, I am still more sure he would not have made these reflections. But he asks for instances. Look at the officers killed and wounded in our recent battles: there are few names to be erased to render it a list of West Point graduates. Who received the first fire of the enemy? Who trained and led the light artillery, so effective on that occasion? The sudden conception and prompt execution which marks the great military mind could not be better displayed than by the infantry officer, who, being charged by cavalry, retired to the chapparel, and placing the backs of his men against the thicket, firmly received, with an undiminished front, their charge, and finally repulsed them.

There is one instance to which I will allude particularly. Lieut. Sackett, of that class denominated as "supernumeraries," the junior brevet second lieutenant of his regiment, and who, therefore, according to the opinion of some here, had no right to remain in the army, lost, in the charge of the second dragoons, his horse, and, by the fall, his sword, also; a Mexican officer attacked him under these circumstances; he disarmed and unhorsed his assailant, and on the horse and with the sword of his enemy, made his way to his company, and again joined in the charge.

If gallantry be all that gentlemen desire, the instances of daring are numerous enough to satisfy them, if they will learn the history of anyone of our campaigns. But, sir, I think there is an unfortunate disposition to undervalue everything which does not exhibit personal daring. It should be remembered that battles are mainly won by that arm which seldom comes into personal conflict, the artillery.

The success of a campaign depends much upon the ability of the general, evinced in his marches and his camps; and no courage, either of himself or troops can compensate for errors made in either, if he has before him a skilful foe. It is the position of General Taylor's camps that constitutes a great portion of their strength. It was the preparation and skilful use of the artillery, which rendered it so efficient—striking terror into the heart of the enemy. For these purposes gallantry alone would not suffice.

Few will believe that the light artillery of the lamented Ringgold could have been dispensed with, and no one can suppose that an uneducated officer would be able to command efficiently an arm in the use of which so much science is involved.

Where is the parallel to be found for Prince Morat as a cavalry leader, the man who rendered himself conspicuous by his gaudy dress, who always returned from a charge with his sword dripping blood and yet never received a wound; but it was not these charges brilliant, dazzling, miraculous as they appear, which gave Napoleon victories It was the deep military science of the emperor, his remarkable attainments as an engineer, and an artillerist which sat as the presiding genius over his campaigns. Need I say that others might be equally instructed yet not be worthy to command, or will anyone infer, save the gentleman before me, that because I believe a military education to be necessary, that I suppose this is all which is required. There are exceptions, men who succeed without education, and others who fail with it, as in every pursuit of life.

Mr. Chairman, I expected the gentleman from Ohio would be relieved from his distrust when the evidence of success, so brilliant, was before him; but no, he shuts out light and knowledge, he hugs the error closely, and I leave him to enjoy the embrace. I regret, sir, that a sense of justice does not prompt him to withdraw the statements made by him, even though they have been printed, now that he must feel they were incorrect, but he refuses. Then I think his readers will generally correct those statements for him. If he sees not, the people of the country generally will see, in what has been done, what is doing, and to be done, the fruits of a professional skill which could not have been produced by the knowledge men acquire in the ordinary avocations of life. It is this combination of the skill of the soldier with the courage and patriotism common to our people, to which I invited attention; and that mind must have been obtuse indeed which could not draw the distinction between ignorance of a particular pursuit, and the inability to learn it. No one can be more sensible than myself of the versatility, the convertibility of the American mind; we are ever changing our pursuits, and instances are constantly occurring of high success by those who have entered late upon a particular profession; but will anyone therefore infer that an early education for the profession, thus late adopted, would have been a disadvantage? Again, sir, I assert my confidence in our army; wherever their country needs their personal exposure, I feel it will be encountered with the same alacrity they showed at Palo Alto, and now, when those white gloves which have been the ground of objection to our officers, have been so deeply died in the blood of the enemy, I trust that justice, generosity, and patriotic sympathy, will unite to give these resolutions an unanimous support.

To Albert G. Brown (PJD)*

WASHINGTON, D.C., JUNE 20, 1846

SIR,

I have the honor to acknowledge, and accept the commission of Colonel in the 1st Regiment of Mississippi Volunteers, received last evening from the hands of your aid-de-camp, Col. J. Roach.

For this most gratifying mark of confidence I return my sincerest thanks.

The unfortunate confusion, and conflict of authority exercised in calling out volunteers to maintain the interests, and defend the honor of our common country, have deprived our State of a full opportunity to evince the zeal and patriotism of her citizens; but sir, in accepting the commission tendered to me as above, I entertain the hope, that an opportunity will be afforded to the 1st Regiment of Volunteers, as the representative of Mississippi in the army of operations, to sustain the military reputation of our State, and to give renewed assurance of that

* Governor of Mississippi, later U.S. representative and senator.

which may be expected of Mississippians, whenever the necessities of our country shall further require their aid. With great respect, I am your obedient servant,

JEFF. DAVIS.

To Lucinda Farrar Davis Davis Stamps (PJD)*

STEAMBOAT NEAR CINCINNATI, OHIO, JULY 8, 1846

MY DEAR SISTER

I am on my way to Vicksburg as Colonel of the Regiment raised in Mississippi for the Mexican War. This movement was unexpected, though I hope not unnecessary, at least it was felt by me as a real compliment to be thus chosen over a field of competitors when absent, and if occasion offers it may be that I will return with a reputation over which you will rejoice as my Mother would have done. Varina and Mary Jane are with me—Mary Jane in fine health, Varina far from well.† I wished to leave her in the North this summer, but she would not consent. If circumstances warranted it I would send her to you. To you and your family alone of all the world could I entrust her and rest assured that no waywardness would ever lessen kindness. She regrets very much that she can not see you all, and has never ceased to remember the kindness of yourself and the girls and Brother Stamps.‡

She will probably stay with her Mother most of the time during which I will be absent. With Eliza she could not be contented, nor would their residing together increase their good feeling for each other.§ This distresses me as you will readily imagine, but if you ever have an opportunity to understand Varina's character, you will see the propriety of the conclusion, and I feel that you will love her too much to take heed of the weaknesses which spring from a sensitive and generous temper. My dear Sister, I do not know how it is that I have not

* JD's sister.
† Mary Jane Bradford Brodhead Sayre, JD's niece.
‡ William Stamps, JD's brother-in-law.
§ Eliza Van Benthuysen Davis, JD's sister-in-law.

written to you often, God knows and I trust you believe there is nothing which I love better.

I intended and perhaps promised to write to little Netty. Kiss her for me and tell her she must permit her Aunt Varina to become fully acquainted with her. She must judge her uncle's wife by observation and not evade the kindest feeling of a warm heart. Remember me affectionately to Brother Stamps and the girls. I will write again. The boat shakes so this is I fear illegible. Farewell, my beloved Sister.

Your brother

Jeffn Davis

To Robert J. Walker (PJD)[*]

New Orleans, Louisiana, July 22, 1846

Dear Friend,

The first detachment of three companies from the Mississippi Rgt. have just sailed. The rifles have not arrived and from a letter sent me by Col. J. Roach it appears that they were not turned over to him but sent in the ordinary way—may I ask of you to make some inquiry concerning this matter .

This evening and to morrow I hope to get the balance of the Rgt. under way—I have put my ow[n] affairs first and in this I have followed certainly a natural order; but the great question upon which I wish to address you concerns others. From all I can discover, the two men of our party who stand first here and hereabouts are Govr. Cass,[†] and Sectry. Walker, the latter would have nothing to fear from the former in a democratic rivalry were it not for the influence exerted by the Custom house officers—they appear odious to the american population and the Surveyor to have influence no where and I will add from all I can learn he don't deserve it—These men hang a dead weight upon you—The Jeffersonian has been touching the Surveyor quite closely about his connexion with a contract he is recommending the government to make with a Capt. Fullerton to run steam b[oats] to

[*] U.S. secretary of the treasury; formerly U.S. senator from Mississippi.

[†] Lewis Cass of Michigan, leading Democratic politician.

Brazos Santiago—you will recollect that I called your attention to his hostility to the "Jeffersonian" it is believed to continue as I am informed by the same authority I gave you at the time I handed a letter to you from the publisher of that paper.

The only democratic paper here could do much good if unembarassed—more harm if rendered hostile to us. You will understand much more from this short letter than I have time in the midst of embarking preperations to write—I am <-of-> decidedly of the opinion that a friend of mine would be benefitted and the party advanced by the removal of surveyor Hayden   Very sincerely your friend
JEFFN. DAVIS

To *Varina Davis* (PJD)

OFF BRAZOS SANTIAGO, JULY 29, 1846

MY DEAR WIFE,

after an extraordinarily quiet voyage we are at anchor, waiting for a Lighter to get ashore on the Brazos Island—Several times I have thought may it not be the calm sea over which we are running is type of my fortune where agitation is to me of far greater moment than in the waters of the gulf—may god have preserved you as calm—your affectionate letter reached just before starting from New orleans. I was much gratified to see that you been engaged in useful and domestic things. However unimportant in themselves each may be, it is the mass which constitutes the business of life, and as it is pursued so will it generally be found that a woman is happy and contented. To one of exacting and devoted temper the cultivation of shrubs furnishes an appropriate and inexhaustible field of employment. I say appropriate because no suspicion of ingratitude or faithfulness can exist towards them.

Joe. is well except the injury to his ancle of which you have been informed—I asked him to write to his Mother he said he had done so.* Present me affectionately to all and receive a Husbands love for sweet Winnie—

---

* Joseph D. Howell, JD's brother-in-law.

Again farewell and again I <-ask-> that the season of our absence may be a season of reflection bearing fruits of soberness, and utility, and certainty of thought and of action. My love for you placed my happiness in your keeping, our vows have placed my hono[r] and respectability in the same hands. K[i]ss Ma and the Children.

Hubbin would kiss the paper he sends to wife, but is in the midst of the men, who though talking & whistling and wondering when the Lighter will come have time enough to observe any thing the Col. Does—I send a kiss upon the wires of love and feel earth, air & sea cannot break the connection

To *Joseph E. Davis* (PJD)

MONTERREY, MEXICO, SEPTEMBER 25, 1846

MY DEAR BROTHER:—

The town is ours after a severe conflict. The Mississippians were brought into action on the 21st and performed some brilliant service. On the 22nd preparations were made, and we held an advance post. On the morning of the 23rd we (the Mississippians) opened the action early, and continued firing and advancing into the town until near sunset, when we were ordered to withdraw. On the 24th propositions having been received to capitulate, Gen. Worth, and Gen. Henderson of Texas, and myself, were appointed commissioners to arrange the terms of capitulation.* We agreed, and the papers have been exchanged. *It was reported to us, by the Mexican General, that Mexico had received commissioners from the United States.*—They were whipped, and we could afford to be generous. We hope soon to return as the war is probably over.

With love to all—I am your brother.

---

* Brigadier General William J. Worth and J. Pinckney Henderson, governor of Texas and major general of Texas Volunteers.

To Robert J. Walker (PJD)

MONTERREY, MEXICO, OCTOBER 12, 1846

If any moral effect could be produced by military achievement enough has been done at this place to produce it. Here we found an Army about double the size of our own; yet we were allowed to approach through a country offering every opportunity that an enterprising officer would ask to check an advancing army; without a battering gun, or a trenching tool, we invested the Town, so strong in its defences, so strong in its natural advantages, as to have been considered impregnable before the recent additions to its works. Indeed it is said that a superstitious confidence existed among the people that Monterey could not be taken. Three days sufficed to make them ask for terms, and the commanding officer even told us at the beginning of the conference that his government had received commissioners from ours, resorting to falsehood as it now appears, to obtain a capitulation.

To Varina Howell Davis (PJD)

MOUTH OF THE RIO GRANDE, DECEMBER 10, 1846

DEAR WINNIE,

I have lost much time as the date of this letter will show you which could I have foreseen the events which have fallen out might have been passed with you. But let us believe that all is ordered for the general good & tutor our minds to act as becomes contributors, to feel as becomes creaturis bound by many obligations to receive with gratitude whatever may be offered, and wait with patience and confidence the coming result.

Thus speak I sweetest wife whilst the winds lash the waves and the waves tumble Jim and the greater part of my baggage on the board the ship, leaving me expectant on the shore and anxious to ascend the River.* For reasoning as above under such circumstances please give me credit.

---

* Jim Green, a slave of Joseph Davis; accompanied JD to Mexico.

It is reported that Genl. Taylor is preparing to move towards Tampico and that the Mississippians are to go with him—Santa Anna is said to be making some demonstration of an attack upon what however is not indicated.*

Letters of Marke are said to have been issued by Mexico and that thirty or forty privateers are fitting out at Havanna to attack some one of our depots. How true this is you know as well as I do, but the probability is increased by the palpable advantage which our defenceless depots offer.

At some time I hope to have an opportunity to introduce you to a Lady friend of mine now staying in New orleans, she is the wife Maj. McCree of the Army. During the absence of her husband she remains with their children at New Orleans, and through our long acquaintance commenced at Prairie du Chien, I have never known her to do an improper act. She gave me a letter to her husband and when he read it he seemed to be happy for two days that we were together, he said it had put him in a good humor with all the world. That letter was written when she was surrounded by annoyances especially disturbing because affecting her children, and was addressed to a husband whom she knew to be chafed by and disatisfied with his situation. One of these days God willing I will give you the history of several of my female acquaintance, of whom I lost trace when I left the army and refound in New Orleans—When in a speculative mood they will furnish food for contemplation. I have seen several volunteers from Monterey they report your brother well—Don't let the whigs find out that I communicated this to you and said nothing about other members of the Regt. I could not find the Bradford letter if you see it in the Room we occupied please send it to me.

My dear wife you have taken upon yourself in many respects the decision of your own course, and remember to be responsible for ones conduct is not the happy state which those who think they have been governed too much sometimes suppose it.

To rise superior to petty annoyances to pity and forgive the weakness in others which galls and incommodes us is a noble exhibition

---

* Major General Zachary Taylor, JD's former father-in-law; Antonio López de Santa Anna, Mexican general and political leader.

of moral philosophy and the surest indication of an elevated nature. To be able to look over the conventionalisms of society yet to have the good sense which skillfully avoids a collision with is the power and the practice I desire in my wife—With the practice and without the power a woman may be respectable. With the power and without the practice she will often be exposed to remarks, the fear of which would render me as a *husband* unhappy. This among other weaknesses which belong to a morbid sensibility I early confessed to you, had I not done so you must after our marriage have discovered it. Please consult Brother Joe. and have such a house built as with his advice you desire, & endeavor to make your home happy to yourself and those who share it with— Before this reaches you I hope your Mother will be with you.

To all our family give my love. Tell Brother Joe. I will write to him soon. There was no cause sufficient to justify your anxiety about the Tennesseans. Farewell, ever with deepest love and fondest hope,

YOUR HUSBAND

To William W. W. S. Bliss (PJD)[*]

SALTILLO, MEXICO, MARCH 2, 1847

SIR:

In compliance with your note of yesterday, I have the honor to present the following report of the service of the Mississippi riflemen on the 23d ultimo.[†]

Early in the morning of that day the Regiment was drawn out from the Head-quarters encampment, which stood in advance of, and overlooked, the town of Saltillo. Conformably to instructions, two companies were detached for the protection of that encampment, and to defend the adjacent entrance to the town. The remaining eight companies were put in march to return to the position of the preceding day, now known as the battle-field of Buena Vista. We had approached to within about two miles of that position, when the report of artillery-firing, which reached us, gave assurance that a battle had commenced.

[*] Chief of staff to Major General Zachary Taylor.
[†] JD's report on the Battle of Buena Vista.

Excited by the sound, the regiment pressed rapidly forward, manifesting upon this, as upon other occasions, their more than willingness to meet the enemy.

At the first convenient place the column was halted for the purpose of filling the canteens with water, and, the march being resumed, was directed towards the position which had been indicated to me, on the previous evening, as the post of our Regiment. As we approached the scene of action, horsemen recognised to be of our troops, were seen running, dispersed and confusedly, from the field; and our first view of the line of battle, presented the mortifying spectacle of a regiment of infantry flying disorganized from before the enemy. These sights, so well calculated to destroy confidence, and dispirit troops just coming into action, it is my pride and pleasure to believe, only nerved the resolution of the Regiment I have the honor to command.

Our order of march was in column of Companies advancing by their centres. The point which had just been abandoned by the regiment alluded to, was now taken as our direction. I rode forward to examine the ground upon which we were going to operate, and in passing <-[illegible]-> through the fugitives, appealed to them to return with us, and renew the fight; pointing to our Regiment as a mass of men behind which they might securely form. With a few honarable exceptions, the appeal was as unheeded as were the offers which, I am informed, were made by our men, to give their canteens of water to those who complained of thirst, on condition that they would go back.

General Wool was upon the ground making great efforts to rally the men who had given way. I approached him, and asked if he would send another regiment to sustain me in an attack upon the enemy before us. He was alone; and after promising the support, went in person to send it.

Upon further examination, I found that the slope we were ascending was intersected by a deep ravine, which, uniting obliquely with a still larger one upon our right, formed between them a point of land difficult of access by us; but which, spreading into a plain towards the base of the mountain, had easy communication with the main body of the enemy. This position important from it's natural strength, derived a far greater value from the relation it bore to our order of battle, and line of communication with the rear. The enemy in number many times greater than ourselves, supported by strong reserves, flanked by cavalry, and elated by recent success, was advancing upon it. The moment seemed to me critical, and the occasion to require whatever sacrifice it might cost to check the enemy.

My regiment having continued to advance was near at hand. I met and formed it rapidly into order of battle; the line then advanced in double quick time, until within the estimated range of our rifles, when it was halted, and ordered to "fire advancing."

The progress of the enemy was arrested. We crossed the difficult chasm before us under a galling fire, and in good order renewed the attack. <-upon the other side.-> The contest was severe,—the destruction great upon both sides. We steadily advanced, and as the distance was diminished, the ratio of loss increased rapidly against the enemy; he yielded, and was driven back on his reserves.

A plain now lay behind us—the enemy's cavalry had passed around our right flank, which rested on the main ravine, and gone to our rear. The support I had expected to join us was nowhere to be seen. I therefore ordered the regiment to retire, and went in person to find the cavalry, which after passing round our right, had been concealed by the inequality of the ground.

I found them at the first point where the bank was practicable for horsemen, in the act of descending into the ravine—no doubt for the purpose of charging upon rear. The nearest of our men ran quickly to my call, attacked this body, and dispersed it with some loss. I think their commander was among the killed.

The regiment was formed again in line of battle behind the first ravine we had crossed; soon after which, we were joined upon our left by Lieut. Kilbourne with a piece of light artillery; and Col. Lane's, the 3d Regiment of Indiana volunteers.

Lieut. Kilbourn opened a brisk and very effective fire: the enemy immediately receded; we advanced, and he retired to the mountain. No senior officer of Lieut. Kilbourn's corps being present upon this occasion, it gives me pleasure to bear testimony to the valuable services he rendered, and to express my admiration of the professional skill and soldierly qualities he manifested.

We now occupied the ground where the Mississippi Regiment first met the enemy. A heavy fire was opened upon us by a battery which the enemy had established near the centre of his line. The Indiana regiment was most exposed and passed from the left into the ravine upon our right.

The artillery retired to the battery from which it had been drawn. I had sent forward some parties, to examine the ground on which we had fought in the morning, for the purpose of bringing in the wounded: when these parties had returned, our Regiment retired by it's left flank, and marched along the bank of the ravine, heretofore noticed, as being on our right. The Indiana regiment, moving down the hollow, was concealed from the view of the enemy, who was probably thereby encouraged to make an attack.

We had proceeded but a short distance, when I saw a large body of cavalry debouche from his cover on the left of the position from which we had retired, and advance rapidly upon us. The Mississippi regiment was filed to the right and fronted, in line across the plain; the Indiana regiment was formed on the bank of the ravine, in advance of our right flank, by which a reentering angle was presented to the enemy. Whilst this preperation was being made, Sergeant Major Miller, of our regiment, was sent to Captain Sherman for one or more pieces of artillery from his battery.

The enemy who was now seen to be a body of richly caparisoned lancers, came forward rapidly and in beautiful order—the files and ranks so closed, as to look like a /solid/ mass of men and horses. Perfect silence, and the greatest steadiness prevailed in both lines of our troops, as they stood at shouldered arms waiting an attack. Confident of success, and anxious to obtain the full advantage of a cross fire at short distance, I repeatedly called to the men not to shoot.

As the enemy approached, his speed regularly diminished, until, when within 80 or 100 yards, he had drawn up to a walk, and seemed about to halt. A few files fired without orders, and both lines then instantly poured in a volley so destructive, that the mass yieded to the blow, and the survivors fled. Captain Sherman having come up with a field piece from his battery followed their retreat with a very effective fire, until they had fled beyond the range of his gun.

Soon after this event, a detachment of our artillery and cavalry moved up on our left, and I was directed to cooperate with it, in an attack upon the enemy at the base of the mountain.

We advanced parallel to this detachment, until it was halted. I then placed our men under such protection, as the ground afforded, from the constant fire of the enemy's artillery, to which we were exposed, to wait the further movement of the force with which we were to act. At this time, the enemy made his last attack upon the right, and I received the General's order, to march to that portion of the field.

The broken character of the intervening ground concealed the scene of action from our view; but the heavy firing of musketry formed a sufficient guide for our course. After marching two or three hundred yards, we saw the enemy's infantry advancing in three lines upon Capt. Bragg's battery; which, though entirely unsupported, resolutely held it's position, and met the attack, with a fire worthy of the former acheivements of that battery, and of the reputation of it's present meritorious commander. We pressed on, climbed the rocky slope of the plain on which this combat occurred, reached it's brow so as to take the enemy in flank and reverse, when he was about one hundred yards from the battery. Our first fire—raking each of his lines, and opened close upon his flank—was eminently destructive. His right gave way, and he fled in confusion.

In this the last conflict of the day, my regiment equalled—it was impossible to exceed—my expectations. Though worn down by many hours of fatigue and thirst, the ranks thinned by our heavy loss in the morning, they yet advanced upon the enemy with the alacrity and eagerness of men fresh to the combat. In every approbatory sense of these remarks, I wish to be included a party of Col. Bowles' Indiana regiment, which served with us during a greater part of the day, under the immediate command of an officer from that regiment, whose gallantry attracted my particular attention, but whose name I regret is unknown to me.

When hostile demonstrations had ceased, I retired to a tent upon the field for surgical aid, having been wounded by a musket ball, when we first went into action. Our Regiment remained inactive until evening, and was then ordered to the encampment of the previous night, under the command of Major Bradford.

We had seen the enemy retire; but his numerical superiority over us would scarcely admit the supposition that he had finally retreated. After my arrival at our encampment, which was some time after dark, I directed Capt. Rogers, with his Company "K." and Lieut. Russell, commanding Company "D." to proceed with their commands to the field of battle, and report to the commanding General for orders. These were the two companies which had been left as a guard at Head-quarters encampment, as stated in the beginning of this report. They had been threatened during the day by a strong detachment of the enemy's cavalry; and had performed all the duties which belonged to their position, as will be seen by the accompanying statement of Capt. Rogers, in a manner creditable to themselves and their regiment; but they were disappointed, because they had not been with us in the battle of the day, and were gratified at the order to march upon night service, and probably to a dangerous post.

Every part of the battle having been fought under the eye of the commanding General, the importance and manner of any service it was our fortune to render, will be best estimated by him: but in view of my own responsibility, it may be permitted me to say in relation to our first attack upon the enemy, that I considered the necessity absolute and immediate. No one could have failed to perceive the hazard. The enemy, in greatly disproportionate numbers, was rapidly advancing. We say no friendly troops coming to our support, and probably none except myself expected reinforcement. Under such circumstances, the men cheerfully, ardently entered into the conflict; and though we lost in that single engagement, more than thirty killed, and forty wounded, the regiment never faltered, nor moved except as it was ordered. Had the expected reinforcement arrived, we could have prevented the enemy's cavalry from passing to our rear, results more decisive might have been obtained, and a part of our loss have been avoided. . . .

To Charles J. Searles (PJD)[*]

BRIERFIELD, WARREN COUNTY, MISSISSIPPI, SEPTEMBER 19, 1847
MY DEAR SIR:

Your highly valued letter of the 3d Inst., came duly to hand, but found me quite sick, and I have not been able at an earlier date to reply to it. Accept my thanks for your kind solicitude for my welfare.

Your past conduct enabled me to anticipate this from you and I am therefore doubly grateful.

The political information you communicate was entirely new to me, and it is only under the belief that the crisis renders important the views of every southern man, that I can account for any speculations having arisen about my opinions as to the next Presidency. I have never anticipated a separation upon this question from the Democracy of Mississippi, and if such intention or expectation has been attributed to me, it is not only unauthorised but erroneous.

That it might become necessary to unite as southern men, and to dissolve the ties which have connected us to the northern Democracy: the position recently assumed in a majority of the non-slave holding states has led me to fear. Yet, I am not of those who decry a national convention, but believe that present circumstances with more than usual force indicate the propriety of such meeting. On the question of Southern institutions and southern rights, it is true that extensive defections have occurred among Northern democrats, but enough of good feeling is still exhibited to sustain the hope, that as a party they will show themselves worthy of their ancient appellation, the natural allies of the South, and will meet us upon just constitutional ground. At least I consider it due to former association that we should give them the fairest opportunity to do so, and furnish no cause for failure by seeming distrust or aversion.

I would say then, let our delegates meet those from the north, not as a paramount object to nominate candidates for the Presidency and Vice-Presidency, but before entering upon such selection, to demand

---

[*] Businessman in Vicksburg, Mississippi.

of their political brethren of the north, a disavowal of the principles of the Wilmot Proviso; an admission of the equal right of the south with the north, to the territory held as the common property of the United States; and a declaration in favor of extending the Missouri compromise to all States to be hereafter admitted into our confederacy.

If these principles are recognized, we will happily avoid the worst of all political divisions, one made by geographical lines merely. The convention, representing every section of the Union, and elevated above local jealousy and factious strife, may proceed to select candidates, whose principles, patriotism, judgement, and decision, indicate men fit for the time and the occasion.

If on the other hand, that spirit of hostility to the south, that thirst for political dominion over us, which within two years past has displayed such increased power and systematic purpose, should prevail; it will only remain for our delegates to withdraw from the convention, and inform their fellow citizens of the failure of their mission. We shall then have reached a point at which all party measures sink into insignificance, under the necessity for self-preservation; and party divisions should be buried in union for defence.

But until then, let us do all which becomes us to avoid sectional division, that united we may go on to the perfection of Democratic measures, the practical exemplification of those great principles for which we have struggled, as promotive of the peace, the prosperity, and the perpetuity of our confederation.

Though the signs of the times are portentous of evil, and the cloud which now hangs on our northern horizon threatens a storm, it may yet blow over with only the tear drops of contrition and regret. In this connection it is consolatory to remember, that whenever the tempest has convulsively tossed our Republic and threatened it with wreck, brotherly love has always poured oil on the waters, and the waves have subsided to rest. Thus may it be now and forever. If we should be disappointed in such hopes, I forbear from any remark upon the contingency which will be presented. Enough for the day will be the evil thereof, and enough for the evil, will be the union and energy and power of the south.

I hope it will soon be in my power to visit you and other friends at

Vicksburg, from whom I have been so long separated. I am, as ever, truly your friend,

JEFFERSON DAVIS.

To Stephen Cocke (PJD)*

WASHINGTON, D.C., NOVEMBER 30, 1847

MY DEAR FRIEND,

your very kind letter of the 7th has just reached me having been forwarded by my Brother,

I truly thank you for the interest you manifest in my election, which is of course a subject upon which I now feel greater interest than I should have done had I remained at home, because to be beaten under present circumstances is to be recalled.

Genl. Foote mentioned to me this morning that he had received a letter informing him that Thompson's friends were endeavoring to incite a feeling in the North by stating that I had opposed his election.† My opinion of Mr. Thompson is known to you and if I had been in his district I should certainly have opposed his nomination, but my notions of propriety caused me to refuse when requested to write to some of my friends and urge them to put him aside by a renomination at a new convention—Briefly, I never interfered in the contest. The report may be of no importance, if however it should appear to you advisable you can say thus much to any of our friends in the Legislature whose opinion may be affected by the underground attack.

The President is in good health & fine spirits, feels confident of being able to dis comfit the enemy as signally at home as abroad. The Southern and Western Whigs are understood to be with us on the War question, which will be in the beginning at least the chief ground of contest. I think the Wilmot Proviso <-n-> will will soon be of the

---

* Friend of JD in Mississippi who was active in Democratic party politics.

† Henry S. Foote, governor and U.S. senator, a major foe of JD in Mississippi politics, and Jacob Thompson, a notable figure among Mississippi Democrats; served in U.S. House of Representatives and as secretary of the interior in President James Buchanan's cabinet.

things which were˙—Cass is heartily with us, and says he always was but saw the necessity last spring of caution, lest the fire which would go out if let alone should be kindled by attempting to extinguish it too suddenly.

I have not been able to find the books and papers which I left here and have no list of Correspondents. I wish at your leisure you would from time to time send me names especially of those we met in our joint canvass—with great regard I am Yr. friend

JEFF'N. DAVIS

Give my respects to Messrs Price and Fall—I will try to write to them this evening—if not ask them to send me the Mississippian, which request I did not make be cause I took as granted they would know my wish upon that point.

JEFF'N. DAVIS

[*To Varina Davis*] (The American Scene: A Panorama of Autographs, 1504–1980)

WASHINGTON, D.C., JANUARY 3, 1848

. . .

Your suspicions and threats are equally unjust and unnecessary.† I have not . . . under the pressure of *grave and important matters* ever shown myself unmindful of your comfort or your welfare . . . nor exhibited a willingness that any one should take from you your *rights as a woman and wife,* nor sought to test your ability to love one who degraded you . . . You had an opportunity when I came to you crippled, so as to be confined to the house, to quarrel with me as much as would have satisfied any ordinary person, and I might have expected that you would have spared me from querulous letters, during my absence.

You proposed to me that I should invite Sister Amanda to live with us and I planned a house for that purpose. Now it becomes in your

---

˙ The Wilmot Proviso proposed to ban slavery in the Mexican Cession; it never passed Congress.

† All ellipses are in the autograph catalog, which has the only known version of this letter.

mind a source of *misery* to live as you proposed; and an injury to you that the house was planned by me. I omit the fact that several plans were submitted to you before one was decided on. I also recollect that you several times told me how unwilling Sister Amanda was to receive as a home any place which she could not transmit to her children, but it did not occur to me that you were the unwilling party, in carrying out a plan proposed by yourself and adopted by me mainly from considerations connected with yourself.

You have been generally sick and unable to take care of the household affairs, often bitter to me because of the irregularities of your servants, and I gladly availed myself of an opportunity to secure for you relief from domestic labors, and a kind companion to watch over and nurse you when I should be absent, and you sick. It was not a plan by which you were to *retire from the rest of the world.* . . .

I have no relation who is capable of a mercenary motive, none who has contemplated our marriage through the medium of pecuniary interest, and I regret that your heart should have suggested such as the feelings of my Sister. . . . My will has been that my death should have you secured in half the income of the property left by me. You are at liberty to anticipate that event, and those terms or an equivalent in any form you prefer, shall be your's. By no act of mine shall you feel yourself bound to a degrading condition, until you cease to love the one who has brought you to it.

4th Jany. 1848. Let there be peace and sincerity between us. In vain have I striven to inspire you with confidence, until the conviction is forced upon me that you never trusted, that our union commenced in doubt. If by the remarks you make about my views as to your retirement from the world you design to draw me out as to your not having come on here with me, I will be frank with you. I cannot expose myself to such conduct as your's when with me here. I cannot bear constant harassment, occasional reproach, and subsequent misrepresentation. I have not forgottin (sic) the old woman with rooms to let, or the multitude attracted by the servants of an angry woman.

You have written me a long letter to prevent me from believing that you have beneficially changed, to crush in me the hope which community and affection built up from materials you did not furnish. . . .

I have heretofore written to you . . . of the possibility of my speedy return to Missi. I do not say home *for without hearts there is no home.* Your words connected with the kisses you placed upon the paper on which you wrote, were enough for the purpose of renewing the wounds your suspicion has so often inflicted. Henceforth I will not answer your assaults or your insults. . . .

To Beverley Tucker (PJD)*

WASHINGTON, D.C., APRIL 12, 1848

MY DEAR SIR,

I have the pleasure to acknowledge the receipt of yours of the 6th Inst. It is with sincere regret that I find my unjustifiable delay in answering your former communication has created a doubt as to the estimation placed upon it. I pray you to accept assurances of the real gratification it gave me and my apology for the delay which has occurred in answering it.

Col. J. P. Taylor, the brother of the genl. was here when your first letter reached, he like myself was grateful for your good services and kind wishes towards Genl. Taylor. It was difficult for me to decide on a channel of communication worthy of yourself and bearing the proper relation to the genl. and myself. The prominent papers here and elsewhere at that time were either hostile to genl. T. or stood aloof from him, neither could be trusted.

I believed that genl. Taylor's true position was on the Democratic side but every thing seemed to drive him from us, my connection with him rendered my efforts especially valueless, and I have now no hope that the Democratic party will avail itself of his strength in the coming contest. The Whigs may, and if so as a necessary consequence his affiliations must be with our opponents. In such case my confidence, admiration, and affection for the man, will be opposed by my convictions, and aherence to measures—Believing it necessary that a candidate should have the organized support of one party or the <-r->

---

* A Virginian and professor of law at the College of William and Mary.

other and that it is impossible for genl. T. to be adopted now by the Democrats, the preliminary contest becomes one for Whig nomination, if in this the better caste of that party should alone be found, and the ultras be driven off a new party might arise from which better things could be expected.

For myself I will confess that I have been disappointed in the course of events, and look despondent upon a progress which I have no power to control or conform to. Your early advocacy of genl. T. cannot fail in any event to be to him a source of gratification and will be remembered by me.

accept my real regrets for the <-momentary-> delay which has caused a misapprehension of my feelings, and be assured of my highest esteem and regard, to which I will add my obligation for having been selected for a correspondent by you. It will give /me/ <-with-> much pleasure to hear from you, and I hope with improved health to be found a more prompt correspondent—Very truly yrs.

JEFFN. DAVIS

To Varina Davis (PJD)

WASHINGTON, D.C., APRIL 18, 1848

. . .

My health is almost restored, very little lameness, and seldom any pain, or other inconvenience except an inability to write for long periods continuously. There was no cause for anxiety about me, and it grieves me that you should have been thus injured either in health or spirits.

I had hoped that with cheerful friends and left in our separation to the full force of your affection for me, you would have enjoyed more equanimity than when we were together. Of disagreeable subjects I hope I have never shown a disposition to speak unnecessarily, and if sometimes unprofitably, it has not been deliberately done except for good ends, thus is it now that I refer to memories to which I recur with pain and for objects which will be apparent. I cannot bear to be suspected or complained of, or misconstrued after explanation, *by you*.

Circumstances, habits, education, combativeness, render you prone to apply the tests which I have just said I cannot bear. You do not wish to destroy my sensibility, or to drive me for relief to temporary stupefaction, and vicious associations; through these channels alone could I reach the condition suited to such treatment as I have received. We are apt by viewing our own heart, to construe our acts differently from others, and conscious of your love for me, you may not have understood how far your treatment of me was injurious. I will only say, that I hoped when you saw that your course if continued would render it impossible for us ever to live together, that my ill health rendering me less able to bear abuse, produced a necessity for separation at a time when a wifes kindness was most needed, and that the dread of constant strife was so great, as not to be overcome by a threat of exposure to the public, of the real cause of my going alone from home; with body crippled, nerves shattered, and mind depressed.—I had hoped your memory instead as you say dwelling on "the weary past and blighted future" would have grappled with substantial facts, and led you to conclusions, which would have formed for your future a line of conduct suited to the character of your husband, and demanded by your duties as a wife. Your two previous letters were very discouraging, this is better, and I have spoken more fully than in the answers to the two last.

I hope soon to hear from concerning affairs at home and the people, very little detail information has been given to me.

You should as a moral duty as a social obligation exercise such prudence and self-control in all things as will conduce to your health physical and mental. If it would be agreeable to you to spend this summer in the North Mrs Walker has kindly proposed to me to let you remain with her at the springs and elsewhere during the recess of Congress*—I need not say that (because I love you) it would always make me happier to be with you, if kind and peaceful.

With love to all our family, I am Affectionately Your husband—Truth & Love ever attend upon you—Good night

(SIGNED) JEFFN. DAVIS.

* Mrs. Robert J. Walker.

To John J. Crittenden (PJD)[*]

MY DEAR GOVR.

I have been long intending to avail myself of your kindness by writing to you, but you know the condition of a Senator during the session of Congress and may be able to estimate the condition of a lazy man thus situated. It is I hope unnecessary for me to say that my sympathies have been deeply enlisted in the case of Maj. Crittenden and what is more important my conviction complete that he has been unjustly treated.

You know Mr. Polk and your view of the manner in which he should be dealt with as shown by your letters has very closely agreed with my own. Wearied by this hesitation I have called for the proceedings in the case and if he holds out it is a case in which the weaker goes to the wall. I think I will beat him and so you may say in confidence to your gallant Son.

My boy Tom, in which style I hope you will recognize Col. Crittenden has been discreet and I think efficient in a cause where feeling might have warped the judgement of an older man.

I regret exceedingly to see that Mr. Clay is to return to the Senate, among many reasons is one in which I know you will sympathize, the evil influence he will have on the friends of Genl. Taylor in the two houses of Congress.[†] Many who would have done very well in his absence will give way in his presence. This will also introduce a new element in the selection of the gens. cabinet. It must be composed of men of nerve and of no Clay affinities.

One instance to illustrate my meaning Berrien of Ga. though well enough without Clay's shadow, would not do under it.

You see that I disregard Mr. C.s pledge to support the administration, he may wish to do so, but can his nature reach so much. The Englishman Baker, who came from the Rio Grande to draw pay,

[*] Notable Kentucky political leader who served in cabinet, in Congress, and as governor.
[†] Henry Clay and Major General Zachary Taylor, at this time president-elect.

mileage and a year's stationery as a member of Congress is here, with recommendations from legislatures for the post of Secty. of War. What would Genl. Taylor say to such impudent dictation and indelicate solicitation. Butler King wants to be Secty. of Navy you know the little Yankee—Andrew Stuart wants to be Secty. of Treasy. the man who proved wool to be a vegetable. I hope you will talk fully with Genl. Taylor he knows very little of our public men personally and will have very little opportunity to observe them after his arrival.

Clayton is true and talks right, has he the necessary nerve,—how would Binney of Philad. do for the Treasy. A. Lawrence is not a Lawyer and is a manufacturer, how would Mr. Lawrence do for Navy, how would Gadsden do for War, how will a Post Master Genl. be selected—˙

The Genl. will need you and I hope to see you here—Loose and hurried as my remarks are, written in the midst of much "noise and confusion" you may from intimate knowledge of all I have treated of, unravel what would be unintelligible to one less informed—Your friend

JEFF'N: DAVIS

To Samuel A. Cartwright (PJD)†

WARREN COUNTY, MISSISSIPPI, JUNE 10, 1849

DR. SIR,

I have the pleasure to acknowledge your's of the 5th accompanying the l[e]tter of W Robertson of the N. O. Standard. I am gratified to learn that Louisiana is about to heve a paper instituted for the purpose avowed, and edited by a genteman of the qualifications and feelings which you inform me belong to Mr. Robertson. It is time for our justification before the uninformed and that we may be understood by posterity as well as by contemporaries that the long continued and

---

˙ Whig politicians: John M. Berrien of Georgia, Edward Baker of Illinois, Thomas Butler King of Georgia, Andrew Stuart of Pennsylvania and Ohio, John Clayton of Delaware, Horace Binney of Pennsylvania, Amos Lawrence of Massachusetts, and James Gadsden of South Carolina.

† Physician and friend of JD who lived in New Orleans.

gross misrepresentations of our slave institutions should be answered. In an evil hour some of the most distinguished of southern stat[es]men admitted that slavery was an evil, this as it is construed takes from us all gro[un]d of defence save that of presen[t nece]ssity, and not only warrants the attempts of others for its abolition but also demands of us constant efforts to remove the obstacles to its abatement.

Speculation can present a condition of society in which government would be an evil, and there have not been wanting those who have contended that there should be no individuality in property. Such opinions and speculations have been generally treated as idle, because inapplicable to the existing state of things, or answered by showing /that/ the advantages which belong to each greatly outweighed the disadvantages to be removed by their destruction. Is not this equally /the/ case with domestic slavery as it exists among us. Even the "odious slave trade," has but saved the African captive from Sacrifice; or transferred him from subjection to a barbarian master, to the milder servitude to a christian, and brought him from the darkness of heathenism to the light of revealed religion. The slave labor of the U.S. h[a]s furnished a cheap material for human clothing, <-[illegible]-> bringing comfort to the indigent by cheaper clothes than could have b[een] otherwise obtained; has increased the supp [ly and?] lowered, therefore, the price of hemp, and of sugar; directly or indirectly conferring important benefits on more than half the civilized people of the globe. It has opened new channels of commerce, and widened old ones; thus bringing different nations into closer intercourse and greater dependence; which is to strengthen the bonds of national amity, and to advance our race in knowledge, industry, security and happiness. Cotton the great staple of the slave holding states, is now the controlling medium of commerce; and between Europe and the U.S., a bond to keep the peace, which it will require much ignorance or vice on the part of their governments to break.

But my respected friend, I do not believe /that/ it is a mistaken policy, or a misguided humanity, or an eager fanaticism which conducts this crusade against our slave institution; but a thirst for political dominion, which adopts the various catch words which may seem best adapted to th[e] different localities of its recruiting rend[ezv]ous.

Under this conviction I have long believed, our only prospect of peaceful adjustment is through such action on the part of /the/ South as will command the attention and excite the reflection of *the masses* of the north. Upon the issue, "shall slavery be extended," we have been and will be beaten in any non slave-holding state. It is not believed /by the north/ that the citizens of the South with any approach to Unanimity will (even to ultimate results) assert and maintain the doctrines which their Representatives have contended for in Congress. Primary assemblies, state conventions, and legislative resolutions may correct this error, in time to save the constitutional rights of the South, and preserve our Union. <-[illegible]-> Such as our Fathers bequeathed it to us, *the Union of equals,* with a common government restricted to its delegated powers. The Masses of the South, must act upon the masses of the North; their politicians, you see, I consider as the vane upon the house top, which tells whence the wind cometh, and veers with the change of the current.

You once mention[ed] some investigations by Mr. Tooley of the Hebrew tex[t] of the Bible. I was struck with your remarks at t[he tim]e, Would not their publication suit the purpose of [the Stan]dard? It will give me much satisfaction to hea[r]. I am your friend &c

JEFF'N: DAVIS

To Malcolm D. Haynes (PJD)*

BRIERFIELD, WARREN COUNTY, MISSISSIPPI, AUGUST 18, 1849
DEAR SIR—
I thank you for your very friendly letter, and it gives me pleasure to comply with your request in relation to the anti-slavery agitation which disturbs the fraternity and peace of the Republic. I regret to hear that there are any, however few, among us who are insensible to the danger with which the rights of the Southern States are threatened. He must have been very unobservant of the legislative, and popular proceedings of Northern States and people, who has not seen

---

* Mississippi editor and officeholder.

enough to convince him that abolitionism is no longer confined to a few fanatics, but is the heart of a great political organization, which in many States holds the balance of power between the two parties of the country, and in some, rules supreme over both. It is no longer the rabble collected about a runaway slave, or moved by the imaginary narratives of vagrant preachers and itinerant spinsters, nor is it the visionary followers of the dreaming philosophy of Rousseau and Bentham, to whom our attention should be directed;* but to the systematic, calculating, sectional organization, which aims at political dominion over us, and strikes at our prosperity, our property, and domestic security. Those thus banded together have taken a variety of names, such as anti-slavery men, non-extensionists, emancipationists, liberty party, freesoil party, &c., but considering them one family, differing somewhat in their mode of attack, but not at all in the final purpose of it, I will refer to them by their patronymic, as abolitionists.

It is about seventeen years since the abolitionists organized for a crusade against the African slavery of the United States. They preached the sin and moral grievance thereof to those States where it did not exist, as a reason why the general government should be called on to abate it. That such a doctrine ever had disciples, is only to be accounted for by the political heresy that ours is an union of the people, the formation of a nation, and a supreme government charged with providing for the general welfare. To those who maintained that it was in an union of States, a confederation of sovereigns, for enumerated objects, and recognized in the general government no other powers than those specifically delegated, or *necessarily* implied, the domestic institutions of any other State than their own could never become a grievance, or be the subject of moral responsibility. In this distinction between the doctrines of centralization and of State rights, is contained the best security for the faithful and willing observance of the guaranties of the constitution; and the probable origin of the apothegm of Mr. Jefferson, that the democracy of the North were the natural allies of the South.† However true this was, however much the result of distinctive principles, the fact does not now exist. We have, at least so far as the domestic

---

* Jean-Jacques Rousseau, French thinker, and Jeremy Bentham, English thinker.

† Thomas Jefferson, Founding Father and president of the United States 1801–09.

institution of slavery is involved, the alliance of neither party at the North. The few politicians who have maintained the faith of non-interference with this domestic question, have either sustained themselves by a personal strength superior to party, or must in future be content with "the private station" which, under such circumstances, is emphatically "the post of honor."

Fanatics and demagogues have inflamed popular passion; it has been fed by sectional pride, and we have to meet the evil which Washington deprecated, the indication of which startled Jefferson like "a fire bell at night," a geographical party. The issue presented to us is a sectional discrimination, alike violative of our constitutional rights, and offensive to our feelings for the institution we inherited, with the arrogant alternative of submission or compulsion. In the spirit of compromise and the confidence of fraternity, the South yielded to the North, by the ordinance of 1787, the whole of the Northwest territory; by the Missouri Compromise, more than half of Louisiana, and by the terms of Texas annexation, the northern part of that State. By the right of the strongest they have taken the whole of Oregon, and by the robber's law, that "he may take who has the power," they now claim New Mexico and California. Before the revolution, the territory of the Southern colonies exceeded that of the Northern nearly four-fold; now the case is reversed, their domain exceeds ours, as estimated, more than a million of square miles: we no longer hear of compromise for sectional equalization, but their cry is that of the unsatisfiable horse leach—give! give!

In the confidence of power, all further compromise is discarded: to submit to further demands thus presented, is to abandon our constitutional rights, and to consent to be subject. If it were true as has been asserted that slaves would not be taken to New Mexico and California if permitted, it would only change the issue presented by the proposition to prohibit them, from injury to insult. But I do not believe it to be true, and that the abolitionist do not, is shown by their whole conduct in Congress, and out of it. See their opposition to the compromise bill of the Senate, called Clayton's bill, by which it was provided that the right of slaveholders of the United States to migrate with their slaves into those territories, should be decided by the United

States courts. See their opposition to the amendment of Senator Walker to the civil appropriation bill which recognised the extension of the constitution, as far as applicable, to those territories. They opposed every measure for the purpose of giving government in the territories, either immediate or prospective, unless it contained a provision forever prohibiting slavery. Often denied as was our constitutional right, they steadily refused to leave the question to the umpire provided to decide in such cases, the Supreme Court of U.S. They claimed the advantage of a law in their favor. Thus showing that they really believed, what they verbally denied, that slaves would be carried to those territories, and that the U.S. Constitution would protect their owners in their possession. Another ground of opposition, one which clearly exposes the political object of its prominent actors, is the influence which they attribute to the presence of slaves, in determining the future institutions of that country. It has been stated in argument against permitting slaveholders to migrate with their property to the territories, that there was such inherent power in the institution, that if a small proportion of the population held slaves they would control the policy of the mass, so as to establish slavery when the territory should become a State. Whilst politicians have been thus laboring for our exclusion, the abolition societies have been also contributing their aid. The N.Y. anti-slavery society announces as "in press for distribution in New Mexico and California," a new edition of the "address to non-slaveholders of the u. States," also "an elaborate address to the inhabitants of California and New Mexico," to show, they say, the comparative value of free and slave labor; they also say they "are advised that several abolitionists have gone thither with a determination to exert all the influence in their power to withstand the encroachments of slavery, and encourage the people in establishing free governments." If Congressional agitation, determining the emigration of slave holders, the Mormon colony, the disbanded regiment of N. York and the resident Mexicans, should cause the first expression of popular opinion to be adverse to the introduction of African slaves, we will no doubt be told that their exclusion is the decree of climate, soil, and production; and the choice of the people. If free from the fears of federal interference, Southern men might form colonies, emigrating in bodies of sufficient size to defend and mutually protect their property from lawless interference, but even this security, which is less than their due, by as much as it falls short of the protection which government owes to all property, a sectional hostilities denies. Whether slaves would be permanently profitable in our Pacific possessions, or become, with the influx of free labor, a tax to their masters, I will not pretend to decide. But if it be true that slavery could not exist in that country, as our opponents habitually assert, what are we to think of the sincerity of their professions for emancipation, when they so strenuously resist the emigration of slaves to a country in which, according to their position, they would soon become free.

. . .

It is time that we should have cointelligence and concert of action, that no consideration should interrupt us in the duty of defence, that we should avail ourselves of all the checks and remedies proper to our present position, and make all the preparation which probable emergencies demand. Trusting, hoping to avert the evils which threaten us, we should be prepared for the worst.

The manufacturing resources of our section should be developed. The press should spread the truth where the Southern side of the question has not been fully presented, and funds should be raised to support it in the expenses thus incurred. Ignorance is the nurse of fiction and prejudice and passion. How great the ignorance, among the masses of the North, is, in relation to the condition of our slaves, appears by the fictions that circulate among them. Such as that marriage among slaves is discountenanced or prohibited, and all their family ties disregarded by their masters. That their bodies are cramped with fetters, or loaded with chains. That the introduction of the Bible is most strictly forbidden.

It is strange almost beyond belief, that any one possessed of reason should not perceive that, from interest, if no higher motive actuated, all those social bonds which would contribute to contentment and morality of the slave would be encouraged by his master. In the least humane view which could be taken, that which would assimilate our slaves to their beasts of burden, they might understand that in manacles and chains the slave would be a tax by his support instead of a profit by his labor or service. But what could be more ridiculous than the idea of prohibiting the Bible to our slaves. If they could read, and would read its sacred pages, where could be found better assurance against the seductions of the abolitionits, than in its lessons of submission and faithful, not eye service, to masters. Its reproof of runaways, and cautions to servants against "fellowship with new fangled teachers," such "as knowing nothing, but doting about questions and strifes of words, whereof cometh envy, strife, railings, evils surmisings, perverse disputings of men of corrupt minds, and destitute of the truth, supposing that gain is godliness: from such withdraw thyself." I Tim., vi. 4, 5.

We rely on the Bible as authority for the establishment of slavery among men, and on the Constitution for its recognition throughout the United States.

It is wholly untrue, as has been stated, that slavery was established by the laws of the States where it is found, and is purely local in its character. All property derives its security of tenure from the laws of the country where it is held, and any property which is prohibited by the laws of certain countries, is to that extent more limited as to locality, than such as being recognized by the universal admission of mankind may be held, acquired, or removed to any part of the inhabited globe. But this distinction has no application to slavery in the U.S. Territories, because slaves being recognized as property by the Constitution of the United States, may be held as such in any part thereof, where it has not been prohibited by competent authority. The question then presents itself, what authority is competent to prohibit slavery in the territories belonging to the United States? I answer, not that of the federal government, not that of the territorial inhabitants during their territorial dependence, but that of the States, in whom this power must remain as sovereign owners, until it has been delegated or surrendered. The general government, as agent of the States, is charged with the power of disposing of the public domain, and of making the needful regulations therefor. This power extends equally to territory (public lands) within the limits of a State, as to that which may be beyond them, and therefore could not have been intended to convey such sovereign power as might determine the relations of persons, and decide what should be property. Where no government existed, other regulations would be needful, than those required under the protection of a State; but in no case could powers be drawn from a grant which, as in the case we are considering, were neither indicated by its terms, germain to its purpose, or supposible as the intent. The territory being the common property of the States, the right of emigrants to occupy it must be derived from this joint ownership, and surely cannot confer on those who may first reach such common property, the power to prescribe the conditions on which others, claiming by the same right, may be admitted to like enjoyment. Those powers which are necessary for police, and security of person and property, belong to the social state, and would of necessity be exercised in the absence of government; for instance, by wrecked mariners upon a desert island. But these natural rights must, in the case of inhabitants of U.S. Territory, be exercised in subordination to the principles of the Constitution, to be recognized and permitted by the general government of the United States. My position, then, is that the authority competent to prohibit slavery in the territories, remain in the sovereign States of the Union, and there I think it should quietly remain, until the people of the territory, by becoming a State, acquire the right to decide the question for themselves. This would be just, because it would give to all an equal opportunity to avail themselves of benefits to which all have an equal right, and expedient, because it would give an opportunity to determine by the laws of climate and production, the policy which would most promote the prosperity of the State.

It is utterly untrue, that slavery in the States is the creature of their enactment. It existed in the colonies and was regulated like other property by the common law of England. It existed before the colonies were founded. It is traced to the earliest period of history, and there we find laws prescribed for its government, as an existing institution. Its beginning is still further back, lost in the mists of a more remote antiquity.

When our Northern brethren drove a profitable trade with the tribes of Africa, for their captive slaves, to be imported and sold in the Southern States, it was enough for them to know where their introduction was not prohibited. The discovery that property in the service of an African was of such peculiar character that it could only exist where it had been previously provided for by municipal law, was reserved for this age of sectional strife, pseudo philanthrophy, speculative philosophy, and political prostitution to make.

The United States constitution recognizing property in slaves, the Congress has no right to discriminate between that and any other species of property. Whether in vessels or in territories, on the high seas, or on the Pacific slope. Wherever our flag floats as the emblem of sovereignty, the citizen of the United States has a right to claim from the general government, the shield of the constitution, and the enforcement of its guarantees. This is all which the South has claimed, and for asserting this right as one which we would not surrender, we have been charged with the design of disunion, by those whose conduct inevitably tends to that catastrophe.

That we have not loved the Union less in the past, than our brethren of the North, let history attest; which of us honor its principles and observe its compromises more, let our present and future conduct determine.

In contending for our constitutional right, we discharge not only a duty to ourselves, and to the Union, but to federative, representative, constitutional liberty, which depends on the success of this government to prove its practicability on an extended scale.

The generation which avoids its responsibility, by permitting the claim of the North to all the territory possessed or to be acquired, will have sown the wind, and left to their children the harvest of the whirlwind. They will have transmitted not Union, but disunion, or submission to the most oppressive species of despotism, that of an irresponsible, sectional majority.

There are many facts and opinions to which I would be glad to avert as connected with this question, but my letter is already so long that I must postpone them until we meet, which I hope will be in the course of next month. With my best wishes for your success, I am very truly, Your friend, &c.,

JEFF. DAVIS.

To W. B. Tebo (JDC)*

BRIERFIELD, WARREN COUNTY, MISSISSIPPI, AUGUST 22, 1849

DEAR SIR:

In your paper of the 8th inst., I perceive a reference to myself which is founded in an error, which I have less hesitation in correcting because of the complimentary terms and distinguished company with which my name is connected. I allude to this paragraph:

"There was a time, it is true, when Quitman's position was obnoxious to the democratic party of the State.† Previous to the extra session of Congress of 1837, he occupied the position of the patriotic Calhoun and his peculiar friends, a position of temporary disagreement or estrangement from the great body of the democratic party. In this he was associated with many of the greatest men of the South (democrats too,) and with many in Mississippi who are now, and have long been considered among the firmest and soundest democrats in the State—Judge C. P. Smith, Dr. Lipscomb, Jefferson Davis, Dr. Hagan, T. B. Woodward and the Hon. Joseph W. Chalmers, and the lamented Col. Andrew L. Martin, then of Tennessee."

At the time referred to I had taken no other part in politics than by casting my vote, and neither before nor since have I had any political associations which placed me in the position of estrangement to the great body of the democratic party. My first vote was cast in favor of General Jackson for President. At subsequent periods I have supported for the same office, Van Buren in 1835, Van Buren in 1840—Polk in 1844—and Cass in 1848.

Political inconsistency is a thing of very little importance to any other than the individual concerned, and except where political principle is involved, is so dependent upon circumstance and association as to afford no evidence of merit.

From my childhood I was attached to General Jackson. My confidence and respect for him increased in after years. My affection and

---

* Editor of the *Natchez Free Trader*.

† John A. Quitman, long friendly with the Davis family and important military and political leader; served as a general officer in the Mexican War, as governor, and as a U.S. representative.

admiration followed him to the grave, and cling to his memory. This feeling induces me to trouble you with the above correction. Very respectfully,

YOUR FRIEND, &C.,
JEF. DAVIS.

To William R. Cannon (PJD)*

WASHINGTON, D.C., JANUARY 8, 1850

MY DEAR SIR,

I have just received your kind and gratifying letter of the 30th Ult.; like yourself I have been for some weeks thinking of writing to you, but have been prevented by the near approach of the time when I would again be submitted to a test by the body of which you are a member. This will probably reach you after that event has transpired or been postponed to a more remote period.

I agree entirely with you in your view about a democratic caucus, and would regret nothing more than that our party should have its organization and harmony disturbed by my name. No office, certainly no candidate is of sufficient importance to justify a course which might lead to such evils. Not having sought either by correspondence or personal interviews to learn the intentions of members in relation to the senatorial election, I am less than most persons would expect informed as to probabilities of the result. I know that various elements have been at work to defeat me, and have seen too often the effect of personal solicitation to underate its power. It is mortifying to me to feel that any section of the state should assume the attitude of opposition to me under the idea that one part of Mississippi is less dear to me than another; but I have the consolation to know that neither my heart or my official conduct justifies such idea.

I have from friends of Barton and some of my particular friends who have conversed with him, received assurances that he was friendly to me, and unless compelled by the presentation of a candi-

* JD's friend and political supporter in Mississippi.

date from his own county would vote for me.* My opinion of him as a frank, honorable man, and my admiration of him as a high toned Democrat have led me to expect good rather than evil from him. Though it would be, as commonly held, a reflection on me, after having served out the remainder of a term, not to be offered a full term, I should attribute it to other causes than a withdrawal of confidence, and consider it only as a means of hastening a step which I would not under any circumstances desire long to defer, that is, a final leave of public station.

The progress of opposition to slavery is evident in both houses of Congress, Demogogues have raised a spirit they dare not face, and which a few who have no other political capital will not allow them to evade. The plan of concealing the Wilmot Proviso under a so called state constitution will be attempted and probably succeed in the case of California, but the question in its former aspect will be presented on New Mexico or some other case. I have no assurance that we will get any northern vote in the Senate except that of Dickinson of N.Y. it is however possible that Sturgeon of Pa. may vote with us in the territorial case.† Neither will vote against California admission as a state, the prohibition of slavery being a fundamental article. The effect is the same, and to my mind the offence the same, unless it be heightened by the insolence exhibited by a few adventurers uniting with a herd as various in color and nearly as ignorant of our government, as Jacobs cattle, to deprive the people of the South from equal participation in the common property of the states.

The action of the southern states has produced much reflection, yet it is not thought by the northern men generally that we are in earnest, they may hug the delusion until it is too late to avoid the precipice on the brink of which I believe we now stand. It is thought by many that /the/ President will if brought to the point, veto the Wilmot proviso, and the fear that it will dissolve the Union induces me to think the opinion correct. otherwise, I would say, that I believe, if Genl. Taylor thinks that the Wilmot proviso would cause dissolution of the union, that he would certainly veto it. I also believe that his party would, if

---

* Roger Barton, Whig politician in Mississippi.

† Daniel Dickinson and Daniel Sturgeon, both U.S. senators.

they knew such would be his course, prevent the test being applied to him, from party considerations which will occur to you. Midshipmen are now assigned to congressional districts, there is I was recently informed but one vacancy from Mi. that was for the 1st Cong. Dist. and has been filled two days since. I am sorry I cannot testify my willingness to serve you by procuring now an appointment for Mr. Brownrig—

Let me hear from you as often as convenient and believe me ever yr friend—

JEFFN DAVIS

Speech in U.S. Senate (JDC)

JANUARY 10, 1850

. . .

Mr. President, I always enter into the discussion of the slavery questions with feelings of reluctance; and only because I am forced into it by those who, having nothing to do with it, nevertheless indecently interfere in our domestic affairs here, I have done so. Sir, it is a melancholy fact, that morning after morning, when we come here to enter into the business of the Senate, our feelings should be harrowed up by the introduction of this exciting and profitless subject, and we be compelled to listen to insults heaped upon our institutions. Sir, there is no man who comes here to represent his constituency for high and useful purposes, and who feels upon himself the obligation of his oath to maintain the Constitution of the United States, who could thus act, from day to day, for the purpose of disturbing the useful legislation of the country—for no other purpose than to insert another brand into the flame which every reflecting, sober man now sees threatens to consume the fabric of our Government. We of the South stand now, as we have always stood, upon the defensive. We raised not this question; but when raised, it is our duty to defend ourselves. For one, sir, my purposes are to keep down this species of excitement, both here and at home. I know the temper of those whom I represent, and they require no promptings to resist aggression or insult. I know their determination. It is well and deeply taken, and will be shown when the crisis comes. They make no threats against anyone, and least of all against the Union, for which they have made such heavy and continued sacrifices. They know their rights, while they feel their wrongs; and they will maintain the one, resent the other, if it may be, will preserve our constitutional Union; but the Union without the Constitution they hold to be a curse. With the Constitution, they will never abandon it. We, sir, are parties to this Union only under the Constitution, and there is no power known in the world that could dictate to my little State a Union in which her rights were continually disrespected and trampled upon by an unrestrained majority. The present generation, sir, will maintain the character their fathers won. They well know how to sustain the institutions which they inherited, even by civil war, if that be provoked. They will march up to this issue, and meet it face to face.

This is our position; you have not respected it. I know yours, and cannot respect it; and knowing it, I came to this session of Congress with melancholy forebodings—with apprehension that it might be the last of our Government. I still trusted, however, in the intelligence and patriotism of the masses, for I have long since said that I put no faith in politicians. I feel that they have raised a storm which they cannot control. They have invoked a spirit which they cannot allay, and dare not confront. And yet I believe that the descendants of the Franklins, the Hancocks, and the Adamses, if they saw our institutions about to be destroyed by a mean and captious exercise of the power of demagogues to press to a fatal extremity aggressions upon our rights by the North, would rise up in their strength, and would enforce the justice and obligations of the Constitution. This is no indication of any confidence which I put in their representatives; with them I am ready to meet this issue face to face; and if the representatives of that people think proper to sow the seeds of dissension, and to inflame the passions and prejudices of one section, whilst they drive the other by every possible provocation to the point of civil war, then all I have to say is, that the representatives of the South, true to their constituency, are prepared to meet the issue here and now. If this is to be the hot-bed of civil war, if from this as a center the evil is to radiate throughout our country, here let the first battle be fought! If gentlemen come here constantly to press upon us, strip us of our rights, move the people of one section of the nation to hostility against the other, I hope that those who have brought the country to this crisis will meet the first test.

Mr. President, it is no part of the business of a southern representative here to deliver panegyrics upon the attachment of his constituents to the Union. We have proved our love of the Union and our devotion to it too often and too long to require such declarations. Let those who feel that it may be doubted make their declarations of fidelity to the Union; we have nothing of the kind to do. If the State of Vermont chooses to send to the Senate of the United States insulting resolutions relating to her sister States, let the Senators and Representatives of that State do their duty in relation to them; and as I say nothing against a sovereign State, I will only say to those Senators that I regret that Vermont has not now such constitutional scruples as actuated her in the war of 1812, and that she does not keep her resolutions within her own limits, in this war of aggression, as she attempted to keep her troops during that war.

I regret that I shall have to part with many friends with whom I have uniformly acted in the Senate, upon the motion, now pending, to print these resolutions. I would agree to print them, however offensive they might be, if the State had sent them to the Senate. The State has a right to speak to the Senate, and be heard. But I accept the argument of the Senator from Georgia, which has improperly, as it seems to me, been called special pleading, that they are the property of the Senators to whom they are directed, and I perceive no obligation requiring them to have been placed before the Senate. They are instructions addressed to them, with reference to their own duties, and might just as well remain in their own pockets as to lie upon the table of the Senate. I hold them to be unjust, to be untrue, offensive, insulting, treasonable to the Constitution; and I will not endorse them by my vote. I have thus briefly stated my reasons.

Speech in U.S. Senate (JDC)

...

I then go on to state what was the case when this Missouri compromise line was applied to the Territory of Louisiana, which was slave territory. The line of 36° 30' was drawn through the territory, and when slavery was prohibited north of that line, the division was complete. It was unnecessary to say anything about the country below, because, saying nothing, slavery existed as theretofore. It was decided by making a division of the territory between the slaveholding and the non-slaveholding States. I have said that, in this case, where the whole territory is in dispute, there should be a distinct application to the one side and to the other, in order that we might have the full benefit of the spirit of the Missouri compromise, in a case unlike that for which it was made; that the citizens of the United States were engaged in controversy as to the right to take a particular species of property into the territories; that this controversy—so painful, injurious, and dangerous in its tendency, and seemingly so irreconcilable—might be adjusted, without compromise of principle, by a division of the territory between the two sections of the Union—the one to have sole possession above, and the other to have equal possession below, the line— for, sir, when you admit slavery into the territory, you do not exclude the white laborer. It is a great fallacy, which has been repeatedly here promulgated, to suppose so. No, sir; slave labor forms the substratum on which white labor is elevated, and he who seeks for that portion of our country where, in fact, as in theory, political equality does exist, must be pointed to the slaveholding States. Such, at least, I know to be the case among all the white men where I reside, and such I cannot believe to be the case where, as in the non-slaveholding States, white men are sunk to menial occupations.

But, sir, the Senator has noticed some closing remarks of that speech, which I hoped would have had a tendency rather to quiet than to excite controversy. Expression was given to the feelings which I have always entertained, of an abiding love for all portions of the country; and no petty sectional hostility toward any, has ever found shelter in my breast. Even that portion of my remarks, the Senator has thought proper to comment on, and, as I think, unkindly. I indicated as the cause of sectional strife—it might be, of the destruction of our happy and happiness-conferring Union—the poor, the despicable antipathy to the South, because of her institution of African bondage. To this he replies, that there is no hostility toward us of the South, because we hold the African race in bondage; but that it is only to the extension of the territory in which the African may thus be held. He has no hostility, then, it appears, to the fact of our holding the African race in bondage in one place, but he has insuperable objections to our doing so in another. Why is this? Is it for the benefit of that race itself? Not at all; for every man must understand that diffusion, not concentration, is for the benefit of the slave. Is it for the benefit of the white race? Not at all; everyone must understand, that as the white population predominates over the black, the safety and happiness of both are secured; and, further, all must understand, that if final emancipation is ever to ensue, it must come when the slaves are few in proportion to the whites inhabiting the country. The number of slaves is rapidly increasing, in a ratio probably equal to the natural increase of the white population in any part of the United States. There is no policy which would perpetuate and rivet that institution forever on this country, so surely as that which confines the slaves to the present limits in which they are held. There must—to render emancipation practicable—be a door opened, by which they may go out; and that door must be toward the equator. All who understand their habits and constitutional peculiarities, must admit this. And yet, the policy is here advocated, day after day, by those who claim to be the peculiar friends of emancipation, to draw around us a barrier to prevent the exodus of the slaves, and dam them up in the small territory which they occupy, where, increasing in number year by year, the impossibility of emancipation will augment also, until he only can deny that the system must be perpetual, who is prepared to see the slave become the master, to convert a portion of the States of this Union into negro possessions, or, to witness the more probable result, of their extermination by a servile war.

. . .

To F. H. Elmore (JDC)*

WASHINGTON, D.C., APRIL 13, 1850

DR SIR:

Since the receipt of your letter we have had some consultation in relation to the proposition you submitted in relation to the Nashville convention. The prevailing opinion is to leave the matter entirely in the hands of the people. My own view is and has been that the convention should meet for preventive purposes. That it is necessary to begin an organization of the South the want of which has left us a divided people, when union and cointelligence was necessary for our safety. The charge which has been made of a design to sever the Southern states from the confederacy but increased the propriety of meeting. If we had no other purpose than to redress past wrongs it would be proper to wait until the measure of our grievances was full; but to check aggression, to preserve the union, peaceably to secure our rights requires prompt action. We should no doubt have greater una[ni]mity, higher resolve if called upon to avenge the blow, than if only required to paralyze the arm upraised to strike. Then it would be the energy of revolution, now it is the preservation of the Constitution.

A postponement is in my opinion, equivalent to abandonment of the Southern convention, and to being hereafter branded as disunionists who were arrested in their purpose. It is needless to add that I cannot aid in the object of postponement. Long since I resolved that if the measure was abandoned it should be by no agency of mine, and have believed that the toryism we now see was only to be put down by the action of the faithful. If a few meet, many will rue the day when they oppose us, and our strength will increase thenceforward—I write freely to you whose aim and feelings I know to be such as I cherish— If a different course be adopted from that which I approve, my cordial wish is that my opinions may prove to have been those of an over excited mind—as ever yr. friend

JEFFN. DAVIS.

* South Carolina political leader and banker.

Speech in U.S. Senate (JDC)

...

I do not propose, Mr. President, at this stage of the bill, and in the known temper of the Senate, to enter into any argument upon its merits or demerits. Although there is a wide field of facts not yet explored, it is not my purpose to enter upon it. I feel that it would be useless. More than that; I should fear to expose myself to an exhibition of that restlessness which has on this question marked the majority of the Senate, and which I do not wish to encounter. But I ask why, and among whom, is the spirit of impatience manifested? Does it proceed from a desire to provide a government for California? No, sir; the records deny that. This impatience is most exhibited by those who, at the last session of Congress, refused, unless with the slavery restriction, to unite with us to give the benefits of a territorial government to California; such a government as was then adapted to their condition; nay more, such a government as is best adapted to their condition now. Then, sir, among that class of Senators the great purpose of giving a territorial government to the people of California was held subordinate to the application of the Wilmot proviso to the bill. Then, and for that reason, Congress failed to give the protection to this people which they had a right to expect at the hands of a just Government, and which they had a right to demand under the treaty of peace with Mexico.

Now, sir, when the people inhabiting that Territory have formed a Constitution, one of the clauses of which prohibits the introduction of slaves, those who refused to give a government under the circustances just named, and, as we have a right to infer, for the reason stated, are now found most earnest in pressing upon us, in violation of all precedent, its admission as a State into the Union. Then are we not compelled to conclude that their policy, both then as now, was governed by the single desire to exclude slaveholders from introducing that species of property into any of the recent acquisitions from Mexico? Is that in accordance with the provision of the Constitution, which secures equal privileges and immunities to all the citizens of the several States of the Union? Is it in accordance with the principle of even-handed justice, if there had been no constitutional obligations? These acquisitions were made by the people of the whole United States, and we are bound to remember that those whom this bill proposes to exclude, contributed more than their fair proportion, both of blood and treasure, to obtain that territory. No, sir, the Constitution forbids justice condemns the course which is pursued, and patriotism and reason frown indignantly upon it. Is it, then, a matter of surprise that we, the suffering party, have shown resentment and made determined opposition? Is it not rather a matter of surprise that that indignation which has blazed throughout the southern States should have been received with such calm indifference by the majority of Congress; that Congress has not only refused to listen, but has treated with scorn the appeal which has been made? Such, however, has been the history of this debate.

But if the motive be denied, then I ask, if not for the reason I have given, why are northern Senators pressing with such eagerness the admission of California? Is it to secure a benefit for their manufactures or navigation? No, sir. They know that when the inhabitants of California become a State they will be a people in favor of free trade, and that their policy will be to invite the shipping of the world, and secure for themselves the cheapest transportation. It is not, then, for purposes of their own interest that they seek her admission. Is it to preserve their political rights under the Constitution? No sir, Now they are in the majority, and they need no addition for such a purpose as that. Then we are forced to conclude that it is for, the purpose of aggression upon the people of the South—that it is an exhibition of that spirit of a dominant party which regards neither the Constitution nor justice, nor the feelings of fraternity which bind them to us, but treads with destroying and relentless step on all considerations which should govern men, wise, just, and patriotic.

And this is the evidence of that love for the Union which is constantly presented to us as a reason why we should abandon the rights, why we should be recreant to the known will of our constituents, why we should disregard the duties we were delegated to perform, and submit to aggression such as freemen have never tamely borne. But, Mr. President, is this the way to avoid danger from the indignation which has been aroused; is this the way to avert the danger of disunion, if such danger exist? That indignation, and that danger, so far as it has been excited, is the offspring of injustice, and this is the maturing act of a series of measures which lead to one end—the total destruction of the equality of the States, and the overthrow of the rights of the southern section of the Union. We, sir, of the South, are the equals of the North by compact, by inheritance, and the patriotic devotion and sacrifices by which the territory from which it is proposed to exclude us was acquired. And when such an outrage excites a manly remonstrance, instead of bringing with it a feeling of forbearance and a disposition to abstain and reflect, it is answered by the startling cry of disunion, disunion! What constitutes the crime of disunion?

This, sir, is a Union of sovereign States, under a compact which delegated certain powers to the General Government, and reserved all else to the States respectively or to the people. To the Union the South is as true now as in the day when our forefathers assisted to establish it; against that Union they have never by word or deed offered any opposition. They have never claimed from this Federal Government any peculiar advantages for themselves. They have never shrunk from any duty or sacrifice imposed by it, nor sought to deprive others of the benefits it was designed to confer. They have never spoken of that constitutional Union but in respectful language; they have never failed in aught which would secure to posterity the unincumbered enjoyment of that legacy which our fathers left us.

Those who endeavored to sap and undermine the Constitution on which that Union rests are disunionists in the most opprobrious understanding of that term; such being the crime of disunion, I ask by whom, and how is this spirit of disunion promoted? Not by those who maintain the Constitution from which the Union arose, and by adherence to which it has reached its present greatness; not those who refuse to surrender the principles which gave birth to the Union, and which are the soul of its existence; not those who claiming the equality to which they were born, declare that they will resist an odious, unconstitutional, and unjust discrimination against their rights.

This, sir, is to maintain the Union by preserving the foundation on which it stands; and if it be sedition or treason to raise voice and hand against the miners who are working for its overthrow, against those who are seeking to build upon its ruins a new Union which rests not upon the Constitution for authority, but upon the dominant will of the majority, then my heart is filled with such sedition and treason, and the reproach which it brings is esteemed as an honor. But, sir, if gentlemen wish to preserve the constitutional Union, that Union to which I and those whom I represent are so ardently attached, I have to say the way is as easy and plain as the road to market. You have but to abstain from injustice, you have but to secure to each section and to all citizens the provisions of the Constitution under which the Union was formed; you have but to leave in full operation the principles which preexisted, created, and have blessed it. Then, sir, if any ruthless hand should be raised to destroy the temple of this Confederacy, with united hearts and ready arms the people will gather around it for its protection; then, sir, it would be indeed a Union of brethren, and not that forced Union which it is sought now to establish and maintain by coercing sovereign States at the point of the bayonet, and reducing the free spirit of the people to submission by the terror of marching armies. By virtue, by confidence, by the unpurchasable affection of the people, by adherence to fundamental principles, and under the direction of the letter of compact and Union, this Republic has grown to its present grandeur, has illustrated the blessings and taught to mankind the advantages of representative liberty. As a nation, it is, though yet in the freshness of youth, among the first Powers of the globe, and casts the shadow of its protection over its citizens, on whatever sea or shore, for commerce or adventure, they may wander. When we see a departure in the administration of the Government from the fundamental principles on which this Union was founded, and by adherence to which it has thus prospered, we have reason to believe the virtue and wisdom of our fathers have departed from the people, or that their agents are unworthy of those whom they represent.

We stand on the verge of an act which is to form an era in the history of our country. Now, for the first-time, we are about permanently to destroy the balance of power between the sections of the Union, by securing a majority to one, in both Houses of Congress; this, too, when sectional spirit is rife over the land, and when those who are to have the control in both Houses of Congress will also have the Executive power in their hands, and by unmistakable indications have shown a disposition to disregard that Constitution which made us equals in rights, privileges, and immunities. When that barrier for the protection of the minority is about to be obliterated, I feel we have reached the point at which the decline of our Government has commenced, the point at which the great restraints which have preserved it, the bonds which have held it together, are to be broken by a ruthless majority, when the next step may lead us to the point at which aggression will assume such a form as will require the minority to decide whether they will sink below the condition to which they were born, or maintain it by forcible resistance.

. . .

I say the case is worse than if the transient inhabitants should, at their own volition, claim to snatch the territory from the United States and appropriate it to themselves. It was not dignified by the impress of popular purpose. If the consequences which are likely to result from this movement were not so grave, we should look upon all the action which occurred anterior to the assembling of that convention, the manner in which the elections were conducted, and in which the ratification of the constitution was expressed, as a farce. In that series of letters, thought to be worthy of being incorporated into a book, written by Bayard Taylor, we are informed that while traveling in one district just before the election, he came near being seized on and elected to the convention *nolens volens*˙—like Teague O'Regan, the hero of Modern Chivalry. That which was intended as a satire on our popular elections might here have been verified.

I do not propose to detain the Senate by entering into evidence of that kind. These and graver facts are abundant, but I know it is useless to produce them. My purpose now, Mr. President, is to make a serious appeal to the Senate against the act which there is but little doubt they are about to perform. In the name of equality, of constitutional right,

˙ *Nolens volens:* willing or unwilling.

of peace, of fraternity, I call upon the majority to abstain. I utter no menace, I foretell no violence; now, as heretofore, I refuse to contemplate or speak of disunion as a remedy. But, sir, "in sorrow rather than anger," at the empty threats which have been made against us, I solemnly warn the majority that they do not look to the South as a field on which victories are to be won without cost, and where the emoluments of conquest are to be obtained without sacrifice. We, sir, are the descendants of those who united with the men of the North ill the revolutionary struggle upon what was to them an abstract principle; we are the descendants of those who cast behind them considerations of safety and interest—who looked danger in the face, and united with your father because they were oppressed. Then, sir, unless it is believed that we are degenerate sons of our glorious sires, in that fact should be found a warning against presuming too far upon the loyalty which, by the sons as by their sires, has been exhibited to the Union. That loyalty is to the Union as established by the Constitution. Sir, they are not bound to the mere form that holds the States together. If I know their character, and have read their history with understanding, they would reject it as a worthless weed whenever the animating spirit of the Constitution shall have passed from the body.

Then, Senators, countrymen, brethren—by these, and by other appellations, if there be others more endearing and impressive than these, I call upon you to pause in the course which pressed by an intemperate zeal, you are pursuing, and warn you, lest blinded by the lust for sectional dominion, you plunge into an abyss in which will lie buried forever the glorious memories of the past, the equally glorious hopes of the future, and the present immeasurable happiness of our common country. It is not as one who threatens, nor as one who prepares for collision with his enemies, but as one who has a right to invoke your fraternal feeling, and to guard you against an error which will equally bear on us both; as one who has shared your hopes and your happiness, and is about to share your misfortunes, if misfortunes shall befall us; it is as an American citizen that I speak to an American Senate—it is in this character that I have ventured to warn you; it is with this feeling that I make my last solemn appeal. . . .

Now, sir, as to the whole argument which the Senator bases upon the proposition, that if the South has lost the balance of power it does not call for disunion I have to say that no one has asked that. We have pointed to the loss of the balance of power as bringing with it another thing. We have pointed to the state of facts in regard to the action of Congress to show that in our opinion that Constitution is already disregarded; and when the temper exists to disregard the Constitution, and the power is possessed to carry that temper into effect, that man must shut his eyes to the future who does not see at once that the consequence is disunion. It is not that one has more power than the other, but the reckless exercise of the power, which authorizes the apprehension of danger; for, sir, if the Constitution had not been disregarded, this new question of the balance of power would never have been introduced. The idea of the balance of power, as it existed originally, was between the States, between the great and monopolizing States and the small ones, and not, between sections. This sectional agitation is the growth of, a subsequent generation to that which formed the Constitution. The danger is one of our own times, and it is that sectional division of the people which has created the necessity of looking to the question of the balance of power, and which carries with it, when that balance is disturbed, the danger of disunion.

To Lowndes County Citizens (PJD)

STEAMBOAT *GEN. SCOTT,* NOVEMBER 22, 1850

...

For your expressions of confidence and estimation, accept assurances of my deepest gratitude, increased, if it be possible, by the consciousness that they are the result of your kindness, not of my service, and are all unmerited save for the unwavering devotion I have felt and feel to the State of Mississippi, the rights the interests, and the honor of my constituents.

The fears which you express of alienation of the people from the yet revered Union of our fathers, and the perversion of the Constitution from its intent and spirit, as consequences of the late action of Congress were the convictions of my mind when the measures to which you refer, were under consideration in the Senate & nerved me in the long opposition I offered to their enactment. It may be said; and from the annals of Congress, demonstrated, that but for sectional rivalry and distortion of the grants of the Constitution from their true purposes, those laws would not have been enacted. The source of the measures will, I think, be increased by their operations. The alienation of the people and the perversion of the Constitution bear to them the double relation of cause and effect.—Yet ingenious demagogues seek to deceive the people of the South, by throwing the responsibility of their present position on those who struggled most to defeat the means by which they have been injured and are required to answer the question, will you resist, or submit to unjust and humilating discrimination against you?

. . .

In this, and in the whole series of measures, there is to be traced the ruling, directing power of hostility to the slave institutions of the South. The Southern men were permitted to pass the fugitive slave bill, which being a law to enforce in the north compliance with a provision of the constitution, should, as far as was necessary, have been tendered and sustained by Northern members. Thus it might have borne to their constituents a respect which it has not received. Whilst by the side of this measure stands the law, in relation to the slave trade in the District of Columbia, offensively discriminating against a particular species of property, placed by the Constitution on at least an equal footing with other property; and which was equally protected by the government, in the earliest days of the Republic; when the equality of the States and the equal privileges of their citizens were rights practically enjoyed. That was the day of fraternity, in contradistinction to sectional strife; before the pseudo philanthropy of British teachers had been entered like a wedge to rend our Union asunder; when no American statesman would have argued for a general law, on the ground that it was demanded by foreign or sectional sentiment; when patrotism would have rebuked into silence the man who for such constitutions would have offended the sensibilities, arraigned the institutions, or invaded the property rights of any portion of our fellow citizens.

If then, and I think it too apparent to admit of an honest doubt, the section which has the controling power in the Government, is hostile to that species of property on which our commercial prosperity depends, and the disturbance of which would involve us in total ruin; and if with the increase of power there is a growing tendency to disregard the checks of the constitution; the time has arrived when all who love the Union or the Constitution should unite to throw an adequate shield over the minority; before it is driven to seek in arms that protection against an aggressive majority which the existing forms of our government fail to afford.

The South needs, and has asked for nothing more than the principles of the Constitution; the rights and immunities the compact was formed to make stable and secure; this much all who recognize this as an Union of equals, with powers conferred for the common benefit and general tranquility are bound to accord, or stand convicted of a wish to change the nature of our government, and binds us to *an Union* which is not *the Union*. The flippent patrizan, and the satelite of power may denounce all who claim sufficent guarantees for the constitutional rights of the South, as impracticable. disorganizing, treasonable, disunionists. Impracticable it is, not if the majority love the Union and the principles from which arose more than the aggrandizement of sectional power. Treasonable it is not. if to be true to one's country, be patriotism, and if it be a duty to maintain, at what ever cost the principles on which our liberty rest, the immovable foundations of truth and justice which will remain to uphold the cause we advocate when we and all of our's are dust.

Our Union was not formed by men who suppliant bent the knee to power; and loved a government only as it was powerful and glorious; nor did they leav us institutions which would be practicable in the hands of men forgetful or careless of the principles on which they were founded. They are the true friends of the Union who resist by all means every invasion on the Constitution, and seek to strengthen every barrier which is found insufficient for the use to which it was appropriated. In the struggle for right against aggressive power, the South will not be alone if she meet the conflict as becomes her cause. The resistance of the colonies made Chatham eloquent in their defence, how much more will every noble spirit be aroused among our Northern brethren, when it shall be attempted to sustain federal usurpation by force, or conquer sovereign States of the Union, and reduce them to territorial subserviency. Those who can contemplate such an event may well point to the sons of a State, thus under the ban, and say " 'tis treason to love her, 'tis death to defend."

I look forward with confidence to the action of Mississippi, and hope it will be sustained by general action in the South; upon which hangs another hope, that the union of the South, will produce a reaction in the public feeling of the North, and that our constitutional union may be preserved, a monument more lasting than brass to our revolutionary fathers; and a temple of true liberty for posterity through countless ages. But if this fondly cherished hope cannot be realized, the union of the South will enable us to preserve the principles on which our federal Union was based, and to transmit to posterity with all the glorious memories of the Union, the principles from which its glory sprung, and to leave the laurels gathered in common toil and danger, unstained by the blood of civil war.

Led on from point to point, I have extended this letter to an unusual length, and must postpone many things which it would be desirable to me to say until we meet. Again permit me to offer my thanks for your kind appreciation, and to assure you that your cheering voice will animate and encourage me in the scenes I expect to encounter; that it will always be heard above the roar of the Northern majority, and be remembered as the reward, one of the poorest capacity may gain by devotion to duty, and the maintenance of the rights entrusted to his care. I am very respectfully, your friend and fellow citizen.

JEFF. DAVIS.

Speech in U.S. Senate (JDC)

FEBRUARY 18, 1851

. . .

Opposition has gone further than I expected. The Senator from Massachusetts says the common sentiment is in opposition to the law, and a Senator who did not address the Senate, but spoke in tones which reached my ear, said "the universal sentiment," strengthening the assertion of the Senator from Massachusetts. If it be so, then it follows that the law is dead, as to that particular State.* As to the particular case which has occurred, I regret it as much as anyone. I regret it, because it is an indication of that downward tendency in the people of the United States, which seems to manifest that they are unworthy of the Government they have inherited. It is a Government which is wholly inoperative whenever the people cease to have sufficient virtue to execute it. Whenever mobs can rule, and law is silenced beneath tumult, this is wholly an impracticable Government. It was not organized as one of force. Its strength is moral, and moral only.

The Government of the United States has power to suppress insurrection and to repel invasion. What insurrection do you suppose is contemplated? Only insurrection against the authority of a State, in which civil government shall be paralyzed by physical power. The occasion, too, must be sudden and ephemeral. If the masses of any State choose, they have the power, and it is undeniable, to change their whole form of government. An insurrection, then, must be one against a State, and a State may seek the aid of the Federal Government to justify it in introducing its power in the State for the purpose of suppressing insurrection. In the better days of the Republic, may I not say the purer days of the Republic, the militia of the States were relied upon for the enforcement of the laws against those who resisted them within the borders of the States. Thus General Washington's Secretary of War called on the militia of Pennsylvania to put down the whiskey insurrection. He did not call on the Army and Navy of the United States.

But, sir, the case in Boston seems to be the legitimate result of an event which occurred not long since, when the officers failed to do their duty, and the marshal who so failed was not removed. What was this but a direct encouragement to a free negro mob to set aside the law, and to oppose the officers if they attempted to execute it? I am not one of those, however anxious I may be to see this law enforced, who would advocate the use of the Army to secure its enforcement. I hold

* Fugitive Slave Law of 1850.

that when any State in this Union shall choose to set aside the law, it is within her sovereignty, and beyond our power. I hold that it would be a total subversion of the principles of our Government if the strong arm of the United States is to be brought to crush the known will of the people of any State in this Union. Such is my theory of this Government. If the people of Massachusetts choose to nullify the law, if they choose to obliterate the Constitution, if they choose to deny the supremacy of the laws of the United States, they will have but one step more to take, and the impulse with which they will be moving will compel them to take it; that is, to declare the authority of the United States abrogated, and the bonds of the Union to be no longer over them. We of the South have been constantly arraigned as those who oppose the Government of the United States, who nullify its laws, and who manifest a violent resistance against their execution. The charge is as untrue as it is common. Look to the history of the country, and find in times past where the laws of this Government have been nullified. Elsewhere they have been; in the planting States never.
. . .

Speech in U.S. Senate (PJD)

FEBRUARY 20, 1851

Mr. Davis, of Mississippi. I shall support the amendment of the Senator from Maine. I think it is evenhanded justice. I do not perceive the least propriety in giving to a member of Congress the right to send to his friends at the expense of the Government such documents as he may think proper to bestow on them, and to leave others either deprived of mailable matter or charged with the expense of paying for its transportation. Nor can there be any justice in requiring that thirty thousand persons shall pay for the transportation of those documents which fall into the hands of one. They are taxed for the benefit of others, not for their own benefit, nor for the benefit of the country at large. I think the amendment sound in principle, and I shall therefore vote for it.

[Thomas J. Rusk urges reconsideration since department heads would retain the privilege.]

Mr. Davis, of Mississippi. I admit there is force in the objection of the chairman of the Post Office Committee; but I think this amendment is carrying out the scriptural injunction. It proposes that we should cast the beam out of our own eyes before we take the mote out of the eyes of others. If we can abolish the franking privilege of members of Congress, we shall soon be able to abolish it altogether. This is the first great step. Justice should begin at home, where I think we can best apply it in this case, if we can apply it at all.

The other statement of the Senator from Maine has great force. This will undoubtedly reduce to a large extent the amount of the printing of documents. We shall no longer print a large number of documents with a view to have matter for circulation, and hereafter we shall only print those which are valuable. If they are worth sending, they are worth paying for.

To *Varina Davis* (PJD)

BRANDON, MISSISSIPPI, MAY 8, 1851

MY DEAR WIFE,

Your claim on my time though first could my heart decide it is interrupted for a longer period than I had anticipated when we parted. Circumstances have pressed me immediately into service of the "Southern Rights Democratic party" and I cannot return to you before the middle of June. A friend will send a despatch to your Father so as to prevent your hastening back on the supposition that I might be waiting for you.

I commenced to talk to you my own dear Winnie but the people are crowding in on me and I have now asked them to sit down and let me close my letter, from another point I will write soon.

God bless you and keep you happy and well prays your Husband.

Speech in Aberdeen, Mississippi (JDC)

...

Col. Davis said that he had heard it said that the poor men, who own no negroes themselves, would all be against the institution, and would, consequently, array themselves on the side of the so called Union men—that the submissionists claimed them. But that he could not believe, that the poor men of the country, were so blind to their own interests, as to be thus cheated out of their privileges, which they now enjoy. That *now they stand upon the broad level of equality with the rich man.* Equal to him in every thing, save that they did not own so much property; and that, even in this particular, the road to wealth was open to them, and the poor man might attain it; and, even if he did not succeed, the failure did not degrade him. That no white man, in a slaveholding community, was the menial servant of anyone. That whenever the poor white man labored for the rich, he did so upon terms of distinction between him and the negro. It was to the interest of the master to keep up a distinction between the white man in his employment, and his negroes. And that this very distinction elevated, and kept the white laborer on a level with the employer; because the distinction between the classes throughout the slaveholding states, is a distinction of color. Between the classes there is no such thing, here, as a distinction of property; and he who thinks there is, and prides himself upon it, is grossly mistaken. Free the negroes, however, and it would soon be here, as it is in the countries of Europe, and in the North, and everywhere else, where negro slavery does not exist. The poor white man would become a menial for the rich, and be, by him, reduced to an equality with the free blacks, into a degraded position; and the distinction, at once, would be made that of—*Property*—of *Wealth*—between the classes, between the *Rich* and the *Poor.* The *rich man,* with his lands, and his other property, and his money, would be a rich man still. The *poor* would be *poor* still, and with much less chance than he now has of acquiring property, because of the numbers of mean and worthless free negroes, in competition with whose labor his own would have to come. And yet the tendency of the doctrines of the submissionists, is directly to invite further aggression from the North, and by this invitation, to bring about this very state of things. The non-slaveholder can see this, as well as the slaveholder. And seeing, and knowing his rights, he will defend and maintain them, as soon, if not sooner, than the rich man will. Then, he did not believe that the submission party had the exclusive right, which they claimed, or expect that the middle and poorer classes would co-operate with them upon this important question, affecting, as it does, their interests—their standing in the community—more than all others.

Col. Davis said that he had always thought, and sincerely believed, that the institution of negro slavery, as it now exists among us, is necessary to the *equality* of the *white* race. Distinctions between classes have always existed, everywhere, and in every country, where civilization has been established among men. Destroy them to-day, and they will spring up to-morrow; and we have no right to expect, or even to hope, that this Southern climate of ours, would be exempt from the operation of this Universal law.

. . .

Speech in Fayette, Mississippi (PJD)

JULY 11, 1851

. . .

He was arraigned not as a disunionist only, but as an archleader of disunion.

He did not know why such terms were applied to him, for he was sure that nothing he had ever done or said could be referred to, to bear out such an application. But when a man charged him with being a disunionist, he should make a monsyllabic answer which was not fit to be used before that assembly, yet which was the only one that ought to be used to his foul assailants. (Cheers.) A disunionist must be made from one of two causes, either interest or prejudice. He could have no prejudice, for since he was sixteen years of age, he had served the federal government. For twelve years he had borne arms for his country;

for five years he had served in the council of the nation. Whatever had been his course of life, all he had done had been for the service of the United States. When called upon, he had always been prepared to serve his country, and his acts had been constituted with the United States. For twelve years, his home had been under the flag of the stars and stripes, and it would indeed be strange, if after this he should desire to become a disunionist. The kind confidence of his fellow-citizens in Mississippi had placed him, he feared, far above his deserts, but he had endeavored to deserve their confidence. He had reached a period of life that caused him to desire no higher honor, nor could any man reach to a higher station, unless he soiled his hands, and bartered away the interests of the South to the fanaticism of Southern opponents— a temptation he hoped ever to resist. (Cheers.) Then what interest had he? He had no ambition to gratify by becoming a disunionist; no higher station to obtain, but he might by such a course, sacrifice the high position he held. Having thus, then, neither interest nor prejudice, what on earth could be an inducement for him to become a disunionist? (Applause.) Had he been willing to have accepted the inducements offered to him, to become a traitor to his constituents, he might have been led into the camp of the "Unionists" and got his reward—he might have gained other laurels, that were but to fade. He might have come home to justify his acts, and his constituents might have appeared satisfied for a time.

But who were the gentlemen that assailed him? He knew not whether they were at that meeting or elsewhere; he was unable to find one of them who had ever lost a drop of blood in defence of his country—or whose acts of patriotism had ever gained them a laured of fame; they were merely those who had basked in the sunshine of pleasure or indulgence, and whose peculiarities were an attachment to office. (Loud cheers.) He claimed his right to be for the Union, because his heart beat for the welfare of his country, but the Union was not so dear to him as Mississippi; and as a choice between secession and political and social degradation, were he asked which he preferred, he would say "secession," and every son of Mississippi with feelings of honor, or a sense of justice in his breast would be with him to the last. (Loud applause.) Was this disunion or disruption that deserved such censure? if it were, why it was the principle of the revolution of '76 and '77, out of which the Constitution arose, being rendered sacred by the blood of those who fell to cement it and who declared that it was right to discountenance a government, when that government became oppressive. The Declaration of Independence recognized the right of secession under circumstances of oppression and injustice. He wanted to see the man who would come forward with arguments to show that if a country has a right to secede from an oppressive government, as the United States did from Great Britain, why States had no right to secede from the federal government under similar circumstances. How could colonies have greater powers than States? And what arguments could those be that denied the right of secession. Mr. Madison had given his opinion. New York and Virginia had both avowed their opinion in favor of the right of secession. Whilst that great and good man who always opposed States coercion, Gen. Washington, in his farewell address discountenanced the perversion of power by one department over another, nor did he ever allude to treason in the sovereign acts of a State, but he left it to this degenerate race to discover that treason could be committed by a sovereignty. Treason in the United States was specifically defined by raising a war against, or giving aid, comfort and assistance to enemies—it was not a crime of sovereignty, or of States, but of a person, and the punishment was restricted to the natural life of the offender. Yet gentlemen in these days went one step farther and talked of the treason of States and the punishment of hanging. What they could mean by hanging a State he did not know, but he did know that a State could provide a rope to hang a traitor, who raised a power against its sovereignty, and instead of any person being engaged in hanging a State, such person might possibly be hanged by a State. (Applause.)

. . .

He had been absent a large portion of his life from Mississippi, but still, in fond recollection, the State recurred to his mind; it had been his fortune to mix in the strife and din of battle; to meet the foe under various circumstances; but whether crouched in the grass or deep morass, or on the more open field, his memory had still wandered back to his parent State—to the days of his childhood—for in Mississippi he had always hoped to make a home. In proportion to the weal and prosperity of the State he had felt a pride and pleasure glowing in his bosom; and in the same respect with her misfortune he had felt depressed. Under that same flag that had so long waved for the Union, and under which there had been so many glorious achievements accomplished, he still marched, so long as that flag was the emblem of justice and equality. If he had ever found the honor of Mississippi assailed—that honor which was as dear to him as his own—if he had ever found her honor attacked or calumniated, he had always rushed to the rescue, as a son would defend the honor of his mother. Perhaps he might be more affected in the disputes that had arisen than they were, inasmuch as he was more closely involved in the struggle, and that he was more excited than many who lived peaceably in their homes, under their present temporary security—but if he were more excited, it arose from the fact that his public career enabled him to see the treacherous and crafty designs of the enemies of the South; and it was also because he saw the dangers and the difficulties by which the South was environed more plainly; but it would be with deep humility if he had to hear that Mississippi reprobated his political acts, not for sacrificing their interests, or submissively surrendering their privileges, but because he had, to the utmost of his ability, defended their rights under the Constitution, and scorned to succumb to the encroachments of a powerful foe.

It was not his wish to let down his constituents, or to act the recreant when in the face of the majority. It was for the people to decide whether they would curtail the power of their representatives, or whether the platform raised by a State convention, should be abandoned or supported. He trusted, however, Mississippi would do that which became her high honor and her self-respect, in order that she might be spoken of abroad as she always had been. For himself he had only to say, that his first and his last allegiance was for the South and Mississippi. His allegiance was reserved for this State, whenever he might be called to any position where his services should be required. In the hour of need, whether upon the field or elsewhere, he would be found by the side of her friends; he would rejoice in her prosperity, and in adversity, throughout the storms that might threaten her; he was with her to the last—(loud applause.) Her honor was his honor, and if she asserted her proper position, he was always ready to maintain it. On every occasion he had defended State sovereignty, and if Mississippi agreed with him, as her son, he still declared for it. Let them, then, have no retreating from their original and just position, and not a corporal's guard throughout the length and breadth of the State, would wish to see injured any one part of the Constitution. If secession presented the only alternative to social and political degradation, he believed Mississippi would adopt the alternative, even had her citizens to leave their widows and orphans alone to weep upon her fields—(applause.)

. . .

To David L. Yulee (PJD)[*]

PALMYRA, MISSISSIPPI, JULY 18, 1851

MY DEAR YULEE,

I have never forgotten your kind request that I should write to you, and long since would have fulfilled my promise if it had been in my power to have written <-just-> what it was desirable to you to hear and to me to communicate. I have visited a large part of the state and have been constantly surprised to find how little the course and temper of the Majority in the last Congress was understood. Foote is as industrious as a bee, and as reckless of truth as himself. The parties in our state were /when I returned/ in great confusion, some for immediate secession; some for retaliation, some for making another attempt to unite the South by a Southern Congress, some for sullen acquiescence, some for avowing contentment if quiet was secured by the compromise, some for joining issue on the compromise bill, and holding all who opposed it responsible for such evils as they might imagine could have resulted from a different state of things if no action had been taken by the federal government. Under such circumstances the least favorable for a forward movement we have entered the canvass for members to the state convention. I feel confident that the Southern

[*] U.S. senator from Florida.

rights men will have a majority but I fear not large enough for a decided policy or for moral effect on our Northern aggressors. Indeed the ground generally taken is that we must maintain our position reaffirm the declarations heretofore made, and wait for cooperation by other planting states. Foote is a Candidate for governor, Quitman opposes him, he cannot get the full vote of our party but circumstances required his nomination unless he would decline. That his vanity would not permit, though it was known to be the wish of a large majority of the Convention which nominated him to run a different person, if Q. could be gotten rid of without seeming to disapprove of him. We have no doubt however of Quitman's election. There is a Yankee influence here as in other new states, when that is crushed we will stand on firmer ground, and unless we do crush it federalism will soon swallow up state rights and wholly change the nature of our government. I think Missi. will do enough to justify me in returning to the Senate, for I need hardly say to you that if she endorses the "compromise" I will seek that post of honor which is found in a private station.

Present me very specially and most kindly to Mrs. Yulee, also to my young friend Charly. Hoping to meet you both next winter accept my best wishes for your prosperity and happiness—As ever your friend

JEFF'N. DAVIS

To Samuel A. Cartwright (PJD)

BRIERFIELD, WARREN COUNTY, MISSISSIPPI, SEPTEMBER 23, 1851
MY DEAR SIR.

I sincerely thank you for your very kind letter, which if it was as you say a departure from professional "etiquette" was certainly an observance of those rules of charity, and good will which [I?] can better appreciate, and on which I certainly [pla]ce a much higher value. I have hesi[ta]ted whether I should go down immediately, and on account of the painful effect produced by exposure to light have decided to wait a few days, perhaps a week longer before I avail myself of your advice which I am sincerely anxious to receive. Since I have been at home, and able to keep myself in a mild and uniform light the inflammation has greatly s[u]bsided, and the sight of that eye which was entirely blind has been partially restored. There is still great irritability in the nerve of the eye, and the cloud which had collected between the coatings of the cornea, and which entirely covered the pupil I am informed has receded so as now to appear like a clear drop of water which swells the cornea on one side (the outside,) and encroaches very little on the pupil, though it covers about a third of the iris. The eye has ceased to weep, and has rather an unnatural dryness, and heat, but without any engorgement of the bloodvessels.

I suffered so much from the glare, and varying light on the steamboat on which I came from Memphis that I have felt unwilling at present to encounter the like exposure. I am using only emollient washes, and take some quinine daily My general health has so much improved t[hat] I suffer little except from extreme debility To one accustomed like yourself to the uni[n]telligible account which the unlearned patient [gives?] of his case it will not seem surprising if I have given you very little idea of my present conditio[n.] Again thanking you for your friendly interes[t] let me assure you of the very high esteem and regard with with which I am your friend

JEFFERSON DAVI[S]

Speech in Jackson, Mississippi (PJD)

JUNE 9, 1852

. . .

He had watched, and he had striven to unite the people of Mississippi upon questions concerning which there should be but one position, as there could be but one interest, but one duty. A blind confidence not warranted by the past, or by passing events, is such fatuity as if the inhabitants of a volcanic mountain, whilst it trembled in token of approaching eruption, should crowd to the crater, and lay themselves down to repose. Let it not be said he was urging a sectional canvass: he was but pleading for principles which pre-existed the Union, and which it was formed to secure, and render perpetual. He did not desire, but most of all he dreaded, a sectional canvass. He feared it was approaching, it might be at hand; but if so, as in every other case of departure from the principles of fraternity and community, the responsibility would not rest upon the Southern minority. If no higher motive restrained them, the impolicy of the weaker section inviting to sectional controversy, was so palpable that he would be stupid indeed, who did not perceive it. The principles upon which he claimed the South should be united, neither belonged to this day, nor to this latitude; they were older than the Union, and capable of extending as far as federative government could be appreciated.

He said he was a party man, had been bred in the paths of Democracy, and had never deviated from them. His creed rested on the capacity of the people to govern themselves, and their right to decide on the form of government under which they would live. That government was but an agency of the people, in ours that agency was direct, and specially limited. He, therefore, who contended for a strict construction of the Constitution, and the rights of the States as sovereign parties to the compact of the Union, was his political brother, called by whatsoever name he might be.

. . .

To William J. Brown (JDC)[*]

WASHINGTON, D.C., MAY 7, 1853

MY DEAR SIR:

I received the "Sentinel" containing your defense of me against the false accusation of disunionism, and, before I had returned to you the thanks to which you are entitled, I received this day the St. Joseph "Valley Register," marked by you, to call my attention to an article in answer to your defense, which was just in all things, save your too complimentary terms.

I wish I had the letter quoted from, that you might publish the whole of that which is garbled to answer a purpose. In a part of the let-

---

[*] Former member of Congress living in Indiana.

ter not published, I put such a damper on the attempt to fix on me the desire to break up our Union, and presented other points in a form so little acceptable to the unfriendly inquirer, that the publication of the letter had to be drawn out of them.

At the risk of being wearisome, but encouraged by your marked friendship, I will give you a statement in the case. The meeting of October, 1849, was a convention of delegates equally representing the Whig and Democratic parties in Mississippi. The resolutions were decisive as to equality of right in the South with the North to the Territories acquired from Mexico, and proposed a convention of the Southern States. I was not a member, but on invitation addressed the Convention. The succeeding Legislature instructed me, as a Senator, to assert this equality, and, under the existing circumstances, to resist by all constitutional means the admission of California as a State. At a called session of the Legislature in 1850, a self-constituted committee called on me, by letter, for my views. They were men who had enacted or approved the resolutions of the Convention of 1849, and instructed me, as members of Legislature, in regular session, in the early part of the year 1850. To them I replied that I adhered to the policy they had indicated and instructed me in their official character to pursue.

I pointed out the mode in which their policy could, in my opinion, be executed without bloodshed or disastrous convulsion, but in terms of bitter scorn alluded to such as would insult me with a desire to destroy the Union, for which my whole life proved me to be a devotee.

Pardon the egotism, in consideration of the occasion, when I say to you that my father and my uncles fought through the Revolution of 1776, giving their youth, their blood, and their little patrimony to the constitutional freedom which I claim as my inheritance. Three of my brothers fought in the war of 1812. Two of them were comrades of the Hero of the Hermitage, and received his commendation for gallantry at New Orleans. At sixteen years of age I was given to the service of my country; for twelve years of my life I have borne its arms and served it zealously, if not well. As I feel the infirmities, which suffering more than age has brought upon me, it would be a bitter reflection, indeed, if I was forced to conclude that my countrymen would hold all this light when weighed against the empty panegyric which a time-serving politician can bestow upon the Union, for which he never made a sacrifice.

In the Senate I announced that, if any respectable man would call me a disunionist, I would answer him in monosyllables.... But I have often asserted the right, for which the battles of the Revolution were fought—the right of a people to change their government whenever it was found to be oppressive, and subversive of the objects for which governments are instituted—and have contended for the independence and sovereignty of the States, a part of the creed of which Jefferson was the apostle, Madison the expounder, and Jackson the consistent defender.

I have written freely, and more than I designed. Accept my thanks for your friendly advocacy. Present me in terms of kind remembrance to your family, and believe me, very sincerely yours,

JEFFERSON DAVIS.

Speech in Philadelphia, Pennsylvania (PJD)

JULY 12, 1853

Hon. JEFFERSON DAVIS responded, and said that he begged leave, on the part of those members of the cabinet who were present, to return their cordial thanks for the compliment tendered them. They stood in the attitude of those who enjoy the advantage of reflected light; yet they did not think they were indebted for the consideration of those present, merely because they were members of the cabinet—it was rather because they were American citizens, and brought within the circle of Pennsylvania hospitality, that compliment was bestowed on them. [Applause] Thanks to the increased facility of intercourse, Pennsylvania hospitality was not to be limited hereafter, as it had been heretofore, by the slow progess of the old wagon and Conestoga horse, nor by the yet more rapid march of the coach, nor by the yet more rapid means of the railroad. No! Socially, Pennsylvania was tied by lightning to every portion of the older settlements of the United States, and with her coal and iron she was about to establish commercial relations with the slope of the Pacific, and to look over into that unknown region of Asia which includes China and Persia. [Tremendous cheering, which prevailed for many minutes.] These were results to be anticipated from the foresight and energy of the people; not to be effected by stretching the powers of the federal government beyond their legitimate sphere. They knew that he belonged to the strict-construction school, which never turned to the right nor to the left to serve any purpose of expediency.

The PRESIDENT [Franklin Pierce](interposing) observed that he was certain of that.*

Mr. DAVIS resumed: Within the limits of the States they would touch nothing in disregard of State sovereignty and right of jurisdiction; and in this he spoke not for himself alone, but also for his honored chief. [Applause.] But when they looked to their recent possessions on the slope of the Pacific, there were two things which arrested attention— the conflicting interests of a different commerce, resulting from the want of easy and rapid communication; and the difficulty of fulfilling one of the great ends of our Union, that of giving adequate protection by mutual defence. Upon the pages of history, running back to the remotest antiquity, nothing is remarked more generally than that mountains have divided nations, and therefore it had been perhaps somewhat fancifully argued, that as the light and shadow fell upon the one side or the other, so would the character of men be modified, and government changed. But had it not been, in the progress of mind in its conflict with matter, that the useful sciences in the United States had advanced—had gained additional force; and had they not reached the period when they could triumph over this natural obstacle—when they could skip the mountains, tunnel them, or pass them by means known to civil engineering, thus combining opposite interests, uniting remote localities, and socially, commercially, and politically binding men together, so that the fluctuations of light should become to them as nothing? [Great applause] He had said that he was a strict constructionist; but he had always mocked the idea that the constitution had one construction within the limits of the United States, and an-

* Franklin Pierce, president of the United States 1853–57.

other outside of them. [Applause.] He had always repelled the supposition that this government could build a road outside of the United States, and could not build one within it Our constitution was formed to bind the States together, to provide for the common defence, to concentrate the power of all for the protection of each, to throw their united shields over every State, over every locality, over every ship and individual of the Union. [Great applause.] The other question, which involved the integrity of the Pacific possessions, was still closer to fraternal feeling and to sense of duty; it was one to which he knew the heart of Pennsylvania would respond—it was the question of protection, which in her strength she had always shown herself willing to throw over the weak. In the event of a war with any of the powerful nations of the earth, California and Oregon are exposed to attack. Fraternity, chivalry, and constitutional obligation would combine to claim for them adequate protection. Could it, with our present means, be given? Could we rely upon an extra-territorial line of communication? If the Pacific possessions should be threatened by a hostile fleet, the government would have no sufficient navy there to interpose for their protection, if that hostile fleet belonged to and fairly represented such a power as England or France. It would take all the navy of the United States to keep a road open which would cross either of the isthmuses of this continent. And while the navy of the United States was thus employed, what would be more easy than for such a maritime power as either of these to strike at those possessions, and rend them from these States, even to the extent of the gold regions which lay behind the coast. If, then, as a purely military question, it is necessary to have an inter-communication, so that the government's munitions of war and men could be thrown upon the Pacific for its defence, the application of the war power of the government to this case would be within the strict limits of the constitution. [Enthusiastic applause.] But if it could be shown, and he always held his opinion open to correction from any quarter, that these means were not required, were not necessary—and by necessary he meant absolutely required—or if any-one would show the other means which would answer as a substitute—how the duties of the government could be performed without this auxiliary more effectively, more economically, with less exercise of the general powers of the government—then, as a strict-construction democrat, he would accept the proposition. [Applause.] Under every ingenious construction which had been placed upon the various powers of the government to bend them to temporary convenience or individual advantage—under every ramification which ingenuity had suggested to supply by isthmus railroads and canals, the wants of commerce resulting from that deficiency of intercommunication—he had insisted that the end should be the discharge of a delegated trust, and that the means should be necessary to the performance of the duty. To defend and maintain the inhabitants and territory of our Pacific possessions was undeniably a delegated trust; and the question was, What means were necessary to the discharge of the duty? In vain had it been attempted to be shown him how the military power of this government, which consisted in the sinews and strong hearts of its citizens, could be used on the slope of the Pacific, unless there was a railroad to transmit it. [Applause.] If, then, it could be done by such means only, and if that hazard existed on the shores ors that ocean, he would say that the rest followed as a consequence. Within the territories belonging to the United States the general government could certainly construct roads for military purposes. This power, so long acted on, would not change its nature with the change of the material to be used in the construction; and it surely constituted no objection if the means employed for a legitimate object should contribute to the increase and development of interests which they were not specially designed to promote. Whether by these or other means effected, he would rejoice in the fulfilment of the anticipation that the smoke of Pennsylvania coal might be seen on the desert waste, beneath the cloud-capped mountains, and Pennsylvania iron, with the very stamp of her own foundries upon it, might be seen creeping in a long serpentine track to the slopes of the Pacific. [Applause.] ...

Speech in New York City, New York (JDC)

JULY 20, 1853

...

But, Mr. Chairman and gentlemen, I feel the impropriety of having extended my remarks thus far, though the subject be one which the place and attendant circumstances could not fail to suggest, and I can only offer you as an excuse for my trespass upon your time the excitement of the scene in the midst of which your kindness has placed me. It is our good fortune now to be thirty-one States, united, with a territory stretching from the Mississippi valley to the Pacific ocean. We have gone on increasing in territory, in strength, in wealth, and, above all, in the application of means for the conquest of mind over matter, with a rapidity which has had no precedent. But we have only commenced. We have but gone thus far to see what is beyond. We have not reached the culminating point of our national destiny. Our country is not yet in the vigor of manhood, but only in its youth.

We have yet great problems, physical and political, to solve. We have, in that controversy to which I referred—that contest between mind and matter—yet to apply all which science can bring to remove obstacles from our path. I refer now to those politico-physical difficulties which separate the Atlantic slope and the valley of the Mississippi from our Pacific possessions. They are separated by a ridge of mountains, a large portion of which is covered with perennial snow. The population of one portion now reaches the other by passing through a foreign country. Will this continue? No, no! To remain united, we must provide the means to bring them more closely together—both as regards time and facility of transportation. The Pacific slope cannot remain permanently in this Union unless such obstacles are removed, any more than these colonies could remain connected with the mother country, with the broad Atlantic to divide, and the slow ships of that day to connect them. Not that blood is to flow or revolution ensue; wise men will seek what it is necessary to do to facilitate the intercourse between the different portions of the nation, and thus to avert the future necessity for political separation. We shall be untrue to the great principles which our fathers bequeathed as a legacy to us if we should attempt to bind our Union together by other than the bonds of fraternity and common interest, or forget that government rests on the consent of the governed. To fulfil our mission, to discharge our duty in the manner appropriate to it, it is necessary to provide the means of intercourse. How is it to be done? The old States are separated from the new-born States on the Pacific by a wide territory—a mountainous district now possessed by roaming bands of Indians.

. . .

To Charles J. McDonald (JDC)*

WASHINGTON, D.C., APRIL 13, 1854

SIR,

I have to acknowledge your letter in relation to the selection of a suitable place, at some point in the South, for a depository of arms, and to the establishment of a government Military Institute in that part of the Union. The views you present in regard to the requirements of a proper site to meet the objects of an Arsenal in that part of the country, are just. It is believed that they are met by the Arsenals already established in the Southern States, viz: at Fayetteville, North Carolina, Charleston South Carolina, Augusta, Georgia, Chattahoochie, Florida, Mount Vernon, Alabama and Baton Rouge, Louisiana. The Arsenal at Augusta, particularly, is regarded as meeting the requirements you suggest. It is healthful, convenient of access, in a position favorable for keeping supplies of arms and ammunition, and in the midst of a large white population of the county and city, with organized volunteer companies at any time available, if needful, for its protection, in aid of the enlisted force of Ordnance soldiers stationed there both as a guard, and as a working party. If it be too far to the East to be relied on by the Western frontier of Georgia, and the States adjacent thereto, then the selection of a site for this particular object would

* Georgia political leader.

probably fall in Eastern Tennessee, as that State has now no United States Arsenal within its limits, and Georgia has the one at Augusta.

As regards the establishment of a Southern Military Academy, if it be intended for the education of Southern youths exclusively, I fear the tendency would be to create and increase sectional jealousies. Experience has shown that the bringing together young men from all parts of the country, at a period of life when they imbibe lasting impressions, create friendships among Northern, Southern, Eastern and Western youths, remembered in after years, and calling up kindly feelings towards the people of each section from their friends of the other. Those who have received their education at West Point, taken as a body, are perhaps more free from purely sectional prejudices, and more national in their feelings than the same number of persons to be found elsewhere in our country. But, if it be intended to have a Southern Academy for youths from every part of the country, this objection, of course, falls, and the question becomes one as to the expediency of providing and maintaining at considerably increased expense more than one school, which is ample for the education of all the Cadets from every part of the Union.

The climate at West Point has not been found, by experience, to affect injuriously the constitutions of youths from the Southern States; and perhaps, the same would be the case with a Southern Academy in regard to those from the North.

VERY RESPECTFULLY, YOUR OBT SERV

JEFF'N DAVIS

SECRETARY OF WAR

To *Joseph G. Totten* (PJD)[*]

WASHINGTON, D.C. AUGUST 19, 1854

MY DEAR SIR,

I have considered the programme of a five years course in the Mil. Academy, and with the deference which belongs to my entire confi-

[*] U.S. Army officer, chief of the Corps of Engineers, and inspector of the U.S. Military Academy at West Point.

dence in the judgement of the Academic board, I offer the follow suggestions for their attention.

That the English studies be postponed to the two last years of the Course. That French be studied in the two first years and Spanish in the <-second and-> third year<-s-> of the course.

The philosophy of our own language is rarely understood by youth<-s-> unless learned through the study of other languages. English grammar, Rhetoric, Logic and composition hang on each other like the links of a chain, whilst geography, History and International law form another class having like dependence on each other.

These seem to be branches required to complete the officer's education and appropiately to belong to Cadets who have stood such tests as prove them competent and worthy.

With these crude remarks I return the papers for such further action as may be found proper and remain Very Resptedy yr obt. Sevt.

JEFFN,, DAVIS.

To Edouard Stoeckl (PJD)[*]

WAR DEPARTMENT, WASHINGTON, D.C., MAY 14, 1855

SIR,

In answer to your verbal enquiries, I have the honor to transmit you the following information. It has long been considered very important to have a wagon body, for army purposes, that could be used in cases of necessity as a boat, or ponton, in crossing the numerous rivers and streams in the wide extent of our country west of the Mississippi river, and at the same time answer all the purposes of an ordinary wagon for transportation, thereby saving expense by dispensing with pontons. In this, through the exertions of Mr. Francis, directed by Colonel Thomas of the Quartermaster Department, I consider we have been successful.

Experiments having been made with it in my presence and that of members of both Houses of Congress, and of officers of the Army and

---

[*] Chargé in Russian legation in Washington.

Navy, which proved satisfactory, I determined to adopt it so far as to order its introduction into the service, and it is now being used on our frontier and in the Indian country.

The weight of the corrugated galvanized metallic body is not greater than that of the ordinary wooden one, while its strength and durability are much greater. But what renders it most valuable is, its being capable of sustaining or floating the carriage (wheels &c) in addition to a moderate load across streams, where the streams are small, it can be used without uncoupling.

For crossing large streams, or rivers, the body can be detached and used as a boat, and by connecting four or six of them with a plank covering, a boat can be made by which the heaviest pieces of field Artillery can be passed over.

They can also be used in the construction of military bridges. Very respectfully   Your Obt Servt

JEFFN DAVIS
SECRETARY OF WAR

To *Joseph E. Davis* (PJD)

WASHINGTON, D.C., AUGUST 25, 1855
MY DEAR BROTHER,

The contract to which you refer for buildings at the Brierfield was authorized by me in general terms. The people seemed to be crowded and Haddick said he could in the state of the crop certainly give such assistance in procuring the heavy timbers as would diminish the expense.* There seemed also to be a necessity for a better store house, and a more commodious hospital; the first I thought it well to build and the second to be obtained by building an overseer's house, and repairing the one then occu[p]ie[d] by him for a hospital. This however to be done after building stables and a new crib, for corn and fodder.

The quarters I proposed to place facing the present line and begining on the ridge /on/ which the store house stands to run divergent

---

* Probably Drury M. Haddick, a recently dismissed overseer at Brierfield.

from the line of the present quarters to a point opposite old Bob's house and if continued then to inline towards the present line of old quarters so that if ever completed the fig- ure would be thus.* The store house having but one door which faced the inner court and was placed like that of the opposite house in the gable end, would /be/ more safe I thought than the present or any other position.

The gin stands were reported defective I did not examine them but suggested that they might be repaired or if that was not possible that new ones should be obtained.

I telegraphed to you some time since in relation to the dismissal of Haddick and I find additional cause for that course in his conduct about the ponies and buggy. Very reluctantly I consented to let his wife go up in the buggy to a place where she could get other transportation, requiring that the buggy should be promptly returned. It was a breach of faith to detain it or to take it a second time. He has written a long letter endeavoring to make the whole case rest on his difficulty with William and in that to represent himself as a very patient and much abused man. He claims a year's salary and to relieve you from all trouble or controversy with the fellow will write to Dr. McElrath who engaged him to have a prompt settlement with him.†   Whilst upon the subject allow me to say that I should deeply regret it if you should believe that Dr. McElrath had designed to conduct himself improperly or disrespectfully to you. It may well have happened that Haddick would seek to produce a misunderstanding between you and Dr. M.; and he who fetches and carries can usually breed strife.

The weather here is and has for some time been rainy and the drought in your neighborhood seems to be an exception to the state of things in evry other section of the country. For some time past I have been residing a few miles in the country, to which I was induced by the sickness of my child, who though drooping and seemingly seriously ill

---

* Old Bob, a favored JD slave.

† Dr. George W. McElrath, a Warren County physician and JD's friend; often acted as JD's agent at Brierfield during the 1850s.

recovered as by a charm as soon as she breathed the pure air of the hills. We are all now as well as usual. Robert arrived here this morning and as soon as he gets his outfit will proceed to his post at old Point Comfort.* I gave /him/ the new tactics, the text book of his Regiment, and will before he leaves perform the ordinarily useless ceremony of giving him some "good advice." He has many high soldierly qualities and as he has never studied enough to test his mental power, I hope for more than you probably expect, if he can be stimulated to earnest exirtion.

I received some time since a very gratifying letter from dear little Lize, and have often intended to answer it; but only one who has seen me /in my present situation/ can appreciate the extent of the interruptions which break up my private correspondence.† At night I can neither read or write without such injury to my sight that I no longer attempt it. affectionately

YOUR BROTHER

To William R. Cannon (PJD)

WASHINGTON, D.C., DECEMBER 7, 1855

A contest involving only the distribution of offices on even the mere question of party supremacy has little chance compared with one which presents a fair issue between the great principles of Democracy and the dangerous and odious heresies of federalism. Centralization claimed a power beyond any thing which Hamilton ever dreamed of when it assumed to prescribe to the states the rule by which the right of suffrage should be measured, and the bones of Jefferson might be imagined to rattle in their last resting place when the people whom he loved and for whom he had labored entertained the idea of trying a political qualification by a religious test.‡

We are all apt to be casuists when our wishes incline to a certain conclusion and distrusting myself, I will not give utterance to consid-

---

* Robert H. Davis, JD's nephew.

† Mary Elizabeth Mitchell, Joseph's granddaughter.

‡ Alexander Hamilton, Founding Father who advocated a strong central government.

erations connecting a personal question with the future of our political creed.

Some of my Friends at home and elsewhere have mentioned me as a candidate for the Vice Presidency, a few even with more zeal than prudence have referred to the Presidency, the first office I would not have, the last is not to be thought of, and a man's friends should not make him ridiculous.

We of the South have been too much disposed to rely on the intrinsic merits of our cause, and to neglect all the necessary defences whilst an active enemy was seizing the outposts preparatory to an attack upon the citadel. Abolitionism would gain but little in excluding slavery from the territories if it was never to disturb that institution in the states, and Northern supremacy in both houses of Congress would not have been pursued through so many years of labor if it had been a thing which was not to be employed against the equal rights of the other section. A direct attack they have too much sagacity to make for that would be met by open resistance, but through the forms of legislation, and ostensibly for the public service, a section having the control of both houses of Congress can gradually work an inequality which will reduce the other section to a tributary condition. We have lost our equality in the Senate, and it is of vital importance that we should endeavor to regain it. We should not allow the Abolitionists to Colonise Kansas by emigrant societies without making an effort to counteract it by throwing in a Southern population, and so of New Mexico. The country on the Pacific is in many respects adapted to slave labor, and many of the citizens desire its introduction. As I have been in the habit of looking to the great interest of the communities to find the cause of their public policy, this case has led me to ask why the advocates of domestic slavery should not have acquired the control of California and Oregon. The answer has seemed to me to be this: The only convenient route for emigrants is now by sea and across the Isthmus, and the vessels for this line of communication start from Northern ports, thus shutting out those who must take with them their servants, their flocks and herds and [thus] securing a Northern Immigration to that country which would first unite our population. If we had a good railroad and other roads making it convenient to go through Texas into New Mexico, and through New Mexico into Southern California, our people with their servants, their horses and their cows would gradually pass westward over fertile lands into mining districts, and in the latter, especially, the advantage of their associated labor would impress itself upon others about them and the prejudice which now shuts us out of that country would yield to the persuasion of personal interest. This border once established from East to West, future acquisitions to the South would insure [*sic*] to our benefit, thus the equality might be regained and preserved which is incumbent [?] to a fair construction of the Constitution and the fulfillment of the great purpose for which our Union was established.

The panacea of 1850 has already lost its efficacy, and the disease it was promised to check for all future time seems to have been rendered chronic by the treatment.

[JEFFERSON DAVIS]

To Collin S. Tarpley (PJD)*

WASHINGTON, D.C., DECEMBER 19, 1855

MY DEAR SIR:

When I received your very kind and interesting letter of the 15th of November, I had hoped it might be possible for me to have returned home in this month, but, in the uncertainty of the case, delayed answering your letter until the present time. The circumstances which surround me now sufficiently establish the fact that I cannot do so without disregarding obligations, among which is prominent my duty to those to whom I am most nearly bound, both by feeling and interest. To the extent of my humble abilities, I have striven to serve our whole country; and, if I have forgotten anything, it has not been my allegiance to Mississippi and my duty to the South. Where ever my personal interest comes in conflict with either, I trust I shall always be ready to sacrifice it. I thank you for your plain advice, for such friendship as you have always evinced for me did not permit me to expect

---

* Attorney in Jackson, Mississippi, who was active in Democratic politics.

that you would speak to me in studied phrase. The disadvantage of being absent when the legislature shall proceed to consider rival aspirants for the United States Senate is clearly perceived by me, and the injury to be inflicted by my defeat for that office is fully appreciated. I shall be happy, however, if the injury is contined to myself; but, as men are but the representatives of ideas, it has no doubt occurred that the effect of such a defeat will have relations far wider than its bearing upon myself. Of those senators who, in 1850, became the objects of special denunciation for their steady adherence to southern rights, all have been endorsed by the people they represented save two—Turney, in whose State the whigs have been ever since in the ascendency, and myself. Yulee was shut out for a time; but Florida has lately done justice to him, and he is again in the Senate.

Others, with better fortune, have remained continually in place, and been re-elected. I have had the satisfaction to believe that the people of Mississippi have been misrepresented, in so far as it has been stated that they had repudiated my course; and for their sake, more than my own, I hope to die thus believing. I have seen something of the manoeuvring to which you refer in the attempts to amuse my friends with the shadow of naming me in connexion with the presidential ticket, and in the declaration that the democratic party north is entitled to the next senator. I am too mindful of my obligations to my friends in the northern part of the State to permit my name to be an obstacle to the accomplishment of any wish they may have in this matter; but there is a broad distinction between a few anxious candidates and the mighty people among whom they live; and I would certainly feel that I had labored to but little purpose if I had now to declare that my love for Mississippi was not graduated by the proximity of its parts to my own dwelling place. I have no means of knowing what will be the probable result; and I could not attempt to affect it by personal solicitation. My position is easily stated, and is that which I have heretofore held; if the legislature should elect me to the Senate, I will accept the honor with pride, and zealously endeavor to discharge the duties of the office. If they should prefer another for their senator, I shall retire to private life, in that position to labor for the honor and interest of our State. Now, as heretofore, I prefer the office of senator to any other, and recent experience has confirmed me in the feeling I expressed to you years ago of total unwillingness to accept any office which Mississippi did not confer. It would certainly be desirable to me that I should not be balloted for if there is any rule founded upon place of residence, or any other paramount consideration, to prevent my election; but that is a matter which I leave to my friends, not only because I am without the information which would enable me to decide the question, but also because, as I cannot ask any member for his vote, or refuse to serve if elected, so I cannot ask anyone to consider me out of the list of candidates.

You have lately canvassed the State, and have had opportunities to know the state of public feeling on this subject. You will be present at the session of the legislature, and your general acquaintance with the members will enable you to tell them whatever they desire to know of my feelings and opinions, as you have long been possessed of both. It is part of man's weakness and vanity to suppose that others preserve a remembrance of what belongs to himself; and thus it appeared to me surprising that members of the legislature should have believed in '54 that I would not accept the office of senator if elected. A little more knowledge of the world might have taught me how, in the busy whirl of politics, men might in less than a year forget the last occasion on which I had surrendered my own personal wishes, interest, and ambition, to serve in a post where my political friends of the South insisted they had special need for me; and how, at a period a little more remote, I had resigned the office, which of all others I preferred, to be a candidate for an office wholly undesirable to me, that I might thus serve my party—may I not say my State?—when the clouds and darkness of a disastrous defeat hung over it.

But if these and other things, which might have assured them as to what course mine might be, were forgotten, I am sure they had not learned that the election of another would be heralded as my defeat, and offered as further confirmation of Mississippi's condemnation of the political course pursued by me when her representative. Very respectfully, your obedient servant,

JEFF. DAVIS.

To William L. Ellsworth (PJD)[*]

WASHINGTON, D.C., JUNE 5, 1856

DEAR SIR,

I have the honor to acknowledge yours of the 3d inst. and to thank you for your very friendly consideration and too high appreciation of myself.

As a part of the present administration, I have singly and sincerely desired and advocated the re nomination of the present Executive, I have believed the best interests of the country could be thus most effectually promoted. If however this should not be possible, then in view of the fact that the Slavery question which now alone disturbs and endangers the harmony of our Union is one which has to be settled at the North, if it is ever to be settled peacably, it appears to me that it would be most advantageous to have in the approaching controversy a Northern leader if one can be selected entirely worthy of the trust. So far then from desiring my own name to be brought before the Convention as a candidate for the Presidency, I have discouraged the idea of looking to the South, for the nominee, unless it should appear that we could in no other way reconcile the conflicting claims of those now prominent for the nomination—all of whom you are aware are northern men. These premises will have already brought your mind to the conclusion that I must decline the complimentary service which you offer to perform in my behalf—But be assured I am not the less grateful for the very kind motive which has prompted you to make the offer. Very Respectfully Your Obt. Servant

JEFFN. DAVIS

---

[*] Probably a native of Connecticut.

To Luther M. Kennett (PJD)[*]

WASHINGTON, D.C., AUGUST 12, 1856

. . .

Having, as requested in your letter, thus presented my views on the report and bill, for improving the navigation of the Western rivers by contract, it may be proper here to state the reasons which have induced the Department in the prosecution of those works to rely on the U.S. Engineers for the plan to be executed, and to retain in their hands the supervision of the work, whether performed by contract or days labor, either or both being used according to the circumstances of each case. It is believed that the public interests will be best subserved by entrusting public works to specially instructed and experienced officers, who, in the execution of their duty, have no interest adverse to that of the Government—whose professional reputation, gained by long years of toil and exposure, is staked on the skilful and successful competion of the works; whose hope of honorable employment—and future advancement in the public service, to which their lives are devoted, give assurance of vigilance and zeal; who have no pecuniary inducement to slight the work, who are urged by all the highest motives—that influence men to the faithful execution of the trusts confided to them.

In conclusion I will say that provision for the permanent or continuous improvement of Western rivers is most desirable, and that without such provision, but small beneficial results are to be anticipated from any plan of operations. No skill can compensate for frequent suspensions, or counteract the evils which must result from interuption in the progress of works before they are complete; and so far as complaints in relation to past expenditures are well founded, I think the true cause is to be found in the want of means to carry out a well devised general system on each river which it is attempted to improve.

Though the report is mainly confined to the removal of snags, logs, wrecks, and sunken rocks, it is well known that the necessities of navi-

---

[*] Businessman in St. Louis.

gation require much more than this. Shoals, bars and natural dams impede the navigation even more than the accidental obstructions proposed to be removed. But the removal of a natural dam, it may be of a sunken rock or a large wreck, may produce a change in the regimen of the river which will create difficulties that did not previously exist; and the construction of a dam to raise the water on a single bar, would probably entail the necessity of another work to answer the consequential effects of the first

The removal of snags for one or two years, though it would produce a temporary benefit, must soon cease to be of any material advantage, if green trees continue to fall in the river and furnish the material to replace the obstacles which had recently been removed. Therefore unless the improvement of the Western rivers be conducted under a general system supported by adequate means for many consecutive years only partial benefits can be expected to result; and we may anticipate that the new evils encountered will be attributed to the work performed in the removal of those obstructions which originally impeded the navigation.

I have not considered it appropriate, in this communication, to offer any suggestions as to the mode by which a fund might be provided for such continuous operations as have been suggested. But the deep interest taken in the whole subject has led me, for many years, to contemplate the adoption of a plan by which the great rivers of the Valley of the Mississippi might be relieved from the interuption and dangers to which their navigation is now subjected. I cannot hope that this end will ever be attained by partial and occasional appropriations, even when expended by the most competent engineers according to the best digested plans but there is still less hope of its being attained by contracts, to be executed, according to the conception of men whose previous pursuits give no assurance of their ability to solve a problem in civil engineering—than which none is more difficult a problem which involves the control of mighty rivers, flowing through alluvial valleys the volume of whose waters vary irregularity with every year and every Season. Very respectfully Yr. ob St.

JEFFN. DAVIS
SEC OF WAR.

To Franklin Pierce [Annual Report of Secretary of War]
(PJD)

. . .

Cavalry cannot be sustained in a state of efficiency unless provided during the winter with stables, grain and hay. At some of the remote posts even the material for construction must be transported a great distance, and the forage can only be furnished at prices which extreme necessity alone will justify. For example: corn delivered at Fort Laramie costs about five dollars a bushel. Infantry garrisons are less expensive, because less forage is required; but, under such circumstances, neither can be sustained except at great cost.

It may be proper further to consider the comparative value of troops thus distributed, and of those serving by detachments from large garrisons quartered in eligible positions. If sufficient garrisons were kept at all the posts now established for the purpose of making expeditions at any time from them among the neighboring tribes, which would require a very considerable augmentation of the present military establishment and a commensurate increase of appropriations for its support, it is not believed that they would be equally effective with marching detachments of the same numerical strength. Their position would be known, their preparations for taking the field would be observed, and a considerable force would necessarily be left behind for the protection of the public property at each military post. The instruction and discipline in quarters would be inferior to that of large garrisons, and the capacity of the troops suddenly emerging from quarters to begin the forced marches of pursuit would be less than that of men inured by a long march and frequent bivouacs to bear fatigue and protect themselves against exposures incident to service in the field. The policy of distribution as at present pursued also involves the frequent construction and abandonment of posts, and with such garrisons as we may expect to have with the present or probable size of the army, involves the employment of all the troops for long periods at constant labor, alike injurious to military instruction and the contentment of the soldier. His compensation at such times is far inferior to that of the common laborer on the frontier, and the prospect of abandoning the position soon after he has made it comparatively comfortable leaves him without an adequate inducement for the sacrifice he is called on to make. A laborer without pay or promise of improvement in his condition, a soldier without the forms and excitement of military life, it is hardly to be wondered at that this state of things should lead to desertion, which has become so frequent as to be one of the great evils of the service. Under the other policy which has been suggested, the troops would be comfortably quartered in the midst of civilization, their summer campaigns would be the field practice of their profession, the temporary dangers and toils of which give zest to a soldier's life; and if to these be added the prospect of a return to the comforts, associations, and means of instruction of a large garrison at a well-established post, it is not seen why the service could not be rendered attractive to persons of military spirit, and it is believed that the efficiency of the troops would be increased proportionally as the expense of supporting them would be diminished.

The occupation of Algeria by the French presents a case having much parallelism to that of our western frontier, and affords us the opportunity of profiting by their experience. Their practice, as far as understood by me, is to leave the desert region to the possession of the nomadic tribes; their outposts, having strong garrisons, are established near the limits of the cultivated region, and their services performed by large detachments making expeditions into the desert regions as required. The marching columns being sufficiently strong to inflict punishment wherever it is deserved, have inspired, it is said, the native tribes with such respect for their power that it has seldom been found necessary to chastise any tribe a second time.

As our present policy rests upon various acts of legislation and the concurrent views of several preceding administrations, a change as radical as that which is here suggested should receive critical examination, and, perhaps, require legislative action before being adopted. The department, if left to the free exercise of its judgment, would have abandoned the policy at present followed, by adopting a few eligible positions, easy of access, and in the midst of a region so productive as to sustain large settlements, from which the bulk of the supplies of the garrisons could be drawn.

. . .

The operations at the national armories have been restricted to the completion of new models for small arms; the alteration of old models to long range rifled arms, and to the preparations requisite for the exclusive manufacture of the adopted new model, of which many of the parts have been fabricated. This model, which is common in its general principles to all our small arms, is a rifled arm, (such as is commonly called the Minié rifle,) with the improvement of a lock, after Maynard's plan, self-priming, when used with the Maynard primers, and as well adapted to use with the percussion cap as the ordinary percussion lock. The alteration of flint lock to rifled arms, with the self-priming lock, has been effected to the limited extent which the means available for the purpose would allow. The results of trials with these arms leave no doubt of the propriety of the measure, which I heretofore recommended, of altering all the old model arms of the United States, including those distributed to States and Territories, by converting them into rifled arms, with the percussion self-priming lock, so as to make them conform to the new model. The arguments then advanced in favor of granting the authority and means for executing this measure have lost none of their force by subsequent reflection and experience. The propriety and necessity of using only the best and most effective arms is obvious. With a population accustomed to the use of arms, familiar with, and competent to judge of their merits or defects, the moral effect of feeling themselves inferior in their armament and equipment would be disastrous. The only point, then, which remains for consideration is, whether the improvements can be applied to our present arms, so as to give to them the desired efficiency. The importance of the improvements and the susceptibility of our arms to receive them are not matters of theory or speculation, but have been proved by actual trial. It is not proposed to hasten, inconsiderately, to the adoption of a scheme of questionable advantage, but one which has undergone various and repeated tests in our own and in other countries, and the merits of which have been practicably established. New models of small arms, with the improvements before mentioned, have been completed, and the alteration of arms of the old model, so as to apply to them all the modern improvements, has been commenced and has progressed far enough to show conclusively that they can be made equal in efficiency to those of the new model. There is in the United States arsenals, and in possession of the States, upwards of half a million of these arms, which have cost between six and seven millions of dollars. In their present condition they are very inferior to the improved arms, and, in order to be made properly efficient and serviceable, they must be altered. It will be remembered that, for many years past, this government has steadily, and at great cost, been filling our arsenals with arms of superior quality, according to any then known standards. Recent improvements have rendered these arms relatively inferior; but, fortunately, we need not lose the fruit of our previous labors. In a short time, with adequate means, we may apply to our present stock of arms these recent improvements, and thus rapidly and satisfactorily give to them the greatest known military efficiency. The propriety of the measure being demonstrated, its execution becomes a mere question of time. Shall it be done as rapidly as practicable, or linger on through the long period of time which will be required to do the work, with the ordinary appropriation? The rapid accomplishment of this work has the advantage of being more economical, for it is obvious that, as the number of arms altered in a given time is increased, the *pro rata* cost is diminished; to which is to be added another and more important consideration, that of being prepared at the earliest period to meet any emergency.

. . .

Since the last annual report the cargo of camels, thirty-two in number, then referred to as being expected, have been landed on the coast of Texas and taken into the interior of the country. Much time was required for their recovery from the effects of a long sea voyage, and but little use has therefore been made of them in the transportation of supplies. On one occasion, it is reported, that a train, consisting of wagons and camels, was sent from Camp Verde to San Antonio, a distance of sixty miles, over a road not worse than those usually found on the frontier, and the result as given is, that the quantity brought back by six camels (3,648 pounds) was equal to the loads of two wagons drawn by six mules each, and the time occupied by the camels was two days and six hours; that by the wagons four days and thirty minutes. On another occasion, the capacity of the camel for travelling over steep acclivities and on muddy roads was tested with the most satisfactory result. Instead of making the detour, rendered necessary in the location of the road, to avoid a rugged mountain, impracticable for wagons, the camels followed a trail which passed directly over it; and a heavy rain occurring whilst they were at the depot to which they had been sent for supplies, the road was rendered so muddy that it was considered impassable by loaded wagons, the train of camels was nevertheless loaded with an average of 328 pounds each, and returned to their encampment, a distance of sixty miles, in two days, suffering, as it is reported, no interruption or unusual fatigue from the mud over which they passed, or the torrents of rain which fell upon them.

These tests fully realize the anticipations entertained of their usefulness in the transportation of military supplies.

The experiment of introducing them into the climate of the United States has been confined to the southern frontier of Texas. Thus far the result is as favorable as the most sanguine could have hoped. Of thirty-four animals imported, two have died—one from accidental injury, and the other from cause unknown. When it is remembered that this is the year of their acclimation, in a climate subject to sudden and violent changes, and of the use by them of herbage very different from that of the countries from which they were imported, there is every reason to believe that as little difficulty will be encountered in the acclimation of the camel as that of the horse or the ox.

The very intelligent officer who was sent abroad to procure them, and who has remained in charge of them, expresses entire confidence, both of their great value for purposes of transportation and of their adaptation to the climate of a large part of the United States.

When we remember that the camel was among the first beasts domesticated by man, it furnishes ground for no little surprise that we should have remained, down to the present day, so little informed of its habitudes and physiology. The information which has been acquired in the progress of this experiment is of a highly interesting character, and must serve to dispel most of those apprehensions which were entertained when it was first proposed to introduce camels into the United States for military purposes. By the kindness of the Secretary of the Navy, I have been again permitted to freight a storeship, on its return voyage from the Mediterranean, with another cargo of these animals, to be purchased from the unexpended balance of the appropriation, and Lieutenant D. D. Porter, of the navy, commanding, was charged with the duty of procuring them, and it is expected that another shipment of about forty in number will be landed during the present winter on the coast of Texas, and sent up to the encampment where those formerly obtained are now located, where we shall have for practical test about seventy animals.

. . .

Speech in Jackson, Mississippi (PJD)

MAY 29, 1857

He was thrice and four times happy to meet again his fellow-citizens of Hinds, and the adjacent country at the capital of the State. Most cordially he thanked them for the medium they had selected to give expression to those sentiments of esteem and affection for him for which he felt profoundly grateful. The honor of the reception was enhanced by the fact that a valued personal and political friend, the popular and talented Governor of Mississippi—a man who had made for himself, during his short career in the federal Senate, an enduring name—a memory which shall last with the records of the Senate—was the medium of that tribute by which he had been so highly honored.

He was proud to be once more in the metropolis of his beloved Mississippi. He was happy to see the unusual development of her agricultural and commercial resources indicating the realization of all that he had hoped for her in future destiny; and he was more than happy to be received into the midst of this improvement and prosperity, not as the politician is commonly received, but with that reward of his highest aspiration, the appreciation and approval of the people. Yes, such was his reception, that it made the flowers of his youthful memory bloom again.

For the past four years, he had been absent, at the call of the elected chief of the nation, to take charge of a department of Government. It was with reluctance that he accepted the position of Secretary of War; and he need not say he did so with assurance that no principle of State Rights Democracy would be contravened. The promise was not broken; the Administration proved unflinchingly true; the pledges to the people were redeemed with a stern fidelity, and the whole country, in its peace, its prosperity and growing regard for the constitutional rights of all sections, were the eloquent witnesses for its good faith and patriotism. From the field of administrative labor, he had come back, but unchanged in heart. Its pulses were ever with Mississippi. And what a country was ours! As a single evidence of its vastness of resource, he would instance the fact, that during the period of the late Administration, more land was ceded by the general government for internal improvement and other legitimate purposes, than a third of France, and still we retain a public domain equal to the entire area of Europe! He thanked Gov. McRae for claiming no more for the Administration than an adherence to the constitution, and he trusted in God that no administration would ever depart from a similar rule of conduct. He was rejoiced to say that it was his conviction that the administration of Mr. Buchanan would not; he had that assurance. And it was his pride to tell them in Washington, when the presidential contest was pending, and the vote of Mississippi was doubted because she had not partaken of the public patronage, that the polar star of Mississippians was *principle*—they cared not for office.

It was but just to say that the late administration had done much to improve our foreign relations. From our immediate neighbors to the remotest point ever reached by the Argonautic expedition, the flag of America commanded the homage of respect, and the name of American was a passport and a protection through the world. In regard to one thing, however, he confessed to disappointment, the legitimate acquisition of the island of Cuba. The failure of that most desirable object was not chargable upon the President. To the lower House of

Congress was all censure attributable in the premises. They withheld supplies, refused even a vote of confidence in the administration; and the next election surged upon the country a curse worse than the locusts of Egypt; a horde of black republicans and knownothings desecrated the hall of congress. The black republicans aimed at the legalization of treason, and from the knownothings nothing was expected. Born of a fantastic nothing, they knew nothing and they done nothing; and that was the total of their history. The Clayton-Bulwer treaty, a diplomatic blunder, threw serious obstacles in the way of an equitable arrangement of our relations with Britain. The Dallas-Clarendon treaty was obnoxious because of the recognition of the English treaty with Honduras, prohibiting slavery in that American State. By the conservatism of the Senate it was amended in that respect; but we are told that England rejects the amended treaty, so that our affairs with that government are still in an unsettled condition. He (Col. Davis) was an advocate of the Monroe doctrine. The attempt of England to exclude slavery from Honduras, was an unwarrantable interference, and it was well that it was resisted, no matter what the hazard.

Within a few years, another event, which lately met with a painful termination, had given hope to the South of the expansion of her institutions. Central America was in a transition state. The people of Nicaragua had revolted against despotism and had invited a well known citizen to their aid. With a Spartan band he answered the summons. But he had other foes to contend with than the native tyrants of the soil. There was palpable British interference under the flimsy guise of protection to British subjects; there was black republicanism at the north pouring in gold, munitions and armaments to the Costa Ricans; and there were the supplies of the patriots cut off, their reinforcements prevented from junction, and such an accumulation of obstacles from powerful cources that successful resistance became impossible, and defeat was the end. He attached no importance to the story that Wm. Walker and his men *capitulated* to the commander of the St. Marys.* He knew her captain well; knew that a more chivalrous gentleman never trod an American battle deck, and knew that the story must be

* William Walker was a leading filibuster; he was executed in Honduras in 1860.

false that he took Walker and his men as prisoners. No, he rescued them from Costa Rican vengeance, threw over them the aegis of our flag, and bore them to their friends. He was glad that the people of Louisiana had given such a welcome to the fillibusters. They were not vanquished; it was but temporary defeat. Clearly, in responding to the call of the oppressed Nicaraguans, they were guiltless of crime, though black republicanism had denounced them as murderers and brigands.

In its domestic policy, the late administration had much to encounter. For instance, there was the slave rescue in Boston. The arm of municipal law was paralyzed. The Marshal could not take a fugitive to the waiting ship; and to the performance of the duty of that federal officer neither state or city authorities gave aid or countenance. A conflict between state and federal power seemed to impend. It was a crisis; but the administration was equal to the delicate and hazardous emergency. The federal authority was coercively interposed, the supremacy of the law was vindicated, and the rights of a southern citizen maintained. But, (said Col. Davis,) we will never have obtained all our rights until the legislation of congress shall amply protect slave as it does all other property. Of that, he was rejoiced to say, he had stronger hopes than ever. The federal opposition of 1851, which so unnaturally prevailed even in the south, to a full measure of our rights, was being reduced to an important minority. There was a healthful reaction at the time, and that reaction was still in progress.

He had ever combatted the "squatter sovereignty" doctrine as a dangerous innovation. And what a harvest we have reaped from that novel tenet. It sent the slavery issue from the halls of congress to the territories, there to generate fraternal strife, bloodshed, and the other unhallowed incidents of civil war, without producing one tangible good. It compelled the administration, in the Kansas difficulties, to interpose the federal arm, notwithstanding the earnest desire that the local civil power, with the ordinary aid of the *posse commitatus*,* would be all sufficient. Such were the results of squatter sovereignty, even as exemplified in a territory where the inhabitants were emigrants from

---

* *Posse commitatus:* the power of the local forces.

the old States; and their tendency should be to convince every citizen of the danger, the fallacy and the impracticability of the doctrine.

In the last presidential contest, we witnessed the great crisis. It was the mightiest effort of the black republican faction, grown up to the colossal proportions of a sectional party. The contest was known to be between democracy and the black republicans. True, there was a third party; but it was like the tub thrown to the whale—it meant nothing. Grandly passed the constitutional Union through that most terrific of all our crisis; and where is that man who does not know, whether he will confess it or not, that the southern democracy saved the Union of equal rights? Yes, in that appalling emergency, when all that we hold dear was jeoparded, they stood like the old guard of Napolean, with the inscription written upon their brows, "the old Guard knows how to die, but never surrenders!" He claimed for Mississippi the van in that grandest of moral combats for the perpetuation of co-equal liberty. Though absent while the contest was upon her, he knew her spirit, he knew her truth and he knew her incorruptibility; and it was this knowledge that led him to tell them, when they feared the result of the conflict here, that his State, while she scorned to swell the pageant and the pomp of power; while she had not her legion of office-seekers at Washington—and he thanked God that she had not—would increase by thousands her majority, for hers was no mercenary liege. She had no thought for place and its emoluments Her purpose was the purer and loftier one of re-inaugurating tried and cherished principles. Mississippians had their reward. It was enough for them to know that they done battle for no phantom—that Buchanan was true.

He (Col. Davis) was no alarmist; he had a contempt for panics and a scorn of panic-makers; but he would tell them that in 1860 the monster crisis was to be met. Then shall American patriotism pass the ordeal of fire. He hoped for the best; but a sense of danger imposed upon him the duty of warning them to prepare for the worst. The time had been when the puling newspapers of the opposition would have denounced him as a traitor for uttering this sentiment. It was a time when patriotism was construed to be submission to degradation and wrong, for the sake of a Union whose soul was perishing away, and which was being perilled only by such submission. He thanked heaven that time was passed. It was not the revolutionary time: O, no, submission was an unuttered word in that day of bold resolve and high achievement. It was a period intermediate between now and then—a "dark age" in our political history. But he need not adjure them to preparation. They were preparing. The iron interlink, now in progress, with Charleston on the Atlantic, was such preparation. The Southern Railroad was originally a conception of John C. Calhoun's. He sought this commercial and social intimacy between Mississippi and South Carolina. And, who would think it? it was stigmatised at the time as a project of *treason!* How flagitious, then, according to the quaint judgment of that day, must be Mississippi's perfidy; for she has made the treason practical—the locomotive traitor is partially on its way! It would bring the South in intimate communion with herself; it would develop her resources within the south; and that was her great need. Mississippi wants factories; he hoped they would spring up in every town and neighborhood all over the State. Ay, *public* factories for arms and ammunition. Virginia, in the epoch of her pride, built them, and it was no treason; but she has permitted their decay, and they are now but vestiges of her power and pristine grandeur. South Carolina built them, and they are still fostered, giving to her people a sense of security, to the State a spirit of independence, to the country a guarantee of her patriotism. Better than any State in the Union is she prepared for the exigencies of war or peace. But the name of South Carolina, most unaccountably to him, seemed always to evoke, in certain quarters even in the south, a peculiar sentiment of dread. What had she done, that gallant sister of the ancient and primitive thirteen, to inspire aversion or incite contumely? Did she falter in the revolution? No. Was she faithless to the constitution? Never—always its defender! but the ignorant culumniator says she nullified. The charge was untrue; she never nullified a federal statute; but her voice has been shrill and clear in the cause of right, and her opposition invincible to wrong. Why charge upon South Carolina the sin of Massachusetts? Massachusetts nullifies both the statute and organic law; South Carolina is consistently obedient to both: yet Massachusetts is eulogized, South Carolina derided.

The democracy (said Col. Davis) have continually new forms of opposition to encounter. That opposition seems to cast its name with the same facility that a snake does its skin; but it is ever the same federalism, centralising and consolidating power in the federal head, and verging the States to provincial degradation. By those characteristics, no matter how illusive its appellation, it cannot fail to be always recognized. To-day—in this age of liberty and enlightenment, and generous trust in the better nature of universal man, it seeks to revive the barbaric idea that the word, stranger, is synonymous with enemy. Hence their proposition to reconstruct the naturalization laws so as to keep the stranger without the pale of citizenship for twenty-one years. Well, who would it exclude—this mis-called "American" policy? Would it keep the mendicant and the criminal from our shores? No, for in no land do they care for political franchises. The beggar comes chiefly for bread, the felon flees the penalties of outraged law. But it would have forbidden our territories such bright and gallant spirits as your Meagher and your Mitchel. Soule would not have tied his worldly wealth in a handkerchief, expatriated himself from France, where he attempted the resurrection of liberty, and sought an asylum in this Republic, where his silvery tongue has spoken only patriotism, as its pure thoughts corruscated from his gifted mind. The vaunted "American" policy would deprive you of men like these, and your gain would be the unchecked influx of the mendicant and the convict. You would have all the evil complained of, despoiled of the countervailing good. A policy so shallow, so illiberal and so ineffectual can never command the adhesion of a majority of generous and high-souled Americans.

Again he would say, Mississippi and Mississippians had his whole heart. That heart was no traveler. Duty may call his person and his spirit afar from the limits of his beloved State, but his affection remains, ever chiding him back to fondest and proudest associations. While life lasted—while his heart had pulses and his spirit energy, it would be his highest pleasure to stand shoulder to shoulder with Mississippians in the hour of danger He would not sympathize with the feelings of him of Lucretia, who when the tempest lashed the ocean into fury, and death yawned in billowy horror upon the mariner, stood calmly in the shelter of a cavernous cliff and enjoyed the peril of the seamen. If there was danger, he would share it; Mississippi's peril was his own. He would aid her in averting or overcoming it, or with her he would perish.

Speech in Mississippi City, Mississippi (PJD)

. . .

He congratulated the audience on the progress and prosperity of the seacoast of Mississippi, and referred to the period when he had seen it an almost unbroken wilderness, when the lofty pines, as they swayed to and fro, sighed mournfully over the solitude which reigned around them; and the streams which drained the grandest forest of ship timber our country contained, as they rolled on to the ocean, complainingly murmured of man's neglect. Now long lines of smiling cottages and cultivated grounds look out upon the sea and court its health-bearing breezes; the ring of the saw and the hammer, the hum of the manufacturing village, the throng of the epicurien, the valetudinarian and the weary denizen of the city give life and activity to the scene, and the solemn dirge of other days is made pensive music in our own. Thus much has been done; it is, however, but the first step in the line of progress which lies before us. Already a valuable trade in timber for foreign markets has commenced; the supply is equal to the absorption of more labor than for centuries can be directed to this branch of industry, when new means of transportation shall render available the forests of the interior.

The railroads projected, and which, it was to be hoped, would be completed in the life-time of those who had conceived the project, would put our sea coast in easy communication with the whole State and bring the commercial world of Mobile and New Orleans into immediate neighborhood. A canal to connect this inner line of navigation with the Mississippi River will give such cheap transportation to and from New Orleans as can not fail to develop the advantages of the harbor of Ship Island, and speedily to conduce to direct the trade between the valley of the Mississippi and the commercial ports of Europe. The beneficial results of those aids to the natural advantages of our seacoast were too evident to require elucidation; and it was, he said, not the least gratifying feature in the view presented, that, while it would tend to enrich our own people, it could not fail to increase the prosperity of our neighbors also. But it was not in the pecuniary aspect alone that these considerations should excite our interest; it was by the development of the resources of the State, by increasing the facilities of intercourse between its various parts, and by giving a common interest and a mutual dependence to the whole, that community feeling, State pride and self-reliance are to be cultivated, all of which were essential to maintain the feeling of State independence, to sustain the rights and fulfil the destiny which we were permitted to hope Mississippi would realize in the future.

. . .

If the discussions by the canvassers and through the press had not silenced our enemies, they had at least conferred one benefit—they had relieved us of Southern apologists who prayed for toleration to African slavery as an admitted evil, but one for the introduction of which we were not responsible, and of which we could not get rid—in admission which not only excused Abolitionists, but which, if true, demanded of every honest man among us that he should co-operate in all well-directed efforts for its abatement. That this relation of labor to capital had defects, he would not deny; that it was subject to abuse by the vicious, the ignorant and the wayward, was true; but so, too, were even the tender relations of parent and child, of husband and wife.

But when he compared it to conditions somewhat similar—to that of apprentices and day-laborers, to the inmates of asylums, poorhouses and penitentiaries, where task masters and police-officers take the place of the domestic government of the plantation—he turned from the humiliation and suffering of his own race, when reduced to that low estate, to the comfort and content which was the usual lot of African slaves in our country, and thankful to the universal principle of self-interest which makes the master usually kind and attentive to the wants of his slave, who, in the language of Holy Writ, "is his money," he (Col. D.) recognized in the institution of domestic slavery the most humane relations of labor to capital which can permanently subsist between them, and the most beneficent form of government that has been applied to those who are morally and intellectually unable to take care of themselves

He held, that after making all the reductions which justice and candor required, if measured by the standard of the practicable and real, African Slavery, as it exists in the United States, was a moral, a social and a political blessing. It had transferred the slave from a barbarian to a civilized master, had taught him the useful arts, and shed upon him the divine light of Christianity. The presence of these laborers of an inferior race elevated the white man, and gave our social condition that freedom from humiliating discrimination and dependence among individuals of our own race, which, where they existed, would leave but the name of political equality.

. . .

Hopefully clinging to that organization which promised something for the safety of the country and which alone could check the progress of sectional hostility, he looked to preparation and action at home as our only sure reliance. Equally opposed to the brainless intemperance of those who desired a dissolution of the Union, and who found in every rustling leaf fresh evidence of volcanic eruption; and to the slavish submission of those who, like the victims of the juggernaut unresistingly prostrated themselves to be crushed, Col. D. said he would, as their Senator, feel himself bound earnestly, faithfully to labor for the preservation of the Union and to guard against the approach of any danger to the Republic. His view of the position of a Representative of a State to the General Government rendered it an obligation that the office should be vacated whenever its duties could not be performed in a spirit of friendship to the Union. His first allegiance was to Mississippi; her fortunes, whether good or evil, must be his own, and wherever she required his services they were wholly at her command. The post to which he had lately been assigned he would hold as a watchful sentinel; he hoped not to disturb their repose by idle alarms, neither could he consent to cry peace when there was no peace, or to avoid the responsibility of arousing them when the tramp of advancing hosts was in his ear.

He said he had a grateful duty to perform in returning his sincere thanks to the people of Mississippi for their long-continued kindness and repeated manifestations of confidence, the last instance of which was his election to the United States Senate at a time when long absence and employment on matters having no especial interest to them, might well have caused him to be overlooked, if not forgotten. For this high evidence of the regard of his friends, he felt a gratitude more deep than he could express, and of which he distrusted his ability to give by his acts due manifestation.

He then urged the necessity of home education, of normal schools, and Southern school-books, as the next step after the mother's pious training in the formation of that character which was essential to progress toward that high destiny to which his anticipation pointed. If, as was sometimes asserted, Governments contain within themselves the elements of their own destruction, as animate beings have their growth, their maturity and decay; if ours, the last, best hope of civil liberty was, like the many experiments which preceded it, to be engulfed in the sea of time, and all for which we now hoped a perpetuity to become part of the history of the last, he hoped on the pages of that volume Mississippi would stand conspicuous for all that was virtuous and noble; that through the waves of fanaticism, anarchy and civil strife, her sons would be the Levites who would bear the ark of the Constitution, and when unable to save it from wreck, that in the pile of its sacred timbers their bones would be found mingled.

Col. Davis concluded by expressing, in the very blandest manner and in the happiest terms, his gratitude for the presence of the ladies; he also thanked his sea coast friends for their manifestations of regard for him.

To Payne & Harrison (PJD)*

BRIERFIELD, WARREN COUNTY, MISSISSIPPI, NOVEMBER 23, 1857
GENTLEMEN.

I have the honor to acknowledge yours of the 30th Inst. In relation to the sale of cotton now in your hands I can suggest nothing beyond the crude opinion heretofore expressed & must leave it to your better information to decide whether to ship or to sell in New Orleans.

Confident of your desire to promote my interest, & fully relying on your Judgment, I shall be quite satisfied with your decision. By the "Adams" I send say fifty bales of cotton to be disposed of as that which you have now on hand.

The opening market led me to hope for fifteen cents as the ruling price of my crop, & though formerly I would have been content with less, I must hold the mercantile world responsible for any disappointment felt if I obtain less, & inflict upon them the penalty of distrusting their bright pictures in the future.

Mr. Clarkson will sometimes order supplies for the place, & at other times supplies for himself & family, for the latter I will be responsible, but wish the bills kept seperate.

Referring to your remarks about the lot of negroes offered by Mr. Christmas, I will explain the meaning of my last letter to have been that I thought from the memorandum sent to my Brother that the proposed reduction mentioned by you was an average of 1000 Dollars instead of the prices therein affixed to each negro except the children not seperately estimated. The two boys estimated at 800 & 900 dollars, as I construed your letter, were in the amended proposition to be raised to the general average of 1000 dollars—which would make the total eleven, instead of twelve thousand nine hundred dollars as first proposed.

I expect to leave tomorrow or next day for Washington. Enclosed please find a list of articles which I will thank you to send per R. W. Adams. Truly yours

JEFFERSON DAVIS

---

* JD's factors in New Orleans.

List of articles for Brierfield plantation to be addressed as usual

One bbl. of Flour
Two   " " Molasses   *For Negroes*
One   " " Sugar
One Sack " Coffee
One Doz. ditching Spades.
Half   " long handled shovels.
Ten pieces of India bagging.
Eight coils " Bale rope

JEFFERSON DAVIS

Speech in U.S. Senate (JDC)

FEBRUARY 8, 1858

...

It is a poor evasion for any man to say, "I make war on the rights of one whole section; I make war on the principles of the Constitution; and yet I uphold the Union, and I desire to see it perpetuated." Undermine the foundation, and still pretend that he desires the fabric to stand! Common sense rejects it. No one will believe the man who makes the assertion, unless he believes him under the charitable supposition that he knows not what he is doing.

Sir, we are arraigned day after day as the aggressive power. What southern Senator, during this whole session, has attacked any portion, or any interest, of the North? In what have we now, or ever, back to the earliest period of our history, sought to deprive the North of any advantage it possessed? The whole charge is, and has been, that we seek to extend our own institutions into the common territory of the United States. Well and wisely has the President of the United States pointed to that common territory as the joint possession of the country. Jointly we hold it, jointly we enjoyed it, in the earlier period of our country; but when, in the progress of years, it became apparent that it could not longer be enjoyed in peace, the men of that day took upon themselves, wisely or unwisely, a power which the Constitution did not confer; and, by a geographical line, determined to divide the Territories, so that the common field, which brothers could not cultivate in peace, should be held severally for the benefit of each. Wisely or unwisely, that law was denied extension to the Pacific ocean. I was struck, in the course of these debates, to which I have not been in the habit of replying, to hear the Senator from New Hampshire, [Mr. HALE] who so very ardently opposed the extension of that line to the Pacific ocean, who held it to be a political stain upon the history of our country, and who would not even allow the southern boundary of Utah to be the parallel of 36° 30', because of the political implication which was contained in it, the historical character of the line, plead as he did, a few days ago, for the constitutionality and legality, and for the sacred character, of that so-called Missouri compromise.

I, for one, never believed Congress had the power to pass that law; yet, as one who was willing to lay down much then, as I am now, to the peace, the harmony, and the welfare of our common country, I desired to see that line extended to the Pacific ocean, and that strife which now agitates the country never renewed; but with a distinct declaration, "go ye to the right, and we will go to the left; and we go in peace and good will towards each other." Those who refused then to allow the extension of that line, those who declared then that it was a violation of principle, and insisted on what they termed non-intervention, must have stood with very poor grace in the same Chamber when, at a subsequent period, the Senator from Illinois, bound by his honor on account of his previous course, moved the repeal of that line to throw open Kansas; they must have stood with very bad grace in this presence, to argue that that line was now sacred, and must be kept forever.

The Senator from Illinois stood foremost as one who was willing, at an early period, to sacrifice his own prejudices and his own interests, if, indeed, his interests be girt and bounded by the limits of a State, by proposing to extend that line of pacification to the Pacific ocean; and failing in that, then became foremost in the advocacy of the doctrine of non-intervention; and upon that I say he was in honor bound to wipe out that line and throw Kansas open, like any other Territory. But, sir, was it then understood by the Senator from Illinois, or anybody else, that throwing open the Territory of Kansas to free emigration was to be the signal for the marching of cohorts from one section or another to fight on that battle-field for mastery? Or did he not rather think that emigration was to be allowed to take its course, and soil and climate be permitted to decide the great question? We were willing to abide by it. We were willing to leave natural causes to decide the question. Though I differed from the Senator from New York, though I did not believe that natural causes, if permitted to flow in their own channel, would have produced any other result than the introduction of slave property into the Territory of Kansas, I am free to admit that I have not yet reached the conclusion that that property would have permanently remained there. That is a question which interest decides. Vermont would not keep African slaves because they were not valuable to her; neither will any population whose density is so great as to trade rapidly on the supply of bread, be willing to keep and maintain an improvident population, to feed them in infancy, to care for them in sickness, to protect them in age; and thus it will be found in the history of nations, that whenever population has reached that density in the temperate zones, selfdom, villenage, or slavery, whatever it has been called, has disappeared. Ours presents a new problem, one not stated by those who wrote on it in the earlier period of our history. It is the problem of a semi-tropical climate, the problem of malarial districts, of staple products. This produces a result different from that which would be found in the farming districts and cooler climates. A race suited to our labor exists there. Why should we care whether they go into other Territories or not? Simply because of the war that is made against our institutions; simply because of the want of security which results from the action of our opponents in the northern States. Had you made no political war upon us, had you observed the principles of our Confederacy as States, that the people of each State were to take care of their domestic affairs, or, in the language of the Kansas bill, to be left perfectly free to form and regulate their institutions in their own way, then, I say, within the limits of each State the population there would have gone on to attend to their own affairs, and have had little regard to whether this species of property or any other was held in any other portion of the Union. You have made it a political war. We are on the defensive. How far are you to push us?

The Senator from Alabama has been compelled to notice the resolutions of his State; nor does that State stand alone. To what issue are you now pressing us? To the conclusion that because within the limits of a Territory slaves are held as property, a state is to be excluded from the Union. I am not in the habit of paying lip-service to the Union. The Union is strong enough to confer favors; it is strong enough to command service. Under these circumstances, the man deserves but little credit who sings paeans to its glory. If through a life, now not a short one, a large portion of which has been spent in the public service, I have given no better proof of my affection for this Union than my declarations, I have lived to little purpose, indeed. I think I have given evidence in every form in which patriotism is ever subjected to a test, and I trust whatever evil may be in store for us by those who wage war on the Constitution and our rights under it, that I shall be able to turn at least to the past and say, "up to that period when I was declining into the grave, I served a Government I loved, and served it with my whole heart." Nor will I stop to compare services with those gentlemen who have fair phrases, whilst they undermine the very foundation of the temple our fathers built. If, however, there be here those who do really love the Union and the Constitution, which is the life-blood of the Union, the time has come when we should look calmly, though steadily, the danger which besets us, in the face.

Violent speeches denunciatory of people in any particular section of the Union; the arraignment of institutions which they inherited and intend to transmit, as leprous spots on the body politic, are not the means by which fraternity is to be preserved, or this Union rendered perpetual. These were not the arguments which our fathers made when, through the struggles of the revolutionary war, they laid the foundation of the Union. These are not the principles on which our Constitution, a bundle of compromises, was made. Then the navigating and the agricultural States did not war to see which could most injure the other; but each conceded something from that which it believed to be its own interest, to promote the welfare of the other.

Those debates, whilst they brought up all that struggle which belong to opposite interests and opposite localities, show none of that bitterness which so unfortunately characterizes every debate in which this body is involved.

...

To F. Bostick (JDC)*

DEAR SIR:

It gives me much pleasure to acknowledge the receipt of your letter of the 1st instant, to which, being still unable to write, I must reply by availing myself of the hand of another.

You ask my views as to what the South should do in the event that Kansas should be finally refused admission into the Union under the Lecompton constitution. Your inquiry shows that you had not, at the date of your letter, learned the action which Congress had taken upon the question of the admission of Kansas under the constitution framed at Lecompton.

The questions which agitated the people of Mississippi when I was last among you, were as to the course the Administration would pursue in relation to the action of the convention in Kansas, and whether the Congress would apply to the application of Kansas the dogma of "No more slave States?" Fortunately for us, neither of the issues on which I took position before my fellow-citizens of Mississippi remains now for consideration.

The Executive, so far from opposing obstacles to the admission of Kansas, because the convention had not submitted the constitution formed by it for the ratification of the people by a popular vote, has used all of his influence to promote favorable action by Congress upon the application of the new State; and the Congress, barring all side pretences, and overthrowing all opposition to the constitution of

---

* Mississippi planter and supporter of JD.

Kansas, because it recognized the right of property in slaves, have decided to admit Kansas into the Union with the constitution framed at Lecompton; thus, at the same time deciding that the recognition of slavery in the constitution of a new State should not exclude her from admission into the Union, and that the inhabitants of a Territory, when assuming the powers and responsibilities of the people of a State, have a right to regulate their domestic institutions in their own way—framing their fundamental law either by delegates assembled in convention, by the people convened in mass, or by any other mode which to them may seem best.

Appended to the constitution as a condition connected with the application for admission into the Union, the convention of Kansas submitted an ordinance which set up extraordinary and inadmissible claims in relation to the public domain, and demanded exorbitant grants of land for educational, railroad and other purposes. These the Congress refused to recognize as a right or to grant as an endowment, at the same time proposing to the people of Kansas terms which, though more moderate, were quite equal to those which had been granted the most favored State at the date of her admission. The only question, then, which remains is, will the people of Kansas accept the terms proposed by Congress, or not? If they accept the terms, then the action of Congress is complete; the constitution having been already received, approved, and the State admitted under it; and the President of the United States, upon notification of the acceptance of the grants conferred, having been authorized, by proclamation, to announce the fact that Kansas is a State in the Union. If the terms offered by Congress be declined, then Kansas remains a Territory of the United States, and, as provided in the act for her admission, must so remain until she has a population which will entitle her to at least one representative in Congress.

The mode in which the acceptance or rejection of the grants offered by Congress in lieu of those claimed by Kansas should be decided, was specified in the act for admission. This was a mere question of policy or convenience, for nothing can be more clear than that, when the conditions annexed to their application for admission had been changed by the Congress, the people of Kansas were not bound by their proposition and had a right to withdraw it, if they believed it to be so materially affected by the change of the conditions as to render admission into the Union no longer desirable to them.

By the act of admission a Territory becomes an equal in the sisterhood of States, and those who claim the right of Congress to modify the constitution of a State asking for admission, or to coerce her to enter the Union under terms unacceptable to the community, offend against the doctrine of State rights, and deny the freedom and equality, which are inseparable from the idea of State sovereignty.

The consequences of admitting a State without a recognition precedent of the rights of the United States to the public domain, are, in my opinion, the transfer of the useful, with the eminent domain, to the people of the State thus admitted without reservation.

The bill first passed by the Senate, like that which became a law, covered the two points which, in my opinion, contained all that was important to the South: First the recognition of the right of the people to exercise entire control over the mode in which they would proceed to form their constitution; second, that the recognition of the right to hold slaves should not be a barrier to the admission of a new State into the Union. As a question of preference between the bill of the Senate, which failed in the House, and that of the Committee of Conference, which became a law, my judgment is in favor of the latter, because it distinctly preserves the rights of the United States, and does not attempt to construe, or seemingly to suggest any modification of the constitution, or to offer any justification for having admitted the State but leaves it to stand as the simple recognition of the right of the people—they having formed a constitution republican in its character—to be admitted into the Union.

The importance which I attached to the success of the measure, and my willingness to incur any responsibility which attached to a participation in it, may be inferred from the fact that though an invalid, whose condition rendered it less than prudent that he should leave his chamber, I went to the Senate for two days in succession, that I might have an opportunity to vote for the bill. Its passage, was then and is now, regarded by me as the triumph of all for which we contended and the success of a great constitutional principle, the recognition of which, though it should bear no present fruit to be gathered by the South, was an object worthy of a struggle, and may redound to our future advantage. By the same means the country was relieved from an issue which, had it been presented as threatened, our honor, our safety, our respect for our ancestors, and our regard for our posterity would have required the South to meet, at whatever sacrifice. I have thus thrown out rather hints that complied with your request to give my views fully, which you will please attribute to the physical embarrassment under which I reply.

VERY RESPECTFULLY AND TRULY, YOURS &C.,

JEFF'N DAVIS.

Speech at Sea on Joseph Whitney (JDC)

JULY 4, 1858

...

First, the Declaration of Independence was read by Sebastian F. Streeter, Esq., of Baltimore, when Senator Davis made an address of singular felicity of diction and impassioned eloquence, and of such a character as to command the admiration of those who listened to it. He commenced by happy allusions to the array of beauty and intelligence that stood before him from all parts of our common country; he then passed in review the condition of the feeble and separate colonies of 1776, and contrasted with it the country now—the only proper republic on earth, as it stood before the world in its wonderful progress in art, and agriculture, and commerce, and all the elements that constitute a great nation. When thus sailing on the Atlantic, looking to the coast of the United States, he was reminded of those bold refugees from British and French oppression who crossed these waters to found a home in what was then a wilderness. The memory, too, arose of the many sorrowing hearts and oppressed spirits since borne over these waves to that refuge from political oppression which our fathers founded as the home of liberty and the asylum of mankind. Her territory, which now stretches from ocean to ocean, contains a vast interior yet unpeopled; and, with a destiny of still further and continued expansion of area, why should the gate of the temple be now shut upon sorrowing mankind? Rather let it be that the gate should be forever open, and an emblematic flag, hereafter as heretofore, wave a welcome to all to come to the modern Abdella—fugitives from political oppression.

. . .

Trifling politicians in the South, or in the North, or in the West, may continue to talk otherwise, but it will be of no avail. They are like the mosquitoes around the ox: they annoy, but they cannot wound, and never kill. There was a common interest which ran through all the diversified occupations and various products of these sovereign States; there was a common sentiment of nationality which beat in every American bosom; there were common memories sweet to us all, and, though clouds had occasionally darkened our political sky, the good sense and the good feeling of the people had thus far averted any catastrophe destructive of our constitution and the Union. It was in fraternity and an elevation of principle which rose superior to sectional or individual aggrandizement that the foundations of our Union were laid; and if we, the present generation, be worthy of our ancestry, we shall not only protect those foundations from destruction, but build higher and wider this temple of liberty, and inscribe perpetuity upon its tablet.

In the course of his beautiful speech, Senator Davis passed a noble eulogium on our mother country; and dwelt on the many reasons why the most cordial friendship should be maintained with her; and he concluded by a tribute to the fair sex—the women—beautiful woman; to the wondrous educational influence as the mother which she exercised over the minds of men. It is ever, at all times, felt and operative—upon the dreary waste of ocean, on the lonely prairie, in the troublous contests at the national halls. And when the arm is moved in the deadly conflicts of the battle-field, and the foe is vanquished, then the gentle influences instilled by women do their work, and the heart melts into tears of pity and prompts to deeds of mercy.

. . .

Speech in Portland, Maine (JDC)

...

Such, in very general terms, is the rich political legacy our fathers bequeathed to us. Shall we preserve and transmit it to posterity? Yes, yes, the heart responds, and the judgment answers, the task is easily performed. It but requires that each should attend to that which most concerns him, and on which alone he has rightful power to decide and to act. That each should adhere to the terms of a written compact and that all should cooperate for that which interest, duty and honor demand. For the general affairs of our country, both foreign and domestic, we have a national executive and a national legislature. Representatives and Senators are chosen by districts and by States, but their acts affect the whole country, and their obligations are to the whole people. He who holding either seat would confine his investigations to the mere interests of his immediate constituents would be derelict to his plain duty; and he who would legislate in hostility to any section would be morally unfit for the station, and surely an unsafe depositary if not a treacherous guardian of the inheritance with which we are blessed.

No one, more than myself, recognizes the binding force of the allegiance which the citizen owes to the State of his citizenship, but that State being a party to our compact, a member of our union, fealty to the federal Constitution is not in opposition to, but flows from the allegiance due to one of the United States. Washington was not less a Virginian when he commanded at Boston; nor did Gates or Greene weaken the bonds which bound them to their several States, by their campaigns in the South.* In proportion as a citizen loves his own State, will he strive to honor by preserving her name and her fame free from the tarnish of having failed to observe her obligations, and to fulfil her duties to her sister States. Each page of our history is illustrated by

---

* Horatio Gates and Nathanael Greene were generals in the Continental army during the Revolution. Both were from northern states but also served in the South.

the names and the deeds of those who have well understood, and discharged the obligation. Have we so degenerated, that we can no longer emulate their virtues? Have the purposes for which our Union was formed, lost their value? Has patriotism ceased to be a virtue and is narrow sectionalism no longer to be counted a crime? Shall the North not rejoice that the progress of agriculture in the South has given to her great staple the controlling influence of the commerce of the world, and put manufacturing nations under bond to keep the peace with the United States? Shall the South not exult in the fact, that the industry and persevering intelligence of the North, has placed her mechanical skill in the front ranks of the civilized world—that our mother country, whose haughty minister some eighty odd years ago declared that not a hob-nail should be made in the colonies, which are now the United States, was brought some four years ago to recognize our pre-eminence by sending a commission to examine our work shops, and our machinery, to perfect their own manufacture of the arms requisite for their defence? Do not our whole people, interior and seaboard, North, South, East, and West, alike feel proud of the hardihood, the enterprise, the skill, and the courage of the Yankee sailor, who has borne our flag far as the ocean bears its foam, and caused the name and the character of the United States to be known and respected wherever there is wealth enough to woo commerce, and intelligence enough to honor merit? So long as we preserve, and appreciate the achievements of Jefferson and Adams, of Franklin and Madison, of Hamilton, of Hancock, and of Rutledge, men who labored for the whole country, and lived for mankind, we cannot sink to the petty strife which would sap the foundations, and destroy the political fabric our fathers erected, and bequeathed as an inheritance to our posterity forever.

. . .

To Arthur C. Halbert (PJD)*

PORTLAND, MAINE, AUGUST 22, 1858

MY DEAR SIR:

I thank you for your kind letter of the 9th inst., enclosing an article copied into the Charleston *Mercury* from the Eufala *Spirit of the South.*†

My curiosity had been excited in relation to that article by the fact that a black republican paper of this State had referred to it as a stricture by the *Mercury* upon a speech made by me at this place, in answer to a complimentary visit; and had improved the occasion to misrepresent the doctrines of the States Rights democracy of the South, and as had been done before, to falsify my conduct as a member of that party. You were not mistaken in supposing that I had said nothing which would justify the comments of the *Spirit of the South*. They are but a bundle of assumptions, and from the first which announces I had gone to Boston, to the last which supposes me to have given up my tried and true friends of 1850 and '51, is without any foundation.

The speech on the steamer was not reported, no notes were taken of it, and I was compelled to decline the request of the passengers that I would write out my remarks, both because I could not stop at Boston, without deranging my plans to the inconvenience of myself and others, and also because my sight was then not sufficiently restored to enable me to write. The publication did not purport to be a report, but was called a sketch, and my recollection is, it did not occupy a fourth of a newspaper column. I could not now give the language employed by me on that occasion; but I have not forgotten the circumstances, neither have I changed the opinions or the feelings then entertained and must, therefore, claim to be rather an accurate judge of what I could not have said, and of the meaning of what I did say.

Being solicited by the passengers to address them when celebrating our national anniversary, they were aware of the fact that my health did not permit me to make any preparation, and were content to re-

---

* Mississippi planter and friend of JD.

† The *Charleston Mercury* was the leading secessionist newspaper in the South.

ceive an address entirely extemporaneous; it was a mixed company, being citizens of many States of the Union, of whose political opinions I was to a great extent uninformed. My remarks were very general, and made without any purpose either to indicate or to assail political theories.

I spoke of British pretensions to search American vessels, of the insults offered to our flag in the Gulf of Mexico, and of the probability that Great Britain had counted on sectional divisions to render our people unable or unwilling to resent the insult, and referred with the satisfaction which I felt, and feel, to the unanimity with which men of all parties, and all sections rallied to the defence of our national flag. Then immediately followed, as it appears in the published sketch, the expression, "and this great country will continue united," which any intelligent reader must see was not the announcement of an independent proposition, but stands as a sort of conclusion that we were to be hereafter, as on the recent occasion referred to, not a weak, distracted country, on whose flag the designing merchant and pseudo philanthropist might trample with impunity, but a powerful people who, however they might wrangle with each other, would still be found united against a foreign foe.

The language which then immediately follows is the sentence which stands at the head of the invective of the Alabama writer, belongs to an idea which is not presented, it is the pride of nationality, adherence to the constitutional union of the States as the instrument through which their concentrated power could be exerted for the purposes for which the union was ordained and established. Our party in Mississippi never was a disunion party. We asserted State Sovereignty, and as a consequence the right of secession, and generally the prerogative of a State to judge in the last resort, as well of her rights as of her remedies; but in 1851, when smarting under the sense of recent injustice, we declared secession to be the last alternative, and that we would not resort to it for the then existing grievances. We apprehended further and greater aggression, and sought to secure cointelligence throughout the South, and to arouse her sons to measures of preparation, haply to ward off impending danger, or otherwise successfully to meet it.

The friends who stood by me then were rendered dearer to me by the trials to which defeat exposed us; I have often vindicated them from the slanderous accusation of having sought to destroy the Union. They are not of the class of politicians who trifling with grave, even solemn subjects, talk of a dissolution of the Union as a holiday affair; and I well remember that men who did thus talk in 1849, deserted us before the close of the struggle of 1851.

But why, in the face of conventions led by native fanatics, and foreign emissaries, and assembled avowedly to destroy the Union, is it that the writer could find no body who might answer the description of a "trifling politician," except the States Rights Democracy of the South? Why is it, when the whole political sea is covered with bubbles, the changelings bow the knee to State Rights in the plenitude of its power, and seek by being absurdly extreme, to seem more devout than the ancient worshipers; and when in another section once honored Democrats are presiding as high priests in the synagogues of the abolitionists, that nothing could be found to whom the name of "musquito" was appropriate except the steady, quiet, true, unwavering defenders of State Rights; whom the writer properly describes as the men who sustained me in the hour of defeat, and elevated me as soon as they had power; and of whom he assuredly and untruly speaks, as the friends whom I had abandoned?

Sometime since a friend wrote to me from Mississippi to inform me that persons politically hostile were representing me as having said on the steamship what my friends denied I had said anywhere. I searched for the public sketch of the remarks made by me on that occasion, and after attentively examining, I sent it to him, I am sorry I have not another copy that I might send one to you, I am sure you would not fail to perceive that it had none of the character of a *report*, and should by any fair man have been treated as it is usual to regard a letter written to describe a public occasion, in which a speech formed a part of the proceedings.

I thank you for your kind wishes in regard to my health, and have the pleasure to inform you that it is much improved, the effect of sea air and a cool summer, has, as was anticipated by my medical advisers, been beneficial both to my general health, and to my sight. With kindest regards, I am, Very truly your friend,

JEFF. DAVIS.

Speech in Portland, Maine (PJD)

SEPTEMBER 11, 1858

...

It was due to the hospitality which he had received at their hands that he should not interfere in their domestic affairs, and he had not failed to remember the obligation; when republicans had introduced the subject of African slavery he had defended it, and answered pharisaical pretensions by citing the Bible, the constitution of the United States and the good of society in justification of the institutions of the State of which he was a citizen; in this he but exercised the right of a freeman and discharged the duty of a Southern citizen. Was it for this cause that he had been signalized as a slavery propagandist? He admitted in all its length and breadth the right of the people of Maine to decide the question for themselves; he held that it would be an indecent interference, on the part of a citizen of another State, if he should arraign the propriety of the judgment they had rendered, and that there was no rightful power in the federal government or in all the States combined, to set aside the decision which the community had made in relation to their domestic institutions. Should any attempt be made thus to disturb their sovereign right, he would pledge himself in advance, as a State-rights man, with his head, his heart and his hand, if need be, to aid them in the defence of this right of community independence, which the Union was formed to protect, and which it was the duty of every American citizen to preserve and to guard as the peculiar and prominent feature of our government.

Why, then, this accusation? Do they fear to allow Southern men to converse with their philosophers, and seek thus to silence or exclude them? He trusted others would contemn them as he did, and that many of our brethren of the South would, like himself, learn by sojourn here, to appreciate the true men of Maine, and to know how little are the political abolitionists and the abolition papers the exponents of the character and the purposes of the Democracy of this State.

...

We of the South, on a sectional division, are in the minority; and if legislation is to be directed by geographical tests—if the constitution is to be trampled in the dust, and the unbridled will of the majority in Congress is to be supreme over the States, we should have the problem which was presented to your Fathers when the Colonies declined to be content with a mere representation in parliament.

If the constitution is to be sacredly observed, why should there be a struggle for sectional ascendency? The instrument is the same in all latitudes, and does not vary with the domestic institutions of the several States. Hence it is that the Democracy, the party of the constitution, have preserved their integrity, and are to-day the only national party and the only hope for the preservation and perpetuation of the Union of the States.

Mr. Jefferson denominated the Democracy of the North, the natural allies of the South. It is in our generation doubly true; they are still the party with whom labor is capital, and they are now the party which stands by the barriers of the constitution, to protect them from the waves of fanatical and sectional aggression. The use of the word aggression reminded him that the people here have been daily harangued about the aggressions of the slave power, and he had been curious to learn what was so described. It is, if he had learned correctly, the assertion of the right to misrate with slaves into the territories of the United States. Is this aggression? If so, upon what? Not upon those who desire close association with the negro; not upon territorial rights, unless these self-styled lovers of the Union have already dissolved it and have taken the territories to themselves. The territory being the common property of States, equally in the Union, and bound by the constitution which recognizes property in slaves, it is an abuse of terms to call aggression the migration into that territory of one of its joint owners, because carrying with him any species of property known to the constitution. The Federal government has no power to declare what is property anywhere. The power of each State cannot extend beyond its own limits. As a consequence, therefore, whatever is property in any of the States must be so considered in any of the territories of the United States until they reach to the dignity of community independence, when the subject matter will be entirely under the control of the people and be determined by their fundamental law. If the inhabitants of any territory should refuse to enact such laws and police regulatsons as would give security to their property or to his, it would be rendered more or less valueless, in proportion to the difficulty of holding it without such protection. In the case of property in the labor of man, or what is usually called slave property, the insecurity would be so great that the owner could not ordinarily retain it.—Therefore, though the right would remain, the remedy being withheld, it would follow that the owner would be practically debarred by the circumstances of the case, from taking slave property into a territory where the sense of the inhabitants was opposed to its introduction. So much for the oft repeated fallacy of forcing slavery upon any community.

If Congress had the power to prohibit the introduction of slave property into the territories, what would be the purpose? Would it be to promote emancipation? That could not be the effect. In the first settlement of a territory the want of population and the consequent difficulty of procuring hired labor, would induce emigrants to take slaves with them; but if the climate and products of the country were unsuited to African labor—as soon as white labor flowed in, the owners of slaves would as a matter of interest, desire to get rid of them and emancipation would result. The number would usually be so small that this would be effected without injury to society or industrial pursuits. Thus it was in Wisconsin, notwithstanding the ordinance of '87; and other examples might be cited to show that this is not mere theory.

Would it be to promote the civilization and progress of the negro race? The tendency must be otherwise. By the dispersion of the slaves, their labor would be rendered more productive and their comforts increased. The number of owners would be multiplied, and by more immediate contact and personal relation greater care and kindness would be engendered. In every way it would conduce to the advancement and happiness of the servile caste.

No—no—not these, but the same answer which comes to every inquiry as to the cause of fanatical agitation. 'Tis for sectional power, and political ascendency. To fan a sectional hostility, which must be, as it has been, injurious to all, and beneficial to none. For what patriotic purpose can the Northern mind be agitated in relation to domestic institutions, for which they have no legal or moral responsibility, and from the interference with which they are restrained by their obligations as American citizens.

...

Speech in Boston, Massachusetts (JDC)

OCTOBER 11, 1858

...

I honor that sentiment which makes us oftentimes too confident, and to despise too much the danger of that agitation which disturbs the peace of the country. I honor that feeling which believes the Constitutional Union too strong to be shaken. But at the same time I say, in sober judgment, it will not do to treat too lightly the danger which has beset and which still impends over us. Who has not heard our Constitutional Union compared to the granite cliffs which face the sea and dash back the foam of the waves, unmoved by their fury. Recently I have stood upon New England's shore, and have seen the waves of a troubled sea dash upon the granite which frowns over the ocean, have seen the spray thrown back from the cliff, and the receding wave fret like the impotent rage of baffled malice. But when the tide had ebbed, I saw that the rock was seamed and worn by the ceaseless beating of the sea, and fragments riven from the rock were lying on the beach.

Thus the waves of sectional agitation are dashing themselves against the granite patriotism of the land. If long continued, that too must show the seams and scars of the conflict. Sectional hostility must sooner or later produce political fragments. The danger lies at your door, it is time to arrest it. It is time that men should go back to the origin of our institutions. They should drink the waters of the fountain, ascend to the source, of our colonial history.

...

Note: usage of 1st person, singular, when referring to self. Heretofore Davis used 3rd person in his public speeches. Could it be that the 3rd person speeches were from newspaper accounts? (see page 177)

Speech in U.S. Senate (JDC)

. . .

I once made a calculation, which was read yesterday to the Senate, of the expense of transportation. I think, in the same report, and if not, in some other, another view of that subject was taken, which exhibited the fact that, after the question of expense had been overcome, there yet remained a difficulty beyond, and that proved it to be an impossibility thus to supply an army on the coast of the Pacific. The reason is brief, and I will state it. The draft animals in crossing this wide belt of desert are compelled to live upon the grass. Grass and water are found only at certain places, and those sometimes so far apart as to make it difficult for a day's journey to span the intermediate space. It very soon follows that, train succeeding train, the grass is consumed or trodden down around all the watering places, and then no more trains can cross the desert until there is another crop of grass. Thus, I say, it is impossible with the present means of transport, to perform our duties of defense towards the coast of the Pacific.

This I hold to be a constitutional obligation upon the United States, and from that I derive whatever of constitutional power we possess for the construction of this road. If the Government of the United States, and the Government of the United States alone, had use for this road; if it had no commercial value; if it was unconnected with agriculture and travel; then I say, the United States would have the power out of its own resources to build the road, and hold it for its own uses. That, however, fortunately, is not our case. It has commercial uses; and it is right that all the interests which are involved in the construction of the road should bear a proportionate share of the burden. The United States is but a party; and as a party it appears both in the original bill and in the substitute. The $10,000,000 which the substitute proposes to advance, and which is to be refunded, is a very small representative of the money which is annually paid for the transportation of mails alone. If to that you add the cost of the transportation of troops and munitions of war for the Army and Navy in time of peace, it will be

found, I think, that in several years that amount has equaled the whole sum which it is proposed here to advance.
. . .

To Franklin Pierce (JDC)

WASHINGTON, D.C., JANUARY 17, 1859

MY DEAR FRIEND,

Your letter relieved of an anxiety created by the absence of any recent intelligence concerning you.

We are dragging on here in a manner significant of no good to the country. Each day renders me more hopeless of effecting any thing for the present or prospective benefit of the country by legislation of Congress. Even more than heretofore members and Senators represent extreme opinions and may increase but cannot allay the ferment which gave to them political life. I am gratified by the view you take of my New England tour. The abolitionists and the Disunionists combined to assail me for the speeches made there. I hope the Southern assailants have been scotched and the others may rail on to their content. That tour convinced me that the field of useful labor is now among the people and that temperate, true men could effect much by giving to the opposite section the views held by the other. The difference is less than I had supposed.

Your old friends in Missi. have not forgotten you and [are] ready to show their appreciation of you on the first occasion. Many said to me that your nomination for the Presidency was their first wish and best hope.

Mrs. Davis was quite happy in our sojourn in Maine and at Boston, but often wished it could have been possible to have found Mrs. Pierce at home. Our children have grown rapidly and the little girl is now quite a companion to me when at evening I go home to forget the past and postpone the future.

Clay and Fitzpatrick were happy to find you still remembered them and both said they would write to you.* I will send you some pa-

* Clement Clay and Benjamin Fitzpatrick, U.S. senators from Alabama.

pers which I hope may be more fortunate in their journey than were those of last year.

Please give my kindest regards to Mrs. Pierce, of whom we speak often and to whose return we look with affectionate solicitude. You may scold me roundly as I deserve for not writing to you more regularly, but do not I pray you fail to give me credit for good resolves and do let me hear from you as often as your convenience will allow.

AS EVER YOUR FRIEND
JEFFN: DAVIS

Speech in U.S. Senate (JDC)

MARCH 2, 1859

. . .

Mr. DAVIS. I reply to the statement, and I reply in no offensive sense. The Senator makes a statement that the white laborers of the South are degraded. I say there was never anything less true, either in the Senate or out of it. I say that the lower race of human beings that constitute the substratum of what is termed the slave population of the South, elevates every white man in our community. I say it is there true that every mechanic asumes among us the position which only a master workman holds among you. Hence it is that the mechanic in our southern States is admitted to the table of his employer, converses with him on terms of equality—not merely political equality, but an actual equality—wherever the two men come in contact. The white laborers of the South are all of them men who are employed in what you would term the higher pursuits of labor among you. It is the presence of a lower caste, those lower by their mental and physical organization, controlled by the higher intellect of the white man, that gives this superiority to the white laborer. Menial services are not there performed by the white man. We have none of our brethren sunk to the degradation of being menials. That belongs to the lower race—the descendants of Ham, who, under the judgment of God speaking to the prophet Noah, were condemned to be servants. To propose that we should change our industrial system, that we should bring the negroes up to a level with the white man, would be such an offense that the lecturer who would come to teach such philosophy would be fortunate indeed if he should escape without some public indignity. One of the reconciling features in the existence of that particular institution called domestic slavery of African bondsmen, is the fact that it raises white men to the same general level, that it dignifies and exalts every white man by the presence of a lower race. I say it in no terms of disparaging comparison with others. I say but what has been with me a deliberate conviction, that it is promotive of, if not essential to, the preservation of the higher orders of republican civilization.

. . .

To William B. Howell (PJD)

BRIERFIELD, WARREN COUNTY, MISSISSIPPI, APRIL 24, 1859
MY DEAR SIR,

I have the pleasure to acknowledge your's of the 21st Inst. and fear you and Ma have allowed your kindness to impose an unecessary trouble on you in taking Julia Ann to your house.*

This being her first departure from the place of her birth it is not wonderful that she should have been subjected to the brutal tricks of the steam Boat servants, but she ought to have known that her trunk was not put on board and not have imposed on you the needless trouble of a search. It will be sent down by this trip of the Boat. I was not prepared for the information that her lameness was the result of a bruise. Negroes only conceal injuries when received in some manner which they fear to relate, and unless her husband struck her she is so quiet that I cannot imagine how she should have received a blow. She was married last fall to Charles the Black-Smith who was purchased by us in New orleans, and whose appearance pleased you so much.

The water has been stationary here for the last twenty four hours,

---

* Slave sent by JD to New Orleans, where Howell lived, for medical treatment.

but as the river is reported to be rising above, the check we experience is no doubt attributable to the break in the Levee at Turner's, Point Pleasant, on the opposite side of the river. A fall of a few inches would enable to save a valuable part of Varina's garden, and is for that reason most desired.

. . .

To J. L. M. Curry (PJD)*

WASHINGTON, D.C., JUNE 4, 1859

MY DEAR SIR,

Inability to work at night and constant engagements during the day delayed attention to your suggestion until near the close of the last Congress. I then decided to present all the speeches which had been the subject of criticism and to that end procured the newspaper reports of the speeches made by me during the last fall and Summer, and gave them to my clerk for publication in pamphlet form. I did not revise them, because such as they were when assailed, it was deemed proper to leave them. The proof sheet seems to have been badly as well as carelessly read, for changes were made and palpable errors of the compositor left.†

On page 34, you will find that the word *Secretary* was changed to *Committee,* the proof reader evidently from historical ignorance supposing he had found an error.

The copy I send with this has been corrected, I will direct others to be mailed to you, but the condition of my eyes will not allow me to correct them.

I was called back from Missi. by the illness of my Wife, she is now convalescent and when she is able to travel we will seek some place in the mountains as a summer retreat and I will return to Missi,

Legislation by congress for the protection of slave property in the

* U.S. representative from Alabama.
† Printed as *Speeches of Hon. Jefferson Davis of Mississippi, Delivered During the Summer of 1858 . . .* (Baltimore, 1859).

territories, and laws in relation to the Slave trade, will probably be the chief topics in our state canvass. There is danger of over action by our friends.

Our right is equality and the duty of the general government is to give adequate protection to every constitutional right which was placed under its care. If existing laws through the Judicial and Executive Depts. give adequate protection, it would be unwise to invite further legislation under the apprehension that they might not hereafter be effectual. The act of 1820 declaring the slave trade to be Piracy was the result of peculiar circumstances then existing. Southern men committed the frequent mistake of yielding to the necessities of the hour a power dangerous to their future safety. It is offensive to us and mischievous in its effects and tendencies.

It's repeal is independent of the question of the reopening of the African slave trade and stands upon a different footing from the questions involved in the act of 1818.

We have gained several positions within a few years, and we should take care to fortify our possession of them. As the smaller of the contending armies it behooves us carefully to reconnoitre ground before we advance to occupy it.

The Black Republicans are getting into disputes with the Americans which will perhaps divide them, this may prevent the nomination of Seward and deprives us of the well defined issue which /with/ an united Democracy I desire to meet at the earliest day—*

I am suffering from a recent surgical operation on my eye and write with difficulty—Very truly yrs

JEFFN,, DAVIS

---

* William Henry Seward, U.S. senator from New York and leading Republican in Congress.

To William A. Buck (JDC)*

WASHINGTON, D.C., JUNE 21, 1859

MY DEAR SIR:

Your kind letter of May 27 was received at this place, and thanking you as a Mississippian for the motive which prompted your inquiry I have the honor to reply by a statement of the facts as a more satisfactory mode than a categorical answer to your questions.

The charge of Mexican cavalry was not anticipated, indeed the presence of such a force on our left was not known until it debouched from a ravine about four hundred yards distant and commenced advancing upon us. The Missi. Regt. was at the time marching to the rear by the left flank and close to the bank of a deep ravine, in which was a Indiana regt. which had taken shelter from the fire of a battery on our right, we being on the left of the line of battle and thrown back perpendicularly to it. The plain on the margin of which we were marching led to the rear of our line of battle and to the road along which communication was kept up with our depot of ammunition and other supplies. Our batteries on the right of the line of battle were unsupported by Infantry and therefore liable to be captured by cavalry charging suddenly from an unexpected quarter.

You will thus see the imperious necessity for checking the advance of that cavalry. For that purpose the Missi. Regt. was formed in line of two ranks across the narrow plain with a portion of the right wing thrown forward and resting on the bank of the ravine.

A message was sent to the Captain of a battery, a short distance in our rear, to move up a section of his guns and form on our flank. In the mean time a portion of the Indiana troops were brought up to the brink of the ravine and formed along the bank. Thus two lines forming a reentering angle presented a disposition the reverse of that usually adopted to resist cavalry. The rule in such cases you are aware would have indicated the refusal of the left wing so as to have offered a salient instead of a reentering angle, as, if time and numbers per-

---

* Cotton factor in Mobile, Alabama.

mitted, the formation of a square. You ask whether this formation was the result of previous design on my part or of the force of a sudden emergency. Our Regt. could have been formed in line instantly by halting and facing to the front. Standing on the brink of a precipitous ravine it would have been absolutely secure against a charge by the Cavalry, but the Cavalry then could have dashed by and have passed the rear.

Their force was so superior to ours that they could have afforded to sacrifice as many men as our fire, under such circumstances could have cost them. It was not therefore the suddenness but the importance of the emergency which entered into the determination of our conduct.

In so far as I had not calculated on that disposition of troops to receive a charge of cavalry, it must be said that there was no previous design, but familiar from a military education and many years of military service with the advantage of a converging fire, it was a natural and ready conclusion from the conviction that our fire would repel the attack; that the troops should be so disposed as to give the greatest effect to our fire at the moment it was opened, hence, the peculiar disposition which has attracted your notice. Your last inquiry, "why was an open angle exposed to the attack," involved the authority for the conviction that the charge would be cheeked by our fire. If that conviction was sufficiently well founded then the formation should have been governed solely by the inquiry how could the fire be rendered most effective; otherwise it was wrong to rely on a single line of two ranks.

. . .

To Edwin De Leon (PJD)[*]

WASHINGTON, D.C., JANUARY 21, 1860

MY DEAR SIR,

I have read your letter with sincere gratification and return my cordial thanks for your kind offer. You express what I would have ex-

---

[*] Lawyer and editor from South Carolina; also consul in Alexandria, Egypt, 1854–61.

pected of you but would have hoped for from few men whom it has been my fortune to know.

I have no wishes or prospects which would justify you in making the proposed sacrifice and for every reason object to your making it. My opinions as you know them would be sufficient to defeat any efforts of my friends to nominate me at Charleston, and should do so as they would impair the ability of the Democratic party to succeed in the next presidential canvass. Since you left us there has been a great advance in public opinion towards the Southern rights creed. We are now all powerful at the South, but are still in a minority at the North. To get as many northern votes as will secure the success of our candidate it will be necessary to recruit largely from the conservative ranks and you will at once perceive that the banner of a radical advocate of southern rights would not in that quarter be sufficiently attractive to produce the result. There will be a hazardous controversy in relation to the resolutions declaratory of the position of the party in relation to the rights of slave holders in the U.S. Territories. The solution which will probably be the only feasible one will be to nominate some one who will be recognized in both sections as true exponent of their opinions. Ex Presdt Pierce will probably best fulfill the conditions. Mr. Dallas might do.* A southern rights man from a planting state would not be accepted by the North without concessions and disclaimers not to be entertained for a moment, and a Southern man with northern leanings as Davy Hubbard expressed would be a submission to which we could only consent as the alternative of submission to a "Black republican."

From both I pray that a good providence and our own self respect will preserve us.

Though it be late permit me to congratulate you on the acquisition of one to divide your sorrows and multiply your joys. At some future day I hope to make the personal acquaintance of Mrs. De Leon and in the mean time offer to her the best wishes of her Husband's friend.

The papers which you no doubt receive will have informed you of the protracted and thus far fruitless struggle to organize the House of

---

* George M. Dallas of Pennsylvania, vice president of the United States 1845–49.

Representatives. No one can now see how the controversy is to be terminated and the Southern members are fast becoming reconciled to their present unorganized condition. As we little to hope and much to deprecate from the action of the present congress—no legislation may be our best estate.

Your Brother Dr. De Leon is here looking quite well, though somewhat the browner for his residence in New-Mexico. A few of your associates in the long siege of '51 are still in the Senate and all remember you with much regard. Let me hear from you as often as your convenience will permit and believe ever most truly your's

JEFFN,, DAVIS

Speech in U.S. Senate (PJD)

FEBRUARY 29, 1860

. . .

But the Senator from New York [William Seward] invokes us by his love for the Union, and in the spirit of fraternity. I have nothing to object to the tone in which he has addressed us, but I wish we could have acts instead of words. Faith might follow something more significant than high-sounding professions of attachment to the Union, and fraternity to its various members. If the Senator would show to us, by his adherence to the Constitution, and his faithful maintenance of the oath he has taken to support it, that we may rely on the pledge which he gives us that the Republican party, bound by its oath, cannot trespass on the rights of any section, our faith might follow, however far behind, such manifestations upon his own part of the good faith which he proclaims to be within the breast of his political party.

But are we to believe these mere professions of the lips whilst he proclaims opposition to one of the most marked features of the constitution? whilst he and those with whom he is associated, not only here, but at home, are endeavoring to trample under foot the laws of the United States enacted in conformity with the Constitution, and to secure one of its provisions—a provision so significant that it has been remarked, and is a part of history, that the Union could not have been formed if it had not been incorporated in the Constitution? The oaths of such men become cheap as custom-house oaths, and we are asked to stake our future security on the mere guarantee which such an oath gives!

But the Senator from New York arraigns those who speak in a certain contingency of providing for their own safety out of the Union, as being in opposition to his love for the Union; and he manifests his incapacity to understand our doctrine of State rights by the very simile which he employs when he speaks of our fathers building a temple wherein they had a collision of opinion as to whether the marble should be white or whether it should be manifold in its color, and at last agreed together— forgetful that our fathers were occupied in providing a common agent for the States, not building up a central government to look over them. The States remained each its own temple. They made an agent. Their controversy was as to the functions and powers of that agent—not as to the nature of the temple in which they should preserve their liberties. That temple is the State governments. Beneath that we sit down as under our own vine and fig tree, secure in our power to maintain our rights.

But the Senator asks, how is it that, whilst we are professing this general fraternity and adherence to the Union, we still assert that if one of his party is elected President, we are ready to dissolve the Union? I do not know who has made that assertion, if it has been made. However, the language employed may have imperfectly conveyed the idea that the position was assumed as the Senator fairly presented it, under the conviction that they spoke of those who sought the Government to use it for their destruction. That was the provocation, that was the contingency, however it may have been expressed, that was the idea I have seen embodied in every resolution of that kind wherever it has been passed. To ask us that we shall sit still, under such a Government, is as though we were to be asked to sit in this Senate Chamber, whilst we knew that some one was destroying the foundation on which it rested; to ask us to rely upon the durability which that foundation had when the building was constructed; to rely confidently on the strength we knew it once to possess, even when we had been advertised that that foundation was being destroyed. Are we not advertised that the Senator and those with whom he cooperates are assailing our constitutional rights? How, then, can we sit quietly? If, instead of sitting here to admire the panel and the pilaster and the typical decorations of the ceiling, one, aware that the foundation was being undermined, should walk out of the Chamber, would you arraign him for endeavoring to destroy the building, or would you level your charges against the sapper and miner who was at work on its foundation? That is the proposition.

Who has been more industrious, patient, and skillful, as a sapper and miner against the foundations of the Constitution, than the Senator himself? Who has been in advance of him in the fiery charge on the rights of the States, and in assuming to the Federal Government the power to crush and to coerce them? Even to-day he has repeated his doctrines. He tells us this is a Government which we will learn is not merely a Government of the States, but a Government of each individual of the people of the United States; and he refers to that doctrine of coercion which the great mind of Hamilton (the mighty intellect of New York, which, in his day, like a lens, gathered in all which could illuminate the subject upon which his mind was concentrated) said was a proposition not to provide for a union of the States, but for their destruction. Such was the view which he who led the forces of the strong Government party took of this idea of enabling the Federal Government to coerce a State. Here the Senator, in advance of that, still mistaking the fundamental principles on which our Government rests, talks about the individual masses coercing the sovereign States of this Union. Sir, when it comes to that, there will be an "irrepressible conflict" indeed; and I have now the faith I have before announced, that, when it comes to that, he will find men loyal to the Government and true to its institutions, residing around his own home, who will arrest his footsteps, and hold him prisoner in the name of liberty and the Constitution.

There is nothing, Mr. President, which has led men to greater confusion of ideas than this term of "free States" and "slave States;" and I trusted that the Senator, with his discriminating and logical mind, was going to give us something tangible, instead of dealing in a phrase never applicable. He applied another; but what was his phrase? "Capital States" and "labor States." And where is the State in which nobody labors? The fallacy upon which the Senator hung adjective after adjective was, that all the labor of the southern States was performed by negroes. Did he not know that the negroes formed but a small part of the people of the southern States? Did he suppose nobody labored but a negro, there? If so, he was less informed than I had previously believed him to be. Negro slavery exists in the South, and by the existence of negro slavery, the white man is raised to the dignity of a freeman and an equal. Nowhere else will you find every white man superior to menial service. Nowhere else will you find every white man recognized so far as an equal as never to be excluded from any man's house or any man's table. Your own menial who blacks your boots, drives your carriage, who wears your livery, and is your own in every sense of the word, is not your equal; and such is society wherever negro slavery is not the substratum on which the white race is elevated to its true dignity. We, however, have no theory to press upon you; we leave you to such institutions as you may prefer; but when you assail ours, we come to the vindication of our institutions by showing you that all your phrases are false; that we are the freemen. With us, and with us alone, as I believe, the white man attains to his true dignity in the Government. So much for the great fallacy on which the Senator's argument hangs. that the labor of the South is all negro labor. and that the white man must there be degraded if he labors; or that we have no laboring white men. I do not know which is his, opinion; one of the two. The Senator has himself resided in a southern State. and therefore I say I believed him to be better informed before he spoke. I must suppose him to be as ignorant as his speech would indicate. No man, however, who has seen any portion of southern society, can entertain any such opinion as that which he presents; and it is in order that the statement he has made may not go out to deceive those less informed than himself, that I offer at this time the correction.

The Senator makes a rather hackneyed argument, that, in asserting our right to go into the Territory and enjoy it, we are seeking to take exclusive possession of it. I shall not dwell on that point further than to say that we have sought to exclude nobody. We have sought not to usurp the Territory to our exclusive possession; we have sought that government should be instituted in order that every person and property might be protected that went into it—the white man coming from the North, and the white man coming from the South, both meeting on an equality in the Territory, and each with whatever property he may hold under the laws of his State and the Constitution of the United States. Such is our position. It is to array a prejudice, which does not justly attach to us, to assume that we have ever sought to exclude any citizen from any State or Territory from going into any Territory and there possessing all the rights which we claim to ourselves.

We have heard time and again this session the same point made against the Democratic party, that they were hedging themselves behind the decision of the Supreme Court. If this had been presented in the beginning, it might have had some fairness; but, after years of conflict, and after we had found it utterly impossible ever to reach a conclusion satisfactory to both sides—in other words. to enact a law which would answer the purpose—we then agreed to postpone a question judicial in its character, and thus agreed to be bound, legislatively and politically, by the decision which that judicial question should receive. Now the Senator pleads to the jurisdiction, as though we had ever asserted that the Supreme Court could decide a political question; but he was bound in honor, and so were all who acted with him, to abide by the decision of an umpire to which they had themselves referred the case. We are willing to abide by it. We but claim from them that to which we pledged ourselves, and that to which they were mutually pledged when this position was taken by the two Houses of Congress.

But the Senator in his zeal depicts the negro slave of the South as a human being reduced to the condition of a mere chattel. Is it possible that the Senator did not know that the negro slave in every southern State was still a person, protected by all the laws which punish crime in other persons? Could the Senator have failed to know that no master could take the life of or maim his slave without being held responsible under the criminal laws of any southern State, and held to a responsibility as rigid as though that negro had been a white man? How, then, is it asserted that these are not persons in the eye of the law, not protected by the law as persons. The venerable Senator from

Kentucky knows very well that this is not law in any State of the Union where slaves are held, but that everywhere they are protected; that the criminal law covers them as perfectly as it covers the white man. Save in the respect of credibility as a witness, there is nothing—
. . .

Mr. Davis. Several southern Senators around have spoken to me to the effect that in each of their States the protection is secured, and a suit may be instituted at common law for assault and battery, to protect a negro as well as a white man. The condition of slavery with us is, in a word, Mr. President, nothing but the form of civil government instituted for a class of people not fit to govern themselves. It is exactly what in every State exists in some form or other. It is just that kind of control which is extended in every northern State over its convicts, its lunatics, its minors, its apprentices. It is but a form of civil government for those who by their nature are not fit to govern themselves. We recognize the fact of the inferiority stamped upon that race of men by the Creator, and from the cradle to the grave, our Government, as a civil institution, marks that inferiority. In their subject and dependent state, they are not the objects of cruelty as they would be if left to the commission of crime, for which they should be incarcerated in penitentiaries and work-houses, and put under hired overseers, having no interest in them and no relation to them, no affiliation, growing out of the associations of childhood and the tender care of age. Is there nothing of the balm needed in the Senator's own State, that he must needs go abroad to seek objects for his charity and philanthropy? What will he say of those masses in New York now memorializing for something very like an agrarian law? What will he say to the throngs of beggars who crowd the streets of his great commercial emporium? What will he say to the multitudes collected in the penitentiaries and prisons of his own State? I seek not, sir, to inquire into the policy and propriety of the institutions of other States; I assume not to judge of their fitness; it belongs to the community to judge, and I know not under what difficulties they may have been driven to what I cannot approve; but never, sir, in all my life, have I seen anything that so appealed to every feeling of humanity and manliness, as the suffering of the poor children imprisoned in your juvenile penitentiaries—imprisoned before they were old enough to know the nature of crime—there held to such punishment as we never inflict save upon those of mature years. I arraign you not for this: I know not what your crowded population and increasing wants may demand; I know not how far it may be the necessary result of crime which follows in the footsteps of misery; I know not how far the parents have become degraded, and how far the children have become outcast, and how far it may have devolved on the State to take charge of them; but, I thank my God, that in the state of society where I reside, we have no scenes so revolting as these.

Why then not address yourselves to the evils which you have at home? Why not confine your inquiries to the remedial measures which will relieve the suffering of and stop the progress of crime among your own people? Very intent in looking into the distance for the mote in your brother's eye, is it to be wondered that we turn back and point to the beam in your own?

Speech in U.S. Senate (JDC)

MAY 8, 1860

The PRESIDING OFFICER, (Mr. Foot in the chair.) If there be no further petitions or reports from committees, the hour for the consideration of the special order being near, the Chair will take it to be the sense of the Senate to proceed to the consideration of that order at the present time.

The following resolutions are now before the Senate as the special order of the day, on which the Senator from Mississippi [Mr. Davis] is entitled to the floor:˙

1. *Resolved,* That, in the adoption of the Federal Constitution, the States adopting the same acted severally as free and independent sovereignties, delegating a portion of their powers to be exercised by the Federal Government for the increased security of each against dangers, *domestic* as well as foreign; and that any intermeddling by anyone

---

˙ For JD these resolutions affirmed fundamental rights protected by the Constitution. They were not a call to action. The Senate passed them in May 1860 with the specification, accepted by JD, that under number five, no conditions existed calling for action.

or more States, or by a combination of their citizens, with the domestic institutions of the others, on any pretext whatever, political, moral, or religious, with a view to their disturbance or subversion, is in violation of the Constitution, insulting to the States so interfered with, endangers their domestic peace and tranquillity—objects for which the Constitution was formed—and, by necessary consequence, tends to weaken and destroy the Union itself.

2. *Resolved,* That negro slavery, as it exists in fifteen States of this Union, composes an important portion of their domestic institutions, inherited from their ancestors, and existing at the adoption of the Constitution, by which it is recognized as constituting an important element in the apportionment of powers among the States; and that no change of opinion or feeling on the part of the non-slaveholding States of the Union, in relation to this institution, can justify them, or their citizens, in open or covert attacks thereon, with a view to its overthrow; and that all such attacks are in manifest violation of the mutual and solemn pledge to protect and defend each other, given by the States respectively on entering into the constitutional compact which formed the Union, and are a manifest breach of faith, and a violation of the most solemn obligations.

3. *Resolved,* That the Union of these States rests on the equality of rights and privileges among its members; and that it is especially the duty of the Senate, which represents the States in their sovereign capacity, to resist all attempts to discriminate either in relation to persons or property in the Territories, which are the common possessions of the United States, so as to give advantages to the citizens of one State which are not equally assured to those of every other State.

4. *Resolved,* That neither Congress nor a Territorial Legislature, whether by direct legislation or legislation of an indirect and unfriendly character, possess power to annul or impair the constitutional right of any citizen of the United States to take his slave property into the common Territories, and there hold and enjoy the same while the territorial condition remains.

5. *Resolved,* That if experience should at any time prove that the judicial and executive authority do not possess means to insure adequate protection to constitutional rights in a Territory, and if the ter-

ritorial government should fail or refuse to provide the necessary remedies for that purpose, it will be the duty of Congress to supply such deficiency.

6. *Resolved,* That the inhabitants of a Territory of the United States, when they rightfully form a constitution to be admitted as a State into the Union, may then, for the first time, like the people of a State when forming a new constitution, decide for themselves whether slavery, as a domestic institution, shall be maintained or prohibited within their jurisdiction; and, "they shall be received into the Union with or without slavery, as their constitution may prescribe at the time of their admission."

7. *Resolved,* That the provision of the Constitution for the rendition of fugitives from service or labor, without the adoption of which the Union could not have been formed, and that the laws of 1793 and 1850, which were enacted to secure its execution, and the main features of which, being similar, bear the impress of nearly seventy years of sanction by the highest judicial authority, should be honestly and faithfully observed and maintained by all who enjoy the benefits of our compact of union; and that all acts of individuals or of State Legislatures to defeat the purpose or nullify the requirements of that provision, and the laws made in pursuance of it, are hostile in character, subversive of the Constitution, and revolutionary in their effect.

. . .

My colleague arraigned that resolution because it did not go far enough. He thought the mere proposition to act when necessary did not meet the case which he said now existed, because he said the necessity had arisen. To that my answer is, that here I ask the Senate to declare great truths to-day, and for all time to come, to bring back the popular judgment to the standard of the Constitution; that I am not seeking legislation in these resolutions; I am but making great declarations on which legislation may be founded. These declarations will be good to-day and to-morrow; they will speak a restraining voice to the Territorial Legislatures. They will speak our sentiments as to the rights of person and property, the obligations and duties of the Constitution. It is for that purpose I introduced them; it is for that purpose I seek the vote of the Senate. At some other time I may institute a comparison between these resolutions and their doctrines, and those of some others before the Senate, particularly those of my colleague, who has twice criticised mine, once very harshly when I was detained by illness from the Senate. I will now only say, however, Mr. President, that his second resolution contains what I consider too near an affiliation with his distinguished friend from Illinois. The admission that every Territory when organized is to exercise legislative power inclines rather too much to the direction of squatter sovereignty. At an earlier period of our history many Territories were organized without a Legislature, with simply a Governor and Council, and if the Territory of Utah was fitted for anything in the form of civil government, a Governor and Council are as much as it ever ought to have had. I thus illustrate my opinion by a case in point.

. . .

To Franklin Pierce (JDC)

WASHINGTON, D.C., JUNE 13, 1860

MY DEAR GENERAL.

Your welcome letter of the 11th Inst relieved me of speculation of your whereabouts as I had seen it stated in the news papers that you were about to go directly to New Hampshire but had not found verification of the statement. It grieves me beyond expression to learn that Mrs. Pierce is ill and Mrs. Davis joins me in expression of our sympathy and affectionate regard.

We all deplore the want of una[ni]mity as to the candidate among our Southern friends and I do not see any satisfactory solution of the difficulty. The darkest hour precedes the dawn and it may be that light will break upon us when most needed & least expected.

If your hope should be realized as to the action of the N.E. and N.Y. delegation in relation to the delegates to be admitted from the South it will have a good effect, if they should otherwise decide in favor of the spurious delegates the Democratic party will become historic.

Our people will support any sound man, but will not vote for a "squatter sovereignty" candidate any more than for a "free soiler."

If northern men insist upon nominating Douglass[*] we must be beaten and with such alienation as leaves nothing to hope for in the future of nationality in our organization.

I have urged my friends to make an honest effort to save our party from disintegration as the last hope of averting ruin from the country. They would gladly unite upon you, or Dallas and would readily be brought to anyone of like character and record.

I urged upon Mr. Minot before he went to Charleston the evil effect of permitting N.H. to be mustered in under the banner of Douglas, but it was of no avail. Matters are now more complicated and men are more unreasonable. Some are unwilling to go into the convention at Baltimore and are disposed to rush blindly on dangers which they feel are at hand but do not appreciate, others see in the crisis only the vulgar struggle of the ins and the outs, and have no fear of a catastrophe whilst a few are willing to abandon the government to get rid of men who are unfaithful to it.

I have never seen the country in so great danger and those who might protect it seem to be unconscious of the necessity. If our little grog drinking, electioneering Demagogue can destroy our hopes, it must be that we have been doomed to destruction.

Hoping soon to see you and in the meantime to hear from you fully I am as ever cordially

YOUR FRIEND
JEFFN: DAVIS

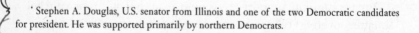

[*] Stephen A. Douglas, U.S. senator from Illinois and one of the two Democratic candidates for president. He was supported primarily by northern Democrats.

Speech in Washington, D.C. (PJD)[*]

JULY 9, 1860

Happy am I to greet this vast multitude, assembled in the cause of our common country. I deeply regret that my physical inability to address you as my heart prompts, requires me to be exceedingly brief. Here for many years it has been my fortune to spend a portion of my time. For four years I was connected with you continually; learned to know your moral attributes; learned to know your peculiar characteristics. I knew how to labor for your natural interests. I trust, therefore, I may be allowed to speak to you of the people of Washington. Some entertain the foolish idea that because you have no vote, therefore you have no right to interfere in the national politics of the day. But you have the deepest interest; that high intelligence which sends forth its promptings to every portion of the country. Why then should not you assemble? Why should you not speak to your fellow-citizens of every portion of the country? Who else so deeply interested in the affairs of the Federal Government? Who else so dependent upon just administration of federal affairs? Who else so deeply interested in having the government administered with full and equal justice to all; and that it should be preserved in those vital energies which give protection whereever legislation exists? But we have heard it said that the democratic party is dead. Dead! Here I lay my hand upon its heart, and in its quick pulsations feel that vitality that sends it to victory. No, it is not dead. Born of the oppression of the mother country, when democracy arose to assert equal rights; baptised in the blood of the Revolution, rocked in the cradle of civil and religious liberty since 1800, it has lived, and lives to-day, with all its vital energies to fulfil the duties of this government, and meet the requirements of 1860. [Applause.] The speaker then proceeded briefly to contrast all the other parties in the country with the democratic.

[*] In this speech JD endorsed the ticket of John C. Breckinridge and Joseph Lane for president and vice president. The breakup of the Democratic party in 1860 resulted in two separate tickets, with Breckinridge and Lane receiving overwhelming support from southern Democrats and very little from northern Democrats.

First, he said, came that spurious and decayed off-shoot of democracy, which, claiming that this Federal government has no power, leaves the people our next greatest evil, despotism; and denies protection to our Constitutional rights. Next comes the party that proclaims the Union and the Constitution, but that dares not tell what the Constitution is—a mere catchword, sounding, but meaning nothing. Then, my friends, there is the "rail-splitter," aptly selected for the purpose, first proclaiming there was an "irrepressible conflict" between the sections; and having proved himself able to rend the yoke, who so fit as he, with such a theory as that, to be selected for the accursed performance of rending the Union? Then, my friends, comes the true democracy, proclaiming the Constitution and the Union, and what that Constitution is; writing your opinions on your banner, throwing it to the winds, and inviting all who believe to command worship at the altar of truth. [Applause.] This banner proclaims the futility of Abe Lincoln's efforts to rend the Union.* Though he did rend the yoke, he will find the Constitution and the Union worse than any black gum in the forest.

Our cause is onward. Our car is the Constitution; our fires are up; let all who would ride into the haven of a peaceful country come on board, and those who will not, I warn that the cow-catcher is down—let stragglers beware! [Cheers.] We have before us in this canvass the highest duty which can prompt the devoted patriot. Our country is in danger. Our Constitution is assailed by those who would escape from declaring their opinions—by those who seek to torture its meaning, and by those who would trample upon its obligations. What is our Union? A bond of fraternity, by the mutual agreement of sovereign States; it is to be preserved by good faith—by strictly adhering to the obligations which exist between its friendly and confederate States. Otherwise we should transmit to our children the very evil under which our fathers groaned—a government hostile to the rights of the people, not resting upon their consent, trampling upon their privileges, and calling for their resistance. But I place my trust in democracy—in that democracy which has borne this country on from its commence-

---

* Abraham Lincoln of Illinois, the Republican candidate for president in 1860.

ment, which has illustrated all its bright passages of history, which has contributed to it all which is grand and manly, all which has elevated and contributed to its progress—the democracy of Washington, of Jefferson, of Jackson, and of Buchanan [great applause] shall be the democracy of the next four years.* [Renewed applause.]

During the entire period of my intercourse with the people of Washington, I do not recollect of ever having seen such a multitude of citizens as those assembled here this evening. But more than that— during the time I have been speaking, as my eye runs over the vast throng before me, I can say never have I seen so quiet, so orderly, so patriotic a concourse of people (judging from the expression of their countenances) as is assembled here to-night. [Applause.]

The national democracy present a ticket to the country which may well inspire the most lofty patriotism. The name of Breckinridge comes down by lineal descent from one who asserted the great principles of 1798, as reaffirmed at Baltimore; and as for Lane, he is too modest to boast of the deeds of his younger days. No doubt he has split a hundred rails to Lincoln's one! [Laughter and cheers.] Let us then be encouraged to go into the conflict, determined to succeed, and transmit to our children the rich inheritance we have received from our fathers unimpaired. [Applause.]

To William Lamb (PJD)†

WASHINGTON, D.C., SEPTEMBER 14, 1860

MY DEAR SIR,

I have the pleasure to acknowledge your's of the 12th inst. and to reply to your inquiries; that I had no objection to the report of the act of the Territorial Legislature of Kanzas to which you refer and should have voted for a bill either repealing, or better still declaring void for want of power derivative or inherent. You are no doubt aware that no such bill was ever in a condition to be voted on.

* James Buchanan, president of the United States 1857–61.
† Virginia newspaper publisher and presidential elector for the Breckinridge-Lane ticket.

The vote on Brown's Amendment to the resolutions of the Democratic Caucus of the Senate is easily explained; and I am surprised that General Wilson's opportunity for Observation did not shield him from misapprehension.* The resolutions were declaratory of fundamental principles and applicable to all cases. The amendment belonged to a special occasion. For the former we had the support of all the democratic senators save two. In relation to the latter there were questions of facts which would weaken our vote and lead to the misconstruction that some of the Northern Democrats other than the two dissented from the principle for which we were contending and which was deemed of vital importance to the South. Practically the amendment could have no value, because the Resolution of the Senate would not alter the case in Kansas nor bind Senators to vote for a bill in future in any greater degree than the general declaration proposed. It may be asked why not make the assertion in a joint resolution, General Wilson must in candor tell you it could not possibly have passed the Ho. of Reps. *Confidentially* I will add that it was known to many of us that the Sup. Court of the territory of Kanzas would whenever a case arose, decide the Anti Slavery law of the Territorial Legislature void; and that the chief justice of the terrytory did not doubt the sufficiency of the *Laws of the U.S.* To furnish a remedy for any invasion of the right of property in a state (?). It would have been bad policy under such circumstances to have had a congressional denial of the right, to precede the hearing of a case for judicial determination.

I have directed the speeches of Senator's Fitch, Toombs and Wigfall to be sent to you that you might see what view was held in the Senate on the movement of Sen. Brown.†

May the kind providence which has sheltered and directed the country in times past be with us still, and may the gallant Old Dominion be found in this dark hour still leading the column of the Constitutional, State rights Democracy to the Defense of sound principles

---

* Albert G. Brown, U.S. senator from Mississippi; Henry Wilson, U.S. senator from Massachusetts.

† Graham Fitch of Indiana, Robert Toombs of Georgia, and Louis Wigfall of Texas, all U.S. senators.

and the preservation of the Union as our Fathers found it. Very truly, yr's,

JEFFN DAVIS.

Speech in Corinth, Mississippi (PJD)

SEPTEMBER 21, 1860

To which he answered, substantially, that he supposed the first question was intended to inquire of him whether he considered Abraham Lincoln a Black Republican—for he regarded himself as instructed by the resolutions of the Legislature of Mississippi, as well as the Democratic Convention of 1859, which declared, in the event of the election of a Black Republican, on the avowed purposes of that organization, Mississippi would regard as a declaration of hostility, and would hold herself in readiness to co-operate with her sister States of the South, in whatever measures they may deem necessary for the maintenance of their rights as co-equals in the confederacy. [He here read the resolutions.] This does not, said the speaker, declare secession as the remedy, nor assume for the South what remedy should be adopted, yet it unquestionably does include a resort to that last alternative of separation. To that position of Mississippi, he had given, and still continued to give his cordial assent. While he thus freely gave his opinions and sentiments, he was not prepared to say that they were the sentiments and opinions of either Breckinridge or Lane; on the contrary, supposed they were not—as, in his opinion, no one entertaining or expressing such sentiments could have received the nomination.

To the second question he said: It was to him a matter of surprise that any one should suppose it necessary to ask him whether he would advise, or in any contingency consent to the use of, coercion upon the sovereign State of Mississippi. Such an inquiry could but be an insult, if he supposed it was made doubting his answer. Such an idea could only exist in the mind of one who reversed the order of things, and supposed the States to be the *creatures* instead of the *creators* of the Federal Government. He referred to the debates in the convention for the formation of the Constitution, upon the proposition to give authority to the General Government to use force in the maintenance of its laws against a resisting State, wherein Hamilton and Madison, so often holding opposite views, concurred that the proposition should not be entertained—denominating it as one not for the formation of a Union, but for the destruction of the States.

He denounced in strong language the craven wretch that could countenance the coercion of a sovereign State by Federal authority.

To the third interrogatory, he answered: That the neck of the author of such an inquiry was in danger of hemp. That the allegiance of each citizen was due to the State of his residence—that his citizenship in the United States resulted from his prior right as one of the citizens of a State, and would necessarily terminate when his State ceased to be of the Union. It was, therefore, an absurdity to hold that he could be justified by any extraneous authority in making war upon the State of which he was a citizen. His opinion was, therefore, that such an act would be treason against the sovereignty to whom he owed his first allegiance. There could be no necessity, according to the Democratic creed, for a judicial decision, as authority to a State declaring her rights violated. For many years the creed of the Democratic party had contained the affirmative of the resolutions of 1798–9, as expounded in Madison's Reports, and he who denies the right of a State to judge in the last resort of its wrongs and the remedies to be applied, repudiated the Democratic creed, and rejects every common sense idea of State sovereignty.

To Robert Barnwell Rhett, Jr. (PJD)[*]

WARREN COUNTY, MISSISSIPPI, NOVEMBER 10, 1860
DEAR SIR:—

I had the honor to receive, last night, yours of the 27th ulto., and hasten to reply to the inquiries propounded. Reports of the election leave little doubt that the event you anticipated has occurred, that

---

[*] Editor of the *Charleston Mercury.*

electors have been chosen securing the election of Lincoln, and I will answer on that supposition.

My home is so isolated that I have had no intercourse with those who might have aided me in forming an opinion as to the effect produced on the mind of our people by the result of the recent election, and the impressions which I communicate are founded upon antecedent expressions.

1. I doubt not that the Gov'r of Missi. has convoked the Legislature to assemble within the present month, to decide upon the course which the State should adopt in the present emergency. Whether the Legislature will direct the call of a convention, of the State, or appoint delegates to a convention of such Southern States as may be willing to consult together for the adoption of a Southern plan of action, is doubtful.

2. If a convention, of the State, were assembled, the proposition to secede from the Union, independently of support from neighboring States, would probably fail.

3. If South Carolina should first secede, and she alone should take such action, the position of Missi. would not probably be changed by that fact. A powerful obstacle to the separate action of Missi. is the want of a port; from which follows the consequence that her trade being still conducted through the ports of the Union, her revenue would be diverted from her own support to that of a foreign government; and being geographically unconnected with South Carolina, an alliance with her would not vary that state of case [*sic*].

4. The propriety of separate secession by So. Ca. depends so much upon collateral questions that I find it difficult to respond to your last enquiry, for the want of knowledge which would enable me to estimate the value of the elements involved in the issue, though exterior to your state. Georgia is necessary to connect you with Alabama and thus to make effectual the coöperation of Missi. If Georgia would be lost by immediate action, but could be gained by delay, it seems clear to me that you should wait. If the secession of So. Ca., should be followed by an attempt to coerce her back into the Union, that act of usurpation folly and wickedness would enlist every true Southern man for her defence. If it were attempted to blockade her ports and

destroy her trade, a like result would be produced, and the commercial world would probably be added to her allies. It is therefore probable that neither of those measures would be adopted by any administration, but that federal ships would be sent to collect the duties on imports outside of the bar; that the commercial nations would feel little interest in that; and the Southern States would have little power to counteract it.

The planting states have a common interest of such magnitude, that their union, sooner or later, for the protection of that interest is certain. United they will have ample power for their own protection, and their exports will make for them allies of all commercial and manufacturing powers.

The new states have a heterogeneous population, and will be slower and less unanimous than those in which there is less of the northern element in the body politic, but interest controls the policy of states, and finally all the planting communities must reach the same conclusion. My opinion is, therefore, as it has been, in favor of seeking to bring those states into cooperation before asking for a popular decision upon a new policy and relation to the nations of the earth. If So. Ca. should resolve to secede before that cooperation can be obtained, to go out leaving Georgia and Alabama and Louisiana in the Union, and without any reason to suppose they will follow her; there appears to me to be no advantage in waiting until the govt. has passed into hostile hands and men have become familiarized to that injurious and offensive perversion of the general government from the ends for which it was established. I have written with the freedom and carelessness of private correspondence, and regret that I could not give more precise information. Very respectfully, Yrs, etc..

JEFF'N DAVIS.

To *J. J. Pettus* (JDC)[*]

MY DEAR SIR,

In my frequent brief and hasty notes I have not replied to your inquiry as to my present opinion in relation to the time when the ordinance of secession of Missi. should take effect. This being a day set apart for "humiliation and prayer" I will assign a part of it to the duty of stating my views on the point of your inquiry.

There are many acts which may be done during this session of Congress if the Black-republicans have a majority in both houses of Congress which must be detrimental to the South. On the 8th the attempt will be made to pass a force bill through the House of Reps. & it will probably succeed. The senate as it now stands can defeat it. A loan bill of huge proportions will be requisite to enable Mr. Lincoln to carry out his policy of coercion. It is important to defeat that measure of finance. Mr. Buchanan will no doubt seek to fill all vacancies occurring in the seceding states by the appointment of northern men, it will be better to reject them than to require our people to expel them; to do this will require all the Southern senators to be present.

Post offices and Post route contractors are necessary to the commercial, political and social relations of our people. To substitute new arrangements for those now existing will require some time. Commercial machinery will be required alike for exports and imports. Even if we should adopt free trade, we must have the ability to clear vessels carrying cargoes to foreign ports. But it is needless to you to enumerate all the points for which provision must be made to avoid the imposition of onerous embarrassments on our people at the period of transition from the old to new governmental relations.

We should not halt, least of all hesitate, the moral power of steady progress must not be impaired, but let us advance with calm deliberation and due regard to all the necessities of the case. If when Lincoln comes to his office he finds no new powers granted for the collection

[*] Governor of Mississippi.

of revenue, no additional force provided for, no funds beyond the accruing revenue, no extraordinary appropriations, he will have little power until the meeting of another congress. He cannot convoke the Congress before next fall, unless he chooses to assemble it in despite of the fact that several of the border slave states have not held an election. To disregard that fact will drive them forthwith into alliance with us, to wait for them gives us the time for preparation which we now most need.

It has therefore seemed to me that it would be well in enacting an ordinance of secession to provide for a temporary continuance of the federal officers and representatives of the state so far as the same may be necessary. It will hardly be possible to inaugurate a government for the new confederacy before the 4th of March, but it should not be postponed to a later date. When on a former occasion I selected that date it was for the two fold consideration, that less than the intervening time would hardly suffice, and that date would present in a palpable form the fact of our resistance to Black republican domination. With this rapid statement of my opinion I leave the case to those to whom its decision belongs, confident that they will judge wisely, and satisfied to abide by and sustain their decision.

Presdt. Buchanan has forfeited any claim which he may have had on our forbearance and support. I regard his treatment of So. Ca. as perfidious, and place no reliance upon him for the protection of our rights or abstinence from hostility to us. In this however do not understand me as alledging a wicked purpose, his evil deeds rather spring from irresolution and an increasing dread of northern excitement. He is said to fear that his house at "Wheatland may be burned, & it is reported that he apprehends impeachment when the withdrawal of Southern senators shall give the Black Repubs. the requisite majority in the Senate to convict him.

Please let me hear from you as often and as fully as your convenience will permit, and believe me ever truly your friend

JEFFERSON DAVIS

To Edwin De Leon (PJD)

MY DEAR SIR,

We are advancing rapidly to the end of "the Union." The cotton states may now be regarded as having decided for secession. South Carolina is in a quasi war and the probabilities are that events will hasten her and her associates into general conflict with the forces of the federal government. The black republicans exultant over their recent success are not disposed to concede any thing, and the stern necessity of resistance is forcing itself upon the judgement of all the slave holding states. The Va. Legislature met yesterday and took promptly and boldly the Southern ground.

Missi. is now in convention I may leave here in a few days, though it is also possible that the state may choose to continue its senators here for purposes of defence against hostile legislation. The confidence heretofore felt in Mr. Buchannan has diminished steadily and is now nearly extinct. His weakness has done as much harm as wickedness would have achieved. Though I can no longer respect or confer with him and feel injured by his conduct yet I pity and would extenuate the offences not prompted by bad design or malignant intent.

Before the 3d of March it will matter little to your people whether it be Buchannan or Lincoln under whom you decline to serve. The South Carolinians who remain under the federal government until then will find the gates of their state closed against them, and if opened it will be to receive them not as Sons hastening home but as foreigners seeking to be incorporated into their body politic. Responding therefore frankly to your inquiry I say the most prompt method of vacating your office will be probably the best. With great regard I am as ever your friend

JEFF'N,, DAVIS

To George W. Jones (JDC)[*]

WASHINGTON, D.C., JANUARY 20, 1861

MY DEAR FRIEND

I have the honor to acknowledge the receipt of your letter & I herewith enclose the reply of the War Department & regret that it is not more in accordance with your wishes in relation to your son's reappointment. I also enclose, as you requested, a Copy of the Congressional Directory which has just been published.

Mississippi has seceded from the Union & I am on the eve of taking my final leave from the general government. This I am sure will excite regret but cannot cause you surprise. I am sorry to be separated from many true friends at the North, whose inability to secure an observance of the Constitution does not diminish our gratitude to them for the efforts they have made. The progress has been steady towards a transfer of the government into the hands of the abolitionists. Many states like Iowa have denied our rights disregarded their obligations, & have sacrificed their true representatives. To us it became a necessity to transfer our domestic institutions from hostile to friendly hands, & we have acted accordingly. There seems to be but little prospect that we will be permitted to do so peacefully but if the arbitrament must be referred to the sword we have resolved to meet it & confident in the justice of our Cause, we trust in the God of our fathers & the gallantry of their sons. I know you will sympathize with us although you cannot act with us, that we shall never find you or yours in the ranks of our enemies—

I AM AS EVER
VERY TRULY
YOUR FRIEND
JEFFN DAVIS

[*] Longtime friend of JD residing in Wisconsin; at this time U.S. minister to Colombia.

To *Franklin Pierce* (PJD)

WASHINGTON, D.C., JANUARY 20, 1861

MY DEAR FRIEND,

I have often and sadly turned my thoughts to you during the troublous times through which we have been passing and now I come to the hard task of announcing to you that the hour is at hand which closes my connection with the United States, for the independence and Union of which my Father bled and in the service of which I have sought to emulate the example he set for my guidance. Mississippi not as a matter of choice but of necessity has resolved to enter on the trial of secession. Those who have driven her to this alternative threaten to deprive her of the right to require that her government shall rest on the consent of the governed, to substitute foreign force for domestic support, to reduce a state to the condition from which the colony rose. In the attempt to avoid the issue which had been joined by the country, the present Administration has complicated and precipitated the question. Even now if the duty "to preserve the public property" was rationally regarded the probable collision at Charleston would be avoided. Security far better than any which the federal troops can give might be obtained in consideration of the little garrison of Fort Sumpter. If the disavowal of any purpose to coerce So. Ca. be sincere the possession of a work to command the harbor is worse than useless.

When Lincoln comes in he will have but to continue in the path of his predecessor to inaugurate a a civil war and, leave a soi disant democratic administration responsible for the fact. Genl. Cushing was here last week and when we parted it seemed like taking a last leave of a Brother.[*]

I leave immediately for Missi. and know not what may devolve upon me after my return. Civil war has only horror for me, but whatever circumstances demand shall be met as a duty and I trust be so discharged that you will not be ashamed of our former connection or cease to be my friend.

[*] Caleb Cushing, Massachusetts Democrat who served as attorney general in Franklin Pierce's cabinet.

I had hoped this summer to have had an opportunity to see you and Mrs. Pierce and to have shown to you our children. Mrs. Davis was sorely disappointed when we turned Southward without seeing you, I believe she wrote to Mrs. Pierce in explanation of the circumstances which prevented us from executing our cherished plan of a visit to you when we should leave West Point.

Mrs. Davis joins me in kindest remembrance to Mrs. Pierce and the expression of the hope that we may yet have you both at our country home. Do me the favor to write to me often, address Hurricane P.O. Warren County, Missi.

May God bless you is ever the prayer of your friend

JEFF'N,, DAVIS

Speech in U.S. Senate (*Farewell Address*) (PJD)

JANUARY 21, 1861

I rise, Mr. President, for the purpose of announcing to the Senate that I have satisfactory evidence that the State of Mississippi, by a solemn ordinance of her people in convention assembled, has declared her separation from the United States. Under these circumstances, of course my functions are terminated here. It has seemed to me proper, however, that I should appear in the Senate to announce that fact to my associates, and I will say but very little more. The occasion does not invite me to go into argument; and my physical condition would not permit me to do so if it were otherwise; and yet it seems to become me to say something on the part of the State I here represent, on an occasion so solemn as this.

It is known to Senators who have served with me here, that I have for many years advocated, as an essential attribute of State sovereignty, the right of a State to secede from the Union. Therefore, if I had not believed there was justifiable cause; if I had thought that Mississippi was acting without sufficient provocation, or without an existing necessity, I should still, under my theory of the Government, because of my allegiance to the State of which I am a citizen, have been bound by her action. I, however, may be permitted to say that I do think she has justifiable cause, and I approve of her act. I conferred with her people before that act was taken, counseled them then that if the state of things which they apprehended should exist when the convention met, they should take the action which they have now adopted.

I hope none who hear me will confound this expression of mine with the advocacy of the right of a State to remain in the Union, and to disregard its constitutional obligations by the nullification of the law. Such is not my theory. Nullification and secession, so often confounded, are indeed antagonistic principles. Nullification is a remedy which it is sought to apply within the Union, and against the agent of the States. It is only to be justified when the agent has violated his constitutional obligation, and a State, assuming to judge for itself, denies the right of the agent thus to act, and appeals to the other States of the Union for a decision; but when the States themselves, and when the people of the States, have so acted as to convince us that they will not regard our constitutional rights, then, and then for the first time, arises the doctrine of secession in its practical application.

A great man who now reposes with his fathers, and who has been often arraigned for a want of fealty to the Union, advocated the doctrine of nullification, because it preserved the Union. It was because of his deep-seated attachment to the Union, his determination to find some remedy for existing ills short of a severance of the ties which bound South Carolina to the other States, that Mr. Calhoun advocated the doctrine of nullification, which he proclaimed to be peaceful, to be within the limits of State power, not to disturb the Union, but only to be a means of bringing the agent before the tribunal of the States for their judgment.

Secession belongs to a different class of remedies. It is to be justified upon the basis that the States are sovereign. There was a time when none denied it. I hope the time may come again, when a better comprehension of the theory of our Government, and the inalienable rights of the people of the States, will prevent any one from denying that each State is a sovereign, and thus may reclaim the grants which it has made to any agent whomsoever.

I therefore say I concur in the action of the people of Mississippi, believing it to be necessary and proper, and should have been bound by their action if my belief had been otherwise; and this brings me to the important point which I wish on this last occasion to present to the Senate. It is by this confounding of nullification and secession that the name of a great man, whose ashes now mingle with his mother earth, has been invoked to justify coercion against a seceded State. The phrase "to execute the laws," was an expression which General Jackson applied to the case of a State refusing to obey the laws while yet a member of the Union. That is not the case which is now presented. The laws are to be executed over the United States, and upon the people of the United States. They have no relation to any foreign country. It is a perversion of terms, at least it is a great misapprehension of the case, which cites that expression for application to a State which has withdrawn from the Union. You may make war on a foreign State. If it be the purpose of gentlemen, they may make war against a State which has withdrawn from the Union; but there are no laws of the United States to be executed within the limits of a seceded State. A State finding herself in the condition in which Mississippi has judged she is, in which her safety requires that she should provide for the maintenance of her rights out of the Union, surrenders all the benefits, (and they are known to be many,) deprives herself of the advantages, (they are known to be great,) severs all the ties of affection, (and they are close and enduring,) which have bound her to the Union; and thus divesting herself of every benefit, taking upon herself every burden, she claims to be exempt from any power to execute the laws of the United States within her limits.

I well remember an occasion when Massachusetts was arraigned before the bar of the Senate, and when then the doctrine of coercion was rife and to be applied against her because of the rescue of a fugitive slave in Boston. My opinion then was the same that it is now. Not in a spirit of egotism, but to show that I am not influenced in my opinion because the case is my own, I refer to that time and that occasion as containing the opinion which I then entertained, and on which my present conduct is based. I then said, if Massachusetts, following her through a stated line of conduct, chooses to take the last step which separates her from the Union, it is her right to go, and I will neither vote one dollar nor one man to coerce her back; but will say to her,

God speed, in memory of the kind associations which once existed between her and the other States.

It has been a conviction of pressing necessity, it has been a belief that we are to be deprived in the Union of the rights which our fathers bequeathed to us, which has brought Mississippi into her present decision. She has heard proclaimed the theory that all men are created free and equal, and this made the basis of an attack upon her social institutions; and the sacred Declaration of Independence has been invoked to maintain the position of the equality of the races. That Declaration of Independence is to be construed by the circumstances and purposes for which it was made. The communities were declaring their independence; the people of those communities were asserting that no man was born—to use the language of Mr. Jefferson—booted and spurred to ride over the rest of mankind; that men were created equal—meaning the men of the political community; that there was no divine right to rule; that no man inherited the right to govern; that there were no classes by which power and place descended to families, but that all stations were equally within the grasp of each member of the body-politic. These were the great principles they announced; these were the purposes for which they made their declaration; these were the ends to which their enunciation was directed. They have no reference to the slave; else, how happened it that among the items of arraignment made against George III was that he endeavored to do just what the North has been endeavoring of late to do—to stir up insurrection among our slaves? Had the Declaration announced that the negroes were free and equal, how was the Prince to be arraigned for stirring up insurrection among them? And how was this to be enumerated among the high crimes which caused the colonies to sever their connection with the mother country? When our Constitution was formed, the same idea was rendered more palpable, for there we find provision made for that very class of persons as property; they were not put upon the footing of equality with white men—not even upon that of paupers and convicts; but, so far as representation was concerned, were discriminated against as a lower caste, only to be represented in the numerical proportion of three fifths.

Then, Senators, we recur to the compact which binds us together;

we recur to the principles upon which our Government was founded; and when you deny them, and when you deny to us the right to withdraw from a Government which thus perverted threatens to be destructive of our rights, we but tread in the path of our fathers when we proclaim our independence, and take the hazard. This is done not in hostility to others, not to injure any section of the country, not even for our own pecuniary benefit; but from the high and solemn motive of defending and protecting the rights we inherited, and which it is our sacred duty to transmit unshorn to our children.

I find in myself, perhaps, a type of the general feeling of my constituents towards yours. I am sure I feel no hostility to you, Senators from the North. I am sure there is not one of you, whatever sharp discussion there may have been between us, to whom I cannot now say, in the presence of my God, I wish you well; and such, I am sure, is the feeling of the people whom I represent towards those whom you represent. I therefore feel that I but express their desire when I say I hope, and they hope, for peaceful relations with you, though we must part. They may be mutually beneficial to us in the future, as they have been in the past, if you so will it. The reverse may bring disaster on every portion of the country; and if you will have it thus, we will invoke the God of our fathers, who delivered them from the power of the lion, to protect us from the ravages of the bear; and thus, putting our trust in God and in our own firm hearts and strong arms, we will vindicate the right as best we may.

In the course of my service here, associated at different times with a great variety of Senators, I see now around me some with whom I have served long; there have been points of collision; but whatever of offense there has been to me, I leave here; I carry with me no hostile remembrance. Whatever offense I have given which has not been redressed, or for which satisfaction has not been demanded, I have, Senators, in this hour of our parting, to offer you my apology for any pain which, in heat of discussion, I have inflicted. I go hence unencumbered of the remembrance of any injury received, and having discharged the duty of making the only reparation in my power for any injury offered.

Mr. President, and Senators, having made the announcement which the occasion seemed to me to require, it only remains to me to bid you a final adieu.

To Alexander M. Clayton (PJD)*

JACKSON, MISSISSIPPI, JANUARY 30, 1861

MY DEAR FRIEND,

Mr. Goodman communicated your kind message and I have in vain endeavored to form a satisfactory reply. The current of events rolls on with such rapidity that the conclusion of today may be inapplicable to the case of to-morrow.

You will have at Montgomery information in relation to the progress of the canvass in the border states which will enable you to judge of the future of the Southern confederacy. If the border slave holding states unite with us there will probably be peaceful separation and we shall have full time to organize our government. Then the civil branch of the Govt. will be the only field for useful labor. But if the cotton states are to maintain their position alone, war is probable and the military branch of the government becomes of paramount importance. If the provisional government gives to the chief executive such power as the Constitution gave to the President of the U.S. then he will be the source of military authority and may in emergency command the army in person. I have said enough to justify me in stating that with the limited knowledge I now possess it is not possible to decide as to what it is best to do in relation to the position I should occupy. The post of Presdt. of the provisional government is one of great responsibility and difficulty, I have no confidence in my capacity to meet its requirements. I think I could perform the functions of genl. if the Executive did not cripple me in my operations by acts of commission or omission. I write as one thinking on paper and say to *you* who will understand me that I would prefer not to have either place, but in this hour of my country's severest trial will accept any place to which my fellow citizens may assign me.

You have a mighty work before you. I trust your colleagues will sustain you and that God will bless your labors. I write in the midst of conversation and in great haste. As ever very sincerely your's

JEFFN,, DAVIS

* Delegate from Mississippi to convention in Montgomery, Alabama, that formally created the Confederate States of America.

Speech in Montgomery, Alabama (JDC)

FEBRUARY 16, 1861

MONTGOMERY, February 16.—A number of model flags were presented to-day and referred. A communication about missiles of war was also referred. A bill was reported from the Committee relative to citizenship, prescribing uniform rules for naturalization, the caption only of which was read. Applications were made for patents and copyrights, which were referred. The balance of the business of the day was transacted in secret session.

SECOND DESPATCH.

MONTGOMERY, February 16.—President Davis' trip from Jackson, Mississippi, to Montgomery , was one continuous ovation. He made no less than twenty-five speeches upon the route, returning thanks for complimentary greetings from crowds of ladies and gentlemen. There were military demonstrations, salutes of cannon, &c., at the various depots.

The Committee of Reception, appointed by the Southern Congress, and also the Committee appointed by the Montgomery authorities, met President Davis about 80 miles from the city and formally welcomed him. Two fine companies from Columbus, Ga., formed an escort to Opelika. The *cortege* reached Montgomery Friday night at ten o'clock. Salvos of artillery greeted his approach, and a very large crowd assembled at the depot, hailing his appearance with tremendous cheering. President Davis, returning thanks, said that he was proud to receive the congratulations and hospitality of the people of Alabama. He briefly reviewed the present position of the South. The time for compromise, he said, had passed, and our only hope was in a determined maintenance of our position, and to make all who oppose us smell Southern powder and feel Southern steel. If coercion should be persisted in, he had no doubt as to the result. We would maintain our right to self-government at all hazards. We ask nothing, want nothing, and will have no complications. If other States should desire to join our Confederation, they can freely come on our terms. Our separation from the old Union is complete. NO COMPROMISE; NO RECONSTRUCTION CAN BE NOW ENTERTAINED. (Tremendous applause.)

A large crowd awaited the President's arrival at the Exchange Hotel. The ladies were equally enthusiastic with the gentlemen. At a quarter before eleven, in response to enthusiastic calls, he appeared on the balcony and said:

Fellow Citizens and Brethren of the Confederate States of America—for now we are brethren, not in name, merely, but in fact—men of one flesh, one bone, one interest, one purpose, and of identity of domestic institutions. We have henceforth, I trust, a prospect of living together in peace, with our institutions a subject of protection and not of defamation. It may be that our career will be ushered in, in the midst of storms—it may be that as this morning opened with clouds, mist and rain, we shall have to encounter inconveniences at the beginning; but as the sun rose, lifted the mist, dispersed the clouds, and left a pure sunlight, Heaven so will prosper the Southern Confederacy, and carry us safe from sea to the safe harbor of constitutional liberty. (Applause.) Thus we shall have nothing to fear at home, because at home we shall have homogeneity. We have nothing to fear abroad, because, if war should come—if we must again baptise in blood the principles for which our fathers bled in the Revolution, we shall show that we are not degenerate sons, but will redeem the pledges they gave to preserve the sacred rights transmitted us, and show that Southern valor still shines as brightly as in the days of '76—in 1812, and in every other conflict.

I was informed by friends that your kindness only required that I should appear before you, fatigued, as I am, by travel—hoarse and unable to speak at length—and I came out merely to assure you of my gratitude for these manifestations of good will. I come with diffidence and distrust to discharge the great duties devolved on me by the kindness and confidence of the Congress of the Confederate States. I thank you, friends, for the kind manifestations of favor and approbation you exhibit on this occasion. Throughout my entire progress to this city I have received the same flattering demonstrations of generous support. I did not regard them as personal to myself, but tendered to me as an humble representative of the principles and policy of the Confederate States. I will devote to the duties of the high office to which I have been called all I have of heart, of head and of hand.

If, in the progress of events, it shall become necessary, and my services shall be needed. in another position—if, to be plain, necessity shall require that I shall again enter the ranks as a soldier, I hope you will welcome me there.

Now, friends, again thanking you for this manifestation of your approbation, allow me to bid you good night.

Speech in Montgomery, Alabama (*Inaugural Address as Provisional President*)* (PJD)

GENTLEMEN OF THE CONGRESS OF THE CONFEDERATE STATES OF AMERICA. FRIENDS AND FELLOW-CITIZENS:

Called to the difficult and responsible station of Chief Executive of the Provisional Government which you have instituted, I approach the discharge of the duties assigned to me with an humble distrust of my abilities, but with a sustaining confidence in the wisdom of those who are to guide and to aid me in the administration of public affairs, and an abiding faith in the virtue and patriotism of the people.

Looking forward to the speedy establishment of a permanent government to take the place of this, and which by its greater moral and physical power will be better able to combat with the many difficulties which arise from the conflicting interests of separate nations, I enter upon the duties of the office to which I have been chosen with the hope that the beginning of our career as a Confederacy may not be obstructed by hostile opposition to our enjoyment of the separate existence and independence which we have asserted, and, with the blessing of Providence, intend to maintain. Our present condition,

---

* On February 9, 1861, the delegates in Montgomery chose a provisional president, JD, and a provisional vice president, Alexander H. Stephens of Georgia. They would serve for one year. In the fall voters in the Confederate States would elect a president and vice president for the six-year term set forth in the Confederate Constitution. In that election JD and Stephens were unopposed.

achieved in a manner unprecedented in the history of nations, illustrates the American idea that governments rest upon the consent of the governed, and that it is the right of the people to alter or abolish governments whenever they become destructive of the ends for which they were established.

The declared purpose of the compact of Union from which we have withdrawn was "to establish justice, insure domestic tranquillity, provide for the common defense, promote the general welfare, and secure the blessings of liberty to ourselves and our posterity"; and when, in the judgment of the sovereign States now composing this Confederacy, it had been perverted from the purposes for which it was ordained, and had ceased to answer the ends for which it was established, a peaceful appeal to the ballot-box declared that so far as they were concerned, the government created by that compact should cease to exist. In this they merely asserted a right which the Declaration of Independence of 1776 had defined to be inalienable; of the time and occasion for its exercise, they, as sovereigns, were the final judges, each for itself. The impartial and enlightened verdict of mankind will vindicate the rectitude of our conduct, and He who knows the hearts of men will judge of the sincerity with which we labored to preserve the Government of our fathers in its spirit. The right solemnly proclaimed at the birth of the States, and which has been affirmed and reaffirmed in the bills of rights of States subsequently admitted into the Union of 1789, undeniably recognize in the people the power to resume the authority delegated for the purposes of government. Thus the sovereign States here represented proceeded to form this Confederacy, and it is by abuse of language that their act has been denominated a revolution. They formed a new alliance, but within each State its government has remained, the rights of person and property have not been disturbed. The agent through whom they communicated with foreign nations is changed, but this does not necessarily interrupt their international relations.

Sustained by the consciousness that the transition from the former Union to the present Confederacy has not proceeded from a disregard on our part of just obligations, or any failure to perform every constitutional duty, moved by no interest or passion to invade the rights of others, anxious to cultivate peace and commerce with all nations, if we may not hope to avoid war, we may at least expect that posterity will acquit us of having needlessly engaged in it. Doubly justified by the absence of wrong on our part, and by wanton aggression on the part of others, there can be no cause to doubt that the courage and patriotism of the people of the Confederate States will be found equal to any measures of defense which honor and security may require.

An agricultural people, whose chief interest is the export of a commodity required in every manufacturing country, our true policy is peace, and the freest trade which our necessities will permit. It is alike our interest, and that of all those to whom we would sell and from whom we would buy, that there should be the fewest practicable restrictions upon the interchange of commodities. There can be but little rivalry between ours and any manufacturing or navigating community, such as the Northeastern States of the American Union. It must follow, therefore, that a mutual interest would invite good will and kind offices. If, however, passion or the lust of dominion should cloud the judgment or inflame the ambition of those States, we must prepare to meet the emergency and to maintain, by the final arbitrament of the sword, the position which we have assumed among the nations of the earth. We have entered upon the career of independence, and it must be inflexibly pursued. Through many years of controversy with our late associates, the Northern States, we have vainly endeavored to secure tranquillity, and to obtain respect for the rights to which we were entitled. As a necessity, not a choice, we have resorted to the remedy of separation; and henceforth our energies must be directed to the conduct of our own affairs, and the perpetuity of the Confederacy which we have formed. If a just perception of mutual interest shall permit us peaceably to pursue our separate political career, my most earnest desire will have been fulfilled. But, if this be denied to us, and the integrity of our territory and jurisdiction be assailed, it will but remain for us, with firm resolve, to appeal to arms and invoke the blessings of Providence on a just cause.

As a consequence of our new condition and with a view to meet anticipated wants, it will be necessary to provide for the speedy and efficient organization of branches of the executive department, having special charge of foreign intercourse, finance, military affairs, and the postal service.

For purposes of defense, the Confederate States may, under ordinary circumstances, rely mainly upon their militia, but it is deemed advisable, in the present condition of affairs, that there should be a well-instructed and disciplined army, more numerous than would usually be required on a peace establishment. I also suggest that for the protection of our harbors and commerce on the high seas a navy adapted to those objects will be required. These necessities have doubtless engaged the attention of Congress.

With a Constitution differing only from that of our fathers in so far as it is explanatory of their well-known intent, freed from the sectional conflicts which have interfered with the pursuit of the general welfare, it is not unreasonable to expect that States from which we have recently parted may seek to unite their fortunes with ours under the government which we have instituted. For this your Constitution makes adequate provision; but beyond this, if I mistake not the judgment and will of the people, a reunion with the States from which we have separated is neither practicable nor desirable. To increase the power, develop the resources, and promote the happiness of a confederacy, it is requisite that there should be so much of homogeneity that the welfare of every portion shall be the aim of the whole. Where this does not exist, antagonisms are engendered which must and should result in separation.

Actuated solely by the desire to preserve our own rights and promote our own welfare, the separation of the Confederate States has been marked by no aggression upon others and followed by no domestic convulsion. Our industrial pursuits have received no check. The cultivation of our fields has progressed as heretofore, .and even should we be involved in war there would be no considerable diminution in the production of the staples which have constituted our exports and in which the commercial world has an interest scarcely less than our own. This common interest of the producer and consumer can only be interrupted by an exterior force which should obstruct its transmission to foreign markets—a course of conduct which would be as unjust toward us as it would be detrimental to manufacturing and commercial interests abroad. Should reason guide the action of the

Government from which we have separated, a policy so detrimental to the civilized world, the Northern States included, could not be dictated by even the strongest desire to inflict injury upon us; but otherwise a terrible responsibility will rest upon it, and the suffering of millions will bear testimony to the folly and wickedness of our aggressors. In the meantime there will remain to us, besides the ordinary means before suggested, the well-known resources for retaliation upon the commerce of an enemy.

Experience in public stations, of subordinate grade to this which your kindness has conferred, has taught me that care and toil and disappointment are the price of official elevation. You will see many errors to forgive, many deficiencies to tolerate, but you shall not find in me either a want of zeal or fidelity to the cause that is to me highest in hope and of most enduring affection. Your generosity has bestowed upon me an undeserved distinction, one which I neither sought nor desired. Upon the continuance of that sentiment and upon your wisdom and patriotism I rely to direct and support me in the performance of the duty required at my hands.

We have changed the constituent parts, but not the system of our Government. The Constitution formed by our fathers is that of these Confederate States, in their exposition of it, and in the judicial construction it has received, we have a light which reveals its true meaning.

Thus instructed as to the just interpretation of the instrument, and ever remembering that all offices are but trusts held for the people, and that delegated powers are to be strictly construed, I will hope, by due diligence in the performance of my duties, though I may disappoint your expectations, yet to retain, when retiring, something of the good will and confidence which welcome my entrance into office.

It is joyous, in the midst of perilous times, to look around upon a people united in heart, where one purpose of high resolve animates and actuates the whole—where the sacrifices to be made are not weighed in the balance against honor and right and liberty and equality. Obstacles may retard, they cannot long prevent the progress of a movement sanctified by its justice, and sustained by a virtuous people. Reverently let us invoke the God of our fathers to guide and protect us in our efforts to perpetuate the principles which, by his blessing, they were able to vindicate, establish and transmit to their posterity, and with a continuance of His favor, ever gratefully acknowledged, we may hopefully look forward to success, to peace, and to prosperity.

To Francis W. Pickens (PJD)*

MONTGOMERY, ALABAMA, FEBRUARY 20, 1861

MY DEAR SIR

Many thanks for your kind expressions and cheering <-associations-> assurances. Their is enough in my situation to discourage one more confident than myself, to suggest the apprehension that he would most disappoint his most sanguine friends—

I hope provision will this day be made for Executive departments and thus enable us to put in train the work of preparation for the duties of the hour. As soon as possible I will in compliance with your wish send an Engineer of Military skill and examine and report on the condition of Charleston harbour. and its works of defence and offence—I am prepared for the criticism which the rash often bestow upon necessary caution, but if success follows and the blood of the brave be thus saved, I will be more than content to have the censure which in the meantime may be encountered. My mind has been for sometime satisfied that a peaceful solution of our difficulties was not to be anticipated, and therefore my thoughts have been directed to the manner of <-making-> rendering force effective—We are poorly prepared for war and have but little capacity for speedy repair of past neglect. Valor is ours and the justice of our cause will nerve the arm of our Sons to meet the issue of—unequal conflict, but we must seek to render the inequality as small as it can be made. I hope to hear from you often and fully, and that you will pardon any failure, which the pressure of public engagements may create on my side of the correspondence. Your very interesting letter addressed to me at Jackson reached me at that place, very truly Your friend

(SIGNED) JEFFN DAVIS

* Governor of South Carolina.

To Anna Ella Carroll (PJD)*

MY DEAR MISS CARROLL:

Thanks for yr Kind letter.

You should not have doubted my desire to see you before leaving and as you had not the reason let me state it. For ten days before <-leaving-> my departure a painful illness confined me to my room, it was necessary to rise from a bed of suffering with an aching head when I started to take leave of the Senate. The effort renewed my "unutterable griefs" and the necessity of immediate return to Missi where I had been appointed to the chief military command caused me to start from D.C. when I should have been in bed I could not or I would have taken leave of you.

It is gratifying to me to learn that Republican gentlemen and ladies speak well of me and there is at least this claim to it, I have not sought to injure them nor in public station neglected the interests of their section or permitted myself ever to contract within smaller limits than the exterior boundary of my country.

But how could you suppose I would ever advocate reconstruction? Was not my leave taking of the Senate announced to be *final*, it was the stern conviction of necessity, the demand of honor which enabled me to utter the heart wringing words.

They were not my utterances but rather leaves torn from the book of fate. Now we have to deal with the present and the future. The North has wanted Canada and the South wants Cuba, the expansion of both may have been restrained by the narrow views of each, let them be left freely to grow casting their branches widely as the Cedar of Lebanon and why not each hereafter rejoice in the prosperity of the other Brother.

There is much more which I would have said but am interrupted and must close with the hope that you will hereafter look to yrself for <-any-> the explanation of any failure on my part and at least know that good motive was not wanting. With highest regard yr friend

JEFF DAVIS.

* Friend of JD who lived in Maryland.

To F. W. Pickens (JDC)

MONTGOMERY, ALABAMA, MARCH 1, 1861

GOV. F. W. PICKENS,

My Dear Sir: I have requested the Secretary of War to inform you fully of the arrangements made and making for the efficient discharge of our duties in connection with the defence of Charleston and the vindication of our rights, territorial and jurisdictional. I use the pronoun our because the cause is common to the Confederate states and near to my heart as if I were a citizen of So. Ca. Genl. Beauregard is full of talent and of much military experience, he has been selected because of his peculiar fitness for the position and because his zeal and gallantry cannot fail to win your confidence and that of the brave men who have given themselves to the service of their country in this hour of its need.[*]

We will confer freely with you and must needs depend upon you for the power to be useful. I have discussed the subject of the works needful as well to prevent the entrance of reinforcements as to reduce Fort Sumter most speedily and at least cost of the blood of our patriotic sons.[†]

I have not despaired of being able to visit you and will avail myself of the earliest occasion when public duties here will permit to do so.

VERY TRULY YOURS,
JEFFERSON DAVIS.

[*] Pierre Gustave Toutant Beauregard, who became a full general in the Confederate army.
[†] A fort in Charleston harbor held by Union forces.

To Brigadier General Braxton Bragg (PJD)[*]

MONTGOMERY, ALABAMA, APRIL 3, 1861

MY DEAR GENL.

The Secty of War communicated to you last night by telegraph our latest information and the suppositions derived from it. It is, there is much reason to believe, with a view to exhibit power and relieve the effect of the necessary abandonment of Sumter that it is proposed to reinforce Pickens, but it is also possible that it may be intended to attempt the reinforcement of both.[†] They will it is said avoid collision with you by landing their forces upon the Island and after the garrison is sufficient will bring in supplies defying your batteries.

You will not have failed to notice that the tone of the Northern press indicates a desire to prove a *military* necessity for the abandonment of both Sumter & Pickens.

It is already asserted that your batteries will not permit the landing of supplies, and soon this may be charged among the short comings of Mr. Buchannan. Per contra there is manifested a desire to show what can be done at Pensacola as proof of what would have been done at Chaleston. In the latter view they may seek to throw both men and supplies into Pickens by landing on Santa Rosa beyond the range of your guns. It is scarcely to be doubted that for political reasons the U.S. Govt. will avoid making an attack so long as the hope of retaining the border states remains. There would be to us an advantage in so placing them that an attack by them would be a necessity, but when we are ready to relieve our territory and jurisdiction of the presence of a foreign garrison that advantage is overbalanced by other considerations. The case of Pensacola then is reduced the more palpable elements of a military problem and your measures may without disturbing views be directed to the capture of Fort Pickens and the defence of the harbor. You will soon have I hope a force sufficient to occupy all

---

[*] Confederate officer and commander at Pensacola, Florida, who would rise to the rank of full general.

[†] Fort on Santa Rosa Island near Pensacola, Florida, held by Union forces.

the points necessary for that end. As many additional troops as may be required can be promptly furnished.

Instruction, organization and discipline must proceed with active operations; you will appreciate the circumstances which rendered such objectionable combination an unavoidable condition. Your batteries on the main shore are I am informed nearly complete and their converging fire may I hope compensate somewhat for their too distant location from the work to be battered. To secure the time necessary for you to effect a breach will it not be necessary to embarrass the use of the guns of Pickens which bear upon your works? Can this be done by a mortar battery placed on the Island so as to take those guns in reverse? In the same connection: could you establish gun batteries on the Island so as to drive off the shipping and prevent a junction of the land and naval forces? A mortar battery, could I suppose be established in a night, secure from fire & from sortie when you have a sufficient force to justify a partition of your army. If that first step /the establishment of a mortar battery/ was permitted you could establish your batteries also, and then carry forward your approaches until you were attacked. Then all your batteries being opened, shells falling in the Fort from front and from rear must prove rapidly destructive to the garrison, and open to you several modes of success—1st. By surrender— Second, By abandonment if you had not been able to command the shipping. Third, By breach of front wall or explosion of glacis mines exposing the work to capture by assault. Fourth. By evacuation on the plea that the means at the disposal of their government had not been sufficient to prevent the investment of the Fort and its reduction by famine.

I have written to you freely and hurriedly because I wished to exchange views with you and felt assured that you would understand that there was no purpose to dictate; and under an entire confidence that your judgement would control your conduct, and could only be influenced by a suggestion, in so far as it might excite a train of thought out of the channel which the constant contemplation of a particular view is apt to wear. Though you are addressed as a Genl upon official matters yet I wish you to regard this not as a letter of the

President but of your old comrade in arms, who hopes much, and expects much for you, and from you. very Respectfully & truly yr's,

JEFFN,, DAVIS

To John A. Campbell (PJD)*

MONTGOMERY, ALABAMA, APRIL 6, 1861

MY DEAR SIR,

Accept my thanks for your kind and valuable services to the cause of the Confederacy and of Peace between those who though seperated have many reasons to feel towards each other more than the friendship common among nations. Our policy is as you say, peace, it is our sentiment also, and surely it must be the interest of both the parties concerned. We have waited hopefully for the withdrawal of garrisons which irritate the people of these states and threaten the respective localities, and which can serve no purpose to the United States unless it be to injure us. So far from desiring to use force for the reduction of Fort Sumter we have avoided any measure to produce discomfort or to exhibit discourtesy, until recently when we were informed that the idea of evacuation had been abandoned and that supplies convoyed by an armed vessel under the command of Capt Stringham had been sent to Fort Sumter, and that Fort Pickens was to be reinforced. Troops have been drawn from the frontier of Texas where they might have been claimed to be necessary to restrain the mexicans and Indians, and have been placed at Taylor & Jefferson where they could only be designed to act against the Confederate States. This is not the course of good will and does not tend to preserve the peace. It is not the preservation of the States, under any possible view of our relations.

It may be that Telegrams are sent here to deceive us and that we not you have been imposed upon, but it is not the part of either wis-

* U.S. Supreme Court justice who became assistant secretary of war in the Confederacy. In Washington in March and early April 1861, he acted as a liaison between Confederate commissioners attempting to negotiate the release of forts still occupied by U.S. forces and Secretary of State William H. Seward, who communicated unofficially with the commissioners.

dom or good neighborhood to continue a state of things so evidently conducive of such results, which thus facilitate collision, and which can answer no other end than to annoy if not to assail us. Were it possible for the US Govt to look beyond the events of a war and to adopt now the terms which after Thousands of lives and Millions of Treasure have been lost they must be content to accept, it would be a triumph of reason over vanity which would in all time testify to the progressive civilization of our age. In any event I will gratefully remember your zealous labor in a sacred cause and hope your fellow citizens may at some time give you acceptable recognition of your service and appreciate the heroism with which you have encountered a hazard from which most men would have shrunk. With equal confidence in our power to meet the political danger of peace, and the physical danger of War I wait the determination of a problem which it belongs to the Govt of the United States to control. I write in haste and confidentially Very faithfully yours

/SIGNED/ JEFF DAVIS.

To *Joseph E. Davis* (PJD)

RICHMOND, VIRGINIA, JUNE 18, 1861

MY DEAR BROTHER,

I have for several days intended to write to you but constant occupation has delayed the fulfilment of the purpose. The war draws nearer to us and daily increases in its proportions. Western Va. is no doubt against us and the counties bordering on the Potomac are to a great extent unsound.

Had the people of this state been as united as those of the cotton states we should have felt less the embarassment of imperfect preparation. Perhaps we might now have been contending for the bank of the Susquehanna instead of retiring from the Potomac. Troops are daily arriving from the South and I hope before long to be able to change from the defensive to an offensive attitude. It will be thus only that we can hope to check the progress of the war by teaching the enemy its evils and discouraging the sending out of their surplus population. The financial difficulty of maintaining the war will give the first sober thought to the North, and it is surprising that so little complaint has been heard. The accounts we have show that they are maddened and now united for our subjugation. The Merchants rave at their diminished trade but blame the South as the cause of all their woe. The Lawyers have forgotten their respect for the judiciary, for preedent, and the written law as shown by the fact that they utter no voice to sustain the venerable Chief Justice in his attempt to vindicate the writ of habeas corpus. It was fortunate that we seperated from a people unfit to possess a free government before our people had too become unworthy to possess the inheritance of community independence with civil & religious liberty.

We have a good house here and expect to occupy it in a few days. I hope you will come and share it with us—Your advice to me always desirable is now more than at any previous period coveted.

My days and much of the nights have been spent in organizing & preparing for the defence of the long and indefensible border of this state. When it is possible to leave here I wish to be on the lines and then if you were here I should feel much relieved as to the condition of my helpless family. God knows what the tide of war may bear to me, nor does the condition of affairs enable me to govern my course by considerations for my family. Varina and the children are well. My own health as good as usual.

Joe. R. Davis is with me and I become daily more pleased with him.* He is discreet, gentlemanly and of sound judgement. The report you have heard of his failure as an officer at Pensacola was certainly unfounded. Genl. Bragg praised him when I was at Pensacola. Subsequently when he was detached to join me, Genl. Bragg complimented him in orders—He /Genl. B./ is not inclined to praise, and is in no degree a courtier.

A letter from Pensacola states that Joe. was not elected to succeed Col. Phillips solely because it was understood that he would not leave his position with me to take command of the Regiment.

Give my love to Sister Eliza and such others of the family as are

* Joseph R. Davis, JD's nephew, who became a Confederate officer and one of his uncle's aides.

with you. Carie wrote a few days since to Varina, she was well and not inclined to run from the Yankees.* Our defences at Norfolk are I hope sufficient to repel any attack which will be made.

Ever affectionately
Your Brother
Jeffn,, Davis

To General Joseph E. Johnston (PJD)†

Richmond, Virginia, June 22, 1861

My Dear Genl.

I congratulate on the brilliant movement of Col. Vaughn's command. To break the line of the B.&O. R.R. was essential to our operations, and if the bridge at Cheat river and the grand tunnel could be destroyed so as prevent the use of that Rail Road for the duration of the war the effect upon public opinion in Western Va. would doubtless be of immediate and great advantage to our cause.

If the enemy has withdrawn from your front to attack on the East side of the mountain it may be that an attempt will be made to advance from Leesburg to seize the Manassas road and to turn Beauregard's position. The recent effort to repair the R.R. from Alexandria to Leesburg may have been with such intent. In that event if your scouts give you accurate and timely information an opportunity will be offered to you by the roads through the mountain passes to make a flank attack in conjunction with Beauregard's column, and with God's blessing to achieve a victory alike glorious and beneficial.

We continue to send forward reinforcements to Mannassas Junction. On Monday & Tuesday a Ballattion of light Artillery will go forward and every effort is made to reach a condition which will enable our forces to shape the campaign by assuming the offensive—

I wish you would write whenever your convenience will permit and give me fully both information and suggestions. Col. Thomas recently undertook to explain to me your wants as one authorized to

---

* Caroline Davis Leonard, JD's niece, who lived in Norfolk, Virginia.

† Confederate full general who at this time commanded at Harpers Ferry, Virginia.

speak for you and to day Mr. Staples communicated his impression of your views, necessities and wishes. I am sure you cannot feel hesitation in writing to me freely and trust your engagements will permit you to do so frequently. With earnest wishes for your welfare & happiness I am very truly your friend

JEFFN DAVIS

To Governor Isham G. Harris (PJD)[*]

RICHMOND, VIRGINIA, JULY 17, 1861

. . . I cordially appreciate the candor with which you have addressed me, and fully recognise the zealous and patriotic spirit which prompted your communication. I deeply regret that the action of this Government, in the appointment of Brigadier Generals in Tennessee, should have been misapprehended, or should be considered as liable to misapprehension. The Government has been guided, in making these appointments, by the sole consideration of the interests of Tennessee, as one of the Confederate States, so far as those interests could be understood here, and I am happy to learn from you, that the appointments already made meet with your entire approval. This is regarded by the Government as an additional and weighty evidence that these have been wisely made. Two of these three were among the number of those previously appointed by your Excellency /and were moreover already the Senior Generals in your State/; the third, Brig. Gen. Donelson was regarded as entitled to the appointment in view of his military education and experience, and high military standing. If, in making these selections, I have seemed to be forgetful of old party distinctions in Tennessee, it was only because I was so much engrossed with the magnitude and supreme importance of the present crisis, that I was led to forget the past, and to regard all good and true men *now,* as belonging to the *one party* of the South, in which *all* are loyal, and *all* are /equally/ entitled to recognition and honor. It was indeed only an extreme desire to *forget* old party distinctions, and to regard all true

---

[*] Governor of Tennessee.

Southerners as now united, in equal participation in a common cause, which led the Government *unconsciously* into *seeming* to observe these distinctions, and to be guided by the recollection of them, in making these appointments. Such, I assure you, was not the motive, but just the contrary. The importance of the considerations which you urge is fully acknowledged, and your candid and friendly suggestions shall not be forgotten in future. The information which you transmit with regard to the state of political Affairs in in Tennessee, and especially with regard to the importance of observing the three great geographical divisions of the State, is thankfully received, and shall not be disregarded. It is the desire of this Government, in conferring its appointments, in Tennessee, as in every other State of the Confederacy, to secure the approbation of a patriotic public opinion, and especially to unite and confirm thereby the loyalty and confidence of the /whole/ people towards the Confederate Government; and so far as this end can be attained, consistently with a supreme regard for the public interests, it shall be the object of constant attention and effort. And I am happy to add, that so far as the State of Tennessee Tennessee is concerned, the Government has so much confidence in your fidelity, and so much respect for your judgment, under your peculiar opportunities for possessing reliable information, that your advice will always be thankfully received, and favorably considered.

In conferring future appointments in Tennessee, the Government will have due regard to the geographic divisions of the State, and to the policy of a fair and equal distribution of the appointments among the Old Parties; and in furtherance of this policy, such suggestions as you may, from time to time, see fit to make, will be gladly received.

. . .

With regard to the measures recommended for the encouragement of Volunteering in Tennessee the Government recognises the paramount importance of this subject, in the present great crisis of our Country, and every encouragement which can be given, consistently with the laws of the Confederate States, shall be cheerfully accorded. Your suggestion with regard to the distribution of the troops, in the several sections of Tennessee, is approved, and shall be observed, so far as possible. No measures, within the power of this Government, shall be neglected, in order to secure and confirm the loyalty of the people of Tennessee.

Your suggestion with regard to the probable intention of the Federal Govt. to take possession, of the Louisville & Nashville R.R., and the military measures necessary to prevent this step, shall receive the early attention of this Government, and, if it is deemed necessary, shall be made the subject of a separate communication.

I am gratified to hear that you have become a candidate for reelection. This is the more honorable to you, as it was not of your own seeking. In heartily wishing you success in the approaching election, in which wish every member of our Government cordially concurs, I beg leave to express the hope, that the good State of Tennessee, and the great Cause of Southern Independence may long have the benefit of your talents, fidelity, and experience, in the public service.

In undoubting confidence of the success of our great undertaking, and cherishing the hope that the whole people of Tennessee may soon be united, as one man, in the cause, I have the honor to be, Sir, Very Respectfully Your obedient Servant,

To T. A. R. Nelson (PJD)*

RICHMOND, VIRGINIA, AUGUST 13, 1861

SIR

I have received your letter of 12th inst. in which you ask to be discharged from arrest and prosecution, and make promise that you will "as a citizen of Tennessee submit to her late action and religiously abstain from any further words or acts of condemnation whatever or opposition to her government"—

The <-rule-> desire <-that actuated-> /of/ this government being <-rather-> to <-reconcile all conflicting-> maintain the Independence it has asserted by <-a common-> /the united/ feeling and action of all its citizens /it has been its policy not/ <-that-> to enter

---

* Tennessee political leader who had opposed secession.

into questions of differences of political opinions heretofore existing;
I am /therefore/ pleased to be spared the necessity of inquiring whether
<-or not-> the accusation against you be well founded or not, vexa-
tious, or not: and to rest content with your submission as a loyal citizen of your State to her recent action in adhering to this Confederacy
and adopting its /permanent/ Constitution by an increased majority—

I have ordered your discharge /& that of your companions/ from
custody—I am &c

JEFF'N,, DAVIS

To General P. G. T. Beauregard (JDC)

RICHMOND, VIRGINIA, OCTOBER 16, 1861

MY DEAR GENERAL:

Enclosed you will find a letter, and slip referred to in it; also another slip derived from a different and, I suppose, a friendly source.
You will be able better than myself to judge of the value or importance of the matter contained in these papers.

A man has been sent up to confer with Genl. Johnston and yourself
in relation to the preparation of Winter Quarters, and the employment of negroes in the construction of a line of entrenchments. The
Secty. of State commended him as a man of great capacity for such
work.

I have thought often upon the questions of reorganization which
were submitted to you, and it has seemed to me, that, whether in view
of disease, or the disappointment and suffering of a winter canton-
ment on a line of defense, or of a battle to be fought in and near your
position, it was desirable to combine the troops, by a new distribution,
with as little delay as practicable. They will be stimulated to extraordinary effort when so organized, in that the fame of their State win be
in their keeping, and that each will feel that his immediate commander will desire to exalt rather than diminish his services. You
pointed me to the fact that you had observed that rule in the case of
the La. & Ca. troops, and you will not fail to perceive that others find
in the fact a reason for the like disposal of them. In the hour of sick-

ness and the tedium of waiting for Spring, men from the same region will best console and relieve each other. The maintenance of our cause rests on the sentiments of the people; letters from the camp complaining of inequality and harshness in the treatment of the men have already dulled the enthusiasm which filled our ranks with men, who by birth, fortune, education, and social position were the equals of any officer in the Land. The spirit of our military law is manifested in the fact that the State organization was limited to the regiment; the volunteers come in sufficient numbers to have Brigadiers, but have only Colonels. It was not then intended (is the necessary conclusion) that those troops should be under the immediate command of officers above the grade of Colonel. The spirit of the law, then, indicates that Brigades should be larger than customary,—the General being the remote commander of the individuals; charged with the care, the direction, the preservation, of the men, rather than the internal police; he has time to visit hospitals, to enquire into supplies, to supervise what others must execute; and the men come to regard him, when so habitually seen, as the friend of the individual; but they also know him in another capacity, and then removed, as it were placed on a pedestal, he seems the power that moves and controls the mass. This is not an ideal, but a sketch of Taylor when General of the Little Army, many of whom would no sooner have questioned his decisions or have shrunk from him in the hour of danger than if he had been their father. The other point was the necessity for unity in the army of the Potomac. The embarrassment was felt, and the sentiment of commanders appreciated, but rivalry running into jealousy is the unavoidable attendant of difference in the discipline, the usage, and the supplies, of camps; how much more so must it be when corps are associated together with the inevitable diversity resulting from control by different minds, and in which a reference is made to distinct antecedents which have never disappeared by a visible transition from the existence under independent heads. I have had applications made to me for transfer from one corps to another; and among the reasons given, was that the sick of one were permitted to go to the hospital, when, under like circumstances, they were in the other, confined to their encampment.

Mr. Benjamin informed me that you had expressed the wish, in the event of your corps being made an undivided portion of the army, to be relieved and sent to New Orleans.* If I had thought you could be dispensed with, it would have given me pleasure long since to have relieved the solicitude of the people of New Orleans by sending you there; but I can not anticipate the time when it would seem to be proper to withdraw you from the position with which you are so intimately acquainted, and for which you have shown yourself so eminently qualified. Nor have I felt that to another could be transferred the moral power you have over the troops you have commanded. My appreciation of you as a soldier and my regard for you as a man can not permit me willingly to wound your sensibility or to diminish your sphere of usefulness. Very truly your friend,

(SIGNED) JEFFN. DAVIS

Message to Confederate Congress (PJD)

RICHMOND, VIRGINIA, NOVEMBER 18, 1861

The few weeks which have elapsed since your adjournment have brought us so near the close of the year that we are now able to sum up its general results. The retrospect is such as should fill the hearts of our people with gratitude to Providence for His kind interposition in their behalf. Abundant yields have rewarded the labor of the agriculturist, whilst the manufacturing industry of the Confederate States was never so prosperous as now. The necessities of the times have called into existence new branches of manufactures, and given a fresh impulse to the activity of those heretofore in operation. The means of the Confederate States for manufacturing the necessaries and comforts of life within themselves increase as the conflict continues, and we are gradually becoming independent of the rest of the world for the supply of such military stores and munitions as are indispensable for war. The operations of the army soon to be partially interrupted by the approaching winter have afforded a protection to the country, and shed a lustre upon its arms through the trying vicissitudes of more

---

* Judah P. Benjamin, a member of JD's cabinet for the entire war. At this time he was interim secretary of war.

than one arduous campaign, which entitle our brave volunteers to our praise and our gratitude.

From its commencement up to the present period, the war has been <-constantly-> enlarging its proportions and expanding its boundaries, so as to include new fields. The conflict now extends from the shores of the Chesapeake to the confines of Missouri and Arizona; yet, sudden calls from the remotest points for military aid have been met with promptness enough not only to avert disaster in face of superior numbers, but. also, to roll back the tide of invasion from the border.

When the war commenced, the enemy were possessed of certain strategic points and strong places within the Confederate States. They greatly exceeded /us/ in numbers, in available resources, and in the supplies necessary for war. Military establishments had been long organised, and were complete; the navy, and for the most part, the army, once common to both, were in their possession. To meet all this, we had to create not only an army in the face of war itself, but also the military establishments necessary to equip and place it in the field. It ought indeed to be a subject of gratulation that the spirit of the volunteers and the patriotism of the people have enabled us, under Providence, to grapple successfully with these difficulties. A succession of glorious victories at Bethel, Bull Run, Manassas, Springfield, Lexington, Leesburg, and Belmont, has checked the wicked invasion which greed of gain and the unhallowed lust of power brought upon our soil, and has proved that numbers cease to avail when directed against a people fighting for the sacred right of self-government and the privileges of freemen. After more than seven months of war, the enemy have not only failed to extend their occupancy of our soil, but new States and Territories have been added to our Confederacy, while instead of their threatened march of unchecked conquest, they have been driven /at more than one point/ to assume the defensive; and upon a fair comparison between the two belligerents as to men, military means, and financial condition, the Confederate States are relatively much stronger now than when the struggle commenced.
. . .

If we husband our means and make a judicious use of our resources it would be difficult to fix a limit to the period during which we could conduct a war against the adversary whom we now encounter. The very efforts which he makes to isolate and invade us must exhaust his means whilst they serve to complete the circle and diversify the productions of our industrial system. The reconstruction which he seeks to effect by arms becomes daily more and more palpably impossible. Not only do the causes which induced us to separate still exist in full force, but they have been strengthened, and whatever doubt may have lingered in the minds of any /must/ have been completely dispelled by subsequent events. If instead of being a dissolution of a league, it were indeed a rebellion in which we are engaged, we might find ample vindication /for the course we have adopted/ in the in the scenes which are now being enacted in the United States. Our people <-have-> /now/ look<-ed-> with contemptuous astonishment on those with whom they had been so recently associated. They shrink with aversion from the bare idea of renewing such a connection. When they see a President making war without the assent of Congress; when they behold judges threatened because they maintain the writ of habeas corpus so sacred to freemen; when they see justice and law trampled under the armed heel of military authority, and upright men and innocent women dragged to distant dungeons upon the mere edict of a despot; when they find all this tolerated and applauded by a people who had been in the full enjoyment of freedom but a few months ago,—they believe that there must be some radical incompatibility between such a people and themselves. With such a people we may be content to live at peace, but the separation is final and for the independence we have asserted we will accept no alternative. The nature of the hostilities which they have waged against us must be characterised as barbarous wherever it is understood. They have bombarded undefended villages without giving notice to women and children to enable them to escape, and in one instance selected the night as the period when they might surprise them most effectually whilst asleep and unsuspicious of danger. Arson and rapine, the destruction of private houses and property, and injuries of the most wanton character even upon non-combatants have marked their forays along our borders and upon our Territory. Although we ought to have been admonished by these things that they were disposed to make war upon us in the most cruel and relentless spirit, yet we were not prepared to see them fit out a large naval expedition with the confessed purpose not only <-of plunder-> /to pillage/, but to incite a servile insurrection in our midst.

If they convert their soldiers into <-criminal-> incendiaries /and robbers/ and involve us in a species of war which claims non-combatants, women and children as its victims, they must expect to be treated as outlaws and enemies of mankind. There are certain rights of humanity which are entitled to respect even in war, and he who refuses to regard them <-upon all occasions-> forfeits his claims, if captured, to be considered as a <-military-> prisoner /of war/ but must expect to be dealt with as an offender against all law human and divine. But not content with violating our rights under the law of nations at home, they have extended these injuries to us within other jurisdictions. The distinguished gentlemen whom, with your approval at the last session, I commissioned to represent the Confederacy at certain foreign courts, have been recently seized by the captain of a United States ship of War on board a British steamer on their voyage from the neutral Spanish port of Havana to England. The /United States/ have thus claimed a general jurisdiction over the high seas, and entering a British ship sailing under its country's flag violated the rights of embassy, for the most part held sacred even amongst barbarians, by seizing our ministers whilst under the protection and /within the/ dominions of a neutral nation. These gentlemen were as much under the jurisdiction of the British Government upon that ship and beneath its flag as if they had been on its soil, and <-the right-> /a claim on the part/ of the United States to <-have-> seize<-d-> them in the streets of London <-was as good as their right-> /would have been as well founded as that/ to apprehend them where they were taken. Had they been malefactors and citizens even of the United States, they could not have been arrested on a British ship or on British soil unless under the express provisions of a treaty and according to the forms therein provided for the extradition of criminals.

But rights the most sacred seem to have lost all respect in their eyes. When Mr. Faulkner, a former minister of the United States /to France/ commissioned before the secession of Virginia, his native State, returned in good faith to Washington to settle his accounts and fulfil all the obligations into which he had entered, he was perfidiously arrested and imprisoned in New York, where he now is. The unsuspecting confidence with which he re<-turned to New York-> /ported to his Government <-he->/ was abused, and his desire to fulfil his trust to them was used to his injury.

In conducting this war we have sought no aid and proposed no alliances offensive and defensive abroad. We have asked for a recognized place in the great family of nations, but in doing so we have demanded nothing for which we did not offer a fair equivalent—The advantages of intercourse are mutual amongst Nations, and in seeking to establish diplomatic relations we were only endeavoring to place that intercourse under the regulation of public law. Perhaps we had the right if we had chosen to exercise it, to ask to know whether the principle that "blockades to be binding, must be effectual" so solemnly announced by the great Powers of Europe at Paris is to be generally enforced or applied only to particular parties.

When the Confederate States at your last session became a party to the declaration reaffirming this principle of international law which has been recognized so long by publicists and Governments, we certainly supposed that it was to be universally enforced. The customary law of nations is made up of their practice rather than their declarations; and if such declarations are only to be enforced in particular instances at the pleasure of those who make them, then the commerce of the world so far from being placed under the regulation of a general law, will become subject to the caprice of those who execute or suspend it at will—If such is to be the course of Nations in regard to this law, it is plain that it will thus become a rule for the weak and not for the strong.

Feeling that such views must be taken by the neutral nations of the Earth, I have caused the evidence to be collected which proves completely the utter inefficiency of the proclaimed blockade of our coast and shall direct it to be laid before such Governments as shall afford us the means of being heard—But But although we should be benefitted by the enforcement of this law so solemnly declared by the great Powers of Europe, we are not dependent on that enforcement for the successful prosecution of the war. As long as hostilities continue the Confederate States will exhibit a steadily increasing capacity to furnish their troops with food, clothing and arms. If they should be forced to forego many of the luxuries and some of the comforts of life, they will at least have the consolation of knowing that they are thus daily becoming more and more independent of the rest of the world. If in this process labor in the Confederate States should be gradually diverted from those great Southern Staples which have given life to so much of the commerce of mankind into other channels so as to make them rival producers instead of profitable customers, they will not be the only or even the chief losers by this change in the direction of of their industry. Although it is true that the /cotton/ supply <-of-> /from/ the Southern States could only be totally cut off by the subversion of our social system; yet it is plain that a long continuance of this blockade might by a diversion of labor and an investment of capital in other employments so diminish the supply as to bring ruin upon all those interests of foreign countries which are dependent on that Staple. For every laborer who is diverted from the culture of cotton in the South, perhaps four times as many elsewhere who have found subsistence in the various employments growing out of its use, will be forced also to change their occupation.

While the war which is waged to take from us the right of self-government can never attain that end, it remains to be seen how far it may work a revolution in the industrial system of the world, which may carry carry suffering to other lands <-contemporaneously with-> /as well as to/ our own. In the meantime we shall continue this struggle in humble dependence upon Providence from whose searching scrutiny we cannot conceal the secrets of our hearts, and to whose rule we confidently submit our destinies. For the rest we shall depend upon ourselves—Liberty is always won where there exists the unconquerable will to be free, and we have reason to know the strength that is given by a conscious sense, not only of the magnitude, but of the righteousness of our cause.

JEFFERSON DAVIS.

To Joseph E. Davis (PJD)

RICHMOND, VIRGINIA, FEBRUARY 21, 1862

MY DEAR BROTHER:

I am in possession of your ever-welcome favors of the 2d and 6th insts. Among my many causes for painful anxiety created by recent disasters in Tennessee, none perplexes me more than your condition. I had realized the embarrassment and loss of removal before your reference to it, and had believed it would not be necessary, but recent events shake my faith. The enemy are for the time occupied with the interior, and I have directed Captain Hollins to move up the river with his fleet In two or three weeks it is expected that some fourteen vessels, to be manned by "river men," will be ready to leave New Orleans for operations against the enemy's gunboats. Beauregard was sent to command and direct the troops and defences on the river above Memphis— and in the adjacent country.

I am the object of such special malignity that the neighborhood would suffer because of my residence there if the enemy should get so far down the river. Your property would be the next to my own an attraction to the plunderers It therefore seems to me that it might be well to send away as far as possible all which is mine, to send away, *even* up the Big Black, your cotton and valuables, and be ready to move your negroes and part of the stock, should a descent be made. O! how I wish to be with you, and fervently do I pray that you were in some place of absolute safety, with your family and mine. All I have, except my wife and children, I am ready to sacrifice for my country. We have very imperfect intelligence of the disaster at Fort Donelson.* I cannot believe that our army surrendered without an effort to cut the invest-

* Major Confederate defeat on February 16, 1862.

ing lines and retreat to the main body of the army. General Johnston's messenger has not reached me; in the meantime I am making every effort to assemble a sufficient force to beat the enemy in Tennessee, and retrieve our waning fortunes in the West.[*]

With love to sister Eliza and the children, and a solemn appeal to you to take counsel of your prudence rather than your courage, I am ever, affectionately,

YOUR BROTHER.

Inaugural Address as Elected President (JDC)[†]

RICHMOND, VIRGINIA, FEBRUARY 22, 1862

Fellow-Citizens: On this the birthday of the man most identified with the establishment of American independence, and beneath the monument erected to commemorate his heroic virtues and those of his compatriots, we have assembled to usher into existence the Permanent Government of the Confederate States. Through this instrumentality, under the favor of Divine providence, we hope to perpetuate the principles of our revolutionary fathers. The day, the memory, and the purpose seem fitly associated.

It is with mingled feelings of humility and pride that I appear to take, in the presence of the people and before high Heaven, the oath prescribed as a qualification for the exalted station to which the unanimous voice of the people has called me. Deeply sensible of all that is implied by this manifestation of the people's confidence, I am yet more profoundly impressed by the vast responsibility of the office, and humbly feel my own unworthiness.

In return for their kindness I can offer assurances of the gratitude with which it is received; and can but pledge a zealous devotion of

[*] Albert Sidney Johnston, a full general in the Confederate army who commanded Department No. 2, which stretched from the western slope of the Appalachians across the Mississippi River, including the states west of the river. He would be killed at Shiloh on April 6, 1862.

[†] JD was inaugurated as provisional president in Montgomery, Alabama, on February 18, 1861. In November he was elected without opposition to the six-year term provided for in the Confederate Constitution. On February 22, 1862 (the birthday of George Washington and the reason for the choice of that day), he was inaugurated as the duly elected president.

every faculty to the service of those who have chosen me as their Chief Magistrate.

When a long course of class legislation, directed not to the general welfare, but to the aggrandizement of the Northern section of the Union, culminated in a warfare on the domestic institutions of the Southern States—when the dogmas of a sectional party, substituted for the provisions of the constitutional compact, threatened to destroy the sovereign rights of the States, six of those States, withdrawing from the Union, confederated together to exercise the right and perform the duty of instituting a Government which would better secure the liberties for the preservation of which that Union was established.

Whatever of hope some may have entertained that a returning sense of justice would remove the danger with which our rights were threatened, and render it possible to preserve the Union of the Constitution, must have been dispelled by the malignity and barbarity of the Northern States in the prosecution of the existing war. The confidence of the most hopeful among us must have been destroyed by the disregard they have recently exhibited for all the time-honored bulwarks of civil and religious liberty. Bastiles filled with prisoners, arrested without civil process or indictment duly found; the writ of *habeas corpus* suspended by Executive mandate; a State Legislature controlled by the imprisonment of members whose avowed principles suggested to the Federal Executive that there might be another added to the list of seceded States; elections held under threats of a military power; civil officers, peaceful citizens, and gentlewomen incarcerated for opinion's sake—proclaimed the incapacity of our late associates to administer a Government as free, liberal, and humane as that established for our common use.

For proof of the sincerity of our purpose to maintain our ancient institutions, we may point to the Constitution of the Confederacy and the laws enacted under it, as well as to the fact that through all the necessities of an unequal struggle there has been no act on our part to impair personal liberty or the freedom of speech, of thought, or of the press. The courts have been open, the judicial functions fully executed, and every right of the peaceful citizen maintained as securely as if a war of invasion had not disturbed the land.

The people of the States now confederated became convinced that the Government of the United States had fallen into the hands of a sectional majority, who would pervert that most sacred of all trusts to the destruction of the rights which it was pledged to protect. They believed that to remain longer in the Union would subject them to a continuance of a disparaging discrimination, submission to which would be inconsistent with their welfare, and intolerable to a proud people. They therefore determined to sever its bonds and establish a new Confederacy for themselves.

The experiment instituted by our revolutionary fathers, of a voluntary Union of sovereign States for purposes specified in a solemn compact, had been perverted by those who, feeling power and forgetting right, were determined to respect no law but their own will. The Government had ceased to answer the ends for which it was ordained and established. To save ourselves from a revolution which, in its silent but rapid progress, was about to place us under the despotism of numbers, and to preserve in spirit, as well as in form, a system of government we believed to be peculiarly fitted to our condition, and full of promise for mankind, we determined to make a new association, composed of States homogeneous in interest, in policy, and in feeling.

True to our traditions of peace and our love of justice, we sent commissioners to the United States to propose a fair and amicable settlement of all questions of public debt or property which might be in dispute. But the Government at Washington, denying our right to self-government, refused even to listen to any proposals for a peaceful separation. Nothing was then left to do but to prepare for war.

The first year in our history has been the most eventful in the annals of this continent. A new Government has been established, and its machinery put in operation over an area exceeding seven hundred thousand square miles. The great principles upon which we have been willing to hazard everything that is dear to man have made conquests for us which could never have been achieved by the sword. Our Confederacy has grown from six to thirteen States; and Maryland, already united to us by hallowed memories and material interests, will, I believe, when able to speak with unstifled voice, connect her destiny with the South. Our people have rallied with unexampled unanimity to the support of the great principles of constitutional government, with firm resolve to perpetuate by arms the right which they could not peacefully secure. A million of men, it is estimated, are now standing in hostile array, and waging war along a frontier of thousands of miles. Battles have been fought, sieges have been conducted, and, although the contest is not ended, and the tide for the moment is against us, the final result in our favor is not doubtful.

The period is near at hand when our foes must sink under the immense load of debt which they have incurred, a debt which in their effort to subjugate us has already attained such fearful dimensions as will subject them to burdens which must continue to oppress them for generations to come.

We too have had our trials and difficulties. That we are to escape them in future is not to be hoped. It was to be expected when we entered upon this war that it would expose our people to sacrifices and cost them much, both of money and blood. But we knew the value of the object for which we struggled, and understood the nature of the war in which we were engaged. Nothing could be so bad as failure, and any sacrifice would be cheap as the price of success in such a contest.

But the picture has its lights as well as its shadows. This great strife has awakened in the people the highest emotions and qualities of the human soul. It is cultivating feelings of patriotism, virtue, and courage. Instances of self-sacrifice and of generous devotion to the noble cause for which we are contending are rife throughout the land. Never has a people evinced a more determined spirit than that now animating men, women, and children in every part of our country. Upon the first call the men flew to arms, and wives and mothers send their husbands and sons to battle without a murmur of regret.

It was, perhaps, in the ordination of Providence that we were to be taught the value of our liberties by the price which we pay for them.

The recollections of this great contest, with all its common traditions of glory, of sacrifice and blood, will be the bond of harmony and enduring affection amongst the people, producing unity in policy, fraternity in sentiment, and just effort in war.

Nor have the material sacrifices of the past year been made without some corresponding benefits. If the acquiescence of foreign nations in a pretended blockade has deprived us of our commerce with them, it is fast making us a self-supporting and an independent people. The blockade, if effectual and permanent, could only serve to divert our industry from the production of articles for export and employ it in supplying the commodities for domestic use.

It is a satisfaction that we have maintained the war by our unaided exertions. We have neither asked nor received assistance from any quarter. Yet the interest involved is not wholly our own. The world at large is concerned in opening our markets to its commerce. When the independence of the Confederate States is recognized by the nations of the earth, and we are free to follow our interests and inclinations by cultivating foreign trade, the Southern States will offer to manufacturing nations the most favorable markets which ever invited their commerce. Cotton, sugar, rice, tobacco, provisions, timber, and naval stores will furnish attractive exchanges. Nor would the constancy of these supplies be likely to be disturbed by war. Our confederate strength will be too great to tempt aggression; and never was there a people whose interests and principles committed them so fully to a peaceful policy as those of the Confederate States. By the character of their productions they are too deeply interested in foreign commerce wantonly to disturb it. War of conquest they cannot wage, because the Constitution of their Confederacy admits of no coerced association. Civil war there cannot be between States held together by their volition only. The rule of voluntary association, which cannot fail to be conservative, by securing just and impartial government at home, does not diminish the security of the obligations by which the Confederate States may be bound to foreign nations. In proof of this, it is to be remembered that, at the first moment of asserting their right to secession, these States proposed a settlement on the basis of the common liability for the obligations of the General Government.

Fellow-citizens, after the struggle of ages had consecrated the right of the Englishman to constitutional representative government, our colonial ancestors were forced to vindicate that birthright by an appeal to arms. Success crowned their efforts, and they provided for their posterity a peaceful remedy against future aggression.

The tyranny of an unbridled majority, the most odious and least responsible form of despotism, has denied us both the right and the remedy. Therefore we are in arms to renew such sacrifices as our fathers made to the holy cause of constitutional liberty. At the darkest hour of our struggle the Provisional gives place to the Permanent Government. After a series of successes and victories, which covered our arms with glory, we have recently met with serious disasters. But in the heart of a people resolved to be free these disasters tend but to stimulate to increased resistance.

To show ourselves worthy of the inheritance bequeathed to us by the patriots of the Revolution, we must emulate that heroic devotion which made reverse to them but the crucible in which their patriotism was refined.

With confidence in the wisdom and virtue of those who will share with me the responsibility and aid me in the conduct of public affairs; securely relying on the patriotism and courage of the people, of which the present war has furnished so many examples, I deeply feel the weight of the responsibilities I now, with unaffected diffidence, am about to assume; and, fully realizing the inequality of human power to guide and to sustain, my hope is reverently fixed on Him whose favor is ever vouchsafed to the cause which is just. With humble gratitude and adoration, acknowledging the Providence which has so visibly protected the Confederacy during its brief but eventful career, to thee, O God, I trustingly commit myself, and prayerfully invoke thy blessing on my country and its cause.

To General Albert Sidney Johnston (PJD)

RICHMOND, VIRGINIA, MARCH 12, 1862

MY DEAR GENERAL:

The departure of Capt Wickliffe offers an opportunity of which I avail myself to write you an unofficial letter. We have suffered great anxiety because of recent events in Ky & Tenn.; and I have been not a little disturbed by the repetitions of reflections upon yourself. I expected you to have made a full report of events precedent and consequent to the fall of Fort Donelson. In the mean time, I made for you such defense as friendship prompted, and many years of acquaintance justified; but I needed facts to rebut the wholesale assertions made against you to cover others, and to condemn my administration. The public, as you are aware, have no correct measure for military operations; and the journals are very reckless in their statements.

Your force has been magnified, and the movements of an army have been measured by the capacity for locomotion of an individual.

The readiness of the people, among whom you are operating, to aid you in every method has been constantly asserted; the purpose of your army at Bowling Green wholy misunderstood; and the absence of an effective force at Nashville, ignored. You have been held responsible for the fall of Donelson, and the capture of Nashville. T'is charged that no effort was made to save the stores at Nashville, and that the panic of the people was caused by the army.

Such representations, with the sad forebodings naturally belonging to them, have been painful to me, and injurious to us both; but worse than this, they have undermined public confidence, and damaged our cause. A full development of the truth is necessary for future success.

I respect the generosity which has kept you silent, but would impress upon you that the question is not personal, but public in its nature. That you and I might be content to suffer, but neither of us can willingly permit detriment to the country. As soon as circumstances will permit, it is my purpose to visit the field of your present operations: not that I should expect to give you any aid in the discharge of your duties as a commander, but with the hope that my position would enable me to effect something in bringing men to your standard. With a sufficient force, the audacity which the enemy exhibits would no doubt give you the opportunity to cut some of his lines of communication, to break up his plan of campaign; and defeating some of his columns, to drive him from the soil, as well as of Tenn. as of Ky. We are deficient in arms, wanting in discipline, and inferior in numbers.

Private arms must supply the first want; time and the presence of an enemy, with diligence on the part of commanders, will remove the second; and public confidence will overcome the third. Genl. Bragg brings you disciplined troops, and you will find in him the highest administrative capacity. Genl. E. K. Smith will soon have in East Tenn. a sufficient force to create a strong diversion in your favor; or if his strength can not be made available in that way, you will best know how to employ it otherwise.[*] I suppose the Tenn. or Miss. rivers will be the object of the enemy's next campaign, and I trust you will be able to concentrate a force which will defeat either attempt. The fleet which you will soon have on the Miss. river, if the enemy's gun boats ascend the Tenn., may enable you to strike an effective blow at Cairo; but to one so well informed and vigilant, I will not assume to offer suggestions, as to when and how the ends you seek, may be attained. With the confidence and regard of many years, I am very truly your friend.

JEFF'N,, DAVIS

To W. M. Brooks (PJD)[†]

RICHMOND, VIRGINIA, MARCH 15, 1862

MY DEAR SIR:

If under other circumstances I might be unwilling to hear criticism of /[my]/ acts, the condition of the country now too fully engrosses all my thoughts and feelings to permit such selfish impatience, and I have read yours of the 25th ult., anxious to gather from it information, and thankful for your friendly remembrance and the confidence your frankness evinces. I acknowledge the error of my attempt to defend all of ~~my~~ /the/ frontier, sea board and inland; but will say in justification that if we had received the arms and munitions which we had good reason to expect, ~~that~~ the attempt would have been successful and the battlefields would have been on the enemy's soil. You seem to have fallen into the not uncommon mistake of supposing that I have chosen to carry on the war upon a "purely defensive" system. The advantage of selecting the time and place of attack was too apparent to have been overlooked, but the means might have been wanting. Without military stores, without the workshops to create them, without the power to import them, necessity not choice has compelled us to occupy strong positions and everywhere to confront the enemy without reserves.

[*] Edmund Kirby Smith, who became a full general.

[†] Alabama lawyer, jurist, and secessionist.

The country has supposed our armies more numerous than they were and our munitions of war more extensive than they have been. I have borne reproach in silence because to reply by an exact statement of facts would have exposed our weakness to the enemy. History, when the case is fully understood, will do justice to the men who have most suffered from hasty judgment and unjust censure. Military critics will not say to me as you do "your experiment is a failure," but rather wonder at the disproportion between the means and the results. You inform me that "the highest and most reputable authors" say that I "have not held a cabinet council for more than four months." I read your letter to a member and exmember of my cabinet to day; they were surprised at the extrav/ag/ance of the falsehood, and did not believe that so much as a week had at any time occurred without a cabinet consultation. I would like to know who the authors of such stories are. Your own estimate of me, I hope, assured you that I would not, as stated, treat the "Secretary of War" as a "mere clerk"; and if you know Mr. Benjamin you must realize the impossibility of his submitting to degradation at the hands of anyone. The opposition here complain that I cling too closely to my cabinet, not, as in your section, that they are disregarded; and the only contempt of the sentiments of Congress which is here alleged against me (so far as I have heard) is that their wish for the removal of two or more members of the cabinet has not been yielded to. Perhaps there might be added dissatisfaction on the part of a few at the promotion or appointment of military officers without consulting the members of Congress in relation to them. Against the unfounded story that I keep the Generals of the army in leading strings may be set the frequent complaint that I do not arraign them for what is regarded their failures or misdeeds, and do not respond to the popular clamor by displacing commanders upon irresponsible statements. You cite the cases of Genls. Johnston and Beauregard; but you have the story *nomine mutata;* and though Genl. Johnston was offended because of his relative rank, he certainly never thought of resigning, and Genl. Beauregard, in a portion of his report which I understand the Congress refused to publish, made a statement for

---

* *Nomine mutata:* with the name changed.

which I asked his authority, but it is surely a slander on him to say that he ever considered himself insulted by me. The grossest ignorance of the law and the facts can alone excuse the statement as to the ill-treatment of Genl. Price by me.* His letters do not permit me to believe that he is a party to any such complaint. If, as you inform me, it is "credibly said" that "I have scarcely a friend and not a defender in Congress or in the Army," yet for the sake of our country and its cause I must hope it is falsely so said, as otherwise our fate must be confided to a multitude of hypocrites. It would be easy to justify the appointments which have been made of Brig. Genls. by stating the reasons in each case, but suffice it to say that I have endeavored to avoid bad selections by relying on military, rather than political recommendations; and upon the evidence of service where the case was one of promotion. It is easy to say that men are proscribed because of their political party. Look for yourself and judge by the men filling the offices whether I have applied party tests. When everything is at stake and the united power of the South alone can save us, it is sad to know that men can deal in such paltry complaints and tax their ingenuity to slander because they are offended in not getting office. I will not follow the example set me and ascribe to them bad motives, but deem it proper to say that the effect of such assaults, so far as they succeed in destroying the confidence of the people in the administration of their Government, must be to diminish our chances of triumph over the enemy, and practically do us more harm than if twice the number of men I can suppose to be engaged in such work were to desert to the standard of Lincoln. You are no doubt correct in your view of the propriety of keeping volunteers in the field, but you will not fail to perceive that, when a small force is opposed to a large one, the alternative is to retreat or fortify some strong position, /and/ as did Genl. Jackson at New Orleans,† thus compensate for the want of numbers. But the strength of an army is not merely dependent on numbers; another element is discipline and instruction. The first duty now is to increase our forces by raising troops for the war, and bringing out

* Confederate major general Sterling Price, former governor of Missouri.

† Andrew Jackson, who was victorious over the British at the Battle of New Orleans, January 8, 1815.

all the private arms of the country for the public defence. If we can achieve our independence, the office-seekers are welcome to the one I hold, and for which possession has brought no additional value to me than that set upon it when, before going to Montgomery, I announced my preference for the commission of a General in the army. Accept my thanks for the kindness which you have manifested in defending me when so closely surrounded by evil reports. Without knowing what are the many things you have supposed me to have done, and which were disapproved, I venture to say, if the supposition was based upon the statements of these "reputable authors" before noticed, that I was more worthy of your defense than you believed when making it. Very respectfully, your friend

(SIGNED) JEFFN. DAVIS.

To General Albert Sidney Johnston (PJD)

RICHMOND, VIRGINIA, MARCH 26, 1862

MY DEAR GENL.

Your's of the 18th Inst. was this day delivered to me by your Aid Mr. Jack, I have read it with much satisfaction. So far as the past is concerned it but confirms the conclusions at which I had already arrived. My confidence in you has never wavered and I hope the public will soon give me credit for judgement rather than continue to arraign me for obstinacy.

You have done wonderfully well and now I breathe easier in the assurance that you will be able to make a junction of your two armies. If you can meet the division of the Enemy moving from the Tenn. before it can make a junction with that advancing from Nashville the future will be brighter if this cannot be done our only hope is that the people of the South West will rally en masse with their private arms and thus enable you to oppose the vast army which will threaten the destruction of our country.

I have hoped to be able to leave here for a short time and would be much /gratified/ to confer with you and share your responsibilities. I might aid you in obtaining troops, no one could hope to do more unless he underated your military capacity. I write in great haste and feel that it would be worse than useless to point out to you how much depends upon you.

May God bless you is the sincere prayer of your friend

JEFFN,, DAVIS

P.S. I send you a Dictionary of which I have the duplicate so that you may communicate with me by cypher telegraphic or written, as follows, First give the page by it's number, second the column by the letter L. M. or R. as it may be in the left hand middle or right hand column, third the number of the word in the column counting from the top.

Thus the word *junction* would be designated by *146.L.208—*

J,D,

To Varina Davis (PJD)

RICHMOND, VIRGINIA, MAY 16, 1862

DEAR WINNIE,

I returned this evening from a long ride through rain & mud, having gone down the James River to see the works and obstructions on which we rely to stop the gun boats. The attack of yesterday has given an impulse to the public and our working parties have been increased so much that a few days will now enable us to effect more than has been done in weeks past. I reached the Fort yesterday /arrived after the firing had ceased/ and found the garrison quite elate at their success and each one prompt to tell that the gun boats were clear gone.

David was under fire and is eloquent in relation to the nervousness of the raw troops, he and the marines being the veterans. Willie Farish has come up but has not told me yet the object of his visit.*

Becca called day before yesterday to take leave but Genl. Jones has been here since and the programme is changed to delay for further developments.

The panic here has subsided and with increasing confidence there

---

* David Bradford, Jr., JD's nephew; Farish was JD's grandnephew.

has arisen a desire to see the city destroyed rather than surrendered. "They lightly talk of scars who never felt a wound" and these talkers have little idea of what scenes would follow the battering of rows of brick houses. I have told them that the enemy might be beaten before Richmond or on either flank and we would try to do it, but that I could allow the army to be penned up in a city. The Boats we ought and I hope are able to stop, their army when reduced to small arms and field pieces I think we can defeat, and then a vigorous pursuit will bring results long wished for but not given to the wind.

I did read Billy's letter and saw that it was idle to argue with him, his course has been chosen and you cannot prove any other to be possible. It is to be regretted but not avoided. He did not reply to my telegram wherefore I conclude a leave of absence would not satisfy him.

We must learn to measure our words with a caution proportionate to the value others place on them, and when you do not feel inclined to walk to state the fact without pleading depression of spirits may serve the quid nunc worse but yourself better. Be of good cheer and continue to hope that God will in due time deliver us from the hands of our enemies and "sanctify to us our deepest distress." As the clouds grow darker and when one after another those who were trusted are detected in secret hostility, I feel like mustering claws were in me, and that cramping fetters had fallen from my limbs. The great temporal object is to secure our independence and they who engage in strife for personal or party aggrandisement deserve contemptous forgetfulness. To me who have no political wish beyond the success of our cause, no personal desire but to be relieved from further connection with office, opposition in any form can only disturb me in so much as it may endanger the public welfare.

It grieves me to hear that Billy is not so well, with the change of his milk a temporary derangement was to be apprehended but it seems to have gone beyond that. Can there be any local cause? Mr. Edwards is a pure and noble old gentleman, to whom I am glad Jeff. has made himself agreeable, even though for no higher motive than the love of cakes. Maggie is a wise child, I wish I could learn just to let people alone who snap at me, in forbearance and charity to turn away as well from the cats as the snakes. Dear little Joey may well attract admiration, and the people who think him like me must have formed complimentary idea of my appearance.*

I miss them as much as when they first went away and you can more than myself desire that our separation were at an end. Kiss them all for me, and tell them Father prays for his children, that God may make them good, loving to each other, and mindful and affectionate to their Mother.

Our church was not fully attended to day, the families have to a great extent left town and the excitement no doubt kept away many men. Mr. Minnegerode was sick, Bishop Johns preached extemporaneously and his address was fervent and appropriate.† I thought him more eloquent than on any former occasion. The resemblance to Mr. Clay in manner is probably accidental.

Give my love to Helen & Lucy. Tell Dr. Gwin not to believe more than half the rumors of good and none of those which are evil.‡

We are getting on in house hold affairs pretty well Mr. Eggeling is very attentive and seemingly efficient.§

Good night dear Wife may every consolation be your's until it shall be our fortune again to be united. Ever affectionately remembered when waking sleep brings you to me in such reality that it would be happier to sleep on.

To Varina Davis (JDC)

RICHMOND, VIRGINIA, MAY 28, 1862

… We are steadily developing for a great battle, and under God's favor I trust for a decisive victory. The enemy are preparing to concentrate in advance by regular approaches; we must attack him in motion, and

---

* JD and Varina's children: William (Billy), Jefferson (Jeff), Margaret (Maggie), and Joseph (Joey).

† The Reverend Charles Minnigerode, rector of St. Paul's Episcopal Church in Richmond and JD's minister; the Reverend John Johns, Episcopal bishop of Virginia.

‡ Helen Davis Keary, JD's niece; family friends Lucy Gwin and her father, William Gwin.

§ Edward G. Eggeling, an employee at the Confederate Executive Mansion.

trust to the valor of our troops for success. It saddens me to feel how many a mother, wife, and child will be made to grieve in bitterness, but what is there worse than submission to such brutal tyranny as now holds sway over New Orleans. . . .

Seeing no preparation to keep the enemy at a distance, and kept in ignorance of any plan for such purpose, I sent for General R. E. Lee, then at Richmond, in general charge of army operations, and told him why and how I was dissatisfied with the condition of affairs.*

He asked me what I thought it was proper to do. Recurring to a conversation held about the time we had together visited General Johnston, I answered that McClellan should be attacked on the other side of the Chickahominy before he matured his preparations for a siege of Richmond.† To this he promptly assented, as I anticipated he would, for I knew it had been his own opinion. He then said: "General Johnston should of course advise you of what he expects or proposes to do. Let me go and see him, and defer this discussion until I return."

. . . When General Lee came back, he told me that General Johnston proposed, on the next Thursday, to move against the enemy as follows: General A. P. Hill was to move down on the right flank and rear of the enemy. General G. W. Smith, as soon as Hill's guns opened, was to cross the Chickahominy at the Meadow Bridge, attack the enemy in flank, and by the conjunction of the two it was expected to double him up. Then Longstreet was to come on the Mechanicsville Bridge and attack him in front. From this plan the best results were hoped by both of us.

On the morning of the day proposed, I hastily despatched my office business and rode out toward the Meadow Bridge to see the action commence. On the road I found Smith's division halted and the men dispersed in the woods. Looking for someone from whom I could get information, I finally saw General Hood, and asked him the meaning of what I saw. He told me he did not know anything more than that they had been halted. I asked him where General Smith was; he said

---

* Lee was a full general and JD's military adviser. Four days later he was appointed commander of the Army of Northern Virginia.

† Major General George B. McClellan, Union commander.

he believed he had gone to a farm-house in the rear, adding that he thought he was ill.

Riding on the bluff which overlooks the Meadow Bridge, I asked Colonel Anderson, posted there in observation, whether he had seen anything of the enemy in his front. He said that he had seen only two mounted men across the bridge, and a small party of infantry on the other side of the river, some distance below, both of whom, he said, he could show me if I would go with him into the garden back of the house. There, by the use of a powerful glass, were distinctly visible two cavalry videttes at the further end of the bridge, and a squad of infantry lower down the river, who had covered themselves with a screen of green boughs. The Colonel informed me that he had not heard Hill's guns; it was, therefore, supposed he had not advanced. I then rode down the bank of the river, followed by a cavalcade of sight-seers, who I supposed had been attracted by the expectation of a battle. The little squad of infantry, about fifteen in number, as we approached, fled over the bridge, and were lost to sight.

Near to the Mechanicsville Bridge I found General Howell Cobb, commanding the support of a battery of artillery. He pointed out to me on the opposite side of the river the only enemy he had seen, and which was evidently a light battery. Riding on to the main road which led to the Mechanicsville Bridge, I found General Longstreet, walking to and fro in an impatient, it might be said fretful, manner. Before speaking to him, he said his division had been under arms all day waiting for orders to advance, and that the day was now so far spent that he did not know what was the matter. I afterward learned from General Smith that he had received information from a citizen that the "Beaver-dam Creek presented an impassable barrier, and that he had thus fortunately been saved from a disaster." Thus ended the offensive-defensive programme from which Lee expected much, and of which I was hopeful.

To Governor Joseph E. Brown (JDC)[*]

RICHMOND, VIRGINIA, MAY 29, 1862

DEAR SIR:

I received your letter of the 8th inst., in due course, but the importance of the subject embraced in it required careful consideration, and this, together with other pressing duties, has caused delay in my reply.

The constitutional question discussed by you in relation to the conscription law had been duly weighed before I recommended to Congress the passage of such a law; it was fully debated in both Houses; and your letter has not only been submitted to my Cabinet, but a written opinion has been required from the Attorney General.

The constitutionality of the law was sustained by very large majorities of both Houses. This decision of the Congress meets the concurrence not only of my own judgment, but of every member of my Cabinet, and a copy of the opinion of the Attorney General herewith enclosed develops the reasons on which his conclusions are based.

I propose, however, from my high respect for yourself and for other eminent citizens who entertain opinions similar to yours, to set forth somewhat at length my own views on the power of the Confederate Government over its own armies and the militia, and will endeavour not to leave without answer any of the positions maintained in your letter.

The main, if not the only purpose for which independent States form unions or Confederations, is to combine the power of the several members in such manner as to form one united force in all relations with foreign powers, whether in peace or in war.

Each State, amply competent to administer and control its own domestic government, yet too feeble successfully to resist powerful nations, seeks safety by uniting with other States in like condition, and by delegating to some common agent the combined strength of all, in order to secure advantageous commercial relations in peace, and to carry on hostilities with effect in war.

Now the powers delegated by the several States to the Confederate

[*] Governor of Georgia.

Government, which is their common agent, are enumerated in the 8th Section of the Constitution; each power being distinct, specific, and enumerated in paragraphs separately numbered. The only exception is the 18th paragraph which by its own terms is made dependent on those previously enumerated, as follows,—"18. to make all laws which shall be necessary and proper for carrying into execution the forego- ing powers &c."

Now the *war powers* granted to the Congress are conferred in the following paragraphs: No.1 gives authority to raise

"revenue necessary to pay the debts, provide for *the common defence* and carry on the government &c."

No. 11—"to declare war, grant letters of marque and reprisal and make rules concerning captures on land and water."

No. 12—"to raise and support armies, but no appropriation of money to that use shall be for a longer term than two years."

No. 13—"to *provide and maintain a navy.*"

No. 14—"to make rules for the government and regulation of *the land and naval forces.*"

It is impossible to imagine a more broad, ample and unqualified delegation of the whole war power of each State than is here con- tained, with the solitary limitation of the appropriations to two years. The States not only gave power to raise money for the common de- fence, to declare war, to raise and support armies (in the plural), to provide and maintain a navy, to govern and regulate both land and naval forces, but they went further and covenanted by the 3d para- graph of the 10th Section not "to engage in war, unless actually in- vaded or in such imminent danger as will not admit of delay."

I know of but two modes of raising armies within the Confederate States, viz.: voluntary enlistment and draft or conscription. I perceive in the delegation of power to raise armies no restriction as to the mode of procuring troops. I see nothing which confines Congress to one class of men, nor any greater power to receive volunteers than conscripts into its service. I see no limitation by which enlistments are to be received of individuals only, but not of companies or battalions, or squadrons or regiments. I find no limitation of time of service, but only of duration of appropriation. I discover nothing to confine Congress to waging war within the limits of the Confederacy nor to prohibit offensive war. In a word, when Congress desires to raise an army and passes a law for that purpose, the solitary question is under the 18th paragraph, viz.: "Is the law one that is necessary and proper to execute the power to raise armies"?

On this point you say,—

"But did the necessity exist in this case? The conscription Act cannot aid the Government in increasing its supply of *arms* or *provisions*, but can only enable it to call a larger number of men into the field. The difficulty has never been to get *men*. The States have already furnished the Government more than it can arm."

I would have very little difficulty in establishing to your entire satisfaction that the passage of the law was not only necessary, but that it was absolutely indispensable; that numerous regiments of twelve months' men were on the eve of being disbanded, whose places could not be supplied by raw levies in the face of superior numbers of the foe, without entailing the most disastrous results; that the position of our armies was so critical as to fill the bosom of every patriot with the liveliest apprehension; and that the provisions of the law were effective in warding off a pressing danger.—But I prefer to answer your objection on other and broader grounds.

I hold that when a specific power is granted by the Constitution, like that, now in question "to raise armies," Congress is the judge whether the law passed for the purpose of executing that power is "necessary and proper." It is not enough to say that armies might be raised in other ways, and that therefore this particular way is not "necessary." The same argument might be used against *every* mode of raising armies. To each successive mode suggested, the objection would be that other modes were practicable, and that therefore, the particular mode used was not "necessary." The true and only test is to enquire whether the law is intended and calculated to carry out the object; whether it devises and creates an instrumentality for executing the specific power granted; and, if the answer be in the affirmative, the law is constitutional. None can doubt that the Conscription law is calculated and intended to "raise armies"; it is therefore "necessary and proper" for the execution of that power and is constitutional, unless it comes in conflict with some other provision of our Confederate compact.

You express the opinion that this conflict exists, and support your argument by the citation of those clauses which refer to the Militia. There are certain provisions not cited by you, which are not without influence on my judgment, and to which I call your attention. They will aid in defining what is meant by "militia," and in determining the respective powers of the States and the Confederacy over them.

The several States agree "not to keep troops or ships of war in time of peace." Art. I. Sec. 10. Par. 3.

They further stipulate that, "a well regulated militia being necessary to the security of a free State, the right of the people to keep and bear arms shall not be infringed." (Sec. 9. Par. 13).

That "no person shall be held to answer for a capital or otherwise infamous crime unless on a presentment or indictment of a grand jury, except in cases arising in the *land or naval forces,* or in *the militia* when in actual service in time of war or public danger" &c. Sec. 9. Par. 16. . . .

What then are militia? They can only be created by law. The arms-bearing inhabitants of a State are liable to become its militia if the law so order, but in the absence of a law to that effect, the men of a State capable of bearing arms are no more militia than they are seamen.

The Constitution also tells us that militia are not *troops,* nor are they any part of the *land or naval forces;* for militia exist in time of peace, and the Constitution forbids the States to keep troops in time of peace, and they are expressly distinguished and placed in a separate category from land or naval forces in the 16th paragraph above quoted; and the words *land and naval forces* are shown by paragraphs 12, 13 & 14 to mean the army and navy of the Confederate States.

Now, if militia are not the citizens taken singly, but a body created by law; if they are not troops,—if they are no part of the army and navy of the Confederacy, we are led directly to the definition quoted by the Attorney General, that militia are "a body of soldiers in a State enrolled for discipline." In other words, the term "militia" is a collective term meaning a body of men organized and cannot be applied to the separate individuals who compose the organization.

The Constitution divides the whole military strength of the States into only two classes of organized bodies; one the armies of the Confederacy, the other the militia of the States.

In the delegation of power to the Confederacy, after exhausting the subject of declaring war, raising and supporting armies, and providing a navy, in relation to all which the grant of authority to Congress is *exclusive,* the Constitution proceeds to deal with the other organized body, the militia, and instead of delegating power to Congress alone or reserving it to the States alone, the power is divided as follows, viz.: Congress is to have power,—"To provide for calling forth the militia to execute the laws of the Confederate States, suppress insurrections, and *repel invasions.* (Sec. 8. Par. 15)

"To provide for organizing, arming, and disciplining the militia, and for governing such part of them as may be employed in the service of the Confederate States; *reserving to the States respectively the appointment of the officers and the authority of training the militia* according to the discipline prescribed by Congress." (Par. 16)

Congress then has the power to provide for organizing the arms-bearing people of the States into militia; each *State* has the power to *officer* and *train* them when organized.

Congress may call forth the militia to execute Confederate laws; the *State* has not surrendered the power to call them forth to execute *State* laws.

Congress may call them forth to repel invasion; so may the State, for the power is impliedly reserved of governing all the militia, except the part in actual service of the Confederacy.

I confess myself at a loss to perceive in what manner these careful and well defined provisions of the Constitution, regulating the organization and government of the militia, can be understood as applying in the remotest degree to the armies of the Confederacy, nor can I conceive how the grant of *exclusive* power to declare and carry on war by armies raised and supported by the Confederacy is to be restricted or diminished by the clauses which grant a *divided* power over the militia. On the contrary, the delegation of authority over the militia, so far as granted, appears to me to be plainly an *additional* enumerated power, intended to strengthen the hands of the Confederate Government in the discharge of its paramount duty,—the common defence of the States.

You state after quoting the 12th, 15th, and 16th grants of power to Congress, that

"These grants of power all relate to the same subject matter and are all contained in the same section of the Constitution, and by a well known rule of construction must be taken as a whole and construed together."

This argument appears to me unsound. *All* the powers of Congress are enumerated in one section, and the three paragraphs quoted can no more control each other by reason of their location in the same section, than they can control any of the other paragraphs preceding, intervening, or succeeding. So far as the subject-matter is concerned, I have already endeavored to show that the armies mentioned in the 12th paragraph are a subject-matter as distinct from the militia mentioned in the 15th and 16th, as they from the navy mentioned in the 13th. Nothing can so mislead as to construe together and as a whole the carefully separated clauses which define the different powers to be exercised over distinct subjects by the Congress.

But you add that,

"by the grant of power to Congress to raise and support armies without qualification, the framer of the Constitution intended the regular armies of the Confederacy, and not armies composed of the whole militia of all the States."

I must confess myself somewhat at a loss to understand this position. If I am right that the militia is a *body* of enrolled State soldiers, it is not possible in the nature of things that armies raised by the Confederacy can "be composed of the whole militia of all the States." The militia may be called forth in whole or in part into the Confederate service, but do not thereby become part of the "armies raised" by Congress. They remain militia, and go home when the emergency which provoked their call has ceased. Armies raised by Congress are of course raised out of the *same population* as the militia organized by the States, and to deny to Congress the power to draft a citizen into the army or to receive his voluntary offer of services because he is a member of the State militia, is to deny the power to raise an army at all, for practically all men fit for service in the army may be embraced in the militia organization of the several States. You seem, however, to suggest rather than directly to assert that the conscript law may be unconstitutional, because it comprehends all arms-bearing men between 18 and 35 years; at least this is an inference which I draw from your expression, "armies composed of the *whole* militia of *all* the States." But it is obvious that if Congress have power to draft into the armies raised by it any citizens at all, (without regard to the fact whether they are, or not, members of militia organizations,) the power must be co-extensive with the exigencies of the occasion or it becomes illusory; and the extent of the exigency must be determined by Congress; for the Constitution has left the power without any other check or restriction than the Executive veto. Under ordinary circumstances the power thus delegated to Congress is scarcely felt by the States. At the present moment, when our very existence is threatened by armies vastly superior in numbers to ours, the necessity for defence has induced a call, not "for the whole military of all the States," not for any militia, but for men to compose *armies* for the Confederate States.

Surely there is no mystery in this subject. During our whole past history, as well as during our recent one year's experience as a new Confederacy, the militia "have been called forth to repel invasion" in numerous instances, and they never came, otherwise than as bodies organized by the States, with their company, field and *general officers;* and when the emergency had passed they went home again. I cannot perceive how any one can interpret the conscription law as taking away from the States the power to appoint officers to their militia. You observe on this point in your letter that, unless your construction is adopted,

"the very object of the States in reserving the power of appointing the officers is defeated, and that portion of the Constitution is not only a nullity, but the whole military power of the States and the entire control of the militia, with the appointment of the officers, is vested in the Confederate Government, whenever it chooses to call its own action 'raising an army' and not 'calling forth the militia.'"

I can only say, in reply to this, that the power of Congress depends on the real nature of the act it proposes to perform, not on the name given to it; and I have endeavored to show that its action is really that of "raising an army," and bears no resemblance to calling forth the militia." I think I may safely venture the assertion that there is not one man out of a thousand of those who will do service under the Conscription Act, that will describe himself while in the Confederate service as being a militia man; and if I am right in this assumption, the popular understanding concurs entirely with my own deductions from the Constitution as to the meaning of the word "militia."

My answer has grown to such a length that I must confine myself to one more quotation from your letter. You proceed :

"Congress shall have power to *raise armies*. How shall it be done? The answer is clear. In conformity to the provision of the Constitution, which expressly provides that, when the militia of the States are called forth to *repel invasion* and employed in the service of the Confederate States, which is now the case, the State shall appoint the officers."

I beg you to observe that the answer, which you say is clear, is not an answer to the question put. The question is, How are armies to be raised? The answer given is, that, when militia are called upon to repel invasion, the State shall appoint the officers.

There seems to me to be a conclusive test on this whole subject. By our Constitution Congress may declare war, *offensive* as well as *defensive*. It may acquire territory. Now, suppose that, for good cause and to right unprovoked injuries, Congress should declare war against Mexico and invade Sonora. The militia could not be called forth in such a case, the right to call it being limited "to repel invasions." Is it not plain that the law now under discussion, if passed under such circumstances, could by no possibility be aught else than a law to "raise an army"? Can one and the same law be construed into a "calling forth the militia," if the war be defensive, and a "raising of armies," if the war be offensive?

At some future day, after our independence shall have been established, it is not improbable supposition that our present enemy may be tempted to abase his naval power by depredations on our commerce, and that we may be compelled to assert our rights by offensive war. How is it to be carried on? Of what is the army to be composed? If this Government cannot call on its arms-bearing population otherwise than as militia, and if the militia can only be called forth to repel invasion, we should be utterly helpless to vindicate our honor or protect our rights. War has been styled "the terrible litigation of nations." Have we so formed our Government that, in this litigation, we must never be plaintiffs? Surely this cannot have been the intention of the framers of our compact.

In no respect in which I can view this law can I find just reason to distrust the propriety of my action in approving and signing it, and the question presented involves consequences both immediate and remote too momentous to permit me to leave your objections unanswered.

In conclusion, I take great pleasure in recognizing that the history of the past year affords the amplest justification of your assertion that, if the question had been whether the conscription law was necessary in order to raise men in Georgia, the answer must have been in the negative. Your noble State has promptly responded to every call that it has been my duty to make on her; and to you personally, as her Executive, I acknowledge my indebtedness, for the prompt, cordial and effective co-operation you have afforded me in the effort to defend our common country against the common enemy.

> I AM VERY RESPECTFULLY,
> YR. OBT. SVT.
> (SIGNED) JEFFN. DAVIS.

To Varina Davis (PJD)

RICHMOND, VIRGINIA, JUNE 11, 1862

MY DEAR WIFE,

Col. Wheeler who you may recollect to have seen in Washington, after his return from Nicaragua, has offered to bear a letter to you, and I have but a few minutes in which to write it.

I am in usual health, though the weather has been very inclement. The roads to the different positions of the army could not be worse and remain passable. The long boots presented by Capt. Keary protect me from mud but the poor horse suffers on every ride. The Green Brier horse which was to be so gentle as to serve your purposes is a fretful rearing animal which it is troublesome for me to ride in the presence of troops. Kentucky is quite gentle compared to Green Brier. The Enemy is entrenching and bringing up heavy guns on the York river Rail Road, which not being useful to our army nor paid for by our Treasury was of course not destroyed.

His policy is to advance by regular approaches covered by successive lines of earthworks, that reviled policy of West Pointism and spades which is sure to succeed against those who do not employ like means to counteract it. Politicians, Newspapers, and uneducated officers have created such a prejudice in our army against labor that it will be difficult until taught by sad experience to induce our troops to work efficiently. The greatest Generals of ancient and modern times have won their renown by labor. Victories were the results. Cezar who revolutionized the the military system of his age, never slept in a camp without entrenching it. France Spain and Great Britain retain to this day memorials of Roman invasion in the Massive works constructed by the Roman armies. But my dear Winnie I did not intend to give you a military lecture or to trouble you with my embarassments. From the fullness of the heart the mouth speaketh.

I will endeavor by movements which are not without great hazard to countervail the Enemys policy. If we succeed in rendering his works useless to him and compel him to meet us on the field I have much confidence in our ability to give him a complete defeat, and then it may be possible to teach him the pains of invasion and to feed our army on his territory. The issues of campaigns can never be safely foretold it is for us to do all which can be done and trustingly to leave our fate to Him who rules the Universe.

We are reinforcing Genl. Jackson and hope to crown his successes with a complete victory over all the Enemy in the Valley of Va.*

Kiss my dear Children, tell them how much their Father loves, how constantly he longs to see them and prays that they may be good and happy.

Brother Joe has been to the Hurricane & Brierfield, he took Joe Mitchell with him I was much distressed when I heard he was going, the exposure at this season in an open boat was very hazardous.† It was from that cause my Father died, when though of many years, his constitution was sound as that of many men at the age of forty. This morning I received the following despatch—date Jackson June 10

"I have just returned from Hurricane brought twelve negroes from Brierfield & fifteen from Hurricane, the measles at Brierfield prevented my bringing more. All came without compulsion'

(SIGNED) J. E. DAVIS

Give my love to Cousin Helen. I have no intelligence of her Husband since that sent by telegram. I have drawn heavily on the time allowed but hope yet to get this off as proposed.

God bless you my dear Winnie and in restore you soon to the arms of your Husband.

To Varina Davis (PJD)

RICHMOND, VIRGINIA, JUNE 13, 1862

DEAREST WINNIE,

Your letter by Mr. Hilliard was received late last night. My heart, sunk within me at the news of the suffering of my angel baby. Your

---

* Thomas J. (Stonewall) Jackson, who became a lieutenant general in the Confederate army.
† Joseph Mitchell, Joseph Davis's grandson.

telegram of 12th gives assurance of the subsidence of disease. But the look of pain and exhaustion, the gentle complaint "I am tired" which has for so many years oppressed me, seems to have been revived; and unless God spares me another such trial, what is to become of me I do not know. Dr. Garnett will I hope reach you this evening. He carries with him what he regards as a specific remedy.

Oh my Wife how I long to be with you in this hour of our distress. My ease, my health, my property, my life I can give to the cause of my country. The heroism which could lay my Wife and children on any sacrificial altar is not mine. Spare us Good Lord.

I was out until late last night on the lines of the Army. The anticipated demonstration was not made and reconnaissance convinces me that the reported movement of the Enemy was unfounded. He keeps close under cover, is probably waiting for reinforcements or resolved to fight only behind his entrenchments. We must find if possible the means to get at him without putting the breasts of our men in antagonism to his heaps of earth.

Beauregard claims by telegram to have made a "brilliant and successful retreat" and pleads his constant occupation as the cause of his delay to reply to the inquiry made through the Adjt. Genl. as to reason for his retreat and the abandonment of the Memphis & Charleston R. Road. —There are those who can only walk a log when it is near to the ground, and I fear he has been placed too high for his mental strength, as he does not exhibit the ability manifested on smaller fields. The news from the Valley of Va. confirms the report of the flight of the Enemy, and the danger to our troops has been mainly passed. We have sent reinforcements who as fresh troops will move in front of the old command. Helen should be less anxious for the future. I wrote to Capt. Keary and expect to hear from him by the first courier who arrives.

Kiss my dear Children, tell them how much I miss them. I saw a little boy yesterday in the street he had his pants rolled up and was wading in a gutter, he looked something like Jeff. and when I persuaded to get out of the water, he raised his sunny face and laughed, but denied my conclusion. Mrs. Greenhow is here, she has her little daughter with her who inquired very affectionately for Maggie, and asked if there were any Yankees where she was. The Madam looks much changed and has the air of one whose nerves were shaken, by mental torture. Genl. Lee's wife has arrived, her servants left her and she found it uncomfortable to live without them.

The postage stamps were sent and have I hope reached you. Farewell my own dear old Wife, write to me fully of my little angel's condition, as well as of your own and the children's health.

Give my love to Helen. Take for yourself a boundless portion of affection from your Husband.

To Col. Wm. P. Johnston (JDC)*

RICHMOND, VIRGINIA, JUNE 14, 1862

GENERAL:

You are hereby directed to proceed to the Head Quarters of the Army commanded by Genl. Beauregard for the purpose of inspection and report. You will report to Genl. Beauregard in person, and hand to him this, your letter of authority as well as of instructions. You will ask of the General, to be communicated to me, the following interrogatories, and having received his reply, will have such conference with him as will enable you thoroughly to inform me as to the several points submitted:

1. I desire to know what were the circumstances and purposes of the retreat from the Charleston and Memphis R.R. to the position now occupied.

2. What is the plan of future operations? And whether an advance of the Army is contemplated and what prospect there is of the recovery of the Territory which has been yielded.

3. Why was it not deemed advisable to occupy the hills north and east of Corinth, and could not a stronger line than that around Corinth have been selected?

4. What was the cause of the sickness at Camp Corinth? Would it have been avoided by occupying the higher ground in front? Has it been avoided by retiring to the present position?

---

* William P. Johnston, one of JD's aides; son of General Albert Sidney Johnston.

5. Was it at no time practicable to cut the enemy's line of communication, so as to compel him to abandon the Tennessee River, or to permit us to occupy Nashville?

6. What means were employed, after the fall of Island 10, to prevent the descent of the Missi. River by the enemy's gunboats? What dispositions were made to defend Memphis, and what was the cause of failure to preserve that most important of our lines of communication?

7. What loss of troops, stores, or arms, occurred at the time of the retreat from Corinth?

RESPECTFULLY YOUR OBT. SVT.

(SIGNED) JEFFN. DAVIS

To Varina Davis (PJD)

RICHMOND, VIRGINIA, JULY 6, 1862

DEAR WIFE

yours of the 4th was delivered last night by Capt. Guthrie, and the enclosures were forthwith sent to Drs. Garnett & Gibson, each answered that he would attend to it. It was a sad blow to me to hear that my little angel was still unwell. Can it be that the milk has any peculiar quality? Have you tried substitutes? I hope a good wet nurse may soon be found, it is safer for one who is moving about. Were it possible for me to leave here I would go to see you and the children, my heart is sick of separation.

Your regret that we did not capture all the Yankees is quite common but very unreasonable, as they being more numerous and better appointed we could neither surround them nor close all the roads against them; but if we had caught them all what could we have done with them? Had all the orders been well and promptly executed there would have been a general dispersion and the remnant which might have been held together could only have reached the James River by first crossing the Chickahominy. Our success has been so remarkable that we should be grateful and believe that even our disappointments were ordered for our gain. McClellan certainly showed capacity in his retreat, but there is little cause to laud a General who is driven out of his entrenchments by a smaller and worse armed force than his own and compelled to abandon a campaign in the preparation for which he had spent many months and many millions of Dollars, and to seek safety by flying to other troops ~~after burning burnt~~ /for cover, burning/ his depots of provisions, and marking his route by scattered arms, ammunition and wagons. The reinforcements sent to him may advance, his army would never have fought us again if we had been left to an even handed settlement of the issue which he made & we joined

The timber for the completion of the Richmond was burned at Norfolk and the work on her has been thus greatly delayed, it is uncertain when she will be finished. The batteries on the river eight miles below here will stop the Gun boats and we must any land force which attempts to take them by attack from the land side.

Our troubles you perceive have not ended but our chances have improved so I repeat be of good cheer. Kiss my dear Children tell them each and all how much I love them Give my love to Helen her anxiety is readily imagined and I am glad she is now relieved

Farewell my dear Wife I would that I were with you in person as I am ever in spirit. May God shield you and restore us to each other soon is the constant prayer of your Husband.

To Col. J. F. Marshall (JDC)[*]

RICHMOND, VIRGINIA, JULY 11, 1862

MY DEAR COLONEL:

Accept my thanks for the very kind terms in which you expressed your congratulations for the recent success of the Confederate arms in the series of battles in which you bore so honorable a part. With sincere regret I learn that you are confined by disease, and very earnestly hope for your speedy restoration to health.

Your view as to our present policy coincides in its main features with my own. Indeed, such has been my purpose for many months,

---

[*] Confederate officer.

and I have silently borne criticism on the supposition that I was opposed to offensive war, because to correct the error would have required the disclosure of facts which the public interest demanded should not be revealed.

We are now endeavoring, with all possible despatch, to reform and recruit our scattered and shattered forces. Reinforcements are expected; recruits are supposed to be on the way from some of the States, and many who were slightly indisposed will probably soon return to duty.

Your figures show that you are not aware of the extent to which our force "present for duty" was reduced: if we could detach the number mentioned and leave a sufficient corps of observation to hold the enemy in check, you are no doubt right as to the effect of the movement. The General is fully alive to the advantage of the present opportunity, and will, I am sure, cordially sustain and boldly execute my wishes to the full extent of his power.*

VERY RESPECTFULLY & TRULY YOURS
(SIGNED) JEFFN. DAVIS

To John Forsyth (PJD)†

RICHMOND, VIRGINIA, JULY 18, 1862

MY DEAR SIR,

I have the pleasure to acknowledge yours of the 2d Inst. and so far from finding any thing to excuse, I have to offer you my thanks for the kind spirit and manifest confidence with which you communicate to me the unfavorable impressions you /have/ found to exist in relation to my policy for the conduct of our military operations.

There could be no difference of opinion as to the advantage of invading over being invaded, if we except that class of politicians who feared to excite the hate of our enemies, and the few others who clung to the /delusive/ hope of aid from our old party-allies at the North. My early declared purpose and continued hope was to feed upon the

---

* The general is Robert E. Lee.
† JD's friend in Mobile, Alabama.

enemy and teach them the blessings of peace by making them feel in its most tangible form the evils of war.

The time and place for invasion has been a question not of will but of power. There have been occasions when it seemed to me possible to make aggressive movements upon detachments of the enemy and they were pointed out to our Generals, but they did not avail themselves of them, and it may be that their caution was wise, at least I have thought it proper to defer much to the opinions of commanders in the field, and have felt the hazard of requiring a General to execute, what he did not favorably entertain. The report to which you refer that I restrained the army after the Battles of Manassas and Leesburg obtained such currency and was doing such injury to our cause, that I asked Genl Johnston, whether I had counselled against pursuit after the battle of Manassas or had at any other time restrained the army from any active operations, which it was possible to attempt. He assured me unqualifiedly in the negative and reiterated his opinion of the impossibility of a pursuit after the battle of Manassas, adding that it was not even contemplated.

I cite from memory, but his letter was read in the Congress and should have prevented the repetition of the falsehood by those who have been most industrious in circulating it. If I have borne unjust criticism in silence and allowed vain men to shift the responsibilities of their grievous failures upon me, it has not been because I, "spurned public opinion or was obstinately deaf to the councils of my ablest co-laborers in the revolution," but because every feeling was subjected to the purpose of success in our struggle for recognized independence. It has not happened so far as my memory serves, that any true friend of our cause has advised me to a change of policy without being answered to his satisfaction. The difference in the beginning being usually the result of untenable premises. Of course I do not include in the term *true friends* that class who make issues for selfish ends and talk for popular effect. My respect for public opinion would have led me, as my personal advantage might have urged me to announce our weakness and want of the munitions of war, but this could not have been done without publishing to the enemy our assailable points, and if I had thus avoided the disapprobation of our people, it would have been a poor exchange for that which I must have acquired, self condemnation. That there should have been much misapprehension as to our ability to achieve what the country desired does, not surprise me for the people have generally no measure of military operations and but little oppertunity to obtain correct information. A General reduced to the necessity of standing on the defensive necessarily conceals his weakness from even his own troops. For example, when I visited the Army of the Potomac, last fall, a Brig Genl. serving there and I who had joined after the battles, gave to me the /his/ opinion that we should advance into the Enemy's country, by turning his works in front of Alexandria and Washington, assuring me that the army was eager to invade. I asked him with what force we could venture to cross the Potomac, he said he would risk the movement with forty thousand men. I then asked him how he would hold the enemy in check in the position from which he then threatened to advance upon Richmond, he said that he believed thirty thousand men would suffice for that, when our army made a demonstration in rear of the enemy's Capital &c. &c. In discussing questions of immediate operations against the Enemy I had that morning called for a report of the effective strength of the Army and it was in round numbers thirty-five thousand. I have remembered the conversation the better, because it has often occurred to me when I have heard of impatience because impossible things were not attempted; and have pitied as much as blamed officers, whose desire to conceal their weakness, led them to the unjustifiable resort of pointing censure against "the Administration" for their own supposed inactivity. Now, Sir, as to the remedy which you propose for existing discontent. Never having preferred defensive to offensive war, but the rather pined for the day when our soil should be free from invasion and our banners float over the fields of the Enemy, with what propriety could I say "we stand upon the defensive no more" and what value would the declaration have unless it was followed by an advance into the enemy's country. And if I could to-night issue orders to an army adequate to the work of invasion, how could I conscientiously gain the public applause by revealing to the enemy the ordeal to which he was about to be subjected, and thus diminishing our chances for success.

I love approbation and will toil on though it be through evil report, to deserve, with the hope that I may gain it. Your friend & fellow citizen

(SIGNED) JEFFN DAVIS.

To General Braxton Bragg (PJD)*

RICHMOND, VIRGINIA, AUGUST 5, 1862

GENERAL.

I have the pleasure to acknowledge yours of the 31st. Ulto. and have read the enclosed letter of my Hon. complainant with mingled feelings of pity and scorn. You have properly appreciated, I have no doubt, his motive both in the first and second instance.

As to your supposition in relation to the newspaper slips, it is proper that I should give you some evidence against your belief of complicity of Judge W. His political antecedents would not bring him into association with the paper making the publication, and if he be capable of such an assault, which I do not think, he would have selected a different medium. The paper was sent to me with a marginal pencil note accusing Mr. Yancey as the author of the article headed: "The Army at Tupelo"; I handed the paper to the Judge, he read it, did not appear to have seen it before, did not dissent from the opinion of the marginal annotationist, and treated it as a scurvy attack on the Administration.

To preserve the liberty of the press, yet restrain its license, is possible only where it is controlled by a sound taste and sentiment in its patrons. To give information to the enemy is an injury but little extenenuated by an improper anxiety to satisfy the curiosity of its readers; and here it has frequently occurred that we have been materially damaged by articles, when the purpose to keep within the prescribed limits as to publications concerning army movements if not real was at least seeming.

You have the misfortune of being regarded as my personal friend,

* At this time commander of the Army of Tennessee.

and are pursued therefore with malignant censure, by men regardless of truth and whose want of principle to guide their conduct renders them incapable of conceiving that you are trusted because of your known fitness for command, & not because of friendly regard. Revolutions develop the high qualities of the good and the great, but they cannot change the nature of the vicious and the selfish. I trust the opportunity will be afforded to you to render the country such service as will compensate you for your long trials and the self denial with which you have labored to support the cause in which we are enlisted.

In General E. K. Smith you will find one of our ablest and purest officers. He has taken every position without indicating the least tendency to question its advantage to himself, without complaint when his prospects for distinction were remote, and with alacrity when dangers and hardships were to be met. His promotions, like your own, have come unsought, and my assurance is complete that the zeal would not have been less had they never been given. Upon your cordial cooperation I can, therefore, confidently rely.

If, as reported, the railroad has been effectually broken in rear of Buell, it may enable you to fight the enemy in detachments. Buell being crushed, if your means will enable you to march rapidly on Nashville, Grant will be compelled to retire to the river, abandoning Middle and East Tennessee, or to follow you. His Government will probably require the latter course, and if so you may have a complete conquest over the enemy, involving the liberation of Tennessee and Kentucky. We have reports here to the effect that a large force has been transferred from Halleck's army in the West for another attack on Richmond. If so we will endeavor to give them full employment in this quarter, so as to prevent any return to the West.[*]

General R. Taylor seemed to be required for Southwestern Louisiana.[†] If he saw you, he gave you fully my views and hopes in relation to that region. He appreciated the compliment of your request that he should be sent to you as a Division Commander.

General Van Dorn has sent General Breckenridge against Baton

---

[*] Major General Don Carlos Buell, Lieutenant General Ulysses S. Grant, and Major General Henry W. Halleck, all Union generals.

[†] Lieutenant General Richard Taylor, JD's former brother-in-law.

Rouge, but reports his command as suffering greatly from the effects of the climate and asks for reinforcements and acclimated troops.* We have none to spare from this Army, but I will endeavor to send, nonetheless, a battalion of Artillerists raised in New Orleans and trained here to the use of heavy guns. The country in East La. and Missi. has been so drained of its population that men cannot be raised there beyond a very limited extent, and until your operations may enable you to relieve the Kentucky troops, I do not see how they can be replaced. Very truly your friend

(SIGNED) JEFFN,, DAVIS

To Generals R. E. Lee, B. Bragg, and E. K. Smith (JDC)

RICHMOND, VIRGINIA, SEPTEMBER 12, 1862†

SIRS:

It is deemed proper that you should in accordance with established usage announce by proclamation to the people of _____‡ the motives and purposes of your presence among them at the head of an invading army, and you are instructed in such proclamation to make known,—

1st. That the Confederate Government is waging this war solely for self-defence, that it has no design of conquest or any other purpose than to secure peace and the abandonment by the United States of its pretensions to govern a people who have never been their subjects and who prefer self-government to a Union with them.

2nd. That this Government at the very moment of its inauguration sent commissioners to Washington to treat for a peaceful adjustment of all differences, but that these commissioners were not received not even allowed to communicate the object of their mission, and that on a subsequent occasion a communication from the President of the Confederacy to President Lincoln remained without answer, although

---

* Major General Earl Van Dorn and Major General John C. Breckinridge.

† The date in *JDC* is incorrect..

‡ The appropriate state, Kentucky or Maryland, would be placed in the blank.

a reply was promised by General Scott into whose hands the communication was delivered.

3rd. That among the pretexts urged for continuance of the War is the assertion that the Confederate Government desires to deprive the United States of the free navigation of the Western Rivers although the truth is that the Confederate Congress by public act, prior to the announcement of the War, enacted that "the peaceful navigation of the Mississippi River is hereby declared free to the citizens of the States upon its borders, or upon the borders of its navigable tributaries"—a declaration to which this Government has always been and is still ready to adhere.

4th. That now at a juncture when our arms have been successful, we restrict ourselves to the same just and moderate demand, that we made at the darkest period of our reverses, the simple demand that the people of the United States should cease to war upon us and permit us to pursue our own path to happiness, while they in peace pursue theirs.

5th. That we are debarred from the renewal of formal proposals for peace by having no reason to expect that they would be received with the respect mutually due by nations in their intercourse, whether in peace or in war.

6th. That under these circumstances we are driven to protect our own country by transferring the seat of war to that of an enemy who pursues us with a relentless and apparently aimless hostility: That our fields have been laid waste, our people killed, many homes made desolate, and that rapine and murder have ravaged our frontiers, that the sacred right of self defence demands that if such a war is to continue its consequences shall fall on those who persist in their refusal to make peace.

7th. That the Confederate army therefore comes to occupy the territory of their enemies and to make it the theatre of hostilities. That with the people of _____ themselves rests the power to put an end to this invasion of their homes, for if unable to prevail on the Government of the United States to conclude a general peace, their own State Government in the exercise of its sovereignty can secure immunity from the desolating effects of warfare on the soil of the State by a separate treaty of peace which this Government will ever be ready to conclude on the most just and liberal basis.

8th. That the responsibility thus rests on the people of _____ of continuing an unjust and aggressive warfare upon the Confederate States, a warfare which can never end in any other manner than that now proposed. With them is the option of preserving the blessings of peace, by the simple abandonment of the design of subjugating a people over whom no right of dominion has been ever conferred either by God or man.

(SIGNED) JEFFN. DAVIS

To Governors F. R. Lubbock of Texas, C. F. Jackson of Missouri, T. O. Moore of Louisiana, and H. M. Rector of Arkansas (JDC)

RICHMOND, VIRGINIA, SEPTEMBER 12, 1862

GENTLEMEN:

I have the honor to acknowledge receipt of your communication of the 28th July which was handed to me by the Hon. G. M. Bryan in the current month.

While deeply gratified by the expression of your confidence in my desire to spare no effort for the relief and protection of our fellow citizens in the trans-Mississippi Dept., I anticipated and relied on your devotion to the cause of our country, and your determination to second any measure adopted for its defence.

The delay which occurred in making arrangements for the proper organization of the trans-Mississippi Department arose from causes some of which are too obvious to require mention, and others are of a nature which cannot now be divulged. It is however not improper to say that while Virginia was pressed by the whole force of the U.S. Government, with our Capitol threatened and even closely invested by the largest and best appointed and commanded army of the enemy, it was impracticable to detach such commanding officers to the trans-Mississippi Department as its importance required.

At no time however had the condition and urgent necessities of that Department ceased to be subjects of deep solicitude, and long before your letter was received and immediately after the defeat and dispersion of the enemy by our gallant soldiers in the battles of the Chickahominy, I selected officers possessing my highest confidence for the command and administration duties of the Department and the Districts composing it.

By the assignment of Maj. Genl. Holmes to command the Department, with Major Genls. Taylor, Hindman and Price to the Districts of Louisiana, Arkansas, and Missouri, aided by a competent staff, I feel assured that the proper military skill, vigor, and administrative ability will not be found wanting.[*]

Large supplies of funds have been sent and will continue to be furnished as the exigencies of the service require, and although not able to give all the aid in arms and munitions of war that would be desirable, a supply has been sent about equal to that asked for in your letter. Some of these supplies have not yet reached their destination and another part was unfortunately lost by capture of a transport steamer by the enemy, yet I feel gratified in being able to state that in every point indicated in your letter, I had anticipated your wishes before its receipt.

On the subject of a Branch Treasury in your Department there will probably be more difficulty in meeting your desires than you are aware of. The law does not now permit it, and I am not sure that the project is feasible. That matter will however be taken into advisement and in the meantime effort will be made (I hope successfully) to prevent any further injury to the service from want of funds.

In conclusion, be assured, gentlemen, that your friendly counsels will always be received with satisfaction, and treated with the deference and consideration to which both personally and officially you are so well entitled. I am fully aware of your superior advantages for obtaining the information necessary for the intelligent guidance of public affairs in the trans-Mississippi Department, and desire you to communicate freely with me. It will always give me pleasure to avail myself of the co-operation which you kindly tender to me.

I AM, VERY RESPECTFULLY,
(SIGNED) JEFFN. DAVIS.

[*] Theophilus Holmes, who would become a lieutenant general; Major General Thomas C. Hindman.

To Benjamin H. Hill (PJD)*

RICHMOND, VIRGINIA, OCTOBER 23, 1862

DEAR SIR.

Your letter of October 12th has been received and I have to thank you for the candor and promptness with which you have advised me of the condition of public affairs in Georgia and Eastern Tennessee.

The state of affairs in East Tennessee presents a very difficult question and one which can be decided only by the consideration of many points.

With every disposition to conciliate the people of that region, still the pressure upon us by the enemy is such as compels us to call into the field all who are able to serve there. To exempt the unwilling would be to offer a premium to disaffection. To allow those who are unreliable in their loyalty to continue in separate organizations would prove a perilous experiment. Dangerous schemers might obtain important posts and the least hazard incurred might be the propagation and perpetuation of a spirit discontented and unfriendly to the Confederacy.

The distribution of this class of men among Regiments of loyal and tried veterans would neutralize their evil influence and in time, perhaps, effect a change in them. On the whole, though not free from objection, this seems the most feasible plan for efficiently organizing the East Tennesseeans. Already some recruits have been received who are much needed to fill up the thinned ranks of the gallant Tennessee Brigade in Va.

I am gratified at the report you give of the favorable tone of public opinion in Georgia relative to the Conscript Act. Nothing could be more unfortunate; not only for the success of the cause in which we are engaged but also for the future reputation of the great State of Georgia than any conflict between the authorities of that State and the Confederate Government on this question. Having full confidence in the constitutionality of the law I rely on the decision of the Supreme

---

* Confederate States senator from Georgia.

Court of Georgia to remove the difficulties that at present embarrass the action of the State authorities.

The recommendations which you make have been referred to the Secretary of War and will receive from him the respectful consideration due to the endorsement they receive. With much personal regard for yourself, as well as high consideration for your public character, I am very truly & respectfully yours

(SIGNED) JEFF'N DAVIS

P.S. Some regiments (said to be five) which have been organized in East Tennessee before the 1st. of October, will be received.

To Lieutenant General E. Kirby Smith (PJD)

RICHMOND, VIRGINIA, OCTOBER 29, 1862

MY DEAR SIR,

Doct. Smith handed me your letter & I have considered it with the respect which any thing you offer always receives. The results in Ky. have been to me a bitter disappointment, but we must deal with the future and using the past as a teacher avoid the common error of critics who employ in judging of events the knowledge acquired after they transpired. I have held long and free conversations with Genl. Bragg he uniformly spoke of you in the most complimentary terms, and does seem to imagine your disatisfaction. He has explained in a direct and frank manner the circumstances of his campaign and has evinced the most self denying temper in relation to his future position. That another Genl. might excite more enthusiasm is probable, but as all have their defects I have not seen how to make a change with advantage to the public service. His administrative capacity has been felt by the army of Missi. his knowledge of the troops is intimate and a new man would not probably for a time with even greater ability be equally useful. Of the Generals, Cooper is at the head of the Bureau, Lee in command of the army in Va. Johnston still disabled by the wound received at seven Pines, Beauregard was tried as commander of the Army of the West and left it without leave when the troops were demoralized and the country he was sent to protect was threatened with conquest.* Bragg succeeded to the command organized the army and marched to your support with efficient troops. The retreat from Ky. was not so bad as that from the camp on the Magnesian lime stone of Corinth. To recover from the depression produced by the failure in Ky. no move seems better than to advance into Middle Tenn. If Buell comes he will be weaker than in Ky. and I hope will be beaten. We may get large accessions of recruits and probably will get supplies which are required for the support of our army. In the mean time the hazard of the capture of Mobile Ala. & Columbus and Vicksburg Missi. demands constant attention. If by passing to the rear of Rozencrantz he shall be checked or compelled to retire the country east of the Missi. river will be relieved.† If on the other hand he should advance to cooperate in an attack on Mobile or Vicksburg your forces will have to aid in that quarter and abandon the less vital point of Middle Tenn. Holmes is getting a large army in Arks. and will I hope be able to attack the Enemy successfully on the west side of the Missi. and embarrass him in the use of the river.

Genl. Bragg cannot move into Middle Tenn. with prospect of success without your cooperation. You are now second in rank and possess to an eminent degree the confidence of the country. Your own corps could not be so usefully led by another commander. How then can I withdraw you or withold your troops? Your Department will remain to you, such part of your force as can be spared from it for the present, you can lead with the army of Genl. Bragg into Middle Tenn.

If I were sure that Genl. Bragg could get say 30.000 new troops in Tenn. I would not hesitate upon your request to assign you to the duty of covering Mobile Columbus and Vicksburg, by placing your army at Selma and Meridian to act as might be necessary. We dare not rely on the promised aid however we may hope to receive it. When you wrote your wounds were fresh, your lame and exhausted troops were before you, I hope time may have modified your pain and that the future op-

---

* General Samuel Cooper, adjutant and inspector general of the Confederate army.

† Union major general William S. Rosecrans.

erations may restore the confidence essential to cheerfulness and security in campaign. I have conversed freely with your friend and he will be able to explain any thing which may be obscure in this, which has been written while he waits for it.

May God direct and protect you is the sincere prayer of your friend. Before closing I will renew my thanks to you and your brave troops for your patient fortitude and heroic daring on the march and in the battle during your campaign in Kentucky. Truly yr's

JEFFN,, DAVIS

To Governor Zebulon B. Vance (PJD)*

RICHMOND, VIRGINIA, NOVEMBER 1, 1862

DEAR SIR.

I have the honor to acknowledge yours of the 25th ult. and regret the disappointment to which some of the recruits of North Carolina have been subjected. I concur with you as to the policy of allowing the Conscripts as far as the state of the service will permit to select the companies and regiments in which they are to serve. The rights secured by law to the volunteer to select his own company was lost, it is true, by enrolment; but the policy was so obvious of associating men together who would best harmonize with each other, that it was my purpose to continue the privilege beyond the limit fixed by the law.

The danger to the coast of N. Carolina and our inability to draw troops from the Army of N. Virginia rendered it proper that the greatest exertion should be made immediately to fill up the regiments in Genl. French's command, but this did not interfere with allowing the conscripts to select among those regiments the one to which they would be assigned, so long as vacancies existed in the companies chosen, & that I expected would have been done. I will send your letter to the War Department with a copy of this reply to you, & hope for the future there will be no ground for dissatisfaction, & that as far as feasible the disappointments to which you refer may be corrected by transfer.

---

* Governor of North Carolina.

I feel grateful to you for the cordial manner in which you have sustained every proposition connected with the public defence, and trust that there will always be such cointelligence and accordance as will enable us to cooperate for the public good.

The Conscript Act has not been popular anywhere out of the Army. There, as you are aware, it served to check the discontent which resulted from retaining the 12 months men beyond the term of their original engagement, and was fairly regarded as a measure equitably to distribute the burthen of public defence; but the State authorities have no where offered any opposition to its execution or withheld their aid except in the State of Georgia & so far as the Cadets of the Military Institute are concerned, in the State of Virgina.

I shall endeavor by judicial decision to settle the questions raised in those two States, & in the meantime, have been cheered by the evidence of a popular sentiment which supports any measure necessary to protect our country & secure our political independence.

Like yourself I have hoped that the party distinctions which existed at a former time would be buried in the graves of the gallant men who have fallen in the defence of their birthright, & that we should all as a band of brothers, strike for the inheritance our fathers left us. With sincere regard, I am yours respectfully & truly—your's

JEFF'N,, DAVIS

To G. W. Randolph, Secretary of War (JDC)*

RICHMOND, VIRGINIA, NOVEMBER 14, 1862

SIR:

I have just received yours of this date in relation to instructions given to Genl. Holmes and their modification by transmission of a copy of my letter of the 12th inst.†

Confusion and embarrassment will inevitably result unless all orders, and directions in relation to movements and stations of troops and officers, be sent through the established channel, the Bureau of

---

* George W. Randolph, Confederate secretary of war March–November 1862.

† Lieutenant General Theophilus Holmes, now commander of the Trans-Mississippi District.

orders and correspondence. In these matters and in all cases of selection of persons to be appointed commissioned officers I have to request a reference before action is taken.

VERY RESPECTFULLY YR. OBT. SVT.
(SIGNED) JEFFN. DAVIS

To G. W. Randolph, Secretary of War (JDC)

RICHMOND, VIRGINIA, NOVEMBER 14, 1862

SIR:

My letter of this date of the meaning of which you are in doubt had reference to the general arrangements of the army.

The removal of an Army, the transfer of a Genl., from the Dept. he had been selected to command, the assignment of Genl. officers, and the highest officers of the supplying and disbursing Departments of the staff, are material to the public defence; and such like cases would all suggest the propriety of reference.

The usage has been free conference, and its advantages are apparent.

The appointment of commissioned officers is a constitutional function which I have neither power nor will to delegate, and much which is disagreeable will be avoided by consultation in the first stage of selection.

VERY RESPECTFULLY,
(SIGNED) JEFFN. DAVIS.

To Governors J. E. Brown of Georgia, R. Hawes of Kentucky,
H. M. Rector of Arkansas, F. R. Lubbock of Texas,
C. J. Jackson of Missouri, I. G. Harris of Tennessee,
John Letcher of Virginia, J. G. Shorter of Alabama,
J. J. Pettus of Mississippi, F. W. Pickens of South Carolina,
John Milton of Florida, Z. B. Vance of North Carolina,
and Thos. O. Moore of Louisiana (JDC)

RICHMOND, VIRGINIA, NOVEMBER 26, 1862

SIR:

The present condition of public affairs induces me to address this circular to the Governors of the several States on a subject of vital importance to our people.

The repeated defeats inflicted on the Federal forces in their attempt to conquer our country have not yet sufficed to satisfy them of the impossibility of success in their nefarious design to subjugate these States.

A renewed attempt on a still larger scale is now in progress; but with manifest distrust of success in a warfare conducted according to the usages of civilized nations, the United States propose to add to the enormous land and naval forces accumulated by them, bands of such of the African slaves of the South as they may be able to wrest from their owners, and thus to inflict on the non-combatant population of the Confederate States all the horrors of a servile war, superadded to such atrocities as have already been committed on numerous occasions by their invading forces.

To repel attacks conducted on so vast a scale, the most energetic action of every department of the Government is directed, but appreciating the great value of the cordial cooperation of the different State governments, and with unfaltering reliance on their patriotism and devotion to our cause, I earnestly appeal to them for all the aid it may be in their power to extend to the officers of the War Dept. in the discharge of their duties within the several States, and for their cooperation in the following important particulars :

1. In the enrollment of the conscripts and the forwarding of them to the proper points of rendezvous.

2. In restoring to the army all officers and men now within the States absent without leave or whose term of absence has expired, or who have recovered from disability and are now able to return to duty.

3. In securing for the use of the army all such necessary supplies as exist within the States in excess of the quantity indispensable for the people at home.

Prompt action in these matters will save our people from very great suffering, will put our army in a condition to meet the enemy with decisive results, and thus secure for us an early and honorable peace on the basis of recognized independence.

In addition to the above urgent matters, I beg respectfully to ask the aid of the Executives of the several States in recommending to the several Legislatures such legislation as will enable the Governors to command slave labor to the extent which may be required in the prosecution of works conducive to the public defence, also the adoption of some means to suppress the shameful extortions now practiced upon the people by men who can be reached by no moral influence and who are worse enemies of the Confederacy than if found in arms among the invading forces. The armies in the field as well as the families of the soldiers and others of the people at home are the prey of these mercenaries, and it is only through State action that their traffic can be repressed. Their condign punishment is ardently desired by every patriot.

I AM, VERY RESPECTFULLY YR. OBT. SVT.

(SIGNED) JEFFN. DAVIS.

To General Robert E. Lee (PJD)

RICHMOND, VIRGINIA, DECEMBER 8, 1862

GENERAL:

I have the pleasure to acknowledge your letters of the 6th & 8th. and have reflected upon the suggestions and information they contain.

Entirely concurring in your views as to the propriety of concentrating all disposable force for the impending struggle on the North and South side of Richmond, I regret that I find so little to be drawn on for that purpose.

In Tennessee and Mississippi the disparity between our armies and those of the enemy is so great as to fill me with apprehension, and I have called on Genl. Holmes to ask him, if it can be safely done, to send reinforcements to Genl. Pemberton.* The campaign in Middle Tennessee promises little more than an increase of our supplies of subsistence.

Genl. J. E. Johnston has been sent to command the western Department, composed of Tennessee Alabama, Mississippi, and the Eastern part of Louisiana. It was believed necessary to have greater cooperation among those armies, and it was sought in this mode to obtain it.

I propose to go out there immediately with the hope that something may be done to bring out men not heretofore in service, and to arouse all classes to united and desperate resistance. Pemberton has fallen back to the Yallobusha, and is preparing there to give the enemy battle. His force is much less than that of the enemy, but I have the most favorable accounts of his conduct as commander, and trust God may bless us, as in other cases seemingly as desperate, with success over our impious foe.

I have been very anxious to visit you, but feeble health and constant labor has caused me to delay until necessity hurries me in an opposite direction.

I have endeavored to have you furnished with whatever I knew you to be in need of. The two 30 pounder Parrott Guns have I suppose reached you, and today the Sec. of War was instructed to have Napoleon Guns made for you, with the suggestion that he should endeavor to get the material without using the valuable small guns which might be found useful on muddy roads or in rapid operations, if the material could be otherwise obtained. The quiet which prevails in the camp of the enemy is probably but the delay for further preparation. McClellan having been removed because he did not advance from the Potomac as a base, it is hardly supposable that his successor will fail to

---

* Lieutenant General John C. Pemberton, commander at Vicksburg.

attempt that movement. Under this view it does not seem~~ly~~ likely that he will so divide his forces as to enable you to attack, or to justify you in dividing yours. You will know best when it will be proper to make a masked movement to the rear should circumstances require you to move nearer to Richmond. At present our information as to the enemies force on the South Side of James River is too imperfect to form an opinion as to his purposes in that quarter. A committee from the North Carolina Legislature visited me recently to propose the organization of a force of exempts, say from five to ten thousand, and to be employed for State defence. They were encouraged to execute the plan, and we may hope thus to receive some increase of numerical strength. If it should be found that the enemy have withdrawn generally from Western Virginia some further increase of our forces on the South Side of James River may be obtained by bringing in three Regiments of Infantry from Marshall and four from the Division lately commanded by Loring. There are also reported to be some twelve or fifteen hundred men in the Northwestern part of N. Carolina. I have directed enquiry to be made that, if it should prove true, they might be added to French's command. Should these expectations be fully realized, the force on the South Side of James River will be so augmented as to relieve you in no small degree from anxiety in relation to that portion of the line.

The fleet, in /(of)/ the preparation of which your scout informs you, is composed to a great ~~degree~~ /extent/ of vessels too deep to enter most of our Southern harbors. The rumor has reached us that it is destined for Brunswick, but I do not perceive an adequate motive for that destination, and of course but little reliance can be placed upon such information as it is practicable for us to obtain in relation to such a matter .

During the period of my absence I shall feel an increasing anxiety to know the events in this quarter, and to have your views in relation to them. You can send me despatches to be forwarded from this place. Col. Lee will accompany me. Col. W. P. Johnston will remain at the office.[*]

---

[*] Two of JD's aides: George Washington Custis Lee (son of R. E. Lee) and W. P. Johnston (son of A. S. Johnston).

I hope to return by New Year. May God bless and preserve you. As ever, your friend

(SIGNED) JEFFN,, DAVIS

To Lieutenant General Theophilus H. Holmes (PJD)

VICKSBURG, MISSISSIPPI, DECEMBER 21, 1862

GENL.:

Enclosed I have the honor to transmit to you copies of letters from Genl. Johnston and from Maj. Genl. Smith in relation to the defence of the Missi. River and to ask your consideration of their contents. It seems to me now clearly developed that the enemy has two principal objects in view, one to get control of the Missi. River, and the other to capture the Capital of the Confederate States. As to the last, our recent successes at Fredericksburg give assurance that at least during the present winter, Richmond may be successfully defended, and at best its capture can only be valuable by the effect which it would produce upon public opinion abroad, and by the destruction of manufactories and other resources very essential to our future efforts. But the control of the Mississsippi River will be not only indirectly valuable to the enemy by the injury which its loss would inflict upon the Confederate States, but directly by furnishing the best possible base for operations in the valley both on the East and West side of the River, by answering the exigent demand of the North Western States for the restoration to them of the unrestricted use of that river, and by utilizing the heretofore fruitless possession of New Orleans. In my former communications to you I pressed the necessity for co-intelligence and cooperation of our armies on the opposite sides of the river. I had hoped that it might have been possible while the river was low to capture Helena and thus give the best security against invasion by water of the territory of Arkansas, but as this has not been effected, I cannot doubt that it has heretofore been impracticable, and the present rise in the river does not permit us to hope that if now taken we should be able to so fortify and arm the place as to make it subserve the purposes indicated. Therefore to prevent the enemy getting control of the Mississsippi and dismembering the Confederacy, we must mainly rely upon maintaining the points already occupied by defensive works; to wit, Vicksburg and Port Hudson. From the best information at command, a large force is now ready to descend the Mississsippi and cooperate with the army advancing from Memphis to make an attack upon Vicksburg. Large forces are also reported to have been sent to the lower Mississsippi for the purpose of ascending the river to attempt the reduction of Port Hudson by an attack on both the land and water sides. The letters enclosed will show you the inadequacy of the forces here to meet the trial to which it will be exposed. If the enemy should succeed in these attempts, he will be then left free to concentrate his forces against your Dept., and though your valor may be relied upon to do all that human power can effect, it is not to be expected that you could make either long or successful resistance. It seems to me then unquestionably best that you should reinforce Genl. Johnston, so as to enable him successfully to meet the enemy, and by his defeat to destroy his power for such future operations against you as would be irresistible by your isolated force, and by the same means to place the army here in such condition as would enable it in turn to reinforce you when the season will /make/ it practicable for you by active operations to expel the enemy from Arkansas, and having secured your rear, to advance to the deliverance of Missouri. I have never been unmindful of the facility with which the enemy could invade Arkansas ~~as~~ by means of the White and Arkansas Rivers, nor underrated the importance of your having the proper works and sufficient garrisons to prevent that movement; but at this season, and in the devastated condition of the country, it seems to me impossible that any large force can invade through the North Western part of Arkansas, and from the forces in that region, I hope you will be able to detach the required number of men to reinforce Genl. Johnston to the extent set forth in the accompanying letters. We can not hope at all points to meet the enemy with a force equal to his own, and must find our security in the concentration and rapid movement of troops. Nothing will so certainly conduce to peace as the conclusive exhibition of our power to hold the Mississippi river, and nothing so diminish our capacity to defend the Trans-Missi. States as the loss of communication between the States on the Eastern and Western sides of the river. I have thus presented to you my views, and trusting alike in your patriotism and discretion, leave you to make the application of them which circumstances will permit. Whatever may be done should be done with all possible dispatch. Very respectfully & truly yr. friend

(SIGNED) JEFFN. DAVIS

Speech in Jackson, Mississippi (PJD)

DECEMBER 26, 1862

Friends and Fellow-Citizens, Gentlemen of the House of Representatives and Senate of the State of Mississippi:

After an absence of nearly two years I again find myself among those who, from the days of my childhood, have ever been the trusted objects of my affections, those for whose good I have ever striven, and whose interest I have sometimes hoped I may have contributed to subserve. Whatever fortunes I may have achieved in life have been gained as a representative of Mississippi, and before all, I have labored for the advancement of her glory and honor. I now, for the first time in my career, find myself the representative of a wider circle of interest; but a circle in which the interests of Mississippi are still embraced. Two years ago, nearly, I left you to assume the duties which had devolved on me as the representative of the new Confederacy. The responsibilities of this position have occupied all my time, and have left me no opportunity for mingling with my friends in Mississippi, or for sharing in the dangers which have menaced them. But, wherever duty may have called me, my heart has been with you and the success of the cause in which we are all engaged has been first in my thoughts and in my prayers. . . . But, speaking to you with that frankness and that confidence with which I have always spoken to you, and which partakes of the nature of thinking aloud, I can say with my hand upon my heart, that whatever I have done, has been done with the sincere purpose of promoting the noble cause in which we are engaged. The period which has elapsed since I left you is short; for the time, which may appear long in the life of man, is short in the history of a nation. And in that short period remarkable changes have been wrought in all the circumstances by which we are surrounded. At the time of which I speak, the question presented to our people was "will there be war!" This was the subject of universal speculation. We had chosen to exercise an indisputable right—the right to separate from those with whom we conceived association to be no longer possible, and to establish a government of our own. I was among those who, from the beginning, predicted war as the consequence of secession, although I must admit that the contest has assumed proportions more gigantic than I had anticipated. I predicted war not because our right to secede and to form a government of our own was not indisputable and clearly defined in the spirit of that declaration which rests the right to govern on the consent of the governed, but because I foresaw that the wickedness of the North would precipitate a war upon us. Those who supposed that the exercise of this right of separation could not produce war, have had cause to be convinced that they had credited their recent associates of the North with a moderation, a sagacity, a morality they did not possess. You have been involved in a war waged for the gratification of the lust of power and of aggrandizement, for your conquest and your subjugation, with a malignant ferocity and with a disregard and a contempt of the usages of civilization, entirely unequalled in history. Such, I have ever warned you, were the characteristics of the Northern people—of those with whom our ancestors entered into a Union of consent, and with whom they formed a constitutional compact. And yet, such was the attachment of our people for that Union, such their devotion to it, that those who desired preparation to be made for the inevitable conflict, were denounced as men who only wished to destroy the Union. After what has happened during the last two years, my only wonder is that we consented to live for so long a time in association with such miscreants, and have loved so much a government rotten to the core. Were it ever to be proposed again to enter into a Union with such a people, I could no more consent to do it than to trust myself in a den of thieves.

... Having been hurried into a war with a people so devoid of every mark of civilization you have no doubt wondered that I have not carried out the policy, which I had intended should be our policy, of fighting our battles on the fields of the enemy instead of suffering him to fight them on ours. This was not the result of my will, but of the power of the enemy. They had at their command all the accumulated wealth of seventy years—the military stores which had been laid up during that time. They had grown rich from the taxes wrung from you for the establishing and supporting their manufacturing institutions. We have entered upon a conflict with a nation contiguous to us in territory, and vastly superior to us in numbers. In the face of these facts the wonder is not that we have done little, but that we have done so much. In the first year of the war our forces were sent into the field poorly armed, and were far inferior in number to the enemy. We were compelled even to arm ourselves by the capture of weapons taken from the foe on the battle-field. Thus in every battle we exchanged our arms for those of the invaders. At the end of twelve months of the war, it was still necessary for us to adopt some expedient to enable us to maintain our ground. The only expedient remaining to us was to call on those brave men who had entered the service of their country at the beginning of the war, supposing that the conflict was to last but a short time, and that they would not be long absent from their homes. The only expedient, I say, was to call on these gallant men; to ask them to maintain their position in front of the enemy, and to surrender for a time their hopes of soon returning to their families and their friends. And nobly did they respond to the call. They answered that they were willing to stay, that they were willing to maintain their position and to breast the tide of invasion. But it was not just that they should stand alone. They asked that the men who had stayed at home—who had thus far been sluggards in the cause—should be forced, likewise, to meet the enemy. From this, resulted the law of Congress, which is known as the conscription act, which declared all men, from the age of eighteen to the age of thirty-five, to be liable to enrolment in the Confederate service. I regret that there has been some prejudice excited against that act, and that it has been subjected to harsher criticism than it deserves. And here I may say that an erroneous impression appears to prevail in regard to this act. It is no disgrace to be brought into the army by conscription. There is no more reason to expect from the citizen voluntary service in the army than to expect voluntary labor on the public roads or the voluntary payment of taxes. But these things we do not expect. We assess the property of the citizen, we appoint tax-gatherers; why should we not likewise distribute equally the labor, and enforce equally the obligation of defending the country from its enemies? I repeat that it is no disgrace to any one to be conscribed, but it is a glory for those who do not wait for the conscription. Thus resulted the conscription act; and thence arose the necessity for the exemption act. That necessity was met; but when it was found that under these acts enough men were not drawn into the ranks of the army to fulfill the purposes intended, it became necessary to pass another exemption act, and another conscription act. It is only of this latter that I desire now to speak. Its policy was to leave at home those men needed to conduct the administration, and those who might be required to support and maintain the industry of the country—in other words, to exempt from military service those whose labor, employed in other avocations, might be more profitable to the country and to the government, than in the ranks of the army.

I am told that this act has excited some discontent and that it has provoked censure, far more severe, I believe, than it deserves. It has been said that it exempts the rich from military service, and forces the poor to fight the battles of the country. The poor do, indeed, fight the battles of the country. It is the poor who save nations and make revolutions. But is it true that in this war the men of property have shrunk from the ordeal of the battle-field? Look through the army; cast your eyes upon the maimed heroes of the war whom you meet in your streets and in the hospitals; remember the martyrs of the conflict; and I am sure you will find among them more than a fair proportion drawn from the ranks of men of property. The object of that portion of the act which exempts those having charge of twenty or more negroes, was not to draw any distinction of classes, but simply to provide a force, in the nature of a police force, sufficient to keep our negroes in control. This was the sole object of the clause. Had it been otherwise, it would never have received my signature. As I have already said, we have no cause to complain of the rich. All of our people have done well; and, while the poor have nobly discharged their duties, most of the wealthiest and most distinguished families of the South have representatives in the ranks. I take, as an example, the case of one of your own representatives in Congress, who was nominated for Congress and elected; but still did a sentinel's duty until Congress met. Nor is this a solitary instance, for men of the largest fortune in Mississippi are now serving in the ranks.

. . .

In considering the manner in which the war has been conducted by the enemy, nothing arrests the attention more than the magnitude of the preparations made for our subjugation. Immense navies have been constructed, vast armies have been accumulated, for the purpose of crushing out the rebellion. It has been impossible for us to meet them in equal numbers; nor have we required it. We have often whipped them three to one, and in the eventful battle of Antietam, Lee whipped them four to one. But do not understand me as saying that this will always be the case. When the troops of the enemy become disciplined, and accustomed to the obedience of the camp, they will necessarily approach more nearly to an equality with our own men. We have always whipped them in spite of disparity of numbers, and on any fair field, fighting as man to man, and relying only on those natural qualities with which men are endowed, we should not fear to meet them in the proportion of one to two. But troops must be disciplined in order to develop their efficiency; and in order to keep them at their posts. Above all, to assure this result, we need the support of public opinion. We want public opinion to frown down those who come from the army with sad tales of disaster, and prophecies of evil, and who skulk from the duties they owe their country. We rely on the women of the land to turn back these deserters from the ranks. I thank the Governor for asking the legislature to make the people of the State tributary to this service. In addition to this, it is necessary to fill up those regiments which have for so long a time been serving in the field. They have stood before the foe on many hard fought fields and have proven their courage and devotion on all. They have won the admiration of the army and of the country. And here I may repeat a compliment I have heard which, although it seems to partake of levity, appears an illustration of the esteem in which Mississippians are held. It happened that several persons were conversing of a certain battle, and one of them remarked that the Mississippians did not run. "Oh no!" said another "Mississippians never run." But those who have passed through thirteen pitched battles are not unscathed. Their ranks are thinned, and they look back to Mississippi for aid to augment their diminished numbers. They look back expecting their brothers to fly to their rescue; but it sometimes seems as if the long anticipated relief would never come. A brigade which may consist of only twelve hundred men is expected to do the work of four thousand. Humanity demands that these depleted regiments be filled up. A mere skeleton cannot reasonably be expected to perform the labor of a body with all its flesh and muscle on it. You have many who might assist in revivifying your reduced regiments— enough to fill up the ranks if they would only consent to throw off the shackles of private interest, and devote themselves to the noblest cause in which a man can be engaged. You have now in the field old men and gentle boys who have braved all the terrors and the dangers of war. I remember an instance of one of these, a brave and gallant youth who, I was told, was but sixteen years of age. In one of those bloody battles by which the soil of Virginia has been consecrated to liberty, he was twice wounded, and each time bound up the wound with his own hands, while refusing to leave the field. A third time he was struck, and the life-blood flowed in a crimson stream from his breast. His brother came to him to minister to his wants; but the noble boy said "brother, you cannot do me any good now; go where you can do the Yankees most harm." Even then, while lying on the ground, his young life fast ebbing away, he cocked his rifle and aimed it to take one last shot at the enemy. And so he died, a hero and a martyr. This was one of the boys whose names shed glory on Mississippi, and who, looking back from their distant camps, where they stand prepared to fight your battles, and to turn back the tide of Yankee invasion, ask you now to send them aid in the struggle—to send them men to stand by them in the day of trial, on the right hand and on the left.

. . .

The issue before us is one of no ordinary character. We are not engaged in a conflict for conquest, or for agrandizement, or for the settlement of a point of international law. The question for you to decide is, "will you be slaves or will you be independent?" Will you transmit to your children the freedom and equality which your fathers transmitted to you or will you bow down in adoration before an idol baser than ever was worshipped by Eastern idolators? Nothing more is necessary than the mere statement of this issue. Whatever may be the personal sacrifices involved, I am sure that you will not shrink from them whenever the question comes before you. Those men who now assail us, who have been associated with us in a common Union, who have inherited a government which they claim to be the best the world ever saw—these men, when left to themselves, have shown that they are incapable of preserving their own personal liberty. They have destroyed the freedom of the press; they have seized upon and imprisoned members of State Legislatures and of municipal councils, who were suspected of sympathy with the South. Men have been carried off into captivity in distant States without indictment, without a knowledge of the accusations brought against them, in utter defiance of all rights guaranteed by the institutions under which they live. These people, when separated from the South and left entirely to themselves, have, in six months, demonstrated their utter incapacity for self-government. And yet these are the people who claim to be your masters. These are the people who have determined to divide out the South among their Yankee troops. Mississippi they have devoted to the direst vengeance of all. "But vengeance is the Lord's," and beneath his banner you will meet and hurl back these worse than vandal hordes.

The great end and aim of the government is to make our struggle successful. The men who stand highest in this contest would fall the first sacrifice to the vengeance of the enemy in case we should be unsuccessful. You may rest assured then for that reason if for no other that whatever capacity they possess will be devoted to securing the independence of the country. Our government is not like the monarchies of the Old World, resting for support upon armies and navies. It sprang from the people and the confidence of the people is necessary for its success. When misrepresentations of the government have been circulated, when accusations have been brought against it of weakness and inefficiency, often have I felt in my heart the struggle between the desire for justice and the duty not to give information to the enemy— because at such times the correction of error would have been injurious to the safety of the cause. Thus, that great and good man, Gen. A. Sidney Johnston, was contented to rest beneath public contumely and to be pointed at by the finger of scorn, because he did not advance from Bowling Green with the little army under his command. But month after month he maintained his post, keeping the enemy ignorant of the paucity of his numbers, and thus holding the invaders in check. I take this case as one instance; it is not the only one by far.

The issue then being: will you be slaves; will you consent to be robbed of your property; to be reduced to provincial dependence; will you renounce the exercise of those rights with which you were born and which were transmitted to you by your fathers? I feel that in addressing Mississippians the answer will be that their interests, even life itself, should be willingly laid down on the altar of their country.
. . .

There are now two prominent objects in the programme of the enemy. One is to get possession of the Mississippi river and to open it to navigation in order to appease the clamors of the West and to utilize the capture of New Orleans, which has thus far rendered them no service. The other is to seize upon the capital of the Confederacy, and hold this out as a proof that the Confederacy has no existence. We have recently repulsed them at Fredericksburg, and I believe that under God and by the valor of our troops the capital of the Confederacy will stand safe behind its wall of living breasts. Vicksburg and Port Hudson have been strengthened, and now we can concentrate at either of them a force sufficient for their protection. I have confidence that Vicksburg will stand as before, and I hope that Johnston will find generals to support him if the enemy dare to land. Port Hudson is now strong. Vicksburg will stand, and Port Hudson will stand; but let every man that can be spared from other vocations, hasten to defend them, and thus hold the Mississippi river, that great artery of the Confederacy, preserve our communications with the trans-Mississippi department, and thwart the enemy's scheme of forcing navigation through to New Orleans. By holding that section of the river between Port Hudson and Vicksburg, we shall secure these results, and the people of the West, cut off from New Orleans, will be driven to the East to seek a market for their products, and will be compelled to pay so much in the way of freights that those products will be rendered almost valueless. Thus, I should not be surprised if the first daybreak of peace were to dawn upon us from that quarter.

. . .

I can then say with confidence that our condition is in every respect greatly improved over what it was last year. Our armies have been augmented, our troops have been instructed and disciplined. The articles necessary for the support of our troops, and our people, and from which the enemy's blockade has cut us off, are being produced in the Confederacy. Our manufactories have made rapid progress, so much is this the case that I learn with equal surprise and pleasure from the general commanding this department, that Mississippi alone can supply the army which is upon her soil.

Our people have learned to economize and are satisfied to wear home spun. I never see a woman dressed in home spun that I do not feel like taking off my hat to her; and although our women never lose their good looks, I cannot help thinking that they are improved by this garb. I never meet a man dressed in home spun but I feel like saluting him. I cannot avoid remarking with how much pleasure I have noticed the superior morality of our troops, and the contrast which in this respect they present to those of the invader. I can truly say that an army more pious and more moral than that defending our liberties, I do not believe to exist. On their valor and the assistance of God I confidently rely.

Speech in Richmond, Virginia (PJD)

JANUARY 5, 1863

FRIENDS AND FELLOW-CITIZENS . . .

I am happy to be welcomed on my return to the Capital of our Confederacy—the last hope, as I believe, for the perpetuation of that system of government which our forefathers founded—the asylum of the oppressed and the home of true representative liberty.

Here, in the ancient Commonwealth of Virginia the great principles of human government were proclaimed by your ancestors; here great battles for freedom have been fought, when the grand system they founded was attempted to be overturned by those who got possession of a government which they could not comprehend, and which, in six months, they see themselves wholly unable to administer.

Anticipating the overthrow of that Government which you had inherited, you assumed to yourselves the right, as your fathers had done before you, to declare yourselves independent, and nobly have you advocated the assertion which you have made. Here, upon your soil, some of the fiercest battles of the Revolution were fought, and upon your soil it closed by the surrender of Cornwallis. Here again are men of every State; here they have congregated, linked in the defence of a most sacred cause. They haved battled, they have bled upon your soil, and it is now consecrated by blood which cries for vengeance against the insensate foe of religion as well as of humanity, of the altar as well as of the hearthstone.

You have shown yourselves in no respect to be degenerate sons of your fathers. You have fought mighty battles, and your deeds of valor will live among the richest spoils of Time's ample page. It is true you have a cause which binds you together more firmly than your fathers were. They fought to be free from the usurpations of the British crown, but they fought against a manly foe. You fight against the offscourings of the earth.—[Applause.]

Men who were bound to you by the compact which their fathers and themselves had entered into to secure to you the rights and principles not only guaranteed by the Declaration of Independence, but rights which Virginia wisely and plainly reserved in her recognition of the government in which she took a part, now come to you with their hands steeped in blood, robbing the widow, destroying houses, seizing the grey-haired father, and incarcerating him in prison because he will not be a traitor to the principles of his fathers and the land that gave him birth.

Recently, my friends, our cause has had the brightest sunshine to fall upon it, as well in the West as in the East. Our glorious Lee, the valued son, emulating the virtues of the heroic Light-horse Harry, his father, has achieved a victory at Fredericksburg, and driven the enemy back from his last and greatest effort to get "on to Richmond." But a few, however, did get on to Richmond.—(Laughter.) A few, I trust, may come from every battle fleid to fulfil the pledge they made that they would come to Richmond—but they will come as captives, not as conquerors. (Applause.)

In the West, too, at Murfreesboro you have gained a victory over hosts vastly superior to our own in number. You have achieved a result there as important, as brilliant as that which occurred on the soil of Virginia; and cotemporaneously at Vicksburg, where they were struggling to get possession of the great artery, the control of the Mississippi river, to answer the demands of the North West. In every combat there they have been beaten, and I trust they will be beaten in future. Out of this victory is to come that dissatisfaction in the North West, which will rive the power of that section; and thus we see in the future the dawn—first separation of the North West from the Eastern States, the discord among them which will paralyze the power of both;—then for us future peace and prosperity.

Every crime which could characterize the course of demons has marked the course of the invader. The Northern portion of Virginia has been ruthlessly desolated—the people not only deprived of the means of subsistence, but their household property destroyed, and every indignity which the base imagination of a merciless foe could suggest inflicted, without regard to age, sex or condition. In like manner their step has been marked in every portion of the Confederacy they have invaded. They have murdered prisoners of war; they have destroyed the means of subsistence of families; they have plundered the defenceless, and exerted their most malignant ingenuity to bring to the deepest destitution those whose only offence is that their husbands and sons are fighting for their homes and their liberties. In one instance, in the Northwestern part of Mississippi, I have heard of them plundering the home of a poor widow, taking her only cow, and then offering her the oath of allegiance as the terms upon which they would furnish her rations. Worthy to be a matron of the Southern Confederacy, she refused it, and when I last heard of her, which was before the enemy was driven from her home, she was living upon parched corn. May God bless her. She is worthy to be a Matron of the Southern Confederacy. (Applause.)—Every crime conceivable, from the burning of defenceless towns to the stealing of our silver forks, and spoons, has marked their career. In New Orleans Butler has exerted himself to earn the execrations of the civilised world, and now returns with his dishonors thick upon him to receive the plaudits of the only people on earth who do not blush to think he wears the human form.* He has stolen millions of dollars in New Orleans from private citizens, although the usages of war exempt private property from taxation by the enemy. It is in keeping, however, with the character of the people that seeks dominion over you, claim to be your masters, to try to reduce you to subjection—give up to a brutal soldiery your towns to sack, your homes to pillage and incite servile insurrection. But in the latter point they have failed save in this that they have heaped if possible a deeper disgrace upon themselves. They have come to disturb your social organizations on the plea that it is a military necessity. For what are they waging war? They say to preserve the Union. Can they preserve the Union by destroying the social existence of a portion of the South? Do they hope to reconstruct the Union by striking at everything which is dear to man? By showing themselves so utterly disgraced that if the question was proposed to you whether you would combine with hyenas or Yankees, I trust every Virginian would say, give me the hyenas.—[Cries of "Good! good!" and applause.]

My friends, constant labor in the duties of office, borne down by care, and with an anxiety which has left me scarcely a moment for re-

---

* Union major general Benjamin F. Butler.

pose, I have had but little opportunity for social intercourse among you. I thank you for this greeting, and hope the time may come soon when you and I alike, relieved of the anxieties of the hour, may have more of social intercourse than has heretofore existed, and that I may come to participate in those quiet enjoyments that one cannot experience when his mind is constantly dwelling upon the struggles of his country. Whilst a man's sympathy is attracted by the sufferings of fellow creatures, whilst every pulse of his heart beats in response to the trials, and every thought is directed to the dangers of his country, there is little time for the cultivation of the social enjoyments that pertain to a time of peace. I can only give this as my excuse for my seldom appearance among you. I can also say, with entire sincerity, that I have nothing to regret, coupled with all the sacrifices which this struggle for the independence of our Confederacy has brought to me. I have borne my full share in the sacrifices of the people of whom I am a part, but I now feel if they had been greater they would have served only to render me more devoted to you. (Applause.)

War is an evil in every form in which it can be presented, but it has its palliating circumstances. This is a new government, formed of independent States, each jealous of its own sovereignty. It is necessary that it should be tried in the severe erucible in which we are being tested, in order to cement us together. The enjoyments and comforts we have been compelled to renounce, the long months of deep anxiety each has felt, the unceasing labors that have tested our united energies, the sacrifices we have been subjected to in common, and the glory which encircles our brow has made us a band of brothers, and, I trust, we will be united forever. (Applause.)

On your soil has the blood of every State been shed—from your soil has gone home the maimed soldier, and the soldier disabled by disease, and to every State of the Confederacy has been borne the story of the hospitality of Virginians; how the kind women have nursed his wasted form and bathed his fevered brow. When in years to come arises the recollection of these kind attentions, his eyes will fill with tears of gratitude and in his heart he will bless the good women of Virginia.

By the firm friendship soldiers from different States have formed and cemented by mutual hardships and dangers; by the glory in which all alike participate; by the congeniality of thought and sentiment, which united us at first in a common destiny, and the thousand events and associations which have since tended to render us more united by all these causes the existence of jealousies and rivalries will be prevented, and when peace and prosperity shall come to us, we will go on assisting each other to develop the great political ideas upon which our Government is based and the immense resources which nature has lavished upon us. Of the former we are awakening to an appreciation of their deep significance. In the latter direction we are displaying unexampled energy. Our mines have been made to yield up neglected wealth, and manufactories start up as if by magic. We are becoming independent in several ways. If the war continues, we shall only grow stronger and stronger as each year rolls on. Compare our condition to-day with that which existed one year ago. See the increasing power of the enemy, but mark that our own has been proportionably greater, until we see in the future nothing to disturb the prospect of the independence for which we are struggling.—One year ago many were depressed and some despondent. Now deep resolve is seen in every eye, an unconquerable spirit nerves every arm. And gentle woman, too, who can estimate the value of her services in this struggle? [Applause.] The mother who has given her son, the wife who has given her husband, the girl who has given her sweetheart, are not all their fingers busy making clothing for the troops in the field, and their words of encouragement a most animating impulse to the soldier? Whilst their prayers go up for the safety of a friend or relative in the field, always coupled with them is the earnest aspiration for the independence of our country. With such noble women at home, and such heroic soldiers in the field, we are invincible. [Applause.]

I thank you my friends for the kind salutation to-night, it is an indication that at some future time we shall be better acquainted. I trust we shall all live to enjoy some of the fruits of the great struggle in which we are engaged. My prayers are for your individual and collective welfare. May God prosper our cause and may we live to give to our children untarnished the rich inheritance which our Fathers gave to us. Good night.

Message to Confederate Congress (JDC)

. . .

The public journals of the North have been received, containing a proclamation, dated on the 1st day of the present month, signed by the President of the United States, in which he orders and declares all slaves within ten of the States of the Confederacy to be free, except such as are found within certain districts now occupied in part by the armed forces of the enemy. We may well leave it to the instincts of that common humanity which a beneficent Creator has implanted in the breasts of our fellow-men of all countries to pass judgment on a measure by which several millions of human beings of an inferior race, peaceful and contented laborers in their sphere, are doomed to extermination, while at the same time they are encouraged to a general assassination of their masters by the insidious recommendation "to abstain from violence unless in necessary self-defense." Our own detestation of those who have attempted the most execrable measure recorded in the history of guilty man is tempered by profound contempt for the impotent rage which it discloses. So far as regards the action of this Government on such criminals as may attempt its execution, I confine myself to informing you that I shall, unless in your wisdom you deem some other course more expedient, deliver to the several State authorities all commissioned officers of the United States that may hereafter be captured by our forces in any of the States embraced in the proclamation, that they may be dealt with in accordance with the laws of those States providing for the punishment of criminals engaged in exciting servile insurrection. The enlisted soldiers I shall continue to treat as unwilling instruments in the commission of these crimes, and shall direct their discharge and return to their homes on the proper and usual parole.

In its political aspect this measure possesses great significance, and to it in this light I invite your attention. It affords to our whole people the complete and crowning proof of the true nature of the designs of the party which elevated to power the present occupant of the Presidential chair at Washington and which sought to conceal its purpose by every variety of artful device and by the perfidious use of the most solemn and repeated pledges on every possible occasion.

. . .

The people of this Confederacy, then, cannot fail to receive this proclamation as the fullest vindication of their own sagacity in foreseeing the uses to which the dominant party in the United States intended from the beginning to apply their power, nor can they cease to remember with devout thankfulness that it is to their own vigilance in resisting the first stealthy progress of approaching despotism that they owe their escape from consequences now apparent to the most skeptical. This proclamation will have another salutary effect in calming the fears of those who have constantly evinced the apprehension that this war might end by some reconstruction of the old Union or some renewal of close political relations with the United States. These fears have never been shared by me, nor have I ever been able to perceive on what basis they could rest. But the proclamation affords the fullest guarantee of the impossibility of such a result; it has established a state of things which can lead to but one of three possible consequences—the extermination of the slaves, the exile of the whole white population from the Confederacy, or absolute and total separation of these States from the United States.

. . .

To General J. E. Johnston (JDC)

RICHMOND, VIRGINIA, JANUARY 22, 1863

GENERAL:

As announced in my telegram, I address this letter to you to explain the purpose for which I desire that you will proceed promptly to the Hd. Qrs. of Genl. Bragg's Army.* The events connected with the late battle at Murfreesboro and retreat from that place have led to criticisms upon the conduct of General Bragg, which induced him to call

---

* In November 1862 Johnston was named commander of the Department of the West, which placed both Bragg and Pemberton under his command.

upon the Commanders of Corps for an expression of opinion, and for information as to the feeling in their commands, in regard to the conduct of General Bragg, and, also, whether he had so far lost the confidence of the Army as to impair his usefulness in his present position. The answers, I am informed, have been but partially given, but are so far indicative of a want of confidence such as is essential to success. Why General Bragg should have selected that tribunal and have invited its judgments upon him, is to me unexplained. It manifests, however, a condition of things which seems to me to require your presence. The enemy is said to be preparing to advance and though my confidence in General Bragg is unshaken, it cannot be doubted that, if he is distrusted by his officers and troops, a disaster may result which but for that cause would have been avoided. You will, I trust, be able, by conversation with General Bragg, and others of his command, to decide what the best interests of the service require, and to give me the advice which I need at this juncture. As that army is a part of your command, no order will be necessary to give you authority there, as, whether present or absent, you have a right to direct its operations, and do whatever else belongs to the General Commanding.

VERY RESPECTFULLY AND TRULY YOURS,
(SIGNED) JEFFN. DAVIS

To Lieutenant General Theophilus H. Holmes (PJD)

RICHMOND, VIRGINIA, JANUARY 28, 1863

MY DEAR SIR:

I avail myself of the opportunity afforded by the departure of Genl. Tappan to acknowledge yours of the 29th. ult. Since that date, I have heard nothing more of the reported advance of the enemy upon Van Buren, and trust it may have been checked by some one of the many causes which seem to me to render the march almost impracticable. I regret very much to observe the increase of disease among your troops, and even more, that desertions have become so frequent. I had hoped that the liberal provisions understood to have been made by the State Legislature would to a great extent have relieved the suffering of the poor, and have quieted the anxiety of the soldiers in regard to the condition of their families. The extortion of which you complain can not be wholly suppressed, but it has seemed to me might best be restrained by State legislation. Prices must always be regulated by the relation of supply and demand, and no law which can be devised can change the effect which will be produced in the enhancement of the price of food where the amount to be sold is too small for the number of consumers. To attempt the remedy which you propose, would create dissatisfaction with the Government, and by destroying the affection and confidence of the people would substitute a greater evil than that for which you propose martial law as a remedy. Congress has, under certain conditions, conferred the power to suspend the writ of habeas corpus; and where suspended, the power of a Genl. to govern by camp regulations would be temporarily increased by the suspension of the ordinary remedies of law against false imprisonment: but neither the suspension of the writ of habeas corpus nor the declaration of martial law, which is the establishment of camp regulations over a place or district, would compel persons having supplies to offer them for sale or transport them to the consumers. Many complaints were made against the attempt to subject the people of Arkansas to a military police. The effort was certainly unwise, and no doubt much of your embarrassment has resulted from the necessity of restoring things to their normal condition. A people called upon to sacrifice everything in resistance to usurpation and oppression should always have before them unmistakeable evidence of a strict regard for their rights on the part of those who invoke their assistance. I rely upon your sound judgment as well as upon your kind temper to unite the people and to make all the resources of the country tributary to the success of the great work which has been entrusted to you.

I have considered your remarks in relation to the proposition to reinforce Genl. Pemberton. If you are correct as to the consequences which would follow, you have properly exercised the discretion which was entrusted to you. The view I then took of the matter was that you might be attacked by the enemy advancing from the Mississippi river, but that no large force could be sent over land against the Northwestern portion of Arkansas, that you had therefore more troops in the latter region than were necessary, and if you had enough on the Arkansas and White rivers, that some might be spared. That was a question which you could better decide on the spot than I at a distance, and therefore it was submitted to you. We have lately received through the Yankee papers an account of the capture of the Post of Arkansas, but as we have nothing from your army, I yet cling to the hope so great a disaster has not befallen us, and this hope is sustained by the knowledge that the enemy have been for some time assembling a large army on the lower Missi. to renew the attack upon Vicksburg. The troops in upper Louisiana have so far, as I can learn, done nothing to impede the operations of the enemy, not even to protect the rail road communication from Vicksburg to Monroe so essential to the efficiency of your command, and to cooperation between the armies east and west of the Mississippi river. The loss of either of the two positions, Vicksburg and Port Hudson would destroy communication with the Trans-Mississippi Department and inflict upon the Confederacy an injury which I am sure you have not failed to appreciate.

Genl. Kirby Smith has been sent to take command of the Department to be composed of Louisiana and Texas. The kind relations which exist between you, though not necessary to either of you to insure a cordial co-operation, will nevertheless contribute to make your intercourse pleasant and your co-intelligence complete. I am looking anxiously for further information in relation to affairs in Arkansas, and hopeful that the Missourians, reported to be coming out in large numbers, are steadily increasing the strength of your army. I still look forward to those successes which I am sure, with a fair opportunity, you will achieve, and to the day when, Arkansas secure, you may advance into Missouri and compel the enemy to look to the defence of the upper Mississippi instead of the conquest of the lower portion of its valley. Very respectfully & truly yrs.

(SIGNED) JEFFN. DAVIS

To General Joseph E. Johnston (PJD)

RICHMOND, VIRGINIA, FEBRUARY 19, 1863

GENERAL,

Your's of the 3d & 12th have been received and considered. I regret that the confidence of the superior officers in Genl. Bragg's fitness for command has been so much impaired. It is scarcely possible in that state of the case for him to possess the requisite confidence of the troops. However truly it may be desired by them, their distrust cannot be concealed. Staff officers will reflect the opinions and feelings of their chief and gradually the impression must be communicated to the whole army. I am truly gratified at the language of commendation which you employ in relation to Genl. Bragg, and at the cheering account you give of the condition and increasing strength of the army of Tenn. When I visited the army, there was no visible sign of discontent with the commander and I had hoped that the disatisfaction created by the events of the Kentucky campaign had given way before calm review of all which had occurred.

It is not given to all men of ability to excite enthusiasm & to win affection of their troops and it is only the few who are thus endowed, who can overcome the distrust and alienation of their principal officers. No one more readily than Genl. Bragg would surrender a desirable position to promote the public interest, and I have not feared any hesitation on his part if he should find that he could better serve his country by a change of position. With the confidence I feel in his ability and zeal you will readily understand the difficulty I find in the question of substitution. You limit the selection to a new man and in terms very embarassing to me, object to being yourself the immediate commander. I had felt the importance of keeping you free to pass from army to army in your Dept. so as to be present wherever most needed and to command in person wherever present. When you went to Tullahoma I considered your arrival placed for as long a period as you should remain there in the immediate command of that army, and that your judgement would determine the duration of your stay. You have borne no part in the investigation of the statements made in relation to the command of Genl. Bragg, other than that which seems to me appropriate to your position of Comdg. Genl. of all the forces of the Dept. The removal of Genl. Bragg would only affect you in so far as it deprived you of his services and might restrain your freedom of movement by requiring more of your attention to that army; therefore I do not think that your personal honor is involved as you could have nothing to gain by the removal of Genl. Bragg. You shall not be urged by me to any course which would wound your sensibility or views of professional propriety, though you will perceive how small is the field of selection if a new man is to be sought, whose rank is superior to that of the Lieut. Genls. now in Tenn. I will expect to hear further from you on this subject.

The condition of affairs in Missi. & La. excites continued anxiety and I am sorry to learn that you have not as full communication from Genl. Pemberton as is desirable. If circumstances permit, a visit from you might be serviceable to the defence of Vicksburg and its approaches. The rise of the river has probably checked any further work on the canal, but it has also opened the line of the Yazoo pass and if it has not been sufficiently obstructed may enable the Enemy to come down the Tallahatchie and get in rear of our position. Nothing has been heard of the plan proposed and which should have been executed before this date for the recapture of the city of ✂︎ ✂︎.* You will have observed the success of the gun boats in passing the batteries at Vicksburg, they will destroy a necessary navigation unless they can be captured, which may be possible by boarding when they land.

The Enemy are leaving the Rappahannock and may design from present indications a change of their line of operations to the South side of James River. Very Respectfully & truly yr's

JEFFN,, DAVIS

---

* New Orleans.

To Congressman A. H. Garland (JDC)*

RICHMOND, VIRGINIA, MARCH 28, 1863

SIR:

I reply to your letter of 21st inst. and to the matters contained in your previous communications of 14th and 18th inst. I state my recollections of what occurred at the meeting between the Arkansas Delegation and myself, for the sole purpose of avoiding the inference that my silence on the subject would be a tacit assent to the accuracy of your recital.

On the 29th January the Arkansas delegation in the House, in answer to a request from me that they would call for conference at the Executive office, were present. Some members of the Cabinet were also present, and a despatch was read to the delegation in which General Holmes requested that martial law should be proclaimed in that State and in the Indian Country. The delegation were understood as recommending that this should be done, and that General Hindman should be recalled, as his presence in command was stated to be very objectionable to the public feeling of the State.

The delegation expressed itself in the kindest terms as to General Holmes, but suggested that after what had occurred in that State, it was very desirable that a new commander, General E. Kirby Smith, should be sent there as soon as it could be done with due regard to the public service.

So certain was it to me and to the members of the Cabinet present that this was the view of the delegation, that I immediately caused the following despatch to be forwarded to Genl. Holmes:

LT. GENL. HOLMES:
RICHMOND, JANUARY 29, 1863
Your despatch of 22d received. The President suspends the writ of habeas corpus in Arkansas and the adjacent Indian country. You will establish the necessary regulations to protect persons and property and to maintain order, but will abstain from any further control over the rights of persons

---

* Confederate States congressman from Arkansas.

or property than is necessary for defensive purposes and military discipline.

BY THE PRESIDENT

(SIGNED)   S. COOPER, ADJT. & INSPR. GENL.

At the same time directions were given to relieve General Hindman from further duties in the Trans-Mississippi District, and that he should repair to Vicksburg for further orders. These directions were executed by the issue of a special order to that effect the next day, 30th January. Soon afterwards, on the 9th of February, the State of Arkansas was united to the military Dept. under command of Genl. Kirby Smith, who as senior officer takes command over Genl. Holmes.

These arrangements were made in accordance with my understanding of the wishes and desires of your delegation, and it plainly appears that I was not mistaken in my interpretation of their views, for on the 2d February, the whole delegation united in a letter to me, setting forth their wishes as follows :

"1st. That you will place Genl. E. Kirby Smith in command of the Trans-Missi. Dept.

2nd. That you withdraw Major Genl. Hindman from command of the army in Arkansas."

In the same letter the delegation said:

"We now respectfully add that we would guard the feelings of Genl. Hindman a faithful and devoted soldier and gentleman, and knowing as we feel we do that he would rejoice at this action and serve with satisfaction under Genl. Smith or wherever you would assign him, and feeling a personal confidence and regard for him, would prefer that you would continue him amongst us, &c &c."

To this statement of facts I will simply add that the law authorizing the suspension of the writ of *habeas corpus* having expired, General Holmes was so informed by me, by letter of 26th February last.

Under these circumstances it will, I am persuaded, appear quite natural to you that I should be surprised at the charge made in your letter of the 14th inst. (which you subsequently explained to have been made without any intention of disrespect to the Chief Magistrate) that "the Representatives and Senators had been surely trifled with and by the Administration," and that "the call on the Senators and Representatives was useless and ridiculous."

I will add one word on the implied complaint of the difficulty of having an interview with me. During the session of Congress, when about one hundred and twenty members of the two Houses are added to the number of the public officers of all the Departments, as well as the Army officers despatched to me on urgent business by their Generals, the entire official day is inadequate to their reception and to the necessary correspondence with both State and Confederate officials in all the States.

It thus happens often that gentlemen of the two Houses find me pre-engaged with other visitors, when it would be convenient to them to confer with me, but I am not aware that I have ever failed to welcome cordially the visit of yourself or any other gentleman of either House, when not deprived of that pleasure by the stress of important public business.

I HAVE THE HONOR TO BE
&C &C
(SIGNED) JEFFN. DAVIS

To *Wm. M. Brooks* (JDC)

RICHMOND, VIRGINIA, APRIL 2, 1863

MY DEAR SIR:

Your letter of the 20th ulto. reached me in due course, and has received careful attention. Your friendly assurance of the extent to which I am honored by the confidence and esteem of my fellow-citizens is a source of sincere gratification, the more acceptable coming from one so well qualified to judge as yourself.

I was not prepared to learn the dissatisfaction which you represent as existing in regard to the assignment of General Pemberton, and I hope that the distrust in his fidelity and ability to which you allude is not as great as you have been led to believe.

I selected General Pemberton for the very important command which he now holds from a conviction that he was the best qualified officer for that post then available, and I have since found no reason to change the opinion I then entertained of him.

If success which is generally regarded in popular estimation as evidence of qualification be so regarded in his case, I am surprised that General Pemberton's merits should still be doubted. With a force far inferior in numbers to the enemy, menaced by attack at several points widely distant from each other, with no naval force to meet the enemy's fleets on the Mississippi and its tributaries, by his judicious disposition of his forces and skilful selection of the best points of defence he has repulsed the enemy at Vicksburg, Port Hudson, on the Tallahatchie and at Deer Creek, and has thus far foiled his every attempt to get possession of the Mississippi river and the vast section of country which it controls.

I think that he has also demonstrated great administrative as well as military ability. He has been enabled to subsist and clothe his army without going out of his own Dept., and though within a recent period some difficulty may have arisen in the transportation of supplies, or some scarcity may have been apprehended which circumstance is, I regret to say, not confined to his command, I think he is not the less commendable for his former success in this regard and that he is entitled to confidence in his ability to overcome the difficulty and procure the requisite provisions for his troops, if indeed such may be practicable.

I still hope that "the suspicions and distrust" which you mention do not exist to any considerable extent, but however this may be, I feel assured that they are "groundless."

With reference to the fact that General Pemberton was born at the North being alleged as a justification of distrust in his fidelity to our cause, I can imagine nothing more unjust and ungenerous.

General Pemberton resigned his commission in the U.S. army, on the secession of Virginia—his adopted State.—He came at once to Richmond and was one of the first officers of the U.S. army who offered his services to Governor Letcher, by whom he was immediately appointed to a field commission. He afterwards entered the service of the Confederate States in which he has risen from step to step to his present position. In addition to the other proofs which he has afforded of his devotion to the cause of the Confederate States, I may add that by coming South he forfeited a considerable fortune.

Your suggestions as to Col. I. W. Garrett shall receive due attention. I recollect him very favorably and have no doubt that your estimate of him is just.

WITH ASSURANCES OF REGARD AND ESTEEM I REMAIN
VERY RESPECTFULLY & TRULY
YOURS
(SIGNED) JEFFN. DAVIS

To *Joseph E. Davis* (PJD)

RICHMOND, VIRGINIA, MAY 7, 1863

MY DEAR BROTHER

I avail myself of the opportunity afforded by the departure of Mr. Barksdale to write to you. I have not heard from you since the present invasion of our section commenced and infer that the known confusion in the mails is the cause of it. You can realize how deeply solicitous I am for your safety.

The despatches leave me in doubt as to the force of the Enemy and the efficiency of the measures taken to meet him. As he must be deficient in transportation great embarassment will necessarily attend any movement into the interior and if our Cavalry are equal to the task of cutting his line of communication and destroying his trains, he must soon be compelled to return to the river even if not beaten in battle. I hope for the latter result though it may not be, until our advance has fallen back to proximity to the main body at Vicksburg.

The battle recently fought on the Rappahannock was certainly a great victory, in view of the thorough preparation of the Enemy and his superiority of numbers, not less than two to one. He is however reinforcing heavily and our Rail Roads are so poor and badly administered that my efforts to reinforce first do not promise well. If the forces ordered up join Genl. Lee in this present condition of the two armies I hope we will destroy Hooker's army and then perform the same operation on the army sent to sustain him.* The withdrawal of

---

* Major General Joseph Hooker, Union commander.

Van Dorn from North Missi. was one of those blunders which it is difficult to compensate for. A *General* in the full acceptation of the word is a rare product, scarcely more than one can be expected in a generation but in this mighty war in which we are engaged there is need for half a dozen. The Enemy are however worse off than ourselves in that regard and hence their failures to effect what upon a calculation must have been admitted was due to their greater armies and better transportation.

I have sent all the force at command and arms for the militia, and though I cannot but be apprehensive, am hopeful that Genl. Pemberton will repel the invader. I hope however to give him further reinforcements, in a very short time.

It is sad to me to know that you and Sister Eliza are in your old age denied the repose required and to feel powerless to give you the personal assistance which in the order of nature is due from me. God I trust will shield you and soon give to our arms entire success.

My health is not good, but has improved so much within the past week that it may be reasonably expected that the recent attack is an end. It commenced with diurnal fever and was followed by bronchitis, the cough only remains of disease, and the present debility is no doubt much due to confinement and anxiety. My official duties have not been suspended at any time except in the matter of personal interviews which inability to talk rendered /it/ necessary to suspend.

I am interrupted and with love to Sister Eliza Lize Joe Nick and others of the family with you, I am ever affectionately

YOUR BROTHER

To General Joseph E. Johnston (PJD)

RICHMOND, VIRGINIA, MAY 24, 1863

I concur in your reliance on the tenacity with which Genl. Pemberton will defend his position, but the disparity of numbers renders prolonged defence dangerous. I hope you will soon be able to break the investment, make a junction & *carry in munitions.* Genl. Rains who has *made valuable inventions* is ordered to you for special service & will I think be useful both *on land* & ~~water~~ *river* Genl. Bragg has probably communicated with you.* If my strength permitted I would go to you.

(SIGNED) JEFF. DAVIS

To General R. E. Lee (JDC)

RICHMOND, VIRGINIA, MAY 31, 1863

...

I wish I knew how to relieve you from all anxiety concerning movements on the York or James river against Richmond while you are moving towards the North and West; but even if you could spare troops for the purpose, on whom could you devolve the command with that feeling of security which would be necessary for the full execution of your designs? I readily perceive the disadvantage of standing still, and surely regret that I can not give you the means which would make it quite safe to attempt all that we desire. That any advantage should have been lost by delay is sad enough where the contest, at best, was so very unequal as to give little room for the exercise of what Genl. Chas. Lee called "that rascally virtue," prudence. I do not know what success we shall have in organizations for local defence, but should it be all which I can hope, you know how far our army will still fall short of the numerical strength of the enemy. Missouri, Kentucky, the most populous portions of Tennessee and Louisiana are contributing nothing to recruit the army. If Genl. Kirby Smith should have success on the West side of the river, he will soon have a large force by volunteers from Mo. and southern La. Genl. Johnston did not, as you thought advisable, attack Grant promptly, and I fear the result is that which you anticipated if time was given. The last intelligence indicates that Grant's army is concentrating on the Yazoo, where he connects with his gunboats and river transportation, and threatens the line of communication between Jackson and Vicksburg. The position, naturally strong, may soon be intrenched, and with the heavy guns which he can bring by water, will require to be reduced by

---

* Brigadier General Gabriel J. Rains, an explosives expert.

some other means than a direct attack. It is useless to look back, and it would be unkind to annoy you in the midst of your many cares with the reflections which I have not been able to avoid. All the accounts we have of Pemberton's conduct fully sustain the good opinion heretofore entertained of him, and I hope has secured for him that confidence of his troops which is so essential to success.

VERY RESPECTFULLY AND TRULY YOURS
(SIGNED) JEFFN. DAVIS

To Senator Robert W. Johnson (PJD)*

RICHMOND, VIRGINIA, JULY 14, 1863

MY DEAR SIR,

Capt Buck delivered to me yours of June the 18th. with the enclosed letter of Judge Watkins, and I thank you for the fullness, and freedom with which you have spoken. Your letter found me in the depth of the gloom ~~with~~ /in/ which the disasters on the Missi River have shrouded our cause. Though it was well for me to know the worst, it pained me to observe how far your confidence was shaken, and your criticism severe on men who I think deserve to be trusted. In proportion as our difficulties increase, so must we all cling together, judge charitably of each other, and strive to bear, and forbear, however great may be the sacrifice, and bitter the trial It is not for man to command success, he should strive to deserve it, and leave the rest to Him who governs all things, and disposes for the best, though to our short vision the Justice may not be visible.

Since the date of your letter the orders for a movement upon ~~the~~ Helena must have satisfied you that Genl. Smith had no idea of abandoning Arkansas, that his attempt to concentrate troops in La. was to prevent the catastrophe which threatened to separate the States of the east, from those of the west, by the loss of the only fortified position, we had on the Missi River. Every consideration rejects the policy of voluntarily surrendering any portion of our territory, and the views

* Confederate States senator from Arkansas.

you express in relation to the Valley of the Arkansas are in accordance with those I have long entertained, and heretofore expressed to our officers in command. Our [pe]ople have not generally realised the magnitude of the struggle in which we are engaged. Had Missouri and Tennessee furnished the number of troops which you say they could now supply if in our possession our banners would be flying on the upper Missi, and the Ohio, and there would have been no question of supplies for the support of the largest army which our necessities could have required, as, if free from invasion, our agricultural products would have greatly exceeded any demand which home consumption could create

I have long seen the importance of establishing manufactures of all munitions of war in the trans Missi dept. Have directed skilled workman to be sent over, and that every inducement should be offered to develop the mines of the country. A foundry, and rolling mill should be located where iron is cheapest, and best, and where the works would be least likely to interruption from hostile invasion. The manufacture, and repair of small arms had probably better be at a different place, a powder mill at another. Tanneries & shoemaking could well be dispersed, and the manufacture of cloth left to domestic industry, to encourage which orders have been given for the importation of cards and facilities offered for the importation of machinery to make them at home.

My information is quite too limited to justify the expression of an opinion as to the best place for a foundry, or for an Arsenal, or for a powder mill. Indeed the only very clear information ever communicated to me was in the report of that much abused officer Brig. Gen. Shoup. Whatever location is best for the country dependent upon the works for supply, will I am sure meet the approval of your judgement, and if the balance be so even that the best informed might differ, you will not I am sure misconstrue the conclusion though it may be different from that at which you would have arrived.

I have called upon Col Gorgas and am waiting for the information which will enable me to reply to Gov. Flannigan's letter in relation to manufactures, and the supply of munitions in the West; and can have no difficulty in giving him the assurance /as to the defence of Arkansas/

which you desire, or feel any doubt that both Genl. Smith, and Genl Holmes will fulfil my purpose to the utmost of their ability.* It would be mad, suicidal for any state of the Confederacy to seek her safety by separation from the rest. I waive the question of faith, and ask what could be hoped for from our brutal enemy /what expected/ but such degradation as to a freeman would be worse than torture at the stake. Proud, honorable men may have opposed the act of secession, but can anyone not fit to be a slave, and ready to become one, think of passing under the yoke of such as the Yankees have shown themselves to be by their conduct in this war—The sacrifices of our people have been very heavy both of blood & of treasure. many like myself have been robbed of all which the toil of many years had gathered, but the prize for which we strive, freedom and independence, is worth whatever it may cost. With Union, and energy, the rallying of every man able to bear arms to the defence of his country, we shall succeed, and if we leave our children poor we shall also leave them a better heritage than wealth—Trusting that God will bless our good cause and that we shall soon have brighter days I am as ever very truly yr. friend

JEFFN,, DAVIS

To Lieutenant General E. K. Smith (JDC)

RICHMOND, VIRGINIA, JULY 14, 1863

SIR:

I sometime since sent you a dispatch invoking your aid to relieve the siege of Vicksburg. Probably before you received it, the disaster which was apprehended had occurred. By the fall of our two fortified places on the Mississippi River, Vicksburg and Port Hudson, your Department is placed in a new relation and your difficulties must be materially enhanced. You now have not merely a military, but also a political problem involved in your command. I have been warned against a feeling which is said to exist in favor of a separate organization on the part of the States west of the Mississippi. Unreasonable

---

* Colonel Josiah Gorgas, Confederate chief of ordnance, who became a brigadier general; Harris Flanagin, governor of Arkansas.

men think they have been neglected and timid men may hope that they can make better terms for themselves, if their cause is not combined with that of the Confederacy. Already, I am told, that dissatisfaction exists in Arkansas and that it has been assumed that you intend to abandon that country, the basis of such supposition being your concentration of troops in Louisiana.

To give to each section all that local interests may suggest will of course be impossible; but much discontent may be avoided by giving such explanations to the Governors of the States as will prevent them from misconstruing your actions, and men are sometimes made valuable coadjutors by conferring with them without surrendering any portion of that control which it is essential for a commander to retain.

Separated from the Eastern States as you now are, your Department must needs be to a great extent self-sustaining. It contains large resources of mineral wealth, but they have been little developed, and I fear there is a great want of skilled labor. To get iron, test its qualities, combine it into the best gun metal and cast ordnance will be one of your first efforts. Some persons skilled in the casting of guns have been sent over. I am not informed what progress they have made.

To manufacture gun carriages and army wagons will also be necessary. These operations may be partly conducted by contract; but you will probably have also to maintain an establishment for that purpose. You will also require a powder mill, and I hope you will be able to procure salt petre and sulphur in the country. Some attempts have been made to establish arsenals for the repair and manufacture of small arms, but the removal and dispersion of the machinery has I fear greatly retarded the successful prosecution of the work.

In selecting the places at which these various operations may be carried on, you will have, to some extent, to defer to the wishes of the people of the different States to have such establishments within their limits. And for other and more weighty consideration it would be advisable so to separate these establishments that not more than one could be destroyed in a single expedition of the enemy.

You will also have to encourage the tanning of leather for the manufacture of shoes and harness, and to stimulate domestic industry in the manufacture of cloths and, if possible, of blankets. And to all this must be added the encouragement in the production of food to support your army and maintain the people. In any view of the case, and especially in connection with an advance into Missouri, it is necessary that the valley of the Arkansas should be kept in such sense of security as to ensure the full cultivation of the land. Of its capacity as a grain growing region, you are sufficiently advised. Of its importance in connection with maintaining the friendly feeling of the Indians, it would be needless to say anything to you, whose years of observation have rendered the subject familiar.

By the use of cavalry accompanied by light batteries, I hope you will be able to prevent the enemy from using the Mississippi for commercial purposes. Beyond that I suppose your operations must be confined to the interior of the country and that, as your means increase, you will be able to prevent the enemy from using the smaller rivers to penetrate the interior .

When you can get a rolling mill established, it may be that iron clad gunboats may be constructed on the Arkansas and Red Rivers, which will enable you in some contingencies to assume the offensive.

I have directed arms and munitions to be sent to you by sea. This will necessarily involve a long line of land transportation; but, under existing circumstances, it is the best which can be done.

Orders have been sent out for the purchase of cotton and woolen cards, and I hope it will be practicable to send some of these to your Department. I would readily give any facilities which we can afford to any one who would introduce machinery into your Department for the manufacture of such cards.

The endurance of our people is to be severely tested, and nothing will serve more to encourage and sustain them than a zealous application of their industry to the task of producing within themselves whatever is necessary for their comfortable existence. And in proportion as the country exhibits a power to sustain itself, so will the men able to bear arms be inspired with a determination to repel invasion.

During the summer months the enemy cannot, I suppose, attempt any extensive operations in the Southern portion of your Department. During the fall the rivers will scarcely be navigable; and the interval will, I hope, enable you to do much in the way of preparation. I have understood that substantial steamboats and good engines have been made at Little Rock and that contracts would be taken for the construction of such, if proposals were invited. Concerning this and all the like subjects of which I have spoken, you are in a situation to obtain correct information and will know how to secure the co-operation of such persons as will be most likely to render your efforts successful. I suppose you will encounter, as we have elsewhere, embarrassment and annoyance from the class of persons who, eager for gain and careless of their country's welfare, engage in illicit trade with the enemy. The little benefit which is derived from such traffic is so greatly overbalanced by the injuries which it inflicts, that, as far as may be, it should be prevented.

I have rejoiced in the success which has attended the operations of your troops in Southwestern Louisiana, and trust it is but the beginning of a career which will extend itself to every portion of your Department and cause your Administration of it to redound equally to the good of our country and your own fame.

We are now in the darkest hour of our political existence. I am happy in the confidence I feel in your ability, zeal and discretion. The responsibility with which you are charged is heavy indeed, and your means I know are very adequate. If my power were equal to my will, you should have all which you require. It grieves me to have enumerated so many and such difficult objects for your attention when I can give you so little aid in their achievement.

May God guide and preserve you and grant to us a future in which we may congratulate each other on the achievement of the independence and peace of our country.

TRULY YOUR FRIEND
(SIGNED) JEFFERSON DAVIS

To General J. E. Johnston (JDC)

RICHMOND, VIRGINIA, JULY 15, 1863

GENERAL:

Your despatch of the 5th inst. stating that you "considered" your "assignment to the immediate command in Mississippi" as giving you a "new position" and as "limiting your authority," being a repetition of a statement which you were informed was a grave error, and being persisted in after your failure to point out when requested the letter or despatch justifying you in such a conclusion, rendered it necessary as you were informed in my despatch of 8th inst., that I should make a more extended reply than could be given in a telegram. That there may be no possible room for further mistake in this matter, I am compelled to recapitulate the substance of all orders and instructions given to you, so far as they bear on this question.

On the 24th November last you were assigned by Special Order No. 275 to a defined geographical command. The description included a portion of Western North Carolina, and Northern Georgia, the States of Tennessee, Alabama and Mississippi, and that portion of the State of Louisiana East of the Mississippi River. The order concluded in the following language :

"Genl. Johnston will for the purpose of correspondence and reports establish his Headquarters at Chattanooga, or such other place as in his judgment will best secure communication with the troops within the limits of his command, and will repair in person to any part of said command, whenever his presence may for the time be necessary or desirable."

This command by its terms embraced the armies under command of General Bragg in Tennessee, of Genl. Pemberton at Vicksburg, as well as those at Port Hudson, Mobile, and the forces in East Tennessee.

This general order has never been changed nor modified so as to affect your command in a single particular, nor has your control over it been interfered with. I have as Commander-in-Chief given you some orders which will be hereafter noticed, not one of them however indicating in any manner that the general control confided to you was restricted or impaired.

You exercised this command by visiting in person the armies at Murfreesboro', Vicksburg, Mobile and elsewhere, and on the 22d January, I wrote to you directing that you should repair in person to the Army at Tullahoma on account of a reported want of harmony and confidence between General Bragg and his officers and troops. This letter closed with the following passage:

"As that army is part of your command no order will be necessary to give you authority there, as whether present or absent, you have a right to direct its operations, and to do whatever belongs to the General Commanding."

Language cannot be plainer than this, and although the different armies in your geographical district were ordered to report directly to Richmond as well as to yourself, this was done solely to avoid the evil that would result from reporting through you when your Head Quarters might be, and it was expected frequently would be, so located as to create delays injurious to the public interest.

While at Tullahoma you did not hesitate to order troops from Genl. Pemberton's army, and learning that you had ordered the division of cavalry from North Mississippi to Tennessee, I telegraphed to you that this order left Mississippi exposed to cavalry raids without means of checking them. You did not change your orders, and although I thought them injudicious I refrained from exercising my authority in deference to your views.

When I learned that prejudice and malignity had so undermined the confidence of the troops at Vicksburg in their commander as to threaten disaster, I deemed the circumstances such as to present the case foreseen in Special Order No. 275, that you should "repair in person to any part of said command whenever your presence might be for the time necessary or desirable."

You were therefore ordered on 9th May to "proceed at once to Mississippi and take chief command of the forces, giving to those in the field as far as practicable the encouragement and benefit of your personal direction."

Some details were added about reinforcements, but not a word affecting in the remotest degree your authority to command your geographical district.

On the 4th June you telegraphed to the Secty. of War in response to his inquiry saying "my only plan is to relieve Vicksburg, my force is far too small for the purpose. Tell me if you can increase it and how much." To which he answered on the 5th, "I regret inability to promise more troops as we have drained resources even to the danger of several points. You know best concerning Genl. Bragg's army, but I fear to withdraw more. We are too far outnumbered in Virginia to spare any &c. &c."

On the 8th June the Secretary was more explicit if possible. He said, "Do you advise more reinforcements from Genl. Bragg? You as Commandant of the Dept. have power so to order if you in view of the whole case so determine."

On the 10th June you answered that it was for the Government to determine what Dept. could furnish the reinforcements; that you could not know how Genl. Bragg's wants compared with yours, and that the Government could make the comparison. Your statements that the Government in Richmond was better able to judge of the relative necessities of the armies under your command than you were and the further statement that you could not know how General Bragg's wants compared with yours,—were considered extraordinary; but as they were accompanied by the remark that the Secretary's despatch had been imperfectly decyphered, no observation was made on them till the receipt of your telegram to the Secretary of the 12th inst., stating,

"I have not considered myself commanding in Tennessee since assignment here, and should not have felt authorized to take troops from that Dept. after having been informed by the Executive that no more could be spared."

My surprise at these two statements was extreme. You had never been "assigned" to the Mississippi command. You went there under the circumstances and orders already quoted, and no justification whatever is perceived for your abandonment of your duties as Commanding General of the geographical district to which you were assigned.

Orders as explicit as those under which you were sent to the West and under which you continued to act up to the 9th May, when you were directed to repair in person to Mississippi can only be impaired or set aside by subsequent orders equally explicit, and your announcement that you had ceased to consider yourself charged with the control of affairs in Tennessee because ordered to repair in person to Mississippi, both places being within the command to which you were assigned, was too grave to be overlooked; and when to this was added the assertion that you should not have felt authorized to draw troops from that Dept. (Tennessee) "after being informed by the Executive that no more could be spared," I was unable to account for your language, being entirely confident that I had never given you any such information.

. . .

To Eliza Cannon Cannon (PJD)[*]

RICHMOND, VIRGINIA, JULY 18, 1863

MY DEAR MADAM

The visit of Govr. Whitfield affords me a safe opportunity to send to you a letter of acknowledgement for your beautiful and most prized present of a Bible.[†] In this copy of the book of life I have found the "Apocrypha" a portion of the scripture with which I had no previous acquaintance and I am truly obliged to you for the introduction.

It needed no visible sign to secure my remembrance of you, yet it is very pleasant to have you thus associated with holy meditation.

Many thanks for your cheering words, though your expressions of confidence and commendation make me feel the more my own unworthiness. In these times of disaster, when my relatives and nearest friends are the objects of most cruel animosity, when my beloved Mississippi is being overrun by the invader I deeply feel my want of that sustaining power which has in times past upheld the just cause, and given to the weak the power to defeat the strong.

I trust the prayers of the righteous will avail and that requisite wis-

[*] Wife of JD's Mississippi friend William R. Cannon.

[†] James Whitfield, Mississippi politician and friend of JD.

dom may be given to me so to discharge the duties devolved upon me, as to redound to the success of our people and to the glory of the giver of all good things.

The original poetry with with which you dedicate the volume to my use has been greatly admired by the few to whom I have been willing to submit it and is treasured by me as being part of yourself. May the Lord preserve your noble son to be a comfort to you in after years and to place his Father's name on the roll of honor which the deeds of this war will leave to future time.

When peace shall again bless our land I trust it may be permitted to me again to see you in your happy home, and I fervently pray for your welfare and happiness now and always. Very Respectfully & truly your friend

JEFFN,, DAVIS

To General R. E. Lee (JDC)

RICHMOND, VIRGINIA, JULY 28, 1863

GENERAL:

Yours of the 24th and 27th have been received. Efforts have been and will continue to be made to send up the convalescents and absentees from your army, and I am well disposed in regard to your suggestion for a general amnesty. Your remarks in relation to the service of enrollment impress me as likely to lead to improvement. Col. Jno. Preston will be here in a day or two to take charge of the Bureau for conscription and I hope will so conduct as to secure better results.

For some time past I have felt the evil to which you refer: the employment of young able-bodied men and in excessive numbers by the Quarter Master's Department for duties which could as well be performed by aged men or disabled soldiers.

The horse shoes you want were sent to you, but I am informed the first lot went to Staunton and would only reach you after being brought back.

You know how rare a quality is that which is esteemed administrative capacity and how much it was needed in our condition. Without stores or workshops or artisans and without even the agricultural habits suited to the wants of this great war, it was needful that a system economizing all supplies should be so administered as to avoid exhaustion. Grain, even pork, can be reproduced annually but where shall we get future supplies of beeves sheep and horses? The hides of the beeves butchered. should have furnished a large surplus of leather, and as our commerce heretofore small is threatened with destruction, the importance of this item increases. The railroads are growing worse, and heavy losses are said to have been sustained, in the Southwest, of locomotives and machinery, which cannot soon, if during the war, be replaced. Our people have proven their gallantry and patriotic zeal,—their fortitude is now to be tested. May God endow them with all the virtue which is needed to save a suffering country and maintain a just cause.

I have felt more than ever before the want of your advice during the recent period of disaster. You know how one army of the enemy has triumphed by attacking three of ours in detail, at Vicksburg, Port Hudson and Jackson. Genl. Johnston, after evacuating Jackson, retreated to the east, to the pine woods of Mississippi, and if he has any other plan than that of watching the enemy it has not been communicated.

Pemberton's army commenced deserting to such extent that he was permitted to give furloughs generally for ten, fifteen, and thirty days; he thinks he will thus secure their future services. The siege at Charleston hastens slowly and General Beauregard calls for reinforcements and heavy guns. Some of both have been sent, but less of each than he asked for. Demonstrations have been made on the Railroad between Wilmington and Petersburg, and General Whiting calls for more troops, especially cavalry. The enemy are reported to be in force again at Suffolk. I think it is the same force which was on the Pamunkey, when Clingman's brigade was sent to Charleston. Colquitt's brigade was sent to Wilmington to replace it. General Whiting on his own responsibility sent two regiments of this Brigade to Charleston; now Beauregard asks for the other two, and Whiting wants Clingman's Brigade returned to Wilmington.

Brigadier General Ransom was sent from Petersburg to Weldon to meet the force said to be advancing upon that place, and when the report of an advance from Suffolk reached here, Brigadier General Jenkins was sent with his Brigade to Petersburg. General S. Jones when about to start for the valley was stopped by an advance of the enemy, and a portion of the force he was to take with him was retained.

The trans-Mississippi Department must now become mainly self sustaining, and will require the exercise of extraordinary powers by the commander, but how far this may extend without involving opposition it is difficult to foresee. To secure efficiency there must be greater promptitude than is attainable if papers are to be sent here by present available routes, yet this war can only be successfully prosecuted while we have the cordial support of the people and this is best secured by close adherence to law and usage. Misfortune often develops secret foes and oftener still makes men complain. It is comfortable to hold some one responsible for one's discomfort. In various quarters there are mutterings of discontent, and threats of alienation are said to exist with preparation for organized opposition. There are others who, faithful but dissatisfied, find an appropriate remedy in the removal of officers who have not succeeded. They have not counted the cost of following their advice. Their remedy to be good should furnish substitutes who would be better than the officers displaced.

If a victim would secure the success of our cause I would freely offer myself, and there are many of those most assailed who would I am sure contend for the place if their sacrifice could bring such reward.

With prayers for your health, safety and happiness, I am

AS EVER, YOUR FRIEND,
(SIGNED) JEFFN. DAVIS.

To General Robert E. Lee (PJD)*

RICHMOND, VIRGINIA, AUGUST 11, 1863

Yours of the 8th. inst. has been received. I am glad to find that you concur so entirely with me as to the want of our country in this trying

* In a letter to JD on August 8, Lee had offered to resign as commander of the Army of Northern Virginia.

hour, and am happy to add that after the first depression consequent upon our disasters in the West, indications have appeared that our people will exhibit that fortitude which we agree in believing is alone needful to secure ultimate success.

It well became Sydney Johnston when overwhelmed by a senseless clamor to admit the rule that success is the test of merit, and yet there has been nothing which I have found to require a greater effort of patience than to bear the criticisms of the ignorant, who pronounce everything a failure which does not equal their expectations or desires, and can see no good result which is not in the line of their own imaginings. I admit the propriety of your conclusions, that an officer who loses the confidence of his troops should have his position changed, whatever may be his ability; but when I read the sentence, I was not at all prepared for the application you were about to make. Expressions of discontent in the public journals furnish but little evidence of the sentiment of an army. I wish it were otherwise even tho' all the abuse of myself should be accepted as the results of honest observation. I say, I wish I could feel that the public journals were not generally partisan nor venal.

Were you capable of stooping to it, you could easily surround yourself with those who would fill the press with your laudations, and seek to exalt you for what you had not done rather than detract from the achievements which will make you and your army the subject of history and object of the worlds admiration for generations to come.

I am truly sorry to know that you still feel the effects of the illness you suffered last Spring, and can readily understand, the embarrassments you experience in using the eyes of others, having been so much accustomed to make your own reconnaissances. Practice will however do much to relieve that embarrassment, and the minute knowledge of the country which you have acquired will render you less dependent for topographical information.

But suppose, my dear friend, that I were to admit, with all their implications, the points which you present, where am I to find that new commander who is to possess the greater ability which you believe to be required. I do not doubt the readiness with which you would give way to one who could accomplish all that you have wished, and you will do me the justice to believe that if Providence would kindly offer such a person for our use, I would not hesitate to avail of his services.

My sight is not sufficiently penetrating to discover such hidden merit if it exists, and I have but used to you the language of sober earnestness, when I have impressed upon you the propriety of avoiding all unnecessary exposure to danger because I felt our country could not bear to lose you. To ask me to substitute you by some one in my judgment more fit to command, or who would possess more of the confidence of the army, or of the reflecting men in the country is to demand an impossibility.

It only remains for me to hope that you will take all possible care of yourself, that your health and strength may be entirely restored, and that the Lord will preserve you for the important duties devolved upon you in the struggle of our suffering country, for the independence which we have engaged in war to maintain. As ever very respectfully & truly yrs.

(SIGNED) JEFFN. DAVIS

To James M. Howry (PJD)*

RICHMOND, VIRGINIA, AUGUST 27, 1863

DEAR SIR:

Your letter of the 25th ult:, brought by Col: Looney, was laid before me a few days ago. I am glad to have received such full information as to your views concerning the affairs of the country, and shall always be gratified to hear from you.

The disasters in Mississippi were both great and unexpected to me. I had thought that the troops sent to the State, added to those already there, made a force large enough to accomplish the destruction of Grant's army. That no such result followed may have been the effect of mismanagement, or it may have been that it was unattainable. An investigation of the causes of the failure is now in progress; though, as the misfortunes have already come upon us, it would afford me but lit-

---

* JD's friend in Mississippi.

tle satisfaction to know that they resulted from bad Generalship and were not inevitable.

Recent events near their own homes have been calculated to produce in some minds the feeling of gloom you speak of. But I have not yet seen cause to waver in the conviction to which I have frequently given expression, that, if our people now show as much fortitude as we are entitled to expect from those who display such conspicuous gallantry in the field, we shall certainly beat the enemy and secure our independence. As some weeks have elapsed since your letter was written, and the progress of the enemy has not been such as was apprehended, I trust that the people of the State have in a measure recovered from their depression.

The recital of your losses during the war pains me. But the firmness with which you bear them—, and the zeal in the country's behalf which characterizes you and all the members of your family, are what I had expected—as well as the loyalty & true-heartedness of the women of the land, upon which you remark.

I beg you to present my compliments to Mrs Howry, with assurances of my admiration for her patriotic devotion. With many thanks for the kind & friendly tone of your letter, and with the best wishes for your welfare, I am, very respectfully & truly your friend & fellow citizen

JEFFERSON DAVIS

To Governor John Milton (JDC)*

RICHMOND, VIRGINIA, SEPTEMBER 1, 1863

GOVERNOR:

Your letter of the 23rd of May, giving reasons why overseers of slaves in Florida should be exempted from liability to military service, reached me by due course of mail, and should have been sooner acknowledged but for the fact that it was mislaid shortly after its arrival and only recently recovered.

---

* Governor of Florida.

Your suggestions received my careful attention and were submitted to the Secretary of War for his consideration in preparing instructions for the enrolling officers.

I have been disposed to do everything I consistently could to comply with your wishes on the subject, prompted as I know they are by a patriotic sense of duty. But you will readily perceive the difficulty of granting general exemptions at a time when our armies are so much in need of recruits.

The prosperous pursuit of agricultural operations, as well as the usual employments of other classes of our citizens, is very much interrupted by an enforcement of the Conscript Act. But the people have ceased to volunteer, and unless the ranks of the Regiments in the field are filled in the manner indicated by Congress we imperil our national existence. It has therefore been impossible for me to grant so general an exemption as you recommend.

Cases of individual hardship have received special consideration and have been relieved as far as practicable.

Orders, too, have been given to the officers of the Bureau of Conscription to grant liberal details of overseers until the crops could be made and gathered. Beyond that I have been unable to go without establishing a dangerous precedent.

It is to be hoped that the action of the enrolling officers under these instructions has been such as to secure to the country the abundant crops of grain planted in Florida during the Spring.

With assurances of my friendly regard, I am

VERY RESPECTFULLY AND TRULY YOURS
(SIGNED) JEFFN. DAVIS.

To General R. E. Lee (JDC)

RICHMOND, VIRGINIA, SEPTEMBER 8, 1863
Have considered your letter. Believe your presence in the western army would be worth more than the addition of a corps, but fear the effect of your absence from Virginia. Did not doubt your willingness

to do whatever was best for the country, and sought your aid to determine that question. Have sent you all additional information to aid your further consideration of problems discussed with you here.

(SIGNED) JEFFN. DAVIS.

Speech at Missionary Ridge, Tennessee (PJD)*

OCTOBER 10, 1863

He began by paying a warm tribute to their gallantry, displayed on the bloody field of Chickamauga, defeating the largely superior force of the enemy, who had boasted of their ability to penetrate to the heart of Georgia, and driving them back, like sheep, into a pen, and protected by strong entrenchments, from which naught but an indisposition to sacrifice, unnecessarily, the precious lives of our brave and patriotic soldiers, prevented us from driving them. But, he said, they had given still higher evidence of courage, patriotism, and resolute determination to live freemen, or die freemen, by their patient endurance and buoyant, cheerful spirits, amid privations and suffering from half-rations, thin blankets, ragged clothes, and shoeless feet, than given by baring their breasts to the enemy.

He reminded them that obedience was the first duty of a soldier, remarking that when he was a youth a veteran officer said to him: "My son, remember that obedience is the soldier's first duty. If your commanding officer orders you to burn your neighbor's house down, and to sit on the ridge-pole till it falls in, do it." The President said, this is an exaggerated statement of the duty, but prompt, unquestioning obedience of subordinates to their superiors could not be too highly commended. If the subordinate stops to consider the propriety of an order, the delay may derange the superior's whole plan, and the opportune moment for achieving a success or averting a defeat may be irretrievably lost.

He alluded to the boast of our enemy that, on the occupation of

---

* Address to the Army of Tennessee.

East Tennessee, they would heavily recruit their army and subjugate us with the aid of our own people; but the boast had not been fulfilled He said the proper course to pursue towards the misguided people of East Tennessee was, not to deride and abuse them, but to employ reason and conciliation to disabuse them of their error; that all of us had once loved and revered the old flag of the Union; that he had fought under its folds, and, for fifteen years, had striven to maintain the Constitution of our fathers in its purity, but in vain. It could not be saved from the grasping ambition for power and greed of gain of the Yankees, and he had to relinquish it. The error of the misguided among us was, that they clung longer than we to what was once a common sentiment and feeling of us all, and, he repeated, they must be reasoned with and conciliated.

In closing, he expressed his deep conviction of our eventual success under the blessing of Providence, and expected the army of Tennessee, when they should resume active operations, not to pause on the banks of the Cumberland, but to plant our banners permanently on the banks of the Ohio.—This, he believed, would be done. As the humble representative of the people he returned their grateful thanks to the army of Tennessee for what they had already accomplished, and fervently invoked the blessing of Almighty God upon all officers and men comprising it.

To the Army of Tennessee (JDC)

MISSIONARY RIDGE, OCTOBER 14, 1863

HEADQUARTERS ARMY OF TENNESSEE

Soldiers: A grateful country has recognized your arduous service, and rejoiced over your glorious victory on the field of Chickamauga. When your countrymen shall more fully learn the adverse circumstances under which you attacked the enemy—though they cannot be more thankful—they may admire more the gallantry and patriotic devotion which secured your success. Representatives of every State of the Confederacy, your steps have been followed with affectionate solicitude by friends in every portion of the country. Defenders of the heart of our territory, your movements have been the object of intensest anxiety. The hopes of our cause greatly depend upon you, and happy it is that all can securely rely upon your achieving whatever, under the blessing of Providence, human power can effect.

Though you have done much, very much yet remains to be done. Behind you is a people providing for your support and depending on you for protection. Before you is a country devastated by your ruthless invader, where gentle women, feeble age, and helpless infancy have been subjected to outrages without parallel in the warfare of civilized nations. With eager eyes they watch for your coming to their deliverance, and the homeless refugee pines for the hour when your victorious arms shall restore his family to the shelter from which they have been driven. Forced to take up arms to vindicate the political rights, the freedom, equality, and State sovereignty which were the heritage purchased by the blood of your revolutionary sires, you have but the alternative of slavish submission to despotic usurpation, or the independence which vigorous, united, persistent effort will secure. All which fires the manly breast, nerves the patriot, and exalts the hero, is present to stimulate and sustain you.

Nobly have you redeemed the pledges given in the name of freedom to the memory of your ancestors and the rights of your posterity. That you may complete the mission to which you are devoted, will require of you such exertion in the future as you have made in the past—continuance in the patient endurance of toil and danger, and that self-denial which rejects every consideration at variance with the public service as unworthy of the holy cause in which you are engaged.

When the war shall have ended, the highest meed of praise will be due, and probably given, to him who has claimed least for himself in proportion to the service he has rendered, and the bitterest self-reproach which may hereafter haunt the memory of any one will be to him who has allowed selfish aspiration to prevail over a desire for the public good. United as you are in a common destiny, obedience and cordial coöperation are essentially necessary, and there is no higher duty than that which requires each to render to all what is due to their station. He who sows the seeds of discontent and distrust prepares for the harvest of slaughter and defeat. To zeal you have added gallantry; to gallantry, energy; to energy, fortitude. Crown these with harmony, due subordination, and cheerful support of lawful authority, that the measure of your duty may be full.

I fervently hope that the ferocious war, so unjustly waged against our country, may be soon ended, that, with the blessing of peace, you may be restored to your homes and the useful pursuits; and I pray that our Heavenly Father may cover you with the shield of his protection in the hours of battle, and endow you with the virtues which will close your trials in victory complete.

JEFFERSON DAVIS.

To Lieutenant General W. J. Hardee (JDC)*

ATLANTA, GEORGIA, OCTOBER 30, 1863

MY DEAR HARDEE:

I regret very much not having seen you before leaving. Delay in receiving information from Genl. Bragg prevented me from communicating with you from Mobile, but hearing that you were on the road, I had hoped to have seen you here. The information from the army at Chattanooga painfully impresses me with the fact that there is a want there of that harmony, among the highest officers, which is essential to success. I rely greatly upon you for the restoration of a proper feeling, and know that you will realize the comparative insignificance of personal considerations when weighed against the duty of imparting to the Army all the efficiency of which it is capable.

With my earners prayers for your welfare, I am

VERY TRULY YOUR FRIEND
(SIGNED) JEFFN. DAVIS

---

* William J. Hardee, Confederate general who served most often in the Army of Tennessee.

Speech in Wilmington, North Carolina (PJD)

The President in reply returned his thanks to the people of Wilmington and to Mr. Wright as their organ, for the cordial welcome they had given him. He was proud to be welcomed by such an enthusiastic concourse of North Carolinians to the soil of the ancient and honored town of Wilmington. He hoped that Wilmington, although frequently menaced, might be forever free from the tread of an invading foe. He knew well the importance of her harbor, now the only one through which foreign trade was carried on, and he trusted that the valor of her people, assisted by the means which the government would send to her defence would be fully adequate for that purpose. He had given for the defence of Wilmington one of the best soldiers in the Confederate army—one whom he had seen tried in battle and who had risen higher and higher as dangers accumulated around him. What other means the government could command had been sent here, and in case of attack such additions would be made to the garrison in men and arms as would, he believed, enable Wilmington to repulse the foe, however he might come, by land or by sea.

The President urged upon all their duty to do a full part in the present great struggle, the issues of which were on the one hand freedom, independence, prosperity—on the other hand, subjugation, degredation and absolute ruin.—The man who could bear arms should do so. The man who could not bear arms, but had wealth, should devote it freely to the support of the soldiers and to taking care of their widows and orphans. Those who for the necessities of civil of government, or for the carrying on of industrial pursuits deemed essential to the country, were exempt from the general service, were still bound to take part in the local defence; even the old man who was unable to bear arms, must, in the course of long years have acquired an influence, which should be exerted to arouse those in his neighbourhood to fresh zeal and renewed exertions in support of the cause in which all are so deeply interested. If we were unanimous, if all did their duty manfully, bravely disinterestedly, then our subjugation would be impossible; but if, neglecting the interests of the country, and only anxious to heap up sordid gain, each man attended only to his own private interests, then would it be found that such gains were accumulated only to fall into the hands of the plundering Yankees. The soldier who had fought bravely for his country, although he could leave his children no other fortune, would leave them rich in an inheritance of honor, while the wealth gathered and heaped up in the spirit of Shylock, in the midst of a bleeding country, would go down with a branding and a curse.

Since the President had last passed through Wilmington he had travelled far and visited many portions of the country, and in some he had found ruin and devastation marking the track of the vandal foe. Blackened chimneys alone remained to mark the spot where happy homes once stood, and smouldering ashes replaced the roofs that had sheltered the widow and the orphan. Wherever the invader had passed the last spark of Union feeling had been extinguished, and the people of the districts which the Yankees had supposed subjugated were the warmest and most devoted friends of the Confederacy.

He had visited the army of the West, had gone over the bloody battle field of Chickamauga, and a survey of the ground had heightened his admiration for that valor and devotion, which, with inferior numbers, had overcome difficulties so formidable, and after two days' fighting had achieved a glorious victory, the routed foe only finding shelter under the cover of night.

He had visited Charleston, where the thunder of the enemy's guns is heard day and night hurling their fiercest fire against Sumter, and still the grand old fortress stands grim, dark and silent, bidding defiance to the utmost efforts of the foe. He had visited the other points about Charleston, and had found the spirit of the people and of the troops alike resolute and determined. The Yankees were anxious to crush what they called the nest of the rebellion. He believed that it would stand, spite of their utmost efforts for its capture. It had his best prayers for its safety. God bless the noble old city!

The President said that in North Carolina, as elsewhere, the contact of the Yankees had thoroughly extinguished every spark of Union feeling wherever they had come. The Eastern portion of the State which had suffered most from the enemy was perhaps the most loyal and devoted portion of the whole State; and North Carolina as a State had not been behind any other in the number of troops she had given to the armies of the Confederacy. In every field, from great Bethel, the first, to Chickamauga, the last, the blood of North Carolinians had been shed and their valor illustrated, and if she had fewer trumpeters than some others to sound her fame, the list of killed and wounded from every battle-field attested her devotion and bore witness to her sacrifices. North Carolina might well be proud of her soldiers in the armies of the Confederacy.

We are all engaged in the same cause. We must all make sacrifices. We must use forbearance with each other.—We are all liable to err. Your Generals may commit mistakes; your President may commit mistakes; *you* yourselves may commit mistakes. This is human and for this proper allowance must be made. We must cultivate harmony, unanimity, concert of action. We must, said the President, beware of croakers—beware of the man who would instil the poison of division and disaffection because this section or that section had not got its full share of the spoils and the plunder, the honors and the emoluments of office. Did we go into this war for offices or for plunder?—did we expect to make money by it? If so, then he and others, who, like him, had lost all—had seen the product of years swept away, had been woefully mistaken. But we had not gone into this war from any such ignoble motives, and no such narrow considerations ought to control appointments. Merit and merit alone should be the criterion. And merit *had* been found, and North Carolinians had received and now held a full proportion of the high positions in the army. He here alluded to General Bragg, a native son of North Carolina.

If, there were those who yielded to despondency, who despaired of the Republic, who were willing to submit to degredation, they were not to be found in the ranks of the army, where all was confidence and determination. Those who complained most, were those who had made the fewest sacrifices, not the soldiers who had made the most.

In the changing fortunes of war, we may for a time be driven back, but with a resolute purpose and united effort we would regain all that we had lost, and accomplish all that we had proposed. Freed from the shackless imposed upon us by our uncongenial association with a people who had proved themselves to be ten times worse than even he had supposed them to be, the Confederate States would spring forward in a career of happiness and prosperity surpassing the dreams of the most sanguine.

The President again returned thanks for his kind and enthusiastic reception, and withdrew.

To Lieutenant General E. Kirby Smith (PJD)

RICHMOND, VIRGINIA, NOVEMBER 19, 1863

GENERAL,

I have the honor to acknowledge yours of Sept. 28th. and have noted your remarks on the condition of your Dept. and its necessities. The Treasury Dept. long since sent out agents with authority and the requisite machinery to effect the ends which you desire in that regard. They were sent by sea and encountered delay; but it is hoped they have since arrived and will relieve you of the embarrassments mentioned in regard to finance operations.

I have directed a supply of arms, say 25,000, to be sent to you across the Missi. & have telegraphed to Genl. Johnston to correspond with you so as to secure your cooperation in giving protection & transportation to the arms after they reach the West side of the river. You have been heretofore advised of the arrangements made to send you arms by way of the Rio. Grande & the disappointments which have been encountered. I rely equally upon your vigilance to discover the purposes of the enemy & upon your energy to counteract them to the full extent of your means. The force of the enemy as estimated by scouts is generally exaggerated. I hope it has been so in this case & if it should be possible to restore confidence among our own people, I trust that desertions will cease and that recruits will flock to your standard.

The evacuation of the valley of the Arkansas no doubt produced, as usual in such cases, desertions from the troops raised in that quarter. If the chances of war should enable you to reoccupy it those men would doubtless return to you. But the reoccupation has a higher importance than this,—that is the only region where you can obtain the requisite supplies to support an army for the defence of Arkansas or for an advance into Missouri. So long as you have no boats to navigate the Arkansas & White rivers those streams may be rendered dangerous to the enemy by the use of submarine torpedoes, & when those rivers are high it would not be practicable for the enemy to transport supplies by land in sufficient quantity to feed an army in Arkansas or S. Western Missouri. There is therefore a double advantage to be derived from holding the valley of the Arkansas and securing its supplies for the use of your army.

. . .

The general truth that power is increased by the concentration of an army is under our peculiar circumstances subject to modification. The evacuation of any portion of territory involves not only the loss of supplies but in eve[ry] instance has been attended by a greater or less loss of troops, & a General, therefore, has in each case a complex problem to solve. With high esteem & cordial good wishes I am very respectfully & truly yours

JEFFN,, DAVIS.

To General Joseph E. Johnston (PJD)*

RICHMOND, VIRGINIA, DECEMBER 23, 1863

GENERAL,

This is addressed under the supposition that you have arrived at Dalton, and have assumed command of the forces at that place. The intelligence recently received respecting the condition of that Army is encouraging, and induces me to hope that you will soon be able to commence active operations against the enemy.

The reports concerning the battle at Missionary Ridge show that our loss in killed and wounded was not great, and that the reverse sus-

---

* Now commanding the Army of Tennessee.

tained is not attributable to any general demoralization or reluctance to encounter the opposing Army. The brilliant stand made by the rear guard at Ringgold sustains this belief.

In a letter written to me soon after the battle, General Bragg expressed his unshaken confidence in the courage and morale of the troops. He says; "We can redeem the past: let us concentrate all our available men, unite them with this gallant little Army, still full of zeal, and burning to redeem its lost character and prestige & hurl the whole upon the enemy, and crush him in his power and his glory. I believe it practicable, and trust I may be allowed to participate in the struggle which may restore to us the character, the prestige, and the country we have just lost. This will give us confidence and restore hope to the country and the Army, whilst it will do what is more important, give us subsistence, without which I do not see how we are to remain united."

The official reports made to my Aide de Camp, Colonel Ives, who has just returned from Dalton, presented a not unfavorable view of the material of the command.[*]

The chief of ordnance reported that notwithstanding the abandonment of a considerable number of guns during the battle, there were still on hand, owing to previous large captures by our troops, as many batteries as were proportionate to the strength of the Army, well supplied with horses and equipment; that a large reserve of small arms was in store at readily accessible points, and that the supply of ammunition was abundant.

Comparatively few wagons and ambulances had been lost, and sufficient remained for transportation purposes, if an equal distribution were made through the different Corps. The teams appeared to be generally in fair condition. The troops were tolerably provided with clothing, and a heavy Invoice of shoes & blankets daily expected.

The returns from the Commissary Department showed that there were thirty days provisions on hand.

Stragglers and convalescents were rapidly coming in, and the

[*] Colonel Joseph C. Ives.

morning reports exhibited an effective total, that, added to the two Brigades last sent from Mississippi, and the cavalry sent back by Longstreet, would furnish a force perhaps exceeding in number that actually engaged in any battle, on the Confederate side, during the present war. General Hardee telegraphed to me on the 11th. Inst: "The Army is in good spirits; the artillery reorganized and equipped, and we are now ready to fight."*

The effective condition of your new command, as thus reported to me, is a matter of much congratulation, and I assure you that nothing shall be wanting on the part of the Government to aid you in your efforts to regain possession of the Territory from which we have been driven. You will not need to have it suggested that the imperative demand for prompt and vigorous action arises not only from the importance of restoring the prestige of the Army, and averting the dispiriting and injurious results that must attend a season of inactivity, but from the necessity of reoccupying the country, upon the supplies of which the proper subsistence of our armies materially depends.

Of the immediate measures to be adopted in attaining this end, the full importance of which I am sure you appreciate, you must be the best judge, after due inquiry and consideration on the spot shall have matured an opinion. It is my desire that you should communicate fully and freely and with me concerning your proposed plan of action, that all the assistance and cooperation may be most advantageously afforded that it is in the power of the Government to render.

Trusting that your health may be preserved, and that the arduous and responsible duties you have undertaken may be successfully accomplished, I remain, Very Respectfully & truly Yours

JEFFN,, DAVIS

* Lieutenant General William J. Hardee.

To Governor Zebulon B. Vance (PJD)

RICHMOND, VIRGINIA, JANUARY 8, 1864

DEAR SIR;

I have received your letter of 30th ulto. containing suggestions of the measures to be adopted for the purpose of removing "the sources of discontent" in North Carolina. The contents of the letter are substantially the same as those of the letter addressed by you to Senator Dortch; extracts of which were by him read to me.*

I remarked to Mr Dortch that you were probably not aware of the obstacles to the course you indicated, and without expressing any opinion on the merits of the proposed policy, I desired him in answering your letter to invite suggestions as to the method of opening negotiations, and as to the terms which you thought should be offered to the enemy. I felt persuaded you would appreciate the difficulties as soon as your attention was called to the necessity of considering the subject in detail. As you have made no suggestions touching the manner of overcoming the obstacles I infer that you were not apprised by Mr. Dortch of my remarks to him.

Apart from insuperable objections to the line of policy you propose, (and to which I will presently advert) I cannot see how the mere material obstacles are to be surmounted. We have made three distinct efforts to communicate with the authorities at Washington, and have been invariably unsuccessful. Commissioners were sent before hostilities were begun, and the Washington government refused to see them or hear what they had to say. A second time I sent a military officer with a communication addressed by myself to President Lincoln. The letter was received by General Scott, who did not permit the officer to see Mr. Lincoln, but who promised that an answer would be sent.† No answer has ever been received. The third time, a few months ago, a gentleman was sent whose position, character, and reputation were such as to ensure his reception, if the enemy were not determined to

---

* Confederate States senator William T. Dortch from North Carolina.
† Brevet Lieutenant General Winfield Scott, commander of the U.S. Army in 1861.

receive no proposal whatever from this government. Vice-President Stephens made a patriotic tender of his services in the hope of being able to promote the cause of humanity, and although little belief was entertained of his success, I cheerfully yielded to his suggestion that the experiment should be tried. The enemy refused to let him pass through their lines or to hold any conference with them. He was stopped before he even reached Fortress Monroe on his way to Washington. To attempt again, (in the face of these repeated rejections of all conference with us,) to send commissioners or agents to propose peace, is to invite insult and contumely, and to subject ourselves to indignity without the slightest chance of being listened to. No true citizen, no man who has our cause at heart can desire this, and the good people of North Carolina would be the last to approve of such an attempt, if aware of all the facts—So far from removing "sources of discontent" such a course would receive, as it would merit, the condemnation of those true patriots who have given their blood and their treasure to maintain the freedom, equality and independence which descended to them from the immortal heroes of King's Mountain and other battle-fields of the revolution.

If then proposals cannot be made through envoys because the enemy would not receive them, how is it possible to communicate our desire for peace otherwise than by the public announcements contained in almost every message I ever sent to Congress? I cannot recall at this time one instance in which I have failed to announce that our only desire was peace, and the only terms which formed a *sine qua non* were precisely those that you suggest, namely, "a demand only to be let alone."—

But suppose it were practicable to obtain a conference through commissioners with the government of President Lincoln, is it at this moment that we are to consider it desirable,—or even at all admissible. Have we not just been apprised by that despot that we can only expect his gracious pardon by emancipating all our slaves, swearing allegiance and obedience to him and his proclamations, and becoming in point of fact the slaves of our own negroes? Can there be in North Carolina one citizen so fallen beneath the dignity of his ancestors as to accept, or to enter into conference on the basis of these terms? That there are a few traitors in the State who would be willing to betray their fellow citizens to such a degraded condition in hope of being rewarded for their treachery by an escape from the common doom, may be true. But I do not believe that the vilest wretch would accept such terms for himself.

I cannot conceive how the people of your State, than which none has sent nobler or more gallant soldiers to the field of battle, (one of whom it is your honor to be,) can have been deceived by anything to which you refer in "the recent action of the Federal House of Representatives"—I have seen no action of that House that does not indicate by a very decided majority the purpose of the enemy to refuse all terms to the South except absolute, unconditional subjugation or extermination—But if it were otherwise, how are we to treat with the House of Representatives? It is with Lincoln alone that we ever could confer and his own partisans at the North avow unequivocally that his purpose in his message and proclamation was to shut out all hope that he would *ever* treat with us on *any* terms. If we will break up our government, dissolve the Confederacy, disband our armies, emancipate our slaves, take an oath of allegiance binding ourselves to obedience to him and to disloyalty to our own states, he proposes to pardon us and not to plunder us of any thing more than the property already stolen from us and such slaves as still remain. In order to render his proposals so insulting as to secure their rejection, he joins to them a promise to support with his army one tenth of the people of any State who will attempt to set up a government over the other nine-tenths, thus seeking to sow discord and suspicion among the people of the several States, and to excite them to civil war in furtherance of his ends.

I know well that it would be impossible to get your people, if they possessed full knowledge of these facts to consent that proposals should now be made by us to those who control the government at Washington. Your own well known devotion to the great cause of liberty and independence to which we have all committed whatever we have of earthly possessions would induce you to take the lead in repelling the bare thought of abject submission to the enemy. Yet peace on other terms is now impossible. To obtain the sole terms to which you or I could listen this struggle must continue until the enemy is beaten out of his vain confidence in our subjugation. Then and not till then will it be possible to treat of peace. Till then, all tender of terms to the enemy will be received as [~~illegible~~] *proof* that we are ready for submission and will encourage him in the atrocious warfare which he is waging.

. . .

To Major General W. H. T. Walker (JDC)*

RICHMOND, VIRGINIA, JANUARY 23, 1864

GENERAL:

I have received your letter with its inclosure, informing me of the propositions submitted to a meeting of the General officers on the 2d inst., and thank you for the information.

Deeming it to be injurious to the public service that such a subject should be mooted, or even known to be entertained by persons possessed of the confidence and respect of the people, I have concluded that the best policy under the circumstances will be to avoid all publicity, and the Secretary of War has therefore written to General Johnston requesting him to convey to those concerned my desire that it should be kept private.

If it be kept out of the public journals, its ill effects will be much lessened.

VERY RESPECTFULLY AND TRULY YOURS
(SIGNED) JEFFN. DAVIS

---

* Division commander in the Army of Tennessee; his letter referred to discussions in the army about the possibility of using slaves as Confederate soldiers.

Message to Confederate Congress (PJD)

You are assembled under circumstances of deep interest to your country, and it is fortunate that coming, as you do, newly elected by the people and familiar with the condition of the various localities, you will be the better able to devise measures adapted to meet the wants of the public service, without imposing unnecessary burthens on the citizen. The brief period which has elapsed since the last adjournment of Congress has not afforded sufficient opportunity to test the efficacy of the most important laws then enacted, nor have the events occurring in the interval been such as materially to change the state of the country.

The unjust war commenced against us in violation of the rights of the States, and in usurpation of power not delegated to the government of the United States, is still characterised by the barbarism with which it has heretofore been conducted by the enemy. Aged men, helpless women and children, appeal in vain to the humanity which should be inspired by their condition, for immunity from arrest, incarceration or banishment from their homes. Plunder and devastation of the property of non-combatants, destruction of private dwellings and even of edifices devoted to the worship of God, expeditions organised for the sole purpose of sacking cities, consigning them to the flames, killing the unarmed inhabitants and inflicting horrible outrages on women and children are some of the constantly recurring atrocities of the invader. It cannot reasonably be pretended that such acts conduce to any end which their authors dare avow before the civilized world, and sooner or later Christendom must mete out to them the condemnation which such brutality deserves. The suffering thus ruthlessly inflicted upon the people of the invaded Districts has served but to illustrate their patriotism. Entire unanimity and zeal for their country's cause have been pre-eminently conspicuous among those whose sacrifices have been greatest. So, the army which has borne the trials and dangers of the war; which has been subjected to privations and disappointments, (tests of manly fortitude far more severe than the brief fatigues and perils of actual combat,) has been the centre of cheerfulness and hope. From the camp comes the voice of the soldier patriots invoking each who is at home, in the sphere he best may fill, to devote his whole energies to the support of a cause, in the success of which, their confidence has never faltered. They, the veterans of many a hard-fought field, tender to their country, without limit of time, a service of priceless value to us, one which posterity will hold in grateful remembrance.

In considering the state of the country, the reflection is naturally suggested, that this is the third Congress of the Confederate States of America. The provisional Government was formed, its Congress held four sessions, lived its appointed term, and passed away. The permanent Government was then organised, its different Departments established, a Congress elected which also held four sessions, served its full constitutional term, and expired. You, the second Congress under the permanent Government, are now assembled at the time and place appointed by law for commencing your session. All these events have passed into history, notwithstanding the threat of our prompt subjugation made three years ago by a people that presume to assert a title to govern States whose separate and independent sovereignty was recognised by treaty with France and Great Britain in the last century, and remained unquestioned for nearly three generations. Yet these very governments, in disregard of duty and treaty obligations which bind them to recognise as independent, Virginia and other Confederate States, persist in countenancing by moral influence, if not in aiding by unfair and partial action, the claim set up by the Executive of a foreign government, to exercise despotic sway over the States thus recognised, and treat the invasion of them by their former limited and special agent, as though it were the attempt of a Sovereign to suppress a rebellion against lawful authority. Ungenerous advantage has been taken of our present condition, and our rights have been violated, our vessels of war detained in ports to which they had been invited by proclamations of neutrality, and in one instance our flag also insulted where the sacred right of asylum was supposed to be secure; while one of these governments has contented itself with simply deprecating by deferential representations the conduct of our enemy in the constantly recurring instances of his contemptuous disregard of neutral rights and flagrant violations of public law. It may be that foreign governments, like our enemies, have mistaken our desire for peace unreservedly expressed, for evidence of exhaustion, and have thence inferred the probability of success in the effort to subjugate or exterminate the millions of human beings who in these States prefer any fate to submission to their savage assailants. I see no prospect of an early change in the course heretofore pursued by these governments; but when this delusion shall have been dispelled, and when our independence, by the valor and fortitude of our people, shall have been won against all the hostile influences combined against us, and can no longer be ignored by open foes or professed neutrals, this war will have left with its proud memories, a record of many wrongs which it may not misbecome us to forgive, some for which we may not properly forbear from demanding redress. In the meantime it is enough for us to know that every avenue of negotiation is closed against us: that our enemy is making renewed and strenuous efforts for our destruction, and that the sole resource for us as a people secure in the justice of our cause, and holding our liberties to be more precious than all other earthly possessions, is to combine and apply every available element of power for their defence and preservation.

. . .

To Joseph E. Johnston (PJD)

RICHMOND, VIRGINIA, JULY 7, 1864

The announcement that your army has fallen back to the Chattahoochee renders more apprehensive for the future—that River if not fordable should not be immediately in your rear & if you cross it will enable the Enemy without danger to send a detachment to cut your communication with Ala & in the absence of the Troops of that Dept to capture the cities, destroy the mines & manufacteries & seperate the states by a new Line of occupation At this distance I cant judge of your condition or the best method of averting calamity. Hopefull of results in Northern Ga other places have been stripped to reinforce your army until we are unable to make further additions & are dependent on your success—efforts have been made & are still making to organize the Reserves as an auxilliary force for state defense You will know what progress has been made in Ga and Ala—

JEFF'N DAVIS

To General R. E. Lee (JDC)

RICHMOND, VIRGINIA, JULY 12, 1864

Genl. Johnston has *failed* and there are strong indications that he will *abandon Atlanta*. He urges that *prisoners* should be removed immediately *from Andersonville*. It seems necessary to *relieve him* at once. Who should *succeed* him? What think you of Hood for the position?

JEFF'N. DAVIS

To Generals Hood, Hardee, and Stewart (JDC)*

RICHMOND, VIRGINIA, JULY 18, 1864

Your telegram of this date received. A change of commander under existing circumstances was regarded as so objectionable that I only accepted it as the alternative of continuance in a policy which had proved disastrous. Reluctance to make the change induced me to send a telegram of inquiry to the Commanding General on the 16th inst. His reply but confirmed previous apprehensions. There can be but one question which you and I can entertain, that is, what will best promote the public good, and to each of you I confidently look for the sacrifice of every personal consideration in conflict with that object. The order has been executed, and I cannot suspend it without making the case worse than it was before the order was issued.

JEFF'N. DAVIS

---

* John Bell Hood, William J. Hardee, and Alexander P. Stewart, corps commanders in the Army of Tennessee. Hood succeeded Johnston as the army's commanding general.

To General Robert E. Lee (PJD)

GENL.

Yours of yesterday recd. Have enquired of the Qr Master Genl. in relation to the question of forage, the supply of which as you are aware was mainly drawn from Southwestern Georgia, communication with which was interrupted by the enemy's recent raid on the Central R.R. That road is again at work, and the Qr Master Genl expects the first lot of corn from Macon since the road was broken will arrive in 4 or 5 days, and that if there be no further interruption that there will be a steady succession in the arrivals from that quarter, and that the amount will be adequate for the supply of your Army—He is quite confident that the Danville and Piedmont /R.R./ can transport all which can be brought to their terminus. One of the difficulties of which he complains is that of getting the corn from the plantations to the Depots, and this, he says is mainly due to the withdrawal of the detailed men, Overseers and farmers from their homes for temporary Military service—

I have had serious apprehension that the source of supply might be exhausted by the retreat of the Army of Tenn:, and the consequent exposure of the Atlanta & Montgomery R.R., the possession of which by the enemy would compel that Army to draw its supplies from the same quarter which is relied on to furnish corn for the Army of Va: West of the Ala: River, there is an abundant supply of corn, large quantities of which are stored along the rail roads and navigable rivers—The reported amount now at Montgomery is 300,000 bus: & the receipts are said to be equal to the amounts sent forward from there daily. Tho' 600 wagons were put on the break on the West Point R.R., and another train of wagons is running from Montgomery to the R.R. at Union Springs. If Genl Hood is successful against Sherman,* and we suffer no serious disaster, so as to deprive us of the supplies in Middle Ala: and east Missi., I think we shall be better able to sustain an Army hereafter than we were in the first year of the war—I di-

---

* Major General William Tecumseh Sherman, Union commander.

rected inquiry to be made for oats in Va. & N. Ca: but have been disappointed, by learning that but a small amount can be obtained. It would seem, therefore, that for the supply of forage, we must mainly rely upon the R.R. connection with the South, by way of Danville & Greensboro: I trust the enemy will not be able to reach that road.

I cannot say I was surprised that the enemy have been able to break the Weldon R.R., tho' I regret that they should have had time to fortify themselves as a consequence of feeble attacks made upon them at the time of their first occupation of it, which, as I understand, was during the absence of the force he had detached to the north side of the James river—Interposed, as he now is, between your Army and Weldon, I have felt increased apprehension lest an attack should be made upon the Wilmington The recent success at Mobile might naturally encourage such an effort. I sent a telegram to Genl. Holmes to urge the preparation of Reserves for immediate service, and a further increase of the force at Wilmington—

The Northern papers clearly indicate the change of plan on the part of Genl Grant which you think suggested by his operations, and they seem to render it quite certain that his movement to the north side of James river was not intended as a feint, but adopted as an easier line under existing circumstances to approach Richmond—I will do whatever is in my power, and in the manner you request, to aid you in defeating the new plan, and I hope you will be as successful as you have heretofore been against this and other Generals of the enemy who have been sent to reduce the Capital of the Confederacy and to humble the pride of Va. Very respectfully & truly yours

(SIGNED) JEFFN DAVIS—

Speech in Macon, Georgia (JDC)

SEPTEMBER 24, 1864

. . .

What though misfortune has befallen our arms from Decatur to Jonesboro, our cause is not lost. Sherman cannot keep up his long line of communication, and retreat, sooner or later, he must. And when that day comes, the fate that befell the army of the French Empire in its retreat from Moscow will be reacted. Our cavalry and our people will harass and destroy his army as did the Cossacks of Napoleon, and the Yankee General, like him, will escape with only a bodyguard.

How can this be the most speedily effected? By the absentees of Hood's army returning to their posts. And will they not? Can they see the banished exiles, can they hear the wail of their suffering country-women and children, and not come. By what influences they are made to stay away it is not necessary to speak. If there is one who will stay away at this hour, he is unworthy the name of Georgian. To the women no appeal is necessary. They are like the Spartan mothers of old. I know of one who has lost all her sons, except one of eight years. She wrote me that she wanted me to reserve a place for him in the ranks. The venerable General Polk, to whom I read the letter, knew that woman well, and said that it was characteristic of her. But I will not weary you by turning aside to relate the various incidents of giving up the last son to the cause of our country known to me. Wherever we go we find the heart and hand of our noble women enlisted. They are seen wherever the eye may fall, or the step turn. They have one duty to perform—to buoy up the hearts of our people.

I know the deep disgrace felt by Georgia by our army falling back from Dalton to the interior of the State; but I was not of those who considered Atlanta lost when our army crossed the Chattahoochee. I resolved that it should not, and I then put a man in command who I knew would strike an honest and manly blow for the city, and many a Yankee's blood was made to nourish the soil before the prize was won.

. . .

The man who can speculate ought to be made to take up his musket. When the war is over and our independence won (*and we will establish our independence,*) who will be our aristocracy? I hope the limping soldier. To the young ladies I would say, when choosing between an empty sleeve and the man who had remained at home and grown rich, always take the empty sleeve. Let the old men remain at home and make bread. But, should they know of any young men keeping away from the service who cannot be made to go any other way, let them write to the Executive. I read all letters sent to me from the people, but have not the time to reply to them.

You have not many men between 18 and 45 left. The boys—God bless the boys—are as rapidly as they become old enough, going to the field. The city of Macon is filled with stores, sick and wounded. It must not be abandoned, when threatened, but, when the enemy come, instead of calling upon Hood's army for defence, the old men must fight, and, when the enemy is driven beyond Chattahoochee, they, too, can join in the general rejoicing.

. . .

It is not proper for me to speak of the number of men in the field. But this I will say, that two-thirds of our men are absent—some sick, some wounded, but most of them absent without leave. The man who repents and goes back to his commander voluntarily, at once appeals strongly to Executive clemency. But suppose he stays away until the war is over, and his comrades return home, when every man's history will be told, where will he shield himself? It is upon these reflections that I rely to make men return to their duty, but if after conferring with our Generals at headquarters, if there be any other remedy it shall be applied.

. . .

Speech in Montgomery, Alabama (JDC)

SEPTEMBER 27, 1864

. . .

He began by expressing a sense of gratitude for the occasion, which the kind attention of the legislature had given him, of appearing before them, and assuring the citizens of Alabama from that Capitol in which the first notes of our existence were issued, of his remembrance and sympathy—He would not attempt to conceal the fact that we have experienced great disasters of late. The enemy have pressed our armies backward into the centre of Georgia, threatened the borders of Alabama, and occupied the bay of Mobile, but the city still stands, and will stand though every wall and roof should fall to the ground. He had been disappointed in all his calculations in Northern Georgia. After sending forward to the army at Dalton all the reinforcements he could collect from every quarter, including the troops from Northern Mississippi, he had confidently expected a successful advance through Tennessee into Kentucky. Had he thought that instead of the forward movement our arms would have retired to Atlanta, he would have left his old lamented and venerated friend, Gen. Polk, to have assailed Sherman upon his flank by North Alabama. But he had yielded to the idea of concentration, and the sequel was anything than what he had been induced to hope.

Yet we were not without compensation for our losses. In Virginia, despite the odds brought against us, we have beaten Grant, and still defiant hold our lines before Richmond and Petersburg. That pure and noble patriot, that great soldier and Christian, General Lee, although largely outnumbered in front, largely outnumbered on his flanks, commanded a body of men who had never known what it was to be whipped, and never stopped to cipher.

The time for action is now at hand. There is but one duty for every Southern man. It is to go to the front. Those who are able for the field, should not hesitate a moment, and those who are not should seek some employment to aid and assist the rest, and to induce their able-bodied associates to seek their proper places in the army.

. . .

There be some men, said Mr. Davis, who, when they look at the sun, can only see a speck upon it. I am of a more sanguine temperament perhaps, but I have striven to behold our affairs with a cool and candid temperance of heart, and applying to them the most rigid test, am the most confident the longer I behold the progress of the war, and reflect upon what we have failed to do, we should marvel and thank God for the great achievements which have crowned our efforts.

. . .

Mr. Davis spoke eloquently of the horrors of war and the sufferings of the people. He desired peace. He had tried to obtain it and had been rudely repulsed. He should still strive, and by the blessing of God and the strong arm of the soldiers, yet hoped to obtain it.

If there be those who hoped to outwit the Yankees, and by smooth words and fair speeches, by the appearance of a willingness to treat or to listen to reunion, hope to elect any candidate in the North, they deceive themselves. Victory in the field is the surest element of strength to a peace party. Let us win battles and we shall have overtures soon enough.

Is there a man in the South in favor of reconstruction? Mr. Davis drew a fine picture of the horrors of reunion, which means subjugation. "All that I have to say," he exclaimed, in concluding this portion of his remarks, "is that the man who is in favor of this degradation, is on the wrong side of the line of battle."

Speech in Augusta, Georgia (JDC)*

OCTOBER 3, 1864

. . .

Ladies and Gentlemen, Friends and Fellow-Citizens of Georgia: At the moment of leaving your State, after having come hither to learn the exact truth as to the late military operations here, I go away much more confident than when I came. I have been to the army, and return imbued with the thought that they are as fully ready now as ever to meet the enemy, and that if all who are absent will return, and those owing service will go, thirty suns will not set before no foot of an invader will press the soil of Georgia.

Never before was I so confident that energy, harmony and determination would rid the country of its enemy and give to the women of the land that peace their good deeds have so well deserved.

Those who see no hope now, who have lost confidence, are to me like those of whose distorted vision it is said they behold spots upon the sun. Such are the croakers, who seem to forget the battles that have been won and the men who have fought; who forget that, in the magnitude of those battles and the heroism of those men, this struggle exceeds all that history records. We commenced the fight without an army, without a navy, without arsenals, without mechanics, without money and without credit. Four years we have stemmed the tide of in-

---

* *JDC* gives October 10, but October 3 is correct date.

vasion, and to-day are stronger than when the war began; better able now than ever to repulse the vandal who is seeking our overthrow. Once we imported the commonest articles of daily use, and brought in from beyond our borders even bread and meat. Now the State of Georgia alone produces food enough not only for her own people and the army within it, but feeds, too, the Army of Virginia. Once we had no arms, and could receive no soldiers but those who came to us armed. Now we have arms for all, and are begging men to bear them. This city of Augusta alone produces more powder than the army can burn. All things are fair: and this Confederacy is not yet, in the familiar parlance of the croaker, "played out," as those declare who spread their own despondency over the whole body politic. (Voice in the crowd, beyond doubt that of a Hibernian, "Three cheers for the Confederacy," which were vociferously given.)

From the accents of that voice, my friend, I see that you have come into this country from one that has itself lost its liberty, and you may well exclaim three cheers for the Confederacy, upon whose success now alone depends the existence of constitutional liberty in the world.—We are fighting for that principle—upon us depends its last hope. The Yankees, in endeavoring to coerce the States, have lost that heirloom of their fathers, and the men of the South alone must sustain it.

Ours is not a revolution. We are a free and independent people, in States that had the right to make a better government when they saw fit. They sought to infringe upon the rights we had; and we only instituted a new government on the basis of those rights. We are not engaged in a Quixotic fight for the rights of man; our struggle is for inherited rights; and who would surrender them? Let every paper guaranty possible be given, and who would submit? From the grave of many a fallen hero the blood of the slain would cry out against such a peace with the murderers. The women of the land driven from their homes; the children lacking food; old age hobbling from the scenes of its youth; the fugitives, forced to give way to the Yankee oppressor, and now hiding in your railroads, all proclaim a sea of blood that freemen cannot afford to bridge.

There is but one thing to which we can accede—separate State independence. Some there are who speak of reconstruction with slavery maintained; but are there any who would thus measure rights by property? God forbid. Would you see that boy, with a peach-bloom on his cheek, grow up a serf—never to tread the path of honor unless he light the torch at the funeral pyre of his country? Would you see the fair daughters of the land given over to the brutality of the Yankees?

If any imagine this would not be so, let him look to the declarations of Mr. Lincoln, the terms he offers; let him read the declarations of the Northern press; let him note the tone of the Northern people; and he will see there is nothing left for us but separate independence.

Who now looks for intervention? Who does not know that our friends abroad depend upon our strength at home? That the balance is in our favor with victory, and turns against us with defeat, and that when our victory is unquestioned we will be recognized, and not till then.

We must do our duty, and that duty is this: Every man able to bear arms must go to the front, and all others must devote themselves to the cause at home. There must be no pleading for exemption. We are fighting for existence; and by fighting alone can independence be gained. Georgia is now invaded.—She is calling for succor, and he who, from Alabama, from Mississippi, from South Carolina, rushes to her aid, strikes, when he strikes for her, a blow for his own home and family. Our Confederate States must lean one upon the other for mutual support. We are, as the poet has said,

"Distinct as the billows, yet one as the sea."

One part must rush to the support of the other. We must beat Sherman, we must march into Tennessee—there we will draw from twenty thousand to thirty thousand to our standard; and so strengthened, we must push the enemy back to the banks of the Ohio, and thus give the peace party of the North an accretion no puny editorial can give.

Words will not now avail. You must consult your hearts, perform more than the law can exact, yield as much as freemen can give, and all will be well. With peace and freedom a glorious career opens for these Confederate States. Relieved from class legislation, free from taxes—indirect it is true, but imposed by your rulers for twenty years past—no longer subject to Northern speculators, grinders of the faces of the poor, and deniers of the rights of men, you will start forward in the brightest of futures.

On each of the former occasions when I was in this State of Georgia, on my way to the army, that army was on the soil of other States; and it is only at this visit that this is the battlefield. I trust that this will not be long so, and that Providence may soon take the war beyond her borders. I trust, too, that our hearts are fixed on following the enemy in his retreat, and then, if negotiations come, they will come in such form as alone we can entertain.

Till then we can have no peace; and yet does anyone suppose this Government is anxious for war? Some have spoken of the executive, and declared that executive hardness and pride of opinion was opposed to any negotiations. Those who think so must imagine me more or less than man. Do they not suppose I have wept over the wounded soldier borne from the field to tell of those who there lay lifeless; that I have not lamented the loss of property by our good and great men; that I have not mourned over the lives that have been offered up? My first effort was for peace, and I sent commissioners to endeavor to arrange an amicable dissolution. From time to time I have repeated efforts to that end, but never, never have I sought it on any other basis than independence. (Enthusiastic applause.) But do I expect it? Yes, I do. (Renewed cheering.)

Brave men have done well before against greater odds than ours, and when were men ever braver?

We will achieve it. How many sacrifices it may take, I cannot tell; but I believe that a just God looks upon our cause as holy, and that of our enemy as iniquitous. He may chastise us for our offences, but in so doing He is preparing us, and in His good Providence will assist us, and never desert the right.

And you, my fair countrywomen, whose past gives assurance of what you will do in the future; you, who have clothed the soldier and sent him forth to battle; who have hung upon the rear of armies, and ever stood ready to succor the wounded; who have lined the wayside to minister to the feeble and pointed the dying to Heaven—you, too, have done your duty. You have given up all. You have sent your husbands, your fathers, your sons, to the army; but you must do more. You must use your influence to send all to the front, and form a public opinion that shall make the skulker a marked man, and leave him no house wherein he can shelter. And you, young ladies, who are yet to marry, let me tell you that when the choice comes between a one-armed or one-legged soldier and one who has grown fat on extortion at home, choose rather to cling to the armless sleeve.

There are some I know who have looked upon Confederate legislation as needlessly harsh. I would that it could have been unnecessary. I would that goods could have been bought in market rather than impressed; that the armies could have been filled by volunteering rather than by conscription; and yet I look upon the latter as the more just. You force all men to make roads, pay taxes, serve on juries; why should not all men fight your battles? My opinion on this subject has not changed. I believed, and believe now, it is just; that it would have been better had it been the policy from the beginning of the war; and I endorse it in all its length and breadth and depth.

Besides, however, these forces we have others. For this the reserves have been organized, and on these, and on the disabled soldiers, who, faithful to the last, will fight, though they cannot march, the defence of this city of Augusta must rest. When your line shall have been completed these forces can hold Augusta against any force but a large army, and when that comes, a large army will be at liberty to meet it, and such an army you shall have. (Great applause.)

Some there are, too, who never set a squadron in the field who yet proffer their advice. They can plan in their closets the campaigns of a general and write the State papers of an executive—I do not gainsay their wisdom, but let them go to the front and there give us the benefit of their services. (Laughter.)

Why criticise a general or rail at the executive? They have ventured all; and everything they have is dependent on the result. Their honor, their reputation, their future, is at stake. If you are assured of their good intent, their steady labor, their constant effort, why destroy confidence in them by railing? In proportion as they err they should be treated with leniency. In proportion as the executive is purblind, should criticism be friendly and error be pointed out calmly. So far as they fall short, just so far do they need support.

. . .

Be of good cheer. In homely phrase, put your shoulder to the wheel, and work while it is day.

. . .

Speech in Columbia, South Carolina (JDC)

...

Among those to whom we are indebted in South Carolina, I have not yet alluded to that peculiar claim of gratitude which is due to the fair country-women of the Palmetto State—they who have gone to the hospital to watch by the side of the sick—those who throng your wayside homes—who have nursed as if nursing was a profession—who have used their needle with the industry of sewing-women—who have borne privation without a murmur, and who have given up fathers, sons, and husbands with more than Spartan virtue, because they called no one to witness and record the deed. Silently, with all dignity and grandeur of patriotism, they have made their sacrifices—sacrifices which, if written, would be surpassed by nothing in history. If all the acts of heroism and virtue of the women of the South could be transmitted to the future, it would present such a record as the world has never seen. All honor, then, I say, to the ladies of the Palmetto State. Their gallantry is only different from that of her sons in this, that they deem it unfeminine to strike; and yet such is the heroism displayed—such the noble demeanor they have exhibited—that at the last moment when trampled upon and it became a necessity, they would not hesitate to strike the invader a corpse at their feet. (Applause.)

It is scarcely necessary for me, at a time like this, to argue grave questions, respecting policy, past, present or prospective. I only ask you to have faith and confidence, and to believe that every faculty of my head and my heart is devoted to your cause, and to that I shall, if necessary, give my life. Let every one in his own sphere and according to his own capacity, devote himself to the single purpose of filling up and sustaining our armies in the field. If required to stay at home, let him devote himself not to the acquisition of wealth, but to the advancement of the common cause. If there is to be any aristocracy in the land after this war, I hope that it will be an aristocracy of those men who have become poor while bleeding to secure liberty. (Applause.) If there are to be any peculiarly favored by public opinion hereafter, I trust it will be those men who have longest borne a musket and oftenest bled upon the battle fields. If there is to be any man shunned by the young ladies when he seeks their favor, I trust it will be the man who has grown rich by skulking.

And with all sincerity, I say to my young friends here, if you want the right man for a husband, take him whose armless sleeve and noble heart betoken the duties that he has rendered to his country, rather than he who has never shared the toils, or borne the dangers of the field. If there still be left any of those military critics who have never spoken of our generals but to show how much better things could have been managed, or of our Government, but to find fault with it, because it never took their advice—in mercy's name let these wise men go to the front and aid us in achieving our independence. With their wisdom and strength swelling our armies, I should have some hopes that I will not be a corpse before our cause is secured, and that our flag would never trail in dishonor, but would wave victoriously above the roar and smoke of battle.

I believe it is in the power of the men of the Confederacy to plant our banners on the banks of the Ohio, where we shall say to the Yankee, "be quiet, or we shall teach you another lesson." Within the next thirty days much is to be done, for upon our success much depends. Within the next thirty days, therefore, let all who are absentees, or who ought to be in the army, go promptly to their ranks. Let fresh victories crown our arms, and the peace party, if there be such at the North, can elect its candidate. But whether a peace candidate is elected or not, Yankee instinct will teach him that it is better to end the war and leave us to the enjoyment of our own rights.

Prayerful for your welfare, confiding in the army of the Confederate States to do that which soft words can never achieve, and in the hope that God will preserve the little ones of all brave men who are in the field, or who are going to it, and trusting that in the future under brighter auspices, it may be my fortune to meet the good people of Columbia, I wish you all for the present farewell. (Applause.)

Message to Confederate Congress (JDC)

RICHMOND, VIRGINIA, NOVEMBER 7, 1864

...

EMPLOYMENT OF SLAVES.

The employment of slaves for service with the Army as teamsters or cooks, or in the way of work upon the fortifications, or in the Government workshops, or in hospitals and other similar duties, was authorized by the act of 17th of February last, and provision was made for their impressment to a number not exceeding 20,000, if it should be found impracticable to obtain them by contract with the owners. The law contemplated the hiring only of the labor of these slaves, and imposed on the Government the liability to pay for the value of such as might be lost to the owners from casualties resulting from their employment in the service.

This act has produced less result than was anticipated, and further provision is required to render it efficacious; but my present purpose is to invite your consideration to the propriety of a radical modification in the theory of the law,

Viewed merely as property, and therefore as the subject of impressment, the service or labor of the slave has been frequently claimed for short periods in the construction of defensive works. The slave, however, bears another relation to the State—that of a person. The law of last February contemplates only the relation of the slave to the master and limits the impressment to a certain term of service.

But for the purposes enumerated in the act, instruction in the manner of encamping, marching, and parking trains is needful; so that even in this limited employment length of service adds greatly to the value of the negro's labor. Hazard is also encountered in all the positions to which negroes can be assigned for service with the Army, and the duties required of them demand loyalty and zeal. In this respect the relation of person predominates so far as to render it doubtful whether the private right of property can consistently and beneficially be continued, and it would seem proper to acquire for the public service the entire property in the labor of the slave, and to pay therefor due compensation rather than to impress his labor for short terms; and this the more especially as the effect of the present law would vest this entire property in all cases where the slave might be recaptured after compensation for his loss had been paid to the private owner. Whenever the entire property in the service of a slave is thus acquired by the Government, the question is presented by what tenure he should be held. Should he be retained in servitude, or should his emancipation be held out to him as a reward for faithful service, or should it be granted at once on the promise of such service; and if emancipated, what action should be taken to secure for the freedman the permission of the State from which he was drawn to reside within its limits after the close of the public service? The permission would doubtless be more readily accorded as a reward for past faithful service, and a double motive for a zealous discharge of duty would thus be offered to those employed by the Government—their freedom and the gratification of the local attachment which is so marked a characteristic of the negro, and forms so powerful an incentive to his action. The policy of engaging to liberate the negro on his discharge after service faithfully rendered seems to me preferable to that of granting immediate manumission, or that of retaining him in servitude. If this policy should recommend itself to the judgment of Congress, it is suggested that, in addition to the duties heretofore performed by the slave, he might be advantageously employed as pioneer and engineer laborer, and in that event that the number should be augmented to 40,000.

Beyond these limits and these employments it does not seem to me desirable, under existing circumstances, to go. A broad moral distinction exists between the use of slaves as soldiers in defense of their homes and the incitement of the same persons to insurrection against their masters. The one is justifiable, if necessary, the other is iniquitous and unworthy of a civilized people; and such is the judgment of all writers on public law, as well as that expressed and insisted on by our enemies in all wars prior to that now waged against us. By none have the practices of which they are now guilty been denounced with greater severity than by themselves in the two wars with Great Britain, in the last and in the present century; and in the Declaration of Independence of 1776, when enumeration was made of the wrongs which justified the revolt from Great Britain, the climax of atrocity was deemed to be reached only when the English monarch was denounced as having "excited domestic insurrections amongst us."

The subject is to be viewed by us, therefore, solely in the light of policy and our social economy. When so regarded, I might dissent from those who advise a general levy and arming of the slaves for the duty of soldiers. Until our white population shall prove insufficient for the armies we require and can afford to keep in the field, to employ as a soldier the negro, who has merely been trained to labor, and as a laborer [under] the white man, accustomed from his youth to the use of firearms, would scarcely be deemed wise or advantageous by any; and this is the question now before us. But should the alternative ever be presented of subjugation or of the employment of the slave as a soldier, there seems no reason to doubt what should then be our decision. Whether our view embraces what would, in so extreme a case, be the sum of misery entailed by the dominion of the enemy, or be restricted solely to the effect upon the welfare and happiness of the negro population themselves, the result would be the same. The appalling demoralization, suffering, disease, and death which have been caused by partially substituting the invader's system of police for the kind relation previously subsisting between the master and slave have been a sufficient demonstration that external interference with our institution of domestic slavery is productive of evil only. If the subject involved no other consideration than the mere right of property, the sacrifices heretofore made by our people have been such as to permit no doubt of their readiness to surrender every possession in order to secure their independence. But the social and political question, which is exclusively under the control of the several States, has a far wider and more enduring importance than that of pecuniary interest. In its manifold phases it embraces the stability of our republican institutions, resting on the actual political equality of all its citizens, and includes the fulfillment of the task which has been so happily begun— that of Christianizing and improving the condition of the Africans who have, by the will of Providence, been placed in our charge. Comparing the results of our own experience with those of the experiments of others who have borne similar relation to the African race, the people of the several States of the Confederacy have abundant reason to be satisfied with the past, and will use the greatest circumspection in determining their course. These considerations, however, are rather applicable to the improbable contingency of our need of resorting to this element of resistance than to our present condition. If the recommendation above made, for the training of 40,000 negroes for the service indicated, shall meet your approval, it is certain that even this limited number, by their preparatory training in intermediate duties, would form a more valuable reserve force in case of urgency than three-fold their number suddenly called from field labor, while a fresh levy could, to a certain extent, supply their places in the special service for which they are now employed.

. . .

NEGOTIATIONS FOR PEACE.

The disposition of this Government for a peaceful solution of the issues which the enemy has referred to the arbitrament of arms has been too often manifested and is too well known to need new assurances. But while it is true that individuals and parties in the United States have indicated a desire to substitute reason for force, and by negotiations to stop the further sacrifice of human life, and to arrest the calamities which now afflict both countries, the authorities who control the Government of our enemies have too often and too clearly expressed their resolution to make no peace, except on terms of our unconditional submission and degradation, to leave us any hope of the cessation of hostilities until the delusion of their ability to conquer us is dispelled. Among those who are already disposed for peace many are actuated by principle and by disapproval and abhorrence of the iniquitous warfare that their Government is waging, while others are moved by the conviction that it is no longer to the interest of the United States to continue a struggle in which success is unattainable. Whenever this fast-growing conviction shall have taken firm root in the minds of a majority of the Northern people, there will be produced that willingness to negotiate for peace which is now confined to our side. Peace is manifestly impossible unless desired by both parties to this war, and the disposition for it among our enemies will be best and most certainly evoked by the demonstration on our part of ability and unshaken determination to defend our rights, and to hold no earthly price too dear for their purchase. Whenever there shall be on the part of our enemies a desire for peace, there will be no difficulty in finding means by which negotiation can be opened; but it is obvious that no agency can be called into action until this desire shall be mutual. When that contingency shall happen, the Government, to which is confided the treaty-making power, can be at no loss for means adapted to accomplish so desirable an end. In the hope that the day will soon be reached when under Divine favor these States may be allowed to enter on their former peaceful pursuits and to develop the abundant natural resources with which they are blessed, let us, then, resolutely continue to devote our united and unimpaired energies to the defense of our homes, our lives, and our liberties. This is the true path to peace. Let us tread it with confidence in the assured result.

JEFFERSON DAVIS.

To *James F. Johnson and Hugh W. Sheffey* (JDC)[*]

RICHMOND, VIRGINIA, JANUARY 18, 1865

GENTLEMEN:

I have the honor to acknowledge receipt of your joint letter of 17th inst., enclosing a resolution of the General Assembly of Virginia, passed on the 17th inst., and communicated to me in confidence, as directed by the Assembly.

This resolution informs me that

"in the opinion of the General Assembly of Virginia, the appointment of General Robert E. Lee to the command of all the Armies of the Confederate States would promote their efficiency and operate powerfully to reanimate the spirits of the Armies, as well as of the people

[*] Members of the Virginia General Assembly.

of the several States, and to inspire increased confidence in the final success of our cause."

In your communication you kindly assure me that "the General Assembly with sincere confidence in my patriotic devotion to the welfare of the country, desire in this critical period of our affairs, by such suggestions as occur to them, and by the dedication, if need be, of the entire resources of the Commonwealth to the common cause to strengthen my hands and to give success to our struggle for liberty and independence."

This assurance is to me a source of the highest gratification, and, while conveying to you my thanks for the expression of the confidence of the General Assembly in my sincere devotion to our country and its sacred cause, I must beg permission, in return, to bear witness to the uncalculating, unhesitating spirit with which Virginia has, from the moment when she first drew the sword, consecrated the blood of her children and all her natural resources to the achievement of the object of our struggle.

The opinion expressed by the General Assembly in regard to General R. E. Lee has my full concurrence. Virginia cannot have a higher regard for him or greater confidence in his character and ability than is entertained by me. When General Lee took command of the Army of Northern Virginia, he was in command of all the armies of the Confederate States by my order of assignment. He continued in this general command as well as in the immediate command of the Army of Northern Virginia, as long as I could resist his opinion that it was necessary for him to be relieved from one of these two duties. Ready as he has ever shown himself to be, to perform any service that I desired him to render to his country, he left it for me to choose between his withdrawal from the command of the Army in the field, and relieving him of the general command of all the armies of the Confederate States.

It was only when satisfied of this necessity that I came to the conclusion to relieve him from the general command, believing that the safety of the Capital and the success of our cause depended in a great measure on then retaining him in the command in the field of the Army of Northern Virginia.

On several subsequent occasions, the desire on my part to enlarge the sphere of General Lee's usefulness has led to renewed consideration of the subject, and he has always expressed his inability to assume command of other Armies than those now confided to him, unless relieved of the immediate command in the field of that now opposed to General Grant.

In conclusion, I assure the General Assembly that whenever it shall be found practicable by General Lee to assume command of all the Armies of the Confederate States, without withdrawing from the direct command of the Army of Northern Virginia, I will deem it promotive of the public interests to place him in such command, and will be happy to know that by so doing, I am responding to their expressed desire.

It will afford me great pleasure to see you, Gentlemen, as proposed in your letter, whenever it may be convenient for you to visit me.

I am,

VERY RESPECTFULLY AND TRULY YOURS,
(SIGNED) JEFFERSON DAVIS

To General P. G. T. Beauregard (JDC)

RICHMOND, VIRGINIA, FEBRUARY 4, 1865

Your three dispatches of yesterday received. The view presented is more discouraging than I had anticipated. The last report I received from Genl. Hardee was of the 8th ultimo. His force seems from your statement to have materially diminished, notwithstanding he at that time expected reinforcements from So. Carolina, and has received a considerable force from the Army of Va. The numbers given for the Corps from the Army of Tennessee are also much smaller than I had been led to expect. You know what was the condition of affairs here when you left Virginia; since then the enemy has received reinforcements, and Genl. Lee has sent detachments to Geo. and So. Car. You can therefore judge of his power to aid you to the extent you propose without abandoning his present field of operations. I will however communicate your dispatches to him, and need not assure you of his readiness to do whatever circumstances will permit to attain your object, the defeat of Sherman. You will assume command of all the forces in the District as defined before your departure to the West; and, should you deem it advisable, will direct Genl. Hardee to resume command of his old Corps when it arrives, and add to it any other forces which may be advantageously associated with it. You will endeavor to obtain from Governor Magrath of So. Car. and Governor Brown of Geo. whatever auxiliary force they can add, and use all available means to restore absentees to the service. From these sources you should be able to obtain a greater number of men than that named in your dispatch as sufficient to enable you to defeat the enemy. You will realize the necessity for the rapid concentration of your forces, and if possible the defeat of the enemy at some point South and East of Branchville and Augusta. To give time for such concentration and for the arrival of reinforcements, every available means must be employed to delay the advance of the enemy, and by operating on his lines of communication to interfere with his supplies.

(SIGNED) JEFFN. DAVIS

To John Forsyth (JDC)

RICHMOND, VIRGINIA, FEBRUARY 21, 1865

MY DEAR SIR:

You will readily understand why, during the session of Congress, my private corespondence should be in arrears. I have now, though it may seem late, to thank you for your letter of 31st Dec.

The article enclosed from the Register and Advertiser is a substantial expression of my own views on the subject of employing for the defence of our country all the able bodied men we have without distinction of color. It is now becoming daily more evident to all reflecting persons that we are reduced to choosing whether the negroes shall fight for us or against us, and that all arguments as to the positive advantages or disadvantages of employing them are beside the question, which is, simply one of relative advantage between having their fighting element in our ranks or in those of our enemy.

On the other topic suggested by you, of making use of this subject as an aid to foreign negotiations, you will appreciate the obligation of reticence imposed on me in those matters; and I can only say that I perceive no discordance in the views you express from what wise policy would dictate. So far, therefore, from obstructing any effort that the government may be or may have been making in the hope of securing our independence, the influence of your journal in the line which you propose to take would be of valuable assistance.

With many thanks for your offer of cordial support in my labors for the success of our common cause, I am,

> VERY RESPECTFULLY AND TRULY,
> YOURS &C.
> (SIGNED) JEFFN. DAVIS

To Governor William Smith (JDC)*

RICHMOND, VIRGINIA, MARCH 25, 1865

GOVERNOR:

Herewith I transmit the requisition made by General Lee in accordance with the suggestion I lately received from you. He informs me that it would have been made sooner if he had known that action on his part was waited for. He had previously written to you, but I infer from the fact that you did not mention his letter that it had failed to reach you.

You have probably noticed that the order issued from the Adjutant General's office, for the organization of colored troops looks only to the acceptance of volunteers, and, in a letter received this evening from General Lee, he expresses the opinion that there should be no compulsory enlistment in the first instance.

My idea has been that we should endeavor to draw into our mili-

* Governor of Virginia.

tary service that portion of the negroes which would be most apt to run away and join the army of the enemy, and that this would be best effected by seeking for volunteers for our own Army. If this plan should fail to obtain the requisite number there will still remain the process of compulsory enlistment.

VERY RESPECTFULLY YOURS
(SIGNED) JEFFN. DAVIS.

To Governor William Smith (JDC)

RICHMOND, VIRGINIA, MARCH 30, 1865

GOVERNOR:

Upon the receipt of your letter of the 27th inst., I had a conference with the Secretary of War, and Adjutant General, in relation to your suggestions as to the published order for the organization of negro troops, and I hope that the modifications which have been made will remove the objections which you pointed out.

It was never my intention to collect the negroes in depots for purposes of instruction, but only as the best mode of forwarding them, either as individuals, or as companies, to the commands with which they were to serve.

The officers at the different posts will aid in providing for the negroes in their respective neighborhoods, and in forwarding them to depots where transportation will be available to aid them in reaching the fields of service for which they are destined. The aid of gentlemen who are willing and able to raise this character of troops will be freely accepted, the appointment of Commanders for reasons obvious to you must depend on other considerations than the mere power to recruit.

I am happy to receive your assurance of success, as well as your promise to seek legislation to secure unmistakably freedom to the slave who shall enter the army, with a right to return to his old home when he shall have been honorably discharged from the military service.

I remain of the opinion that we should confine our first efforts to getting volunteers, and would prefer that you would adopt such measures as would advance that mode of recruiting, rather than that concerning which you make inquiry, to-wit: by issuing a requisition for the slaves as authorized by the Statutes of Virginia.

I have the honor to be with great respect,

YOUR OBEDIENT SERVANT,
(SIGNED) JEFFN. DAVIS

To General R. E. Lee (JDC)

RICHMOND, VIRGINIA, APRIL 1, 1865

SIR:

I have been laboring without much progress to advance the raising of negro troops. You must judge how far you can consistently detach officers to recruit. I called for the recommendations made by you, and so few names were presented that I infer you do not find it desirable to rely on officers sent to recruit for their own commands; therefore have directed that orders be given to the Commanders of "Reserves" in the several States to employ their officers to recruit negroes. If there be an officer or soldier to whose command, the masters would prefer to entrust, and the slaves would prefer to go, he can be appointed when the company or battalion reaches its destination.

I have prepared a circular letter to the Governors of the States, invoking their aid as well by appeals to the owners as by recommendations to the Legislatures, to make the most liberal provisions for those who volunteer to fight for the safety and independence of the State.

I have asked often but without satisfactory reply how many of the exchanged prisoners have joined the Army. Your force should have been increased from that source, eight or ten thousand men.

The desire to confer with you would have caused me to go to Petersburg before this date, but for the pressure which recent events have put upon me, and the operations in your vicinity prevented me from inviting you to come here.

Today the Secretary of War presents propositions from the proprietors of the Tredegar works which impress me very unfavorably. We will endeavor to keep them at work, though it must be on a reduced scale. There is also difficulty in getting iron even for shot and shell, but hope this may for the present be overcome by taking some from the Navy which under the altered circumstances may be spared.

Last night we had rumors of a general engagement on your right; your silence in regard to it leads to the conclusion that it was unwarranted.

General Holmes returned immediately to Genl. Johnston. I could reply in general terms to the message he brought me, and as there was a supposed misunderstanding on your part of the views of Genl. Johnston, I advised him to go on and see you.

The reports, especially those of newspaper correspondents, had encouraged me to hope for a better condition and prospect in N.C. than was presented in the statement which General Holmes was directed to make to me. The arrival of the men left behind on the march from Mississippi will, I hope, improve the tone, as well as increase the military power there.

The question is often asked of me "Will we hold Richmond," to which my only answer is, if we can, it is purely a question of military power.

The distrust is increasing and embarrasses in many ways.

RESPECTFULLY YOURS,
(SIGNED) JEFFN. DAVIS

To the People of the Confederate States of America (JDC)

DANVILLE, VIRGINIA, APRIL 4, 1865

The General-in-Chief of our Army* has found it necessary to make such movements of the troops as to uncover the Capital, and thus involve the withdrawal of the Government from the city of Richmond.

---

* Robert E. Lee.

It would be unwise, even if it were possible, to conceal the great moral, as well as material injury to our cause that must result from the occupation of Richmond by the enemy. It is equally unwise and unworthy of us, as patriots engaged in a most sacred cause to allow our energies to falter, our spirits to grow faint, or our efforts to become relaxed, under reverses however calamitous. While it has been to us a source of national pride, that for four years of unequalled warfare, we have been able, in close proximity to the centre of the enemy's power to maintain the seat of our chosen Government free from the pollution of his presence; while the memories of the heroic dead, who have freely given their lives to its defence, must ever remain enshrined in our hearts; while the preservation of the capital, which is usually regarded as the evidence to mankind of separate existence, was an object very dear to us, it is also true, and should not be forgotten, that the loss which we have suffered is not without compensation.

For many months the largest and finest army of the Confederacy, under the command of a leader whose presence inspires equal confidence in the troops and the people, has been greatly trammeled by the necessity of keeping constant watch over the approaches to the capital, and has thus been forced to forego more than one opportunity for promising enterprises.

The hopes and confidence of the enemy have been constantly excited by the belief, that their possession of Richmond would be the signal for our submission to their rule, and relieve them from the burthen of a war which, as their failing resources admonish them, must be abandoned if not speedily brought to a successful close.

It is for us; my countrymen, to show by our bearing under reverses, how wretched has been the self-deception of those who have believed us less able to endure misfortune with fortitude, than to encounter danger with courage.

We have now entered upon a new phase of a struggle, the memory of which is to endure for all ages, and to shed ever increasing lustre upon our country. Relieved from the necessity of guarding cities and particular points, important but not vital to our defence with our army free to move from point to point, and strike in detail the detachments and garrisons of the enemy; operating in the interior of our own country, where supplies are more accessible, and where the foe will be far removed from his own base, and cut off from all succor in case of reverse, nothing is now needed to render our triumph certain, but the exhibition of our own unquenchable resolve. Let us but will it, and we are free; and who in the light of the past, dare doubt your purpose in the future?

Animated by that confidence in your spirit and fortitude, which never yet has failed me, I announce to you, fellow countrymen, that it is my purpose to maintain your cause with my whole heart and soul; that I will never consent to abandon to the enemy one foot of the soil of any one of the States of the Confederacy; that Virginia, noble State, whose ancient renown has eclipsed by her still more glorious recent history; whose bosom has been bared to receive the main shock of this war; whose sons and daughters have exhibited heroism so sublime as to render her illustrious in all time to come; that Virginia, with the help of the people, and by the blessing of Providence, shall be held and defended, and no peace ever be made with the infamous invaders of her homes by the sacrifice of any of her rights or territory.

If by stress of numbers, we should ever be compelled to a temporary withdrawal from her limits, or those of any other border State, again and again will we return, until the baffled and exhausted enemy shall abandon in despair his endless and impossible task of making slaves of a people resolved to be free.

Let us not then respond, my countrymen, but, relying on the never failing mercies and protecting care of our God, let us meet the foe with fresh defiance, with unconquered and unconquerable hearts.

(SIGNED) JEFFERSON DAVIS

To Varina Davis (JDC)

DANVILLE, VIRGINIA, APRIL 5, 1865

MY DEAR WIFE,

I have in vain sought to get into communication with Genl Lee and have postponed writing in the hope that I would soon be able to speak to you with some confidence of the future—On last Sunday I was called out of church to receive a telegram announcing that Gen'l Lee could not hold his position longer than till night and warning me that we must leave Richmond, as the army would commence retiring that evening—I made the necessary arrangements at my office and went to our house to have the proper dispositions made there—Nothing had been done after you left and but little could be done in the few hours which remained before the train was to leave.

I packed the bust and gave it to John Davis who offered to take it and put it where it should never be found by a Yankee—I also gave him charge of the painting of the heros of the Valley—both were removed after dark—The furniture of the house was left and very little of the things I directed to be put up, bedding & groceries, were saved. Mrs Omelia behaved just as you described her, but seemed anxious to serve and promised to take care of everything, which may mean some things.

The Auctioneer returned account of sales $28.400—Could not dispose of the carriages—Mr Grant was afraid to take the carriage to his house &c. &c. I sent it to the depot to be put on a flat. At the moment of starting it was said they could not take it in that train but would bring it on the next train. It has not been heard from since—I sent a message to Mr Grant that I had neglected to return the cow and wished him to send for her immediately—Called off on horseback to the depot, I left the servants to go down with the boxes and they left Tippy—Watson came willingly, Spencer against my will, Robert Alf V. B. & Ives got drunk—David Bradford went back from the depot to bring out the spoons and forks which I was told had been left—and to come out with Genl Breckenridge, since then I have not heard from either of them—

I had short notice, was interrupted so often and so little aided that the results are very unsatisfactory.

The people here have been very kind and the Mayor & Council have offered assistance in the matter of quarters, and have very handsomely declared their unabated confidence—I do not wish to leave Va, but cannot decide on my movements until those of the army are better developed.

I hope you are comfortable and trust soon to hear from you. Kiss my dear children.

I weary of this sad recital and have nothing pleasant to tell. May God have you in his Holy keeping is the fervent prayer of

YOUR EVER AFFECTIONATE—
HUSBAND

J. D. Howell is here though I have not seen him, he & Joe Nick came together as a guard to Treasury specie—

To *Varina Davis* (JDC)

GREENSBORO, NORTH CAROLINA, APRIL 14, 1865

DEAR WINNIE

I will come to you if I can—Everything is dark—you should prepare for the worst by dividing your baggage so as to move in wagons If you can go to Abbeville it seems best as I am now advised—If you can send everything there do so—I have lingered on the road and labored to little purpose—My love to the children and Maggie—God bless, guide and preserve you, ever prays

YOUR MOST AFFECTIONATE
BANNY.*

I sent you a telegram but fear it was stopped on the road. Gen. Bonham bears this and will [tell] you more than I can write—As his horse is at the door and he waits for me to write this—again and ever yours—

---

* A term of endearment used by Varina for JD.

To *Varina Davis* (JDC)

CHARLOTTE, NORTH CAROLINA, APRIL 23, 1865

MY DEAR WINNIE.

I have been detained here longer than was expected when the last telegram was sent to you. I am uncertain where you are and deeply feel the necessity of being with you, if even for a brief time, under our altered circumstances.

Govr. Vance and Genl. Hampton propose to meet me here, and Genl. Johnston sent me a request to remain at some point where he could readily communicate with me. Under these circumstances I have asked Mr Harrison to go in search of you and to render you such assistance as he may. Your brother William telegraphed in reply to my inquiry, that you were at Abbeville and that he would go to see you. My last dispatch was sent to that place and to the care of Mr Burt.[*]

Your own feelings will convey to you an idea of my solicitude for you and our family, and I will not distress by describing it.

The dispersion of Lee's army and the surrender of the remnant which remained with him, destroyed the hopes I entertained when we parted. Had that army held together, I am now confident we could have successfully executed the plan which I sketched to you and would have been today on the high road to independence.

. . .

Genl. Johnston had several interviews with Sherman and agreed on a suspension of hostilities, and the reference of terms of pacification. They are secret and may be rejected by the Yankee Government. To us, they are hard enough, though freed from wanton humiliation, and expressly recognizing the State Governments, and the rights of person and property as secured by the Constitutions of the United States and the several States.

. . .

[*] Lieutenant General Wade Hampton; Burton Harrison, JD's private secretary; Armistead Burt of Abbeville, South Carolina, a JD supporter.

The issue is one which it is very painful for me to meet. On one hand is the long night of oppression which will follow the return of our people to the "Union"; on the other, the suffering of the women and children, and carnage among the few brave patriots who would still oppose the invader, and who, unless the people would rise en-masse to sustain them, would struggle but to die in vain. I think my judgment is undisturbed by any pride of opinion, I have prayed to our Heavenly Father to give me wisdom and fortitude equal to the demands of the position in which Providence has placed me. I have sacrificed so much for the cause of the Confederacy that I can measure my ability to make any further sacrifice required, and am assured there is but one to which I am not equal—My wife and my Children—How are they to be saved from degradation or want is now my care.

During the suspension of hostilities you may have the best opportunity to go to Mississippi, and there either to sail from Mobile for a foreign port or to cross the river and proceed to Texas, as the one or the other may be more practicable. The little sterling you have will be a very scanty store and under other circumstances would not be coveted, but if our land can be sold, that will secure you from absolute want. For myself, it may be that, a devoted band of Cavalry will cling to me, and that I can force my way across the Mississippi, and if nothing can be done there which it will be proper to do, then I can go to Mexico, and have the world from which to choose a location.

Dear Wife, this is not the fate to which I invited [you] when the future was rose colored to us both; but I know you will bear it even better than myself, and that, of us two, I alone, will ever look back reproachfully on my past career. I have thus entered on the questions involved in the future to guard against contingencies. My stay will not be prolonged a day beyond the prospect of useful labor here, and there is every reason to suppose that I will be with you a few days after Mr Harrison arrives.

. . .

To Varina Davis (TR)

FORTRESS MONROE, VIRGINIA, AUGUST 21, 1865

MY DEAR WIFE,

I am now permitted to write to you, under two conditions viz: that I confine myself to family matters, and that my letter shall be examined by the U.S. Atty. Genl. before it is sent to you.

This will sufficiently explain to you the omission of subjects on which you would desire me to write. I presume it is however permissible for me to relive your disappointment much in regard to my silence on the subject of future action towards me by stating that of the purpose of the authorities I know nothing.

To morrow it will be three months since we were suddenly and unexpectedly separated, and many causes prominent among which has been my anxiety for you and our children have made that quarter in seeming duration long, very long. I sought permission to write to you that I might make some suggestions as to your movements and as to domestic arrangements. The first and most important point, has in the mean time been so far decided by the journey of the older children that until a key is furnished to open what is now to me unintelligible I can only speak in general terms in regard to your future movements. It is to be inferred that you have decided and I think wisely not to return to our old home, at least in the present disturbed condition of society. Thus you have the world before you but not where to chose, as the loss of our property will require the selection to be, with a view to subsistence. Should I regain my liberty before our "people" have become vagrant there are many of them whose labor I could direct so as to make it not wholly unprofitable. Their good faith under many trials, and the mutual affection between them and myself make me always solicitous for their welfare and probably keeps them expectant of my coming. Should my fate be not to return to that country you can best be advised by Brother Jos. as to what and how it should be attempted, if any thing may be done. Always understand however that I do not mean that you should attempt in person to do any thing in the matter. I often think of "old Uncle Bob" and always with painful anxiety. If Sam. has rejoined him he will do all in his power for the old man's comfort and safety.

The Smith land had better be returned to the heirs.* No deed was made and the payments were for moveable effects and for interest; their right to the land which alone remains therefore clearly revives since I am most unable to make the payment which is I believe due, and shall be unable to fulfil the engagements hereafter to mature; therefore the sooner the case is disposed of the better. Please write to my Brother for me in such terms as you can well understand I would use if allowed to write to him myself.

In like manner please write to my Sisters. I asked Jeff. V. when he & I parted, to join you as soon as he could and to remain with you; he could render you much assistance as well by his intelligence as his discretion. Have you heard from him? The servant reported by the newspapers to be with the children in New York, is I suppose Robert, indeed so hope.

Ellen came ashore, and it must have embarrassed you greatly under the circumstances as to lose her before you could get another. Jim. reported here that he knew where we had buried a large sum of gold at or near Macon.† This I heard after he had gone and in such manner as created the impression that he had gone on the same ship with you. The ready conclusion was that he had returned with assurances of zeal and fidelity to you and expecting to find an opportunity to rob your trunks. This greatly disturbed me until I found that he had gone by way of Raleigh. Then remembering his complaint that he was not to be furnished with transportation from here; another explanation of his fiction was afforded more creditable at least to his cunning. I have the prayer book you sent, but the memorandum placed in it was witheld. The suit of dark grey clothes has also been received. It was like

---

* Land in Hinds County, Mississippi, bought by Joseph Davis for JD during the war.

† Jefferson Van Benthuysen, nephew of Eliza Davis; Robert Brown, former slave of JD who remained with the family; Ellen McGinnis, a free servant of Varina Davis, who was with the Davises when they were captured; Jim is probably James H. Jones, a free black servant captured with the Davises.

you in moments of such discomfort and annoyance as those to which you were subjected, to be careful about my contingent and future wants. Some day I hope to be able to tell you how in the long, weary hours of my confinement, busy memory has brought many tributes to your tender and ardent affection. The confidence in the shield of Innocence with which I tried to quiet your apprehensions and to dry your tears at our parting, sustains me still. If your fears have proved more prophetic than my hopes, yet do not despond—"Tarry thou the Lord's leisure; be strong, and he will comfort thy heart."

Every day twice or oftener I repeat the prayer of St. Chrysostom and assemble you all, each separately noted, on the right side is Winnie, then Polly, Big Boy, Billie, then L.P. held by Aunty and sometimes, as affection numbers the line, "the Little man" is found between his Brothers. x x x x x __ __ __ __ __ __.*

I daily repeat the hymn I last heard you sing. "Guide me" &c. It is doubly dear to me for that association. The one which follows it in our Book of Common prayer is also often present to me. It is a most beautiful lesson of humility & benevolence.

I have had here first occasion to realize the kindness of my fellow man. To the Surgeon and Regtal. Chaplain I am under many obligations. The officers of the Guard and of the Day have shown me increased consideration, such as their orders would permit. The unjust accusations which have been made against me in the newspapers of the day might well have created prejudices against me. I have had no opportunity to refute them by proof nor have I sought to do so by such statements of chronological and other easily to be verified facts which I might perhaps have been induced to make under other circumstances; I can therefore only attribute perceptible change to those good influences which are always at work to confound evil designs. Be not alarmed by speculative reports concerning my condition. You can rely on my fortitude, and God has given me much of resignation, to His blessed will.

If it be His pleasure to reunite us, you will I trust find that His Fa-

---

* Xs and dashes in original.

therly correction has been sanctified to me, and that even in exile and obscurity I should be content to live unknown, quietly to labor for the support of my family; and thus to convince those who have misjudged me, that self-seeking and ill regulated ambition are not elements of my character.

Men are apt to be verbose when they speak of themselves and suffering has a rare power to develop selfishness; so I have wandered from the subject on which I proposed to write and have dwelt upon a person whose company I have for sometime past kept so exclusively that it must be strange if he has not become tiresome.

Under the necessity before stated, and during our separation, you will have temporarily a place of abode where you will not be wounded by unkind allusions to myself, where you will have proper schools for the children, and such social tone, moral and intellectual, as will best conduce to their culture. As well for yourself as for them you should endeavor to find a healthy vocation. To you a cold climate has been most beneficial, such also will best serve to strengthen the constitution of the children; and though the mind may hold mastery over the body, yet a strong frame is a great advantage to a student, and still more to him who in the busy world is called upon to apply his knowledge. If the news gatherer has rightly concluded that the children were on their way to Canada, I suppose it must have been under some intermediate arrangement. You will sufficiently understand the necessity for your presence with them and you must not allow your affectionate solicitude for me to interfere with your care for them.

It has been reported in the newspapers that you had applied for permission to visit me in my confinement, if you had been allowed to do so the visit would have caused you disappointment at the time, and bitter memories afterwards. You would not have been allowed to hold private conversation with me and if we are permitted to correspond freely in relation to personal matters, not connected with public affairs, it would be a great consolation, and with it I recommend you to be content.

Your stay in Savannah has been prolonged much beyond my expectation and I fear beyond your comfort. I do not know whether you are still there, but I hope your whereabouts may be known at Washington and will ask that this letter may there receive the proper address.

Have the articles belonging to *you personally* and which were seized at the time of our capture been restored? You are aware that I have had no opportunity to present the case, and therefore you have had the unusual task of attending to it yourself. Money derived from the sale of your jewelry and the horses presented to you by Gentlemen of Richmond could hardly be put on the same footing with my private property, and as little could they be regarded as public property, the proper subject of capture in war. The Heads of Executive Departments accustomed to consider questions of law and of fact, would I supposed take a different view of the transaction from subaltern officers of the Army.

You will realize the necessity of extreme caution in regard to our correspondence. The quid nuncs if they learn you have received a letter from me will no doubt seek to extract something for their pursuit, and your experience has taught you how little material serves to spin their web.

Have you been sick? On the 21st of July little Maggie appeared to me in a most vivid dream, warning me not to wake you &c. &c. You know how little I have been accustomed to regard like things. Here such visions have been frequent, nor have they always been without comfort.

I am reluctant to close this first letter to you after so long an interval; but am warned that I may be abusing privilege, as what I write is to be read by those to whom the labor will not be relieved by the interest which will support you.

If my dear Margaret is with you give her my tenderest love, she always appears to me associated with little Winnie. Kiss the Baby for me, may her sunny face never be clouded, though dark the morning of her life has been.

My dear Wife, equally the centre of my love and confidence, remember how good the Lord has always been to me, how often he has wonderfully preserved me, and put thy trust in Him.

Farewell, may He who tempers the wind to the shorn lamb, whose most glorious attribute is mercy, guide and protect and provide for my distressed family; and give to them and to me that grace which shall lead us all to final rest in the mansions where there is peace that passeth understanding.

Once more farewell, Ever affectionately

YOUR HUSBAND
JEFFERSON DAVIS

To Varina Davis (TR)

FORTRESS MONROE, VIRGINIA, SEPTEMBER 26, 1865
MY DEAR WIFE,

Your much wished for letter of the 14th Inst. reached me yesterday and to day I have been furnished with writing materials to enable me to reply. Your well known and beloved hand brought comfort to me before the envelop was broken. The spirit which attends me waking and sleeping seemed to be brought more into a oral presence. Your letter informs me of much which you did not intend to communicate. I hope you are better now than when you wrote, as the weather must be less oppressive. One of the causes of my anxiety that you should go with the children was the expectation that your health would suffer if you remained in that hot, crowded, and to you strange place. The assurance given on the Clyde that you were no longer under restraint, though it was modified when thereupon I proposed that you should leave that ship and take passage on one bound to a northern port, still left me under the belief that when you reached Savannah you would be free to go elsewhere, and I have been always led to suppose that your stay there was voluntary. Though not so related, the logic of events leads to the conclusion that you too have been a prisoner. Your inquiry by telegraph was answered by Genl. Miles, and from him I learned at the same time that your address was Augusta; I hope his dispatch reached you and relieved your anxiety in regard to my health.* My letter to you written at that time gave you so full an account of my disease that it will not be necessary in this to notice it further than to say, that though it has reappeared in a modified form there is no cause for

---

* The *Clyde* was the ship that transported the Davises from Savannah to Fortress Monroe; Major General Nelson Miles, commander of Fortress Monroe.

apprehension. My kind Physician, called in the chief Medical Director who recently visited this Post, and the result of their consultation was that change to better quarters should be recommended. If their recommendation should secure to me a purer and drier atmosphere I think there will be a prompt and material improvement in my health. But as I have said to you heretofore have confidence in my ability to bear much and to bear long, above all be not disturbed by the unwarranted statements of those newsgatherers who would earn their living by coining the tears of the afflicted. Such people if they are here, have no access to me, and can have no reliable information; if to make themselves acceptable to their employers they invent stories painful to you, remember the motive and apply it as a test. It is true that I did not wish you to know entirely the rigors of my imprisonment and regret that you should have learned them; it is true that my strength has greatly failed me; and the loss of sleep has created a morbid excitability; but an unseen hand has sustained me and a peace which the world could not give, and has not been able to destroy, will I trust uphold me to meet with resignation whatever may befal me.

You do not mention Margaret and by saying your Ma. has not written to inform you about the children, it is to be inferred that Margaret did not go with them. Your praise of Robert is very grateful to me. I felt sure of him when giving him a parting charge. That which seems in him to be bad temper is rather a spirit of independence, an uncourtly virtue but in time of trial a better reliance than submissive compliance. I am glad that Billy is his favorite not only because he is most helpless, but also because I am haunted by the suspicions that Betsy treated him harshly when an infant and I thought I saw the effect on him afterwards. When he is numbered in the little group of prayer, my heart *usually* starts convulsively as though he appealed to me for protection. I have not heard of My Ellen, but she might be very near without my knowing it, and this, however desirous she might be to serve. Catharine no doubt repented, and if she could control her angry passions would do better; but that is improbable, and when angry she is as little to be trusted as an insane person.ˑ

ˑ Betsy, a JD slave in the Executive Mansion who ran away in 1864; My Ellen, Ellen McGinnis; Catherine (last name unknown), a nurse in the Davis household in Richmond.

With you however I rejoice in the truth and faithfulness of those humble friends; it is to your kindness and justice the best tribute which could be offered. It was similar manifestation on the part of the negroes at home that has caused me to feel so anxious for their welfare. Had they been willing to leave us and have done so without coercion it would have caused me far less regret. I should have reckoned them greater losers by the change than ourselves. Their honesty will I trust be duly rewarded here and hereafter.

This is not the first time that we have found our humblest friends, the truest when no longer selfishly prompted. Yet I would not ascribe the defections of the higher class so much to treachery and deceit, as to timidity and avarice. Wishing to be relieved of responsibility for the past they offer in proof either of their little identification with the cause of the Confederacy or of their repentance for such connection; their censure, their accusation or their avowed hostility to the man on whom they lately conferred the highest office in their representative government, and who by performing the duties of that station has been rendered the object of special vengeance. If one is to answer for all upon him it most naturally and properly falls. If I alone could bear all the suffering of the country and relieve it from further calamity, I trust our Heavenly Father would give me strength to be a willing sacrifice; and if in a lower degree some of those who called me (I being then absent) to perform their behests, shall throw on me the whole responsibility; let us rejoice at least in their escape, expecting for them a returning sense of justice, when the stumbling blocks of fear and selfishness shall have been removed from their path.

In any event we have the satisfactory evidence that the class referred to is but a small portion of the people. The great mass accepting the present condition of affairs as the result of the War, and directing their attention to the future issues which are involved in the changes produced, would bury the inevitable past with the sorrow which is unmingled with shame.

As in my former letters I can only say that I have no information as to the purpose of the authorities in regard to myself. Neither as to accusation or proceeding.

I thank you for attention to my Brother, and grieve that it is not in my power to serve him. Gladly would I labor for him. There can I suppose be no question as to the restoration of his land. He did not leave home to enter the Service of the Confederacy, neither was the place abandoned. Persons were left in charge of each of the *three* quarters, and if they did not retain possession and cultivate some crop, it must have been because they were dispossessed by force. I refer to the River lands.

The amount of cotton which is promised on those places could have been easily produced without destroying the lawns. But will it be gathered? If my brother would get some competent agent to attend to the division of the land and the receipt of rents, the place should yield a revenue sufficient to support him in comfort at some more agreeable residence than that will hereafter be. I hope you will soon have definite information as to the children, winter is approaching and they are in a very cold climate. Dear little P.C. it is hard for me to realize that she has names for people. It must be a severe trial for her to teeth in a hot climate and crowded as you must have been in Savnh.

God grant that she may pass through the ordeal. Kiss her for one who loves her dearly though she does not know who he is. I did not doubt that your friends in Richmond would follow you with their prayers, and am glad that so many wrote to you. What became of Mrs. O'Melia and how did she do?*

Our kind neighbors sent me some time since a bunch of cigars and a bottle of brandy. A reminder of the big glass of julep. Dr. Simmons who you may recollect as a surgeon in the Old Army, a friend of Dr. Wood, son in law of Mr. Gittings of Balto. is now Medical Inspector of this Dept. & is stationed at Richd. He was here some time since and I have cause to be thankful to him for subsequent kindness. My little friend who has so kindly attended to sending my meals and looking after my clothes when sent to wash, has gone to the Moravian school near to Easton. I requested her Father to let Mary Jane know of her. She used to ride on horseback and in my daily walk I sometimes saw her. If I had known how to get it I would have given your fine saddle to her.

---

* An Irish widow who became Varina Davis's housekeeper during the war.

My dear Winnie I felt how anxious you would be to be with me if you knew that I was sick and in pain. Need I say that every pang reminded me how often your soft touch and loving words had soothed me in like times of suffering.

How sadly I felt that public cares and frequent absence and preoccupation with disagreeable subjects had prevented me from making even the poor return which it was in my power to give. That time so long looked for when we should be apart from the world, and quietly occupied with objects of common interest to us, seemed to rise before me like the "convenient season" of the impenitent. I have prayed if it be the will of our Father that it might yet be given to me, to show you how much and how truly I am yours, and with such poor measure as I could mete, to return when you were sick your services in kind. My good Wife, the Lord will care for you. There always seems to me to be an assuring answer when I pray especially for you. The needy and the sorrow stricken who have been relieved and soothed by you, smooth your way to the favor of Him who shows mercy to the merciful. My heart is sustained by the conviction that we shall meet again in this world, that even before human judgement my innocence of wrong to my fellow man will prevail, though many seek my destruction. The bigotry which gave power to false witnesses and frightened truth from the presence of the Judges, though it lives, no longer reigns. Be hopeful and again I say "tarry thou the Lord's leisure."

May the Lord guide and comfort you, ever prays with all the fervor of devoted affection your Husband,

JEFFERSON DAVIS

P.S. I met Mr. Clay in our walk, he asked me to give his love to you and the children. He is now in better health, but is much changed. Hair and beard quite grey. Jno. Mitchell is here.* I saw him in like manner. He looks thin and feeble, is said to be consumptive. We are not allowed to visit each other or to converse when we meet in the open air. When Mr. Clay was quite sick I earnestly desired to be with him.

D.

---

* Clement C. Clay, who also was imprisoned at Fortress Monroe; Jonathan Mitchell, a prisoner at Fortress Monroe who was released in October.

To Varina Davis (TR)

FORTRESS MONROE, VIRGINIA, OCTOBER 20, 1865

MY DEAR WIFE,

Yesterday brought me your letters of Sept. 4 and Oct. 1 with note of Oct. 2 and enclosures, viz. Letter from Ellen, one from Jeff., and circular of the Academy at Sault au Recollet. Though the tours could not be those employed in happier hours, they were consolatory to me and retired many of my distressing anxieties. You of course understood that in the absence of the requisite data I did not intend on former occasions to do more than suggest what would be preferable if no impediment existed. Not imagining that you would be restricted to a place which I had stated was objectionable on account of the evil effect which the climate would produce and in which you would be an entire stranger. I only fear the hardship of your being required to go there and feeling that your constant care was needful to our small children. I expressed the wish that you would go with them to some place where they and you would be more advantageously situated. You have done what seems to me the best under the circumstances and I trust God will so order all things as to justify the actions taken by it's future results.

Chafed by harsh restraints and agonized by fears for me, it may have been naturally expected that a nervous woman would give expression to her feelings and seek to make her griefs known to her Husband's friends, perhaps it was therefore that detectives were put around you; and I am proud of your self denial, and grateful that the sickness consequent has had no worse effect upon you and your infant. We should not be surprised that those whose palms itch for gold should attribute to me a like vice, and therefore may have hoped by watching you to find hidden treasure. Newspapers publish silly accounts of large sums of specie possessed by me and abandoned, of course every intelligent man knows that my office did not make me the custodian of public money, but such slanders impose on and serve to inflame the ignorant, the very ignorant who don't know how public money was kept and how drawn out of the hands of those who were responsible for it. My children as they grow up and prove the pressure of poverty, must be taught the cause of it; and I trust they will feel as I have, when remembering the fact that my Father was impoverished by his losses in the War of the Revolution.

The religion we possess has this peculiar characteristic, that just in proportion as we advance in preparation for the world to come, is our happiness in this increased. Our injuries cease to be grievous in proportion as Christian charity enables us to forgive those who trespass against us, and to pray for our enemies. I rejoice in the sweet, sensitive nature of my little Maggie, but I would she could have been spared the knowledge which inspired her "grace" and the tears which followed its utterance. As none could share my suffering, and as those who loved me were powerless to diminish it, I greatly preferred that they should not know of it. Separated from my friends of this world, my Heavenly Father has drawn nearer to me. His goodness and my unworthiness are more sensibly felt, but this does not press me back, for the atoning Mediator is the way and his *hand* upholds me.

I trust Maggie will be happy, her loving temper will suit the government of the Nuns, and they will probably soon become attached to each other. When I was a child the kindness of the Friars so won upon my affection that impression has never been effaced, but has the rather extended from them to their whole church. Her letter to me has not arrived, nor has your's of Sept. 1st which you mention as having enclosed to be forwarded. The big boy has not improved much in his writing but the warm heart was not to be hidden or hushed by his want of skill clerkly. You have no doubt answered his inquiry but when you write to him again tell him how glad I was to see his letter, how anxious I am that he should be a good boy and learn fast, how much I love him and how constantly I pray for him. Where is Robert? Would he not be more useful to you under the present condition of the family than elsewhere. I hope your Ma. is comfortably situated and that she and Billy will get on well together, but unless he has a good nurse you know she will overwork herself. Give my love to her when you write and to Margaret who is I suppose there. You will know how to express my feelings for both of them.

Joe. D & S. have not disappointed and if you should hereafter require the services of either of them they will no doubt come as fully at your command as when they recently came to you unbidden.* Please write to Ellen for me thank her for the kind true hearted letter she wrote to me. This in the spirit I honor and expected from her, may she never be shaken in her confidence in the supremacy of justice and the protecting power of innocence. Little Winnie in the photograph grows more like herself than she seemed when it first came. My Winnie's sadness continues. May a brighter sun lighten her heart and enliven her picture.

I will try to get the commentaries of which you write. Would like to read the same books with you, but under present circumstances this would be difficult and objectionable. Difficult because I have little field for selection and objectionable because entertaining books, poetry and romance would excite, whereas my effort is to keep sentiment subdued and to live in the region of driest fact, I would not have you reduced to the same fare, as mingling with the world the impressions of poetry and romance come as a relief and do not remain to injure.

Dear Le Pi's hair came safely and softly lies with me, you are now in that condition which is the symbol of occupation.† May you soon have all your cares and objects of love about you again.

Brother Joe. should not I think return to the river place. All is changed, he will be troubled beyond his strength by the confusion which must exist, an Agent will suit the new regime much better than the old one. If he goes back why not take the Brierfield House. He can claim possession, as owner of the land. But my decided opinion is that in the existing condition neither he nor Lize should stay there. I cannot write to him.

The saddest effect which has been produced on me is in impaired memory. Accustomed to rely on it with confidence it is painfully embarrassing to me, especially as to names and dates. In regard to events it is less felt and by association only can I measure time. This year came in on Sunday and thus the tables in the Prayer book serve as a Calendar. A circumstance to which I am much indebted. Have you re-

---

* Joseph R. Davis and Joseph Davis Smith, M.D., nephews of JD.

† Le Pi and Piecake were nicknames for JD and Varina's youngest child, Varina Anne Davis.

tained our family Bible? If so the dates you ask for are there. 1859 &
1864 must be the years. The month of the first was I think April & day
18th—the last was Saturday preceding the meeting of Congress—I
have nothing to refer to in aid of memory. It was very kind of those
friends. Pardon me I cannot. xxx (For say, three months after I was imprisoned here two hours of consecutive sleep were never allowed to
me,) more recently it has not been so bad, but it is still only broken
sleep which I get at night, and by day my attention is distracted by the
passing of the Sentinels who are kept around me as well by day as by
night. I have not sunk under my trials, am better than a fortnight ago
and trust shall be sustained under any affliction which it may be required of me to bear. My sight is affected but less than I would have
supposed if it had been foretold that a light was to be kept where I was
to sleep, and that I was at short intervals to be aroused and the expanded pupils thus frequently subjected to the glare of a lamp. You have
repeated the request for a description of my situation and I complied
in part. Already regret having done so and hope you will be satisfied of
the correctness of the rule heretofore observed. Of my occupation a
brief account will suffice. In the morning as soon as dressed I read the
morning prayer (family) sometimes adding a chapter of the New Tes-
tament and a Psalm. After breakfast read, at this time Bancroft's History of the United States. Soon after 11 read the morning service, on
Sundays, Wednesdays & Fridays, add the Communion service, the Collect, Epistle and Gospel and the Litany. In the afternoon read whatever book occupies me and when Genl. Miles comes, go out to walk
say, for an hour on the parapet. In the evening read the Service as appointed. Family prayer at night. To the morning & evening service a
modified form of the prayer for a person going to sea and of the prayer
for a person under affliction are always added. Of food I am quite satisfactorily supplied by the Doctor's family, and my appetite is to blame
for any want of appreciation. My cot is now comfortable and I have
plenty of water and fire—Do not imagine horrible things and suffer
vicariously for me. If President Johnsoin ever finds out the exact state
of the case, I think he will remove the most disagreeable features in
the discipline and until then or some other change, be assured I will
bear it with the patience that lightens burdens, and expect me to get

better rather than worse. There is soon to be a change of the garrison here, I will be sorry to part from many of the officers—but as they are to go home I should rejoice for such as are entitled to my gratitude. Au reste, as I cannot control so I may hope it will be for the better.

William's conduct surprises me. I will only say of it that it was unlike either his Father or his Mother, and of him that I wish never to hear of him again. I am sorry you did not see Sam; when he joins "old Bob" there will be supplied to him the only thing he needs, judgement.

Tom. & Charley expressed to you what is I believe the feeling of all our family negroes. I hope their fidelity will be duly rewarded and regret that we are not in a situation to aid and protect them.˙ There is I observe a controversy which I regret as to allowing negroes to testify in court. From Brother Joe, many years ago, I derived the opinion that they should then be made competent witnesses, the jury judging of their credibility; out of my opinion on that point arose my difficulty with Mr. Cox, and any doubt which might have existed in my mind was removed at that time.† The change of relation diminishing protection, must increase the necessity. Truth only is consistent, and they must be acute and well trained, who can so combine as to make falsehood appear like truth when closely examined. After full consideration I believe Jim innocent and that the story was the invention of a lower man having higher position.

I have not seen Jordan's critique and am at a loss to know where that game was played and was lost by my interference.‡ If the records are preserved they dispose summarily of his romances past, passing, and to come. Be not distressed by the conduct of those who wilfully misrepresent, neither of the others whose timidity but not their will consults. If those whom I have served turn against me theirs is the shame, and time will make them feel it. The events were of a public character and it is not possible for men to shift their responsibility to another. Every one who has acted must have made mistakes, and the frank acknowledgement of his errors will be the best defence he can make to the public and the only one beneficial to his conscience. Let him who

---

˙ William, Sam, Old Bob, Tom, and Charley were former slaves of JD.

† Owen B. Cox, an overseer at antebellum Brierfield.

‡ Thomas Jordan, wartime chief of staff for General P. G. T. Beauregard.

has changed his theory confess it, let him whose opinions are unchanged conform his action to the changed circumstances, and both
classes may preserve their integrity and live and work in harmony.
Our life is spent in choosing between evils and he would be most unwise
who would refuse the comparative good thus to be obtained. History is
ever repeating itself, but the influence of Christianity and letters has
softened its harsher features. The wail of the destitute women and children who were left on the shore of Cork after the treaty of Limerick,
still rings in the ears of all who love right and hate oppression; but bad
as was the treatment of the Irish then, those scenes, of which you were
reading not long before you left Richmond, enacted by Philip of Spain
in the low countries were worse. The unfortunate have always been
deserted and betrayed; but did ever man have less to complain of when
he had lost power top serve. The critics are noisy—perhaps they hope
to enhance their words by loud crying. The multitude are silent, why
should they speak save to Him who hears best the words most secretly
uttered. My own heart tells me the sympathy exists, that the prayers
from the family hearth have not been hushed. Then be ye, not charitable, but loving and confiding still to those from whom I have received much more than I deserved and as you know far more of
official honors than I desired.

Little Polly will I suppose resume French, the boy has probably forgotten much and will be almost a beginner. If the course of the school
is to put boys early at Latin I would not object. It is the root of the languages of Southern Europe and enters highly into the etimology of
our own; but the argument for it's study most conclusive with me is
that it is the best exercise for the mind of which a small boy is capable.
Strange though it may seem I have generally found when a school boy,
that those from warm countries would expose themselves most to cold
and for a time at least would bear it best. It will be well that care
should be taken to prevent our children from being thus injured. Some
of our friends might get the little dog, especially if it's history is not
known. Horrible you say, I answer generally true. The individual may
be an exception of that I know nothing, though his reputation for gallantry is suggestive of generosity and humanity. I have asked for the
Schomburg Catte family and Cummings Scripture readings—the lat-

ter I hope the chaplain might have. The Psalter and Lessons for the day will give us that daily reading in common which you suggest. It is not easy for me to know the hour except by the relieving of Sentinels which is every two hours beginning at 9 A.M. When in the casemate I constructed on the floor of the embrasure a partial dial, here it is not practicable. To me hours are alike, but to you there will be frequent occurences, visitors, domestic employments &c, &c which will not leave you entire command of your time. When I read though you should not be at the same time reading or praying with me, I will know you have been or will be uttering the same words, engaged with the same thoughts. There are other things of which I would write yet do not. The events in your letter are understood, I think thoroughly, but it would avail nothing to comment on them.

It is generally true that complaint diminishes the capacity to hear, certainly it does the freedom of inquiry into the nature of the grievance.

It was not my intention to have entered on a third sheet yet I must stop before having written of many things affecting us all. Imprisonment in solitude gives much time for speculation, but in this rapidly changing current of events thoughts not having fresh data are little worth.

Kiss the Baby for me, may God grant to me the sight of you both, may he preserve you from all harm in this world and gives us all grace to meet in Heaven as we assemble especially in my prayers twice or oftener daily.

Farewell my dear Wife. You have a key to my heart and know its unuttered feelings. That God may remember us in mercy, and grant our petitions as His wisdom will provide ever prays with unchanging devotion your Husband

JEFFERSON DAVIS

To *Varina Davis* (TR)

FORTRESS MONROE, VIRGINIA, JANUARY 16, 1866
MY DEAR WIFE,
. . .

The condition of society as described in Georgia is lamentable enough, and I fear it is much the same generally in the planting states. It is probable that our friend will find it worse, rather than better in Texas. He will not probably take his family there before making a personal inspection. Why do not well informed persons state the case fully and truly to Presdt. Johnson, his knowledge of the negro character and of the kind relations which formerly existed between the slaves and their masters, would enable him readily to perceive the appropriate remedies for present disorders.* Though in view of the excitement and blindness of the "Radicals" it may not be practicable to do all which sound policy would otherwise dictate, the worst grievances surely would be abated if rightly understood. There cannot be many so fanatical that for the sake of keeping armed negroes as a military police, they would render the lives of white women and children insecure and destroy what little of property the devastation of war has left. However wisely conducted the transition of the negro from his state of dependence to that of self control, must involve serious difficulties; if speculative theory, experimenting without special information, is to direct the change, those to the manor born will easily foresee the result. The resolute will, calm temper and practical sense which seek to extract good from unavoidable evil may if left unobstructed, save enough from the wreck to prevent the country from lapsing into desert. The efforts now being made to import laborers may be finally beneficial, but at first Europeans will be unskilful in that agriculture, and must be acclimated before they can be productive.

I had feared that our negroes would be disturbed by the introduction of others among them, but could not have imagined that they would be driven away from their home by those pretending to be their

* Andrew Johnson, president of the United States 1865–69.

especial advocates. What a beast he must have been who turned old Uncle Bob out of his house, to find where he could a shelter for the infirmities of more than a hundred winters. That claim was manifest. Of the truth, the fidelity the piety which had so long secured him the respect of all who knew him, a stranger might plead ignorance. Were one in proper position, to bring the case to the notice of the authorities I cannot believe such conduct would be tolerated. The chief of the bureau would probably correct it as I understand his policy has been to induce the negroes to remain at their old homes. An agent *suited* to such work would probably be able by proper representations to remove the evils complained of at the H. & B.

17th—I have been suffering from neuralgia in the head and the usual effect upon the eyes causes me to write at intervals. Do not be disturbed, the attack is not serious, indeed considering the circumstances, it is rather to be wondered at that I am not worse. More than heretofore I use caution in all things, so that my strength may be preserved for whatever awaits me. Once a day it is still permitted to me to walk in the open air & though the time is brief the result is beneficial.

I would be obliged to you for the suggested shade for the eyes. Your ingenuity and handicraft has so often come to my relief that hope always hangs thereon. Since the attack of erysipelas my nose has not been equal to the pressure of the goggles.

I have the pocket comb you put in a case for me, so that you will have no occasion to attend to your offer in that regard. It is dear to me by every mark and association.

. . .

18th—The newspapers will have informed you of events at Washington, for obvious reasons I will make no comment, save to point you to the unavoidable conclusion that you can no longer cherish the hope which was formerly indulged. Strengthen your heart for the high responsibilities imposed on you & go forward on the path of duty, accepting every providence with the comforting assurance that it must be right. Truth is powerful and the common sense of justice recoils, after the paroxism of passion subsides, from continuance in wrong doing. Then I say, of the final result of any proceeding against me, be hopeful; my conduct has been too public, too consistent to be perverted, after slanderers are confronted by true witnesses.

It is hard for me to be reconciled to the trials to which my Wife and little children are exposed, but I trustingly pray that God will hide them under the shadow of his wings until earth's calamities are over-passed.

I will be glad when you are removed beyond the reach of the brutal cruelty of such statements and suggestions as those which have so disturbed you. They are crosses which you cannot bear and I have seen in your letters their evil as well as painful effect upon you. By dwelling on them, they grow into more than their real importance.

It was to remove a stumbling block that I referred to the parable, but from your answer perceive that my treatment was injudicious, and regret the error. The gifts with which men are divinely endowed are various, and the requirements of the Lord are never beyond the range of possibility; for he knows our infirmities and judges of our motives. These man cannot know, and is therefore forbidden to judge. We hope & pray for God's forgiveness on the ground of true repentance, and as we cannot tell in the case of those who trespass against us, whether the repentance is true or feigned, we are bound to accept the seeming. That is possible, is it not easy, for virtue far short of the God like or saintly examples of the Redeemer and the first Christian martyr. I struggle, not always successfully, against my temptations, and often feel how much communion with you, would aid my efforts to walk in the way of the Fathers commandments.

In my isolation a daily experience enables me to realize the heart warming influence of little Winnie's presence with you. Frequent thinking of her enables me to imagine her growth and progress. She is now associated in my mind with the memory of Sister Ann and the sadness which Ellen described confusedly mingles with thoughts of the child.

Kiss the little angel for me. Did she keep her baby, tear it up or lose it. Farewell dear Wife. There is a great satisfaction in feeling that you know most of that which I would write but do not. And it is perhaps fortunate that the restraint exists as it is one of the pressures upon feelings which it is necessary for me to control by every means within my power. May He that will not break a bruised reed, guide and comfort you. Your loneliest hour will not be alone for there is no emotion which does send my spirit to hover about the object of its dearest affection.

Again dear Wife farewell. Your Husband

JEFFERSON DAVIS

To Varina Davis (TR)

FORTRESS MONROE, VIRGINIA, FEBRUARY 3, 1866

MY DEAREST WIFE,

...

I have just heard that Mr. Clay is dieing, and regret it as well on account of my kind feeling for him and the respect which amiable character commanded as because he was one of those on whom I felt I could rely to vindicate my character from some of the accusations made against me, after Mr. Crittenden there was no one to whom I talked so much and so freely concerning the sectional troubles in 1860–1. With Mr. Crittenden I daily conferred when we served on the compromise committee in that winter, the record of which shows who it was who opposed every effort at accommodation.

Mr. Buchannan in his book has verified the judgement of his Pennsylvania acquaintance who ascribed to him vindictiveness as his absorbing trait. I then thought they were unjust but must admit as it was their wont to say, that they knew him better than I did. While employing argument to convict Genl. Scott of an offence and rhetoric to intensify its heinousness he commits against me the very offence of which he accuses Genl. S. When he says Southern Senators and especially Jefferson Davis became alienated because of his annual message of 1860, who would imagine that the criticism of the especial J.D. had been made to the writer on the rough draft of his message and in such friendly spirit as to lead to several modifications. That the known relations between us had caused two of his Cabinet to send me an urgent despatch to come immediately to Washington when the Message was in course of preparation. And that after the Message had been delivered, repeated conferences between us were held in regard to affairs in South Carolina. At last being made painfully aware that I had been treated with unfairness and put in a false position by using assurances given to me, as a means of restraining others; I did, and therefore did terminate all friendly intercourse; though even as late as the receipt of the telegrams giving an account of the firing on the Star of the West, I went to him and made another effort to induce him to adopt a line of action which seemed to me most likely to avoid collision and to give the best prospect for a peaceful solution. I hope he has forgotten much, and only wish his memory had been better or worse. He retained the telegrams for the purpose of taking copies, to be used in a proposed Cabinet meeting & returned them.

As my memory serves me, his Message of 1860 had a great deal to commend it, and in ordinary times that which was most objected to by southern men, would have been dismissed as a discussion upon terms, verbology. Censure so unreasonable has pursued this old man in his retirement, that I had come to remember the good to the exclusion of the evil, I wish he had left me that pleasure.

. . .

Since the time when mention was made of my suffering from neuralgia of the head, and dyspepsia the latter has been diminished by more proper diet and the former has subsided even more rapidly. Again let me urge you not to allow yourself to be disturbed by rumors in relation to me, they are so unreliable that you could not believe them if favorable and should not be distressed at those which are otherwise. On the night of the thirtieth I was sitting before the fire because I could not sleep and had a startling optical illusion, such as you know were common in fever; but to my vision, I saw little Pollie walk across the floor and kneel down between me and the fire in the attitude of prayer, I moved from consequent excitement and the sweet vision melted away. I have not called it a dream because not conscious of being asleep, but sleep has many stages, and that only is perfect sleep which we call Death.

To use your expressive phrase I am hungry for the children's little faces and have habitually to resist the power of that and other tender feelings which may not be gratified.

. . .

[FEBRUARY 4]

When our family group is in imagination gathered together with one accord to make our common supplication, each member stands before me with such distinctness and life as only could be understood by one of like constitutional idiosyncrasy. Except my dear "ittie Paie" they are all unchanged, and so I wish to keep them. Under your sweet recitals of her sayings and doings little Winnie grows before me, and I try to realize her voice that I may mingle it with that which charmed me so many years ago, and which through all the varied scenes of my subsequent life has been ever my ear, waxing sweeter, not fainter, for it does not die away in the distance. My dear Winnie it is not for me to forgive you, but to ask for your forgiveness. We are all weak, erring, willful, sinful creatures, I should have been less so than you being older and stronger, but in justice I feel that it was the reverse, and that it is I who have to ask because I love much that much may be forgiven. Of you I have endless succession of memories all clothed in a fond Wife's tenderness, judicious care, effective aid and graceful cheering to my heart when saddest and least attractive. Though torn from you, we are not divided, you are seen in the darkness as in the light. God has joined us and will I trust unite us before we go hence forever. Give my tenderest love to all near and dear to me when you unite to them, tell my children how much I think of them pray for them and hope from them. Kiss ittie Paie and make know who it is for. God bless and sustain you under your heavy burdens. Let us trust that he will find it expedient to give to us our hearts desire in this world. The blackest cloud soonest is dissolved, and despair is often on the border of relief. Know that my love is always around and with you, that my prayers are fervent for you and my hopes run unceasingly to you as the rivers to the Sea. Farewell dearest Farewell,

DEVOTEDLY YOUR HUSBAND,
JEFFERSON DAVIS

To Frank H. Alfriend (PM)*

Strictly confidential

MY DEAR SIR,

Absence from this place has prevented me from earlier receiving and acknowledging your's of the 22d Ulto. Having always been very reluctant to give an account of my own deeds it has resulted that the sketches so far as I have seen them of my life anterior to my entrance into Congress are very defective and often erroneous. In the last two years several notices of my service on the northern frontier have been published in the newspapers, the minuteness of which show that they must have been written by some one who served with me. One of them announced the object of showing how events deemed of sufficient interest to be preserved had been passed over as though nothing had occurred to distinguish the service from that of the ordinary life at a frontier post.

I do not know that there was anything in current proceedings of the Senate which does sufficiently appear in the debates of the period concerning which you first inquire viz 1857–8–9. You will recollect that in 1850 the party opposed to the "extension of slavery" as was denominated the asserted right to take Slaves into the territories of the U.S. refused to recognize the Mo. Compromise, and that they were joined by those who claimed for the inhabitants of the common territory the right to decide whether slave property should be taken to and held in such territory. When the territory of Kanzas was to be organized those who under the name of "popular sovereignty" had voted with the Abolitionists in 1850 and defeated the efforts of Southern men to preserve and apply the "Mo. Comp." preserved their consistency in the organization of Kanzas by repealing the Mo. Comp. restriction. The Southern men having seen that "Compromise" repudiated by the North in 1850 and having then yielded to the legislation which decreed it to be a nullity voted with those who subsequently advo-

---

*Author of the first biography of JD, published in 1868.

cated a general declaration of its nullity. It was but the consequence logically flowing from the Acts of 1850. It has been as unjust to charge it to the Representation of the South, as to the Administration of Mr. Pierce. The first struggled hard against the acts which necessarily produced it and the second knew nothing of the measure until it had been agreed upon by the Committees of the two Houses of Cong. on territories. The change thus produced between my resignation from and return to the Senate—1851–1857 is the only thing to which I can refer you as explanatory of whatever may have suggested to you the idea of an under current.

The committee specially raised Sess. 1860–1 by the Senate, to consider the "Crittenden Compromise" and to devise if practicable the means of pacification, submitted a report of their proceedings which was ordered to be printed. I left the Senate before it was issued and have not seen it. I suppose you may readily obtain a copy of it, and it is to be regretted that the debates in Committee were not also reported. The propositions and votes will however show that the Southern members were ever ready to accept any proposition which saved the honor of the South; and with the exception of Douglass the Northern members rejected every proposition which it could by any one have been supposed would allay the discontent, remove the distrust and prevent the passage of ordinances of Secession by many of the Southern States. Mr. Crittenden and myself frequently went together from the Com. room and he was indignant and often times hotly denunciatory of what we both regarded as a purpose to prevent any adjustment which either of us believed would have a pacifying effect on the country. Few believed as fully as myself that a long and bloody war would surely follow the exercise of the sovereign right of State revocation of its grants and withdrawal from the Union.

Hence it followed that I was not only as you observe conciliatory in spirit, but was deeply anxious to avoid the issue if it could be consistently done with due regard to the rights the safety and the honor of the South. There was a time when some, who are now favored by those who still persecute me, criticized censoriously my avowed attachment to the Constitutional Union of our Fathers. My hope of an honorable peacable settlement was not abandoned until the report of the Com.

to which reference was made above. You will see in a speech of Mr. Douglass about that time reference to my votes and declarations in Com. and his arraignment of the other side for their rejection of every proposition and their refusal to propose any thing. As nothing had been done to prevent secession or to remove the impression that it was a necessary resort, it was forseen that the state by whose commission I sat in the U.S. Senate would soon notify me of her withdrawal from the Union. I waited to perform the duty of announcing that fact and formally to vacate the seat which was a sign of the equality and sovereignty of the states as well as of the adherence of each to the league by which she voluntarily became united to the others.

It has been said that the Southern Senators should have remained because with their northern allies they could have controlled the hostile administration soon to be inaugurated. To admit that the people had chosen their Executive in hostility to the South is to fix the responsibility of the separation where those referred to did not intend to place it. The majority in the House already and soon it would be the same in the Senate reduced the plan to a war on the Govt. by persons holding trusts in it and accredited by the states to it. My view of the position of a Senator would not have permitted me to pursue that line of conduct. In the debates (I think of 1850) I stated my theory of the obligation of one representing a state in the Congress of the States; and holding it to be a point of honor not to occupy such relation with the object of hostility to the govt. I announced in connection with an allusion to a secret slander and covert insinuations that I would answer in monosyllables any one who charged me with being a disunionist. To represent a state adhering to the Union and use the position to make war on the govt. or to retain a seat in Congress when the state had by its sovereign fiat revoked its grants and withdrawn from the league, were either of them such offences as belong to the last stage of decadence in political morality & personal honor. The first congress of the Confederation defined treason, and there was unmistakably declared the doctrine to which the founders of the Union steadily adhered, the paramount allegiance of the citizen to his state. The departure from that creed has been the source of all our ills.

The proceedings of the Sen. Com. of 1860–1 will show you that

I was willing to accept the Crittenden compromise if northern men would in good faith adjust on that plan.* The votes there and the debates in the two Hos. of Cong. will show that the great body of the northern members were inflated by the success of their sectional campaign and would make no terms with the threatened South.

I have not seen the article of Thos. Jordan to which you refer, and am only surprised that he should have come so near to the truth as appears from your citation. In the fall of 1860 after the Legislature of Missi. had been called to meet in extraordinary session, as was understood to consider the propriety of ordering a convention to provide for the security of the state by separation from the Union or otherwise; and before the day for its meeting, I received a telegram from two of Mr. Buchannan's cabinet urging me to come at once to Washington. The motive, as subsequently appeared, was to obtain my aid in connection with the Presdt's message.

I saw Mr. Buchannan and was invited by him to read the rough draft of his message. It was unecessary to assure him of my desire to preserve and defend the *Constitutional* Union, I think no one who knew me, would have believed that I would attend the Session of Cong. with any different feeling. Mr. Buchannan kindly listened to all my suggestions and so far as I saw or believed had the same purpose in view which animated me.

The relation was confidential and I can only say that I regretted when his message was sent to Congress to find that it differed in some respects from the draft as I last saw it. The remarks made by me on his message show how unfortunate I deemed some of those new passages.

I have no books to which to refer and write from memory entirely. You will readily understand how difficult it is to recall events accurately, except in their main features, and I have therefore only attempted to state the substance generally.

Writing in haste and being now so near the hour of closing the mail that I cannot revise, I fear that you may find my letter less clear and satisfactory than is desirable, but your knowledge of the events referred to, will I hope render the statements intelligible to you.

---

* The select Senate Committee of Thirteen charged to find a resolution to the crisis of the Union; it failed to do so.

Thanking you for the personal interest evinced in my defence, I am very truly your's

JEFFERSON DAVIS

To Howell Cobb (JDC)*

LENNOXVILLE, QUEBEC, CANADA, JULY 6, 1868

MY DEAR SIR,

The proceedings against me having left a longer interval in which to cast about for some employment by which to support myself and family, I have decided to go to Liverpool to see what may be done in establishing a commission house, especially for cotton and tobacco. An English man of very high character and social position who has been extensively engaged in the India trade as a commission merchant has proposed to me a partnership under the belief that I could obtain assurance of the shipments of the staple of our own country, with such assurance I would be willing to attempt a new pursuit confident that if the business was strictly that of commissions my friends would incur no risk, and I might hope for all increasing income. I write to you to inquire what may be expected in regard to shipments by your friends and neighbors.

I expect to leave here on or before the 20th inst. and to take passage the 25th from Quebec, consequently your answer would not reach me at the latter place later than the 24.

Mrs. Davis is my amanuensis, as I had the misfortune to fall and break two of my ribs ten days ago, and am quite feeble from the effects of the fall.

With kind regards to Mrs. Cobb and the family, believe me

VERY SINCERELY
YOUR FRIEND,
JEFFN. DAVIS.

* Friend of JD and formerly a notable Georgia political leader.

To Varina Davis (UA)

BALTIMORE, MARYLAND, OCTOBER 15, 1869

DEAR WIFE

Your letter reached me here and gave me great joy, for it seemed a very long time since we parted and I could hardly hope that you would realize my anxiety to hear from and of you. Brother Joe is so feeble that I wish to save him from the fatigue of a journey by land, and we sail in a few hours on the *Cuba* for New Orleans. Mrs. Duke had called with her little boy inquire for you and to send you her regards.

Your friends by the battalion have called and inquired for you.

Your letter to Lize came under cover to me this morning.

I have sent the receipt for Mary's box to its address and I hope her Uncle will soon notify her of its safe arrival.

My friends here are anxious to do some thing for us, and don't like the idea of my going into business—but you know my feelings and can judge of replies—I will go soon after reaching Missi to Memphis and confer with the insurance Co. on their proposition. The rail road which was offered to me in La. has been sold under execution and bought by a New York man.

Our property at Brierfield is no longer to be thought of as concerning me or you or our heirs—Chas. Brodhead did not come to see me and it did not seem worth while or perhaps judicious that I should enter into the business matters between him and yourself as they now stand.* If he had wanted my advice at inspection he would have sought it.

Kiss my own Winnie Anne many times for her Father. Your next letter will I suppose give me news of little Pollie and the boys.

Love to Margaret from whom I hope to hear soon.

In much haste and in frequent interceptions I close this with prayers for your welfare and happiness and am ever affectionately

YOUR HUSBAND

---

* In 1867 Brierfield, with JD's agreement, and Hurricane were sold by Joseph Davis to Ben Montgomery and two of his sons, all former slaves of Joseph; Charles Brodhead was married to a niece of JD.

To Varina Davis (UA)

VICKSBURG, MISSISSIPPI, NOVEMBER 9, 1869

DEAR WIFE

Yours of Oct 2nd and 11th had been forwarded to this place and were waiting for me when I arrived yesterday.

It was a grievous disappoint to me to learn that Maggie was threatened with a disease of the spine.* Of course under such circumstances you could not properly have sent to a public school. May God grant to care and judicious treatment and entire restoration. Whatever can be done without injury to her health in the way of studies will be well, but to preserve her from constitutional infirmity must be the great object.

I stopped at Bayou Sara and after visiting Sister Anna and Joe went to see Sister Lucinda then went with Hugh to Homochitto and the next day to Natches, where I took a boat for this place.

Sister Anna is quite feeble but walks better than when you saw her. Sister Lucinda is unchanged. Mr. Stamps is much the same as two years ago. They all spoke of you with warmest affection and Hugh seemed ready to start at once for you and the children. Little Helen insisted that she had a right to expect you and little Winnie be with me.† Something you said to her appeared to be the foundation of her claims. Many of your early friends inquired for you, none more considerably than Mrs. Boyd the Wife of the Preacher and the daughter of Mr. Reily.

I saw your Aunt Frances and your cousins in Natches.‡ Miss Nancy Davis & Mrs. Shiff charged me with kind messages for you, as did so many others that it would be a long letter which enumerated them. Many friends in New Orleans wished me to settle there and spoke of good things in the future for me, but all contingent, yet they generally deprecated my connection with life insurance business.

---

* JD's daughter Margaret.

† JD's sister Anna and nephew Joseph Smith; his sister Lucinda and brother-in-law William Stamps; his nephew Hugh Davis and niece Helen Davis.

‡ Frances Sprague.

If I had fewer necessities or more means I would in deference to their sentiments decline the offer of the Co. but soberly, indeed sadly, looking at my needs as well as those of others near and dear to me, I am inclined to "gather gear by every wile that is justified by honor."[*]

A letter from the President of the Co. was waiting for me here asking to meet them on the day in the afternoon of which I arrived. I wrote to him and telegraphed this morning. It may be that I will leave on the next train, if not will go in three days according to the reply of Mr. Wicks.[†]

There is a desire to serve me and benefit themselves by so doing on the part of several Companies, the work I would prefer the Southern Pacific Rail Road, it is thought will be offered to me if the needful means and combinations can be made to carry out the work. I dislike to lose but there was also the consideration that my past services having identified me mainly with the South West, my Sons would in this region start with whatever advantage would be derived from that fact. It is therefore more in view of the possible interest of the Company than of my own that a future removal to Baltimore has been contemplated. Somewhat tediously I fear, you have been put in possession of the data on which to form a decision to your own residence, and as your wishes must exercise an important influence on my action, I wish you would communicate them as early and as freely as can be convenient.

I forgot to mention that offers have been made to aid me with money to resume the business of cotton planting, and Joe. when here pressed that upon me as the best thing to be done.

To my dear Winnie Anne I send a Kiss given with her father's tenderest love, her sweet letter and the outline of her hand brought strongly before me the sacrifice which circumstances have imposed upon me. Tell my own little Pollie that she is ever remembered in my prayers and often very often her sweet face is before me.[‡] I am glad that Margaret has a change of scene and hope she will be benefitted by it.[§]

[*] Carolina Life Insurance Company; JD served as president 1869–73.
[†] M. J. Wicks, president of Carolina Life Insurance Company before JD.
[‡] Polly or Pollie was another nickname for JD's daughter Margaret.
[§] Margaret Howell, Varina's sister.

When you see her and Jeff. and little Billy tell them how very dear they are to me. Thanks for your kind care in giving the photographic satchel, but I wish for later likenesses of yourself and Margaret and Maggie and Jeff. I dreamed you were by me darning my socks and asked what I expected to do without your assistance. Here I was again interrupted. And this being already a long and rambling letter I will not inflict another sheet upon you. Brother Joe. told me one day in a connection not complimentary that I was the least of a Bourbon he knew because both learning and forgetting many things. I do try to do what is before me and find it more pleasant to look to the future than to the past. Please remember. . . .*

To Varina Davis (UA)

MEMPHIS, TENNESSEE, NOVEMBER 23, 1869

DEAR WIFE,

Your interesting letter, last date Nov. 3. reached me at this place, having arrived at Vicksburg after my departure. Of affairs there I have nothing to add to my letter written before leaving. On my arrival here I stated to the Company the fears entertained of my ability to fulfill their expectations by establishing a branch of their company at Baltimore. It was proposed to exhibit to me their books and to have a conference with me after I had examined them. At the next meeting I stated my views and found the directors willing to conform to them. There the question was asked whether I believed my influence would be greater if in charge of a parent than a branch institution. I could but say that it would probably be greater if in charge of a parent institution. And it was proposed then that I should accept the offer which had been previously made by the President to resign in my favor. The point of delicacy was quite removed and being satisfied of the solidity of the institution and the character of the Directors I placed myself at their disposal and withdrew. The result was soon afterwards communicated to me that I had been unanimously elected President of the

---

* Remainder of letter has not survived.

Co. with a salary of twelve thousand dollars per annum and travelling expenses.

I have entered on the duties of the office and will try to extend the operations of the company to the Eastward so as to increase the income as well as the security of it.

A residence in Memphis will not probably be agreable to you, but it gives me the prospect of means which will enable you to live elsewhere until all things may combine to give us a less restrained choice.

It is possible that after a year it may be found desirable to transfer the present institution to Baltimore as a larger monetary and commercial centre, but this will depend upon the success of the Co. here and the prospects of business in the Atlantic states.

There are many handsome residences near to this city which have been offered to me but I have not had time to look at them, except from the road when driving past them.

I am now at the "Peabody Hotel" a good house kept by an acquaintance of former years and would be comfortably situated if there were more quiet. Jos. R. Davis came up to see me from his present home in Bolivar country, and staid several days.* I miss him greatly now. He spoke most affectionately of you and the children.

Genl. Wade Hampton with his Wife and three youngest children have been here for several days. Both Genl. and Mrs. Wade Hampton charged me to give their regard to you, and their son McDuffie took your address that he might send you his photograph, and write to you. William Warfield and his Wife asked me to give their kind remembrance to you.† So many others have done the same that I must ask to suppose them delivered.

The political condition of Tenn. is now so good that no further trouble is anticipated and this winter it is said that all the obnoxious legislation of the Radicals when in possession of this state government will be repealed. The negroes hereabout are said to be quiet and the security from thieving and violence to be about the same as in former years. You know that was not equal to the safety in England or France.

---

* JD's nephew.
† Maryland friends of the Davises.
‡ from Columbia, S.C., founder of "Hampton's Legion"

I am much relieved by the favorable account of the health of my dear little Pollie, and of her improvement in the subjects of her studies. The second however important is to be regarded as subordinate to the first. I would not deprive you of the joy Winnie Anne brings to you when she comes in, so do not envy you, but wish it were mine also. Tell her I am trying to get "a good house and to stop wandering about" as she advised and that the kiss she sent to me will help me to work until I make one fit for her.

Jeff. wrote to me a very good letter which was forwarded to me and which will be answered as soon as leisure permits.

The cordiality of the people has been so actively manifested as to leave me little time and to render me as tired as when we were in the New York Hotel. Many persons ask me when you are coming and before I answer the question it is well that we should reason together. Your remarks as to the desirableness of a residence which would secure to our children associations beneficial to them are fully concurred in; but if you forget others will not fail to remember the difference, between a man of business, and a Soldier, or a Planter, or a Senator, or a cabinet minister, or a President, or even an exiled representative of an oppressed people. The difference between these classes would be greater in London than in Liverpool, in Liverpool than in Baltimore, in Baltimore than in Memphis, and lastly would be greater in Baltimore against the Agent than the Head of the Company. Thus it would be for the benefit of those for whom I live if I go to Baltimore, it should be as the President of a Company rather than as the agent administering the branch of a company. I have compounded with my pride for the material interest of my family, and am ready to go on to the end as may best promote their happiness. So now having laid down the premises, let us proceed with the conclusion.

You can remain in Europe and give the children the advantage of the Schools there for some time to come, or you can when the season is favorable to crossing the ocean come to Maryland and put the boys with Mr. Brand and Maggie at school in Baltimore where you will find a pleasant residence; or you may leave the boys at Mr. Brand's and come here with the girls to stay with me for all except the summer months.

You can judge better than myself as to the probable suitableness of this climate for yourself and Margaret and Maggie and Winnie and that should be the ruling consideration in the selection of a home.

While I live there is reason to believe the money necessary for an economical mode of living will be at my command, and subject to your order. So choose freely—

So my dear Winnie Anne I send a kiss given with her Father's tenderest love, her sweet letter and the outline of her hand brought strongly before me the sacrifice which circumstances have imposed upon me. Tell my own little Pollie that she is ever remembered in my prayers and often very often her sweet face is before me. I am glad that Margaret had a change of scene and hope she will be benefitted by it. When you see her and Jeff. & little Billy tell them how very dear they are to me. Thanks for your kind care in giving me the photographic satchel, but I wish for later likenesses of yourself and Margaret and Maggie & Jeff: I dreamed you were by me darning my socks and asked what I expected to do without your assistance. Then I was again interrupted. And this being already a very long and rambling letter will not inflict another sheet upon you. Brother Joe. told me one day in a connection not complimentary that I was the least of a Bourbon he knew because both learning & forgetting many things. I do try to do what is before me & find it more pleasant to look to the future than to the past.

Please remember me to Mary & to Mrs. Williams and Bessy & Hetty. God bless them and every body else who cares for you. I wish you would go to Mr. Hope's or some other such place that you may not be hereafter bored by people who describe country life in England. This should reach you before Xmas and I send you the good wishes of the season and the offering of love grown old but not decayed. In my prayers you are personally summoned as joining in the petition. Whatever may be our fate on earth I trust our father in Heaven will receive us into the same mansion, and that He may guide and preserve you is the fervent prayer of your Husband.

To W. T. Walthall (JDC)*

MEMPHIS, TENNESSEE, MARCH 14, 1873

MY DEAR SIR,

Some of the Agents of our Company have expressed the opinion that the organization of local boards of trustees would be of advantage to them, and authority has been given for that purpose.† If it would aid you to have such Boards say in Mobile & Montgomery you can select and nominate persons to be appointed as Trustees. I do not know whether Genl. Browne, before he left here, sent you a copy of the resolution of the Board of Directors on that subject and therefore state, that the qualification for a Trustee is that he shall take a policy for $5,000 or that he shall be a stockholder to the amount of $1,000.

The Committee on agencies have called on me for a statement of receipts and disbursements on account of the several agencies, and one of the clerks is now engaged in the preparation of the required statement.

Please let me hear from you as to the prospect of this season's business in your district. I would like to have whatever may serve me in the event of the statement being unfavorable in your case. This not merely because of my personal regard for you, but also because of my confidence in your ability to do as much as another, whether that be great or small.

VERY TRULY YOUR FRIEND
JEFFERSON DAVIS

---

* Former Confederate officer living in Mobile, Alabama, who would become JD's chief assistant in preparing *The Rise and Fall of the Confederate Government.*

† Carolina Life Insurance Company.

To W. T. Walthall (JDC)

MEMPHIS, TENNESSEE, MARCH 27, 1873

MY DEAR MAJ. WALTHALL,

Since my last in answer to your's of the 19th Inst., I have conferred with the committee on agencies, in regard to the several matters presented in your letter. Each was adopted as proposed by you, of which the Secretary will officially notify you. The want of money has been felt in this region as you describe it to have been in your's, and a consequent failure of our expectations of new business has been the result. This state of affairs sufficiently accounts for the difficulty in getting good solicitors. Mr. Powell wrote to me that an agent could he thought do well in his embryo city of Birmingham and I invited him to nominate one having the requisite qualifications. He has not replied.

Mr. Jno. K. Barton, jr wrote to me from Opelika, asking on the part of the Baptists who were building for a female college at that place, that he should be made a special agent to get insurance to warrant a loan of money, needed to complete their buildings. We are still in correspondence with him. Do you know any thing of him? To obtain the good will of a sect sufficiently strong to lead in the foundation of a College may be useful in getting other business in that section.

As ever with best wishes for you and your's I am your friend

JEFFERSON DAVIS

To A. J. Beresford Hope (JDC)*

MEMPHIS, TENNESSEE, MAY 15, 1873

. . .

The political condition of this country grows worse. The true character of the government has been subverted, the maxim of the party in power is that "the will of the majority is the law of the land." Than which nothing could be less like the theory of the compact of Union,

---

* Member of Parliament and formerly pro-Confederate.

or a wider departure from the idea of security under a written constitution. Universal suffrage has brought in its train endless evil. Ignorance and depravity are making us the byword of nations. It is a common occurrence to hear reflecting men say, that the separation of these colonies from the Mother country has proved a misfortune to us. A few years ago the expression of such an opinion was never heard.

We of the South enjoyed the castigation inflicted on the pretentious trickster Cushing, for his publications in regard to the Geneva arbitration. Adopting the designations of _____ Lord Lothian, Jacob having despoiled Esau, naturally sought the stores of Laban. Not finding swagger likely to avail, he returned to his own role of craft, and has succeeded so well that he may be expected to renew his attempt.

It is a hard choice between the present blundering ministry and the succession of one who cannot unite and lead the conservatives to the accomplishment of their ends.

With sincere regard & esteem I am very truly your's

JEFFERSON DAVIS

To Mrs. S. A. Ayres (MVHR)*

MEMPHIS, TENNESSEE, AUGUST 19, 1874

MY GOOD AND DEAR FRIEND,

Your Kind and most welcome letter was duly received. It was truly cheering to my care worn heart to have your congratulations on my safe return. Though it was for the benefit to be expected from a sea voyage that I went abroad, my stay on shore was pleasant and beneficial to my health. You ask me how I was received elsewhere than in England, and I answer one must have been in Scotland to know the full import of "a Highland welcome." Among the many pleasant memories left to me, is my ramble in the land of Burns. The white thorn was in bloom, the fields were gaudy with the furze "unprofitably gay" and the modest crimson tipped daisy clustered with the gowans, buttercups and wild hyancinths. The cottage in which Burns was born is neatly

---

* A friend of JD who was living in Keokuk, Iowa.

kept for show, and Kirk Alloway now quite a ruin, unfit even for the witches dance, still stands to remind of Tam O'Shanters ride.* The Landlady of the tavern where Tam and Souter Johnny had their drinking bout courteously invited [me] to sit in the chair Tam occupied on that night made famous by Burns. The "auld Brig" across the bonny Doon yet stands though severely marked by time but beneath it runs the sparkling bright and fresh as ever, reminding us of Tennison's brook. The Ruins one meets in Europe, and sometimes buildings in good repair which were constructed before Columbus sailed on his voyage of discovery most forcibly reminds one of our country how new we are.

And what reflection could be more sad than that which finds in our moral decadence cause to apply the bon mot which Diderot made upon Russia. But you did not ask for reflections on our own land & times. Your position as to that oath shows you to have passed the stage of discussion on our affairs, and I am very glad that your proud adherence to principle was not detrimental to your pecuniary interest. But to return I found every thing quiet and prosperous in France. Paris inside of the fortifications had suffered little damage by the war, and the people seemed comfortable and happy. They are nominally Republican and though you might deny their right to be so called, it probably means so much as that monarchy if reestablished will be of short duration.

We have suffered much here from the heat of the summer and I wish it were practicable for me to go [to] that cool retreat of which you sent me a description. Then I might have the pleasure of seeing you again and telling you as much as you would be willing to hear of things and persons seen abroad. Accept my congratulations on the evident prosperity in business of your Husband and Sons. So true is it that it is the first step which costs, that Mr. Girrard is reported to have said, he founded it harder to make his first hundred dollars than his last hundred thousand.

I am truly obliged to you for the offer of one of your ancient coins, but must decline it, because the loss of everything I had collected, by the events of the war, discourages me at my advance age from at-

---

* The Scottish poet Robert Burns, a great favorite of JD.

tempting to renew the work; further it may be added that my residence is not sufficiently permanent to give the proper security to so valuable a relic as that which you offer. Some day perhaps it may be granted to me to see your collection and to enjoy each and all as your property.

You ask if I would accept the buttons you offer and I assure you as a token of your friendship they would be gladly received, the more so however if you would instead of the proposed initials, combine the letters so as to indicate as well the donor as the receiver.

It will always give me true pleasure to hear from you and with the hope that we may meet again in this world, I am faithfully and most Respectfully

YOURS
JEFFERSON DAVIS

To W. T. Walthall (JDC)

MEMPHIS, TENNESSEE, APRIL 26, 1875

MY DEAR SIR,

I am thankful to you for your kind letter of the 20th ulto. and for efforts to find the letter of Dr. Yandell. The published letter I have been informed was a modification of the Mss. mailed for publication in England, but yet enough remained to show that the cause of the Confederacy was subordinate to the purpose to magnify his Chief Genl. J. E. Johnston by blaming the administration.

The desire you express in regard to the vindication of the principles for which our battles were fought is the first object of importance with me. But poverty does not permit me to make it first in the order of things to be attempted. The transfer of the "Carolina" L. Ins. Co. to the "Southern Life," while I was absent and in disregard of my opinion, cost me $15.000, that being the amount of my stock, and note since paid; and that loss from my small means has kept me from that time to this in anxiety, and thus far unsuccessful effort, to provide for the future wants of my family.

Your kind offer to aid me by fragmentary labor may excuse me for saying that in the proposed work, I should if possessed of sufficient means to offer you a salary, have requested your assistance. Perhaps my fortunes may improve, from the wreck made by the War I may yet get something, but confidentially I will tell you that those who should have been first to regard my interests are as eager to appropriate the wreck as the yankees were to make it. But I only intended to say that if the courts can be expected to view *my case* without prejudice there is reason to hope for improvement in my condition and for leisure and rest for work on the history. Like yourself I have argued against the idea of leaving history to posterity. While admitting that the future historian may alone be able to write without bias and therefore to make a history in the higher sense of the word, surely unless contemporaries furnish the material, posterity cannot judge of events and describe their causes.

   With great regard I am ever truly your friend

JEFFERSON DAVIS.

Speech in New Orleans, Louisiana (JDC)

MARCH 7, 1876

LADIES AND GENTLEMEN:

   Veterans of the war with Mexico, my friends and fellow soldiers, it is with no common emotions that I look upon you, the few survivors of that gallant host, who in their early manhood surrendered their ease and personal interest, to serve their country's need. And it is sad, while reviving the memories of your glorious career, that existing circumstances should force us to remember how soon the gratitude of your country, which with loud acclaim welcomed your return from a foreign war, has grown so cold that the survivors are compelled by private effort to raise funds for the relief of your decayed and unfortunate comrades. But there is a consolation in feeling that he who treads the path of duty for duty's sake walks under a shield which the slings and arrows of adversity cannot destroy, and has in the conscious rectitude of his own heart a balm for the worst wounds the world can inflict. There was a time when to be a soldier in the war with Mexico was a passport throughout the length and breadth of the land. Why is it then these veterans are without the poor reward of a pension? It is not my purpose to review the course of the Government. It is not mine to arouse the public to censure. It is mine, however, as a friend and comrade of these men, to proclaim aloud the injustice under which they suffer, and to urge the yet possible reparation. I would, my friends, if time and physical ability had sufficed, out of the respect which I bear you and the cause which I here represent, have prepared an address for this occasion. Circumstances did not permit me to do so, but I have not failed, at least, to show my consideration by preparing some brief notes, and for the rest must rely on the inspiration of your presence.

It is one of the characteristics of the human mind to dwell rather upon the pleasant than the painful, and in nothing is this so true as in the soldier's memory. In no instance as far as my acquaintance goes is there any condition of life where the path so blooms with the flowers of affection and fidelity as that of the soldier, marked though it be with privation and danger, with disease and death. And this Association for the benefit of those who have fallen into misfortune sufficiently attests the truth of the proposition I make, and adds to the already full measure of your claim to regard.

The theme which you have presented for my consideration this evening does not suggest the discussion of any particular campaign or battle, but a general view of the moral and material results of the war. And therefore I shall not attempt to describe any battle; shall not enter into those scenes of carnage, crowned as they were with the glory of American arms, in the war with Mexico; but shall speak to you first of the moral elements, and of the material results afterwards.

. . .

Thus far, my friends, I have but briefly sketched some of your military glory; I now come to grander achievements. In the possession of the Capital of the country, the question was what would the Americans do,—would they hold possession, and claim the country as their own by conquest? Would they claim these people as subjects by ordeal of battle? No, no, not so. It is my pride as an American to remember that you made a treaty of peace, and took not one rood of land by conquest. By that treaty of peace you withdrew from the Capital, you surrendered the territory that you held by military possession, and the territory you acquired by treaty you paid for with your money. Never did any country present a grander moral spectacle according to my estimate than ours did on that occasion; nor did our soldiers less exemplify those noble attributes. Wherever our troops marched, all the rights of property were respected, never was any non-combatant disturbed. The troops never did take anything from them without just compensation. In the villages we passed through we got what we required and paid for it at the market price of the country. These are some of the moral elements. Let us pass to the material results. A material result of the war with Mexico was the acquisition by purchase of that great land of California, a land of promise and of golden fulfilment. Not only has the gold of California been poured into your treasury as a material result of this war, but exploration and development of the whole territory lying between the Mississippi Valley and the Pacific Coast is a consequence of the acquisition. It has thus made us one of the greatest contributors in the world in adding to its specie. Nevada certainly, and perhaps Idaho, produces more silver than the famous land of Peru, and if our country has not specie sufficient to redeem all the greenbacks afloat, that is one of the results which I may not ascribe to the war with Mexico. Then there was another material result, the necessity of connecting by railroads the country already occupied with that which had been recently acquired, led to the surveys and construction; and another, we hope, is soon to be built to connect your city of New Orleans with the Pacific Coast. These are some of the material results which have followed from the war with Mexico; nor are they all, for the progress in Texas is fairly ascribable to the same cause, and the railroad I spoke of being built will be the means of still further developing the vast resources of that State, and New Orleans may become in commerce what her natural position fairly ascribes to her. Then, my friends, this progress in and beyond the Valley of the Mississippi is opening up other vast resources which again are connected with the material results of the war with Mexico.

When all these railroads are completed, stretching across the continent, the quickest line of commerce will be across the Territory of the United States, and the Mississippi Valley will be the Central Station. Yours is a mission not to propagandize, or by force to extend your Empire. The diversity of the climate of your valley, the different lights and shadows of its mountain borders on the East and on the West proclaim for you a cosmopolitan future, and the great and varied productions of your country announce your permanent policy to be that of peace and trade with the nations. Yours is a higher mission than political propagandism or territorial conquest. It is to feed the hungry, to clothe the naked, to shelter the homeless, and to offer a field of profitable labor to every energetic, industrious wanderer of the Caucasian race. To one born in the Mississippi Valley, after the acquisition of Louisiana had given unity to the commercial and political relations of the inhabitants of the wide spread territory, it was natural if he grew up with wishes expanded as his native valley. Happy is it for him if the experience of age enables him to weave a garland of hope around the anticipations of youth, to see manufacturing cities surpassing the wealth of Tyre and Sidon, and granaries by the side of which the world supplying the stores of the Pharaohs would seem diminutive. At no distant day, your city, situated at the point where ocean and river meet, where the productions of all the country drained by the Mississippi find the best route to the markets of Southern and Central America, as well as of Western Europe, should, may we not say must, become one of the principal commercial centers of the world. You have only to be true to yourselves to command that which by the endowment of nature, fairly belongs to you. And in your progress to power, in the midst of your achieved prosperity, let us ask that you remember the part of it which may justly be regarded as consequences of the achievements of your soldiers in Mexico. But brilliant as were the deeds performed, important as were the results which followed directly and indirectly, and just as your claim may be on the gratitude of the present and future generations of the veterans and representatives of the army in Mexico, I would say they have a glory surpassing all which was acquired on the field of battle. They came from a foreign war waged against a people of different origin, language and habits. They came from a conquered country where corporations and individuals possessed much personal and portable wealth. They came with hands empty of plunder, they came with hearts free from the stain of injustice or cruelty to the helpless, they left behind them no widow of a non-combatant husband slain on the family hearth, they left no orphans destitute because of the destruction or appropriation of their property by the invading army. They came back poorer than they went, except in that which is the true soldier's treasure—*honor, HONOR.*

They brought to the altar of their country the priceless sacrificial offering of fame without spot or blemish, and these are the men who have not yet been considered worthy of a pension. Whether they came unscathed in battle, or whether they came upon crutches, they were both the same, and they have whatever else they may have lost, that which has not a value to be measured in this world's goods, self respect and a good name, which challenges the denial of the world. There is much more, my friends, that I would be glad to say to you, but as I mentioned to you, I am suffering physically, and must now draw to a close;—but first, you will pardon me for addressing some words to the veterans who sit behind me.

Few, my friends, we are in numbers, and time with its ceaseless course must soon bear us to the ocean of Eternity. Right glad am I to have had this opportunity to meet you, proud am I to feel that the love of soldiers' memories rooted deep in the affections have been proof against the trials you have borne. If we were for a moment to be captives to the memories of the past, we would again recall friends that are with us no more, Again would we sit around the cheerful camp fire, hear the exhilarating rattle of the small arms and the deafening roar of the artillery. Again would we stand surrounding the little hillocks where sleep the brave we loved so well. But shall we mourn for them? They died amid the shout of victory, their last look was upon the advancing flag of their country for which if they had had a hundred lives they would willingly have surrendered them all. Peace to their ashes, glory to their memories. May that kind future which the good Father promises to those who love Him attend you, and your closing career be as calm and happy as its commencement was brilliant and honorable. I thank you, ladies and gentlemen.

To W. T. Cordner (JDC)[*]

. . .

When yon invited me to accept the Presidency of the American Dept. and proposed a fixed salary with contingent emolument, I could not have supposed that the Parent Society was without an assured revenue, least of all was that suggested by an invitation to forward an estimate of the advance we would require to support the Dept. during the first year of its operations. Your telegram declaring the modification I proposed to your Rules & Bye laws, formed the basis on which our reorganization was founded; but this was soon followed by a letter from the Executive Committee wholly inconsistent with that basis. These and other matters might have been discussed with possible advantage to the Society had you and Mr. Lawson gone to the chief office of the American Dept. when you were sent by the Parent Society in London, to confer with us. In default of that, I was sent to London. On my arrival there, it was stated that you had so entirely managed the past affairs of the Society, that your presence was needful in making arrangements for the future, and that you were expected to return in three weeks. After delays and sometimes failures to attend called meetings, for a period of say four months, it was finally decided to reconstruct the Society by giving to it the form of a stock Co. and a Committee was appointed to draft a programme for that purpose. The programme was submitted to me, and some alterations made in it at my suggestion. I left for the Continent & was absent about a fortnight. On my return the Chmn. of the Executive Com. called on me and read to me a scheme for a Mortgage Bank to be established in New York, which he said had been received from you, and was approved by Mr. Crossley, Presdt. of the Parent Society as a substitute for it. I was indignant at the manner in which I had been treated, failed to see how

---

[*]Executive with the Mississippi Valley Society, a company based in London with an American branch in New Orleans. It was designed to spur investment and trade. In January 1876 JD agreed to head the American branch, but the company failed by the end of the year.

the proposed Bank was to promote direct trade with the Missi Valley, to aid in securing emigration to it, or to induce the increase of shipping to the Port of New Orleans. Therefore as foreign to the Mission on which I was sent to London, I declined to be associated with the proposed scheme.

As an addition to the Banks of New York, willing to lend money on mortgage security, and seeking such investments in the Missi. Valley it may be beneficial to our people and so I wish it success; but surely that is not akin to the objects for which we were invited to form branches of the London Society, or to the work in which you asked me to cooperate. Had you informed me that the Parent society had so far failed that it had become necessary to close it's office in London, the Society in New Orleans would not have sent me to confer with the London Board as to future cooperation between the European and American Departments.

Had you earlier informed me that it had devolved on you, personally, to furnish funds for the current expenses of the society, and that pecuniary losses had rendered you unable to fulfil your undertaking, I should have ceased to hope for any thing from the society and been better prepared to meet the disappointment which has been encountered.

YOURS RESPECTFULLY
JEFFERSON DAVIS

To Rev. J. William Jones (JDC)[*]

MISSISSIPPI CITY, MISSISSIPPI, MAY 15, 1877

MY DEAR SIR—

I have read with great satisfaction the back numbers of the *Papers of the Southern Historical Society.* The future historian, to do justice to our cause and conduct, will require the material which can only be furnished by contemporaneous witnesses, and a great debt is due to the Society, and especially to you, for what you have done and are doing

[*] Former Confederate chaplain; secretary of the Southern Historical Society and editor of the society's *Papers*.

to save, while there is yet time, the scattered records and unwritten recollections of the events of the war against the Southern States.

Various causes, and not the least among them, such entire confidence in the righteousness of our cause as give assurance of a favorable verdict, have prevented our people from presenting, or even carefully preserving, the material on which the verdict must be rendered by future generations.

The Society has done much in exposing and refuting the current slanders in regard to treatment of prisoners of war. That was most needful for the restoration of good feeling, and should be welcome, beyond the limits of the vindicated, even to all who respect truth and eschew deception.

There are many brilliant exploits, concerning some of which there are no official reports extant. In such cases, the recollection of actors would be a valuable contribution to our war history. You have done so much to excite a willingness to furnish the material for history, that it may be hoped you will be able to draw from those to whom it is rather a dread than a pleasure to see themselves "in print," special statements, such as any one can prepare who can write a business letter. It is not style, but facts which are to be regarded.

With the hope that the interest felt by the public in the patriotic work of the Society will be increased by the manifestation of its power for usefulness, and with cordial regard for you personally,

I AM, YOURS FAITHFULLY,
JEFFERSON DAVIS.

To W. P. Johnston (JSH)*

MISSISSIPPI CITY, MISSISSIPPI, NOVEMBER 18, 1877

MY DEAR FRIEND,

My absence was prolonged beyond my expectation when I wrote to you from Memphis. On my return yours of the 5th Inst. was received and the Mss. found and promptly read.† I have made some pencil crosses on the margin to point your examination of the passages on which the subjoined remarks are offered.

P. 1—When the war began and the fact was realized of actual conflict, there was want of appreciation of the danger and of the means necessary for defense rather than lethargy of the South.

P. 16—The mixed arms and varied ammunition was a source of inefficiency and confusion, rather than of "disorganization."

2nd p. 16—The opportunity to import arms never existed. Our agents were before those of the North in the markets of Europe, serviceable arms were not to any considerable extent for sale, so they made contracts for manufacture, as rapidly as was practicable. Had we waited until the men who subsequently blamed us for not importing arms, had become satisfied that there would be war, the agents of the north would have been in advance of us, with the contractors whose works we employed after buying all the arms on hand. There were reported to be a large number of French muskets for sale, we had them examined, they were condemned arms of which an expert reported that they would be more dangerous to the men using them, than those against whom they might be used.

p. 13—I do not know what sort of preparation the Govt. neglected. It can hardly refer to absence of exertion to create manufactories of the munitions of War, and if to efforts to increase the army, you will recollect the steady flow of reinforcements to the army with which you were serving, after the first battle of Manassas. True they only

---

* One of JD's wartime aides.

† The manuscript referred to was Johnston's biography of his father, Albert Sidney Johnston, which was published in 1878.

supplied the waste of that in inaction, so that the effective force was about equal in Oct. to what it had been in July.

p. 19—If arms not men was the difficulty, it could not have been wise to issue the arms to men enrolled for short terms. Men for the war might well have been just in camps to wait for arms, and in the meantime to be instructed, disciplined and nursed through the usual diseases, but reasons are numerous in addition to those mentioned by the Secretary of War against adopting that course toward volunteers for short periods and who being unarmed could render in the meantime no service.

p. 22—In the temper ascribed to the people, confidence in the all sufficient force of Genl. Johnston might have encouraged enlistments, instead of preventing them.

p. 23—Of all men those least likely to reenlist would, I think, be such as had served a short tour. Did you ever hear of sixty day men wanting to try another tour. Those who went from Missi. to Columbus, Ky. would serve for an example. Was the willingness to reenlist at the expiration of their term exhibited by the 12 Mos. men. If such had been the fact, the conscript act would not only have been unnecessary, but offensively unjust, as to those who had served 12 months and were willing to continue.

p. 24—If to take 12 mos. men would prevent recruitment for the War, and if only unarmed men were received for the War more of that class could be obtained than could be armed in any foreseen period, the policy seemed clearly indicated.

p. p. 25 & 26—The "importance and the danger of the situation in Tenn." was not unseen or unmeasured by at least one member of the Confederate Govt, the one of whose opinions you had the best opportunity to judge, and to whom it had not been the habit to ascribe the belief that there would be no war, or a small war, or that diplomacy or foreign intervention would suffice for our case. Before I was inaugurated I announced the belief that the war would be long and bloody, and spoke of the necessity for keeping the war out of our interior. After Middle Tenn. and Ky. were in the hands of the enemy, and East Tenn. was open to him there was yet a part of that importance not overlooked in the beginning which remained, the mountain chain running from Ala. to Lynchburg. The barrier of what has been called the Switzerland of the South, and my fault was, not having failed to see its value, but not being able to carry out my wishes and convictions. It was the fate of the Administration to be considered able to defend every assailed place, & to be criticized by everyone who saw but one of the many places to be covered. It was easy to say other places were less important, and it was the frequent plea, but if it had been heeded as advised, dissatisfaction, distress, desertions of soldiers, opposition of State Govts. would have soon changed "apathy" into *collapse.* I hope it may never be your misfortune to conduct a war and a political campaign as a joint operation, but until you have such an experience, you cannot rightly measure the trials to which the Confederate Gov't. was subjected, and on how slender a foundation the structure was made to stand, when powerfully assailed not only from without, but within by a cabal whose acts are beginning to be visible. I will send your Mss. by this mail. I am as ever yours

JEFFERSON DAVIS

To Crafts J. Wright (JDC)[*]

MISSISSIPPI CITY, MISSISSIPPI, JANUARY 10, 1878

MY DEAR FRIEND,

. . .

I will frankly tell you why I cannot emerge from my present obscurity—or leave the dead past to bury its dead. That past of my life for which I am most censured and for which I am so bitterly hated, was dictated by convictions against which my interests and ambition were most opposed. I cannot say I am sorry or ask for pardon, for that which were it to be done over, I would do again, and when I see the government drifting from the moorings of those who made it and believe that the departures are fatal to the peace, and happiness and liberty of Posterity, I can and will say nothing, which will lead anyone,

---

[*] West Point classmate and lifelong friend of JD.

who trusts me, to suppose that I am content with the present or the future it forebodes. I have no taste for declamation and do not wish to vaunt my love for the constitution as it was made, and interpreted by the Fathers of the Federation, and therefore, it has been easy for me to keep quiet, and allow the best current of Politicians to flow past me without any action on my part to attract their attention. I would be glad "to allay feelings prejudicial to the public interest" and to contribute if I might to a restoration of the Government to its original character. If the opportunity should ever occur, doubt not it will be seized. Should you conclude to present the petition for an adequate pension, please notify me that I may aid you as suggested. With kindest regards to your Wife, I am ever cordially yours,

JEFFERSON DAVIS.

To Jubal Early (DU)*

BEAUVOIR, MISSISSIPPI, APRIL 7, 1878

MY DEAR SIR:

Please accept my Thanks for your kind letter of the 18th ulto; You were right in supposing that I thought a much larger number of re inforcements had been sent than your estimate between the 21st of July & the 20th October 1861. Hence the surprise I have felt, that the army was not materially increased between those dates. Upon the question of discipline the means of enforcing it I depart from your opinions & my experience as a commander of volunteers has led me to the conclusion that with proper instruction & vigilance on the part of officers capital punishment would be rarely necessary. I held then as I do now that desertion properly defined meant a total abandonment of the colours, & that in it there were two grades—one where the purpose was to join the enemy the other where it was merely to escape from service but in most, if not in all the cases where my authority was interposed—to prevent an execution, the proof showed

---

* Former Confederate lieutenant general.

that it was much a case of absence without leave, & that the party intended to return. The brigading troops by States was the consequence of the absence of any national character in our confederation & the fact that State pride was the highest incentive for gallant & faithful service. No small part of the difficulty of our situation was the absolute necessity of consulting public opinion instead of being guided simply by military principles. The inexpediency of removing a popular, though incompetent general from command led to electioneering by high officers and other practices for which in a well regulated and fully sustained government the commissioners if not the head, should have paid the penalty. In reviewing the question I would say leniency to high officers rather than to some poor private who slipped off to attend to a suffering family, was the error that impaired discipline & fidelity to duty. Let me assure you that you need not apprehend harshness on my part in reviewing the conduct of any of our own men. I would rather forget their failures than exhibit them to others.

AS EVER CORDIALLY YOUR FRIEND
JEFFERSON DAVIS

Mrs. Davis sends her kindest regard & hopes for another visit.

J.D.

To J. C. Derby (JDC)*

BEAUVOIR, MISSISSIPPI, MARCH 12, 1879

MY DEAR SIR,

Accept my thanks for your kind letter of the 4th Inst. as well as for the Copy of the "Sun" containing the report of the Potter committee and a synopsis of the debate in the Senate referring to me.

I had been so specific in my instructions to Maj. Walthall that he should not bind me to furnish Mss. on or before any particular date, that my disappointment on being called on for "copy" was expressed

* Editor with D. Appleton and Company; instrumental in the completion of *The Rise and Fall of the Confederate Government.*

to him distinctly, but the "annoyance" he wrote of was not at the terms of your letter.

All of your correspondence with me, has been most gratifying & I have been frequently indebted to you for aid in the matter of published material. Please accept my renewed thanks for your courteous and useful attention.

Mr. Chandler waited long to resent what he considered an insult, when we were together in the Senate, and he by his "impertinence" received the only notice I ever gave him.

I hope, as you suggest, to survive the attacks of such as he, and trust our constitutional government may suffer no permanent injury, at the hands of ignorant and corrupt officials who may occasionally fill high places.

Maj. Walthall is steadily working, both in compiling & copying, as well as in corresponding with those who can furnish "reports" &c. &c.

We were told long ago that of making books there was no end. I am making the first experiment in that manufacture and am very desirous to bring it to an end.

Unanticipated obstructions have retarded the progress of the work, already beyond the period at which I expected to close my part of the undertaking.

WITH SINCERE REGARD & ESTEEM
I AM FAITHFULLY
JEFFERSON DAVIS

To W. T. Walthall (JDC)

NEW ORLEANS, LOUISIANA, JULY 4, 1879

MY DEAR FRIEND,

The dreaded event has occurred. Mrs. Dorsey ceased to breathe about 4 o'clock A.M.[*] She was known to be dying early in the night. With labored breathing but otherwise painlessly she passed the night. She had been for some days expecting death, was resigned, calm and hopeful.

[*] Sarah Ellis Dorsey, friend and benefactress of JD; she owned Beauvoir and bequeathed it to him.

She said she was at peace with the world, and feared not to meet her God. She took the communion and hopefully looked beyond this life to a better state. She was pleased to receive your message and sent loving remembrance to your family, and self.

After she was unable to converse, her mind remained entirely clear and composed. In repeating to her the beatitude Blessed are the pure in heart for they shall see God, she responded by repeated motion of the head.

You know more than most others how self sacrificing she was, how noble in sentiment, how grand in intellect, but you cannot know how deeply grateful I am to her for years of unvarying kindness & service & therefore cannot realize how sorrowfully I feel her loss.

We leave tomorrow evening on the packet for Natches, after the interment I shall return without delay.

You will I know regard it as a labor of love, and it will also be a favor to me, if you will write an obituary notice for the Sea Shore Gazette and for any other papers you may choose.

Please give my cordial regards to each of your household and believe me

FAITHFULLY
JEFFERSON DAVIS.

To Crafts J. Wright (LAM)

BEAUVOIR, MISSISSIPPI, AUGUST 30, 1879

MY DEAR CRAFTS,

Yours of the 26th has been this day received. When your previous letter arrived I was too ill to acknowledge it.

The slips enclosed exhibit a malignity only equalled by their mendacity. I did not forward your petition but wrote to you that I thought a passage in it might be rendered more clear, as you may remember. In writing to several Southern men I did use substantially the language said to have been *endorsed* on your petition. The brute who could make of the sentiment matter for complaining reproach must have been rendered as blind by his malice as a rattle snake by it's poison in August.

Your "Tribune" is stolidly capable of any virulence, which human depravity could sink to. Whether they who have to act on your case are mean enough to be affected by my advocacy of you, so as to turn against you for that reason has to be seen. I am doubtful, because I remember when the south adopted *Greely* who had been the apostle of the negrophobists alias abolitionists, they thereupon and as it seemed therefore dropped him, as an Ephraim gone over to false gods.*

I hope that despite the shabby dogs of your section that your eyes may not be closed before you have seen the spirit of justice in the seat of power, and gentlemen where low bred money seeking knaves have unfortunately been. I trust it may be my good fortune to have a visit from you. Not claiming that all of our people are as good as they ought to be, I believe they are such as would have suited you, and such as you would feel to be *your* brethren now.

I am living quietly and have no desire to return to the vulgar scramble of the present state of politics. Public life never had any other charm for me than the hope it offered of being useful in a sense as broad as our ocean bound territory; the slips you sent show how futile that hope would be to me now. I do not desire, nor intend "to go to Washington." May God open the eyes of the people so that they may before it is too late, preserve the Liberty and local self government their Father's of the Revolution secured, and left as a legacy to their posterity. With love to your Wife and children I am ever your friend

JEFFERSON DAVIS

---

* Horace Greeley, editor of the *New York Tribune* and Democratic–Liberal Republican party candidate for president in 1872.

To R. C. Holland (JDC)*

BEAUVOIR, MISSISSIPPI, JULY 25, 1881

MY DEAR SIR,—

Accept my kind thanks for your kind letter of the 28th ult. In reply to your inquiry I would say:

The States cannot be deprived of their reserved rights except by their own action in a general convention, such as formed by the Constitution.

As each State did by its own consent delegate certain powers and reserve the rest, so must each State grant any additional power as the only means by which it can be justly deprived of it.

Force may prevail over right, but cannot destroy truth.

The exercise of a power to coerce a State cannot give to that act constitutional authority, but it has been so acquiesced in, that the remedy of secession by an oppressed minority must be considered impracticable.

The South never asked for more than a fair construction of the Constitution as interpreted by the men who made it, and if in the future that can be secured we may be content, though we cannot surrender a right even while admitting our inability to maintain it.

I was much gratified by the expression of your opinion in regard to the past, and tender to you my sincere regards.

RESPECTFULLY AND TRULY YOURS,

JEFFERSON DAVIS.

* Professor at Roanoke College in Virginia and Confederate veteran.

To Mrs. John Dement (JDC)*

BEAUVOIR, MISSISSIPPI, FEBRUARY 4, 1883

MY DEAR FRIEND:

Of the many who will offer you condolence in your recent bereavement, there is not one who sympathizes more deeply with you than he who long years ago claimed the privilege of the sacred name of friend.

Widely and long we have been separated, but your image has not been dimmed by time and distance.

The gallantry and noble bearing of your deceased husband was known to all who, like myself, were on the frontier of Illinois during the campaign against Black Hawk, and from your brother, Augustus, and your friend, General Jones, I heard of him in after years.†

As your husband, he was to me the object of special interest, and it was a great gratification to me to learn that he was so worthy to be your life companion.

If you have preserved enough of the pleasant memories of one springtime to care for one who flitted with you over the flowers of youth's happy garden, it will give me sincere gratification to hear from you and to learn of the welfare of yourself and children.

With cordial regard for you and yours, and renewed assurance of my deep sympathy, I am ever,

FAITHFULLY YOUR FRIEND,
JEFFERSON DAVIS

---

* Friend of JD during his service as a young army officer.
† Black Hawk was a Sauk warrior who gave his name to a conflict with the U.S. Army—the Black Hawk War—in 1832.

Speech Before Mississippi Legislature in Jackson, Mississippi (JDC)

MARCH 10, 1884

FRIENDS AND BRETHREN OF MISSISSIPPI: In briefest terms, but with deepest feeling, permit me to return my thanks for the unexpected honor you have conferred on me. Away from the political sea, I have in my secluded home observed with intense interest all passing events, affecting the interest or honor of Mississippi, and have rejoiced to see in the diversification of labor and the development of new sources of prosperity and the increased facilities of public education, reason to hope for a future to our State more prosperous than any preceding era. The safety and honor of a Republic must rest upon the morality, intelligence and patriotism of the community.

We are now in a transition state, which is always a bad one, both in society and in nature. What is to be the result of the changes which may be anticipated it is not possible to forecast, but our people have shown such fortitude and have risen so grandly from the deep depression inflicted upon them, that it is fair to entertain bright hopes for the future. Sectional hate concentrating itself upon my devoted head, deprives me of the privileges accorded to others in the sweeping expression of "without distinction of race, color or previous condition," but it cannot deprive me of that which is nearest and dearest to my heart, the right to be a Mississippian, and it is with great gratification that I received this emphatic recognition of that right by the representatives of our people. Reared on the soil of Mississippi, the ambition of my boyhood was to do something which would redound to the honor and welfare of the State. The weight of many years admonishes me that my day for actual service has passed, yet the desire remains undiminished to see the people of Mississippi prosperous and happy and her fame not unlike the past, but gradually growing wider and brighter as years roll away.

'Tis been said that I should apply to the United States for a pardon, but repentance must precede the right of pardon, and I have not repented. Remembering as I must all which has been suffered, all which has been lost, disappointed hopes and crushed aspirations, yet I deliberately say, if it were to do over again, I would again do just as I did in 1861. No one is the arbiter of his own fate. The people of the Confederate States did more in proportion to their numbers and means than was ever achieved by any in the world's history. Fate decreed that they should be unsuccessful in the effort to maintain their claim to resume the grants made to the Federal Government. Our people have accepted the decree; it therefore behooves them, as they may, to promote the general welfare of the Union, to show to the world that hereafter, as heretofore, the patriotism of our people is not measured by lines of latitude and longitude, but is as broad as the obligations they have assumed and embraces the whole of our oceanbound domain. Let them leave to their children and children's children the grand example of never swerving from the path of duty, and preferring to return good for evil rather than to cherish the unmanly feeling of revenge. But never question or teach your children to desecrate the memory of the dead by admitting that their brothers were wrong in the effort to maintain the sovereignty, freedom and independence which was their inalienable birthright—remembering that the coming generations are the children of the heroic mothers whose devotion to our cause in its darkest hour sustained the strong and strengthened the weak, I cannot believe that the cause for which our sacrifices were made can ever be lost, but rather hope that those who now deny the justice of our asserted claims will learn from experience that the fathers builded wisely and the Constitution should be constructed according to the commentaries of the men who made it.

It having been previously understood that I would not attempt to do more than to return my thanks, which are far deeper than it would be possible for me to express, I will now, Senators and Representatives, and to you ladies and gentlemen, who have honored me by your attendance, bid you an affectionate, and it may be, a last farewell.

To George C. Hodges (JMH)[*]

BEAUVOIR, MISSISSIPPI, JUNE 19, 1884

MY DEAR SIR

The very kind terms of your letter and the purpose of your enquiry do not permit me to adhere to my usual practice of abstaining from active participation in the political questions of the day. Briefly then I respond.

The Democratic party had its origin in resistance to latitudinarian construction of the Constitution by which powers not delegated were usurped. It is a well-known historical fact that the Constitution could not have been ratified but for the confident expectation of the adoption of the 10th Amendment, thereby & in many other ways was manifested the purpose of the States when they formed the more perfect union was to appoint an agent for enumerated objects a[nd] to limit his powers to the grants which they expressly made. Unless therefore there can be found among the enumerated powers a grant to take money out of the Treasury & apply it to the support of schools, an act making such an appropriation must be unconstitutional and be in the nature of those usurpations which caused the political revolution of 1800 and out of which arose the Democratic party. The argument which has been used to justify the educational bill to which you refer is an instance of the general fact that one false step necessitates another. The unauthorized emancipation of the slaves of the South & the bestowal of the franchise upon the emancipated Negro, each alike inexcusable whether regarded as a matter of right or of policy, is now the basis of the argument that these incompetent suffragans must be educated.

With such a record, may we not expect the Federal agent for the preservation of its own ill gotten power, will prescribe the character of the education, see to it that the teachers are fit instruments for the work; & with school books manufactured for the purpose, poison the

---

[*] South Carolinian who had written to JD asking his opinion in regard to the Blair Bill, the first attempt to provide federal money for public education; it never passed Congress.

minds of the children to whom we were to transmit the legacy our Fathers left us.

RESPECTFULLY YOURS,
JEFFERSON DAVIS

To J. L Power (JDC)*

BEAUVOIR, MISSISSIPPI, JUNE 20, 1885

"DEAR SIR,—

Among the less-informed persons at the North there exists an opinion that the negro slave at the South was a mere chattel, having neither rights nor immunities protected by law or public opinion. Southern men knew such was not the case, and others desiring to know could readily learn the fact. On that error the lauded story of "Uncle Tom's Cabin" was founded, but it is strange that a utilitarian and shrewd people did not ask why a slave, especially valuable, was the object of privation and abuse? Had it been a horse they would have been better able to judge, and would most probably have rejected the story for its improbability. Many attempts have been made to evade and misrepresent the exhaustive opinion of Chief-Justice Taney in the "Dred Scott" case, but it remains unanswered.

From the statement in regard to Fort Sumter, a child might suppose that a foreign army had attacked the United States—certainly could not learn that the State of South Carolina was merely seeking possession of a fort on her own soil, and claiming that her grant of the site had become void.

The tyrant's plea of necessity to excuse despotic usurpation is offered for the unconstitutional act of emancipation, and the poor resort to prejudice is invoked in the use of the epithet "rebellion"—a word inapplicable to States generally, and most especially so to the sovereign members of a voluntary union. But, alas for their ancient prestige, they have even lost the plural reference they had in the

---

* Mississippi newspaper publisher and Confederate veteran.

Constitution, and seem so small to this utilizing tuition as to be described by the neutral pronoun "it"! Such language would be appropriate to an imperial Government, which in absorbing territories required the subjected inhabitants to swear allegiance to it.

Ignorance and artifice have combined so to misrepresent the matter of official oaths in the United States that it may be well to give the question more than a passing notice. When the "sovereign, independent States of America," formed a constitutional compact of union it was provided in the sixth article thereof that the officers "of the United States and of the several States shall be bound by oath or affirmation to support this Constitution," and by the law of June 1, 1789, the form of the required oath was prescribed as follows: "I, A B, do solemnly swear or affirm (as the case may be) that I will support the Constitution of the United States."

That was the oath. The obligation was to support the Constitution. It created no new obligation, for the citizen already owed allegiance to his respective State, and through her to the Union of which she was a member. The conclusion is unavoidable that those who did not support, but did not violate the Constitution, were they who broke their official oaths. The General Government had only the powers delegated to it by the States. The power to coerce a State was not given, but emphatically refused. Therefore, to invade a State, to overthrow its government by force of arms, was a palpable violation of the Constitution, which officers had sworn to support, and thus to levy war against States which the Federal officers claimed to be, notwithstanding their ordinances of secession, still in the Union, was the treason defined in the third section of the third article of the Constitution, the only treason recognized by the fundamental law of the United States.

When our forefathers assumed for the several States they represented a separate and equal station among the powers of the earth, the central idea around which their political institutions were grouped was that sovereignty belonged to the people, inherent and inalienable; therefore, that governments were their agents, instituted to secure their rights, and "deriving their just powers from the consent of the governed, whence they draw the corollary that whenever any form of government becomes destructive of these ends it is the right of the people to alter or abolish it," etc. What was meant by the word "people" in this connection is manifest from the circumstances. It could only authoritatively refer to the distinct communities who, each for itself, joined in the declaration and in the concurrent act of separation from the government of Great Britain.

By all that is revered in the memory of our Revolutionary sires, and sacred in the principles they established, let not the children of the United States be taught that our Federal Government is sovereign; that our sires, after having, by a long and bloody war, won community-independence, used the power, not for the end sought, but to transfer their allegiance, and by oath or otherwise bind their posterity to be the subjects of another government, from which they could only free themselves by force of arms.

RESPECTFULLY,
JEFFERSON DAVIS.

To Edward Bailey (JDC)[*]

BEAUVOIR, MISSISSIPPI, JANUARY 15, 1886
DEAR SIR,

I have this evening received your letter of the 8th Inst. and the Christian spirit in which you write leads me to reply hoping that I may remove what I think is a misconception of my position. I certainly did not mean that the war was not to me, a cause of regret. I labored before its inception with all the power I possessed, as my speeches in the U.S. Senate and my action on a select Committee in Jan. 1861, clearly prove, to avert, if practicable, the catastrophe of war. I believed then, and do now, that the states possessed sovereignty and therefore had a right to withdraw from any league into which any of them had entered. My opinion was that secession would, but should not, produce war. When Mississippi passed her ordinance of secession, I felt I no longer had any right to remain in the Senate as her representative & therefore withdrew. As a citizen of Missi. I owed her my

[*] Baptist minister in Philadelphia, Pennsylvania.

allegiance and went home to serve the State as her needs might require. When the General Govt. in violation of the Constitution attempted to coerce the State, I served her as best I might. On her part it was a war of defense, the only kind of war which I believed justified by Man's duty to his Fellow and to his God.

Now my dear Sir with this introduction you will need no argument to show you that with my convictions unchanged, 1 could not repent for all I had done, or attempted to do for the maintenance of the Constitutional and natural rights of the State, to whom my first duty was due, under the limitations of Man's obligations to his Maker.

If I had desired war, had provoked war, had not endeavored after the Confederacy was organized, by a commission to find a peaceful solution of all pending issues, then I should have much cause to repent of sins of commission and omission, but your reading has no doubt taught you that the facts are otherwise. In my book, entitled "Rise and Fall of the Confederate Government" I have more fully than it would be possible to do in a letter, presented my view of the whole subject. If suffering for the cause I espoused could produce repentance, I have surely borne enough for that end, but martyrs have gloried in their faith when yielding up their lives for its assertion and if I mistake not your character, you would scorn the man who recanted and called it repentance. You seem impressed by my assertion in this connection, that if it were to do over again I would do as I have done. Surely Sir, believing myself to have been right you would not have me to say or to feel otherwise Looking beyond the prejudice and malice of men, I trust my case to Him who knoweth the hearts of men and, "Doeth all things well."

Accept my thanks for your prayers for I am not self-righteous enough to believe I do not need them and believe me Sir,

VERY RESPECTFULLY YOURS,
JEFFERSON DAVIS.

To F. R. Lubbock (JDC)*

MY DEAR FRIEND:

Yours of the 12th inst., with its inclosures, has been received. I have hitherto declined to answer any of the many inquiries made for my opinion on the Constitutional Amendment, now pending in Texas. My reason for not replying was an unwillingness to enter into a controversy in which my friends in Texas stood arrayed against each other. In departing from the rule heretofore observed, I trust that it will not be an unwarrantable intrusion.

Reared in the creed of Democracy, my faith in its tenets has grown with its growth, and I adhere to the maxim that "The world is governed too much."

When our fathers achieved their independence, the cornerstone of the government they constructed was individual liberty, and the social organizations they established were not for the surrender, but for the protection of natural rights. For this, governments were established, deriving their just powers from the consent of the governed. This was not to subject themselves to the will of the majority, as appears from the fact that each community inserted in its fundamental law a bill of rights to guard the inalienable privileges of the individual.

There was, then, a two-fold purpose in government: protection, and prevention against trespass by the strong upon the weak, the many on the few.

The world had long suffered from the oppressions of government under the pretext of ruling by divine right and excusing the invasion into private and domestic affairs on the plea of paternal care for the morals and good order of the people.

Our sires rejected all such pretensions, their system being: Government by the people for the people, and resting on the basis of these general propositions, I will briefly answer the inquiry in regard to the Prohibition Amendment at issue.

---

* Former JD aide and former governor of Texas.

"Be ye temperate in all things" was a wise injunction, and would apply to intolerance as well as to drunkenness. That the intemperate use of intoxicating liquors is an evil, few, if any, would deny. That it is the root of many social disorders is conceded; but then, the question arises, what is the appropriate remedy, and what the present necessity? To destroy individual liberty and moral responsibility would be to eradicate one evil by the substitution of another, which it is submitted would be more fatal than that for which it was offered as a remedy. The abuse, and not the use, of stimulants, it must be confessed, is the evil to be remedied. Then it clearly follows that action should clearly be directed against the abuse rather than the use. If drunkenness be the cause of disorder and crime, why not pronounce drunkenness itself to be a crime and attach to it proper and adequate penalties. If it be objected that the penalties could not be enforced, that is an admission that popular opinion would be opposed to the law; but if it be true that juries could not be empannelled who would convict so degraded a criminal as a drunkard, it necessarily follows that a statutory prohibition against the sale and use of intoxicants would be a dead letter.

The next branch of the inquiry is as to the present necessity.

I might appeal to men not as old as myself to sustain the assertion that the convivial use of intoxicants, and the occurrence of drunkenness had become less frequent within the last twenty years than it was before. The refining influence of education and Christianity may be credited with this result. Why not allow these blessed handmaidens of virtue and morality to continue unembarrassed in their civilizing work. The parties to this discussion in your State have no doubt brought forward the statistical facts in regard to the effect produced in other States by this effort to control morals by legislation, and I will not encumber this letter by any reference to those facts.

You have already provision for local prohibition. If it has proved the wooden horse in which a disguised enemy to State sovereignty as the guardian of individual liberty was introduced, then let it be a warning that the progressive march would probably be from village to State and from State to United States.

A governmental supervision and paternity, instead of the liberty the heroes of 1776 left as a legacy to their posterity. Impelled by the affection and gratitude, I feel for the people of Texas, and the belief that a great question of American policy is involved in the issue you have before you, the silence I had hoped to observe has been broken. If the utterance shall avail anything for good, it will compensate me for the objurgations with which I shall doubtless be pursued by the followers of the popularism of the day. I hope the many who have addressed me letters of inquiry on the subject will accept this as an answer, though somewhat long delayed.

FAITHFULLY YOURS,
(SIGNED) JEFFERSON DAVIS.

Remarks in Mississippi City, Mississippi (JDC)*

[UNDATED], 1888

Mr. Chairman and Fellow Citizens: Ah, pardon me, the laws of the United States no longer permit me to designate you as fellow citizens, but I am thankful that I may address you as my friends. I feel no regret that I stand before you this afternoon a man without a country, for my ambition lies buried in the grave of the Confederacy. There has been consigned not only my ambition, but the dogmas upon which that Government was based. The faces I see before me are those of young men; had I not known this I would not have appeared before you. Men in whose hands the destinies of our Southland lie, for love of her I break my silence, to speak to you a few words of respectful admonition. The past is dead; let it bury its dead, its hopes and its aspirations; before you lies the future—a future full of golden promise; a future of expanding national glory, before which all the world shall stand amazed. Let me beseech you to lay aside all rancor, all bitter sectional feeling, and to make your places in the ranks of those who will bring about a consummation devoutly to be wished—a reunited country.

* Final public address.

To James H. Jones (NC)*

MR. JAMES H. JONES,

I was very glad to receive your letter with its assurances of kind remembrance, and it gave pleasure not only to me, but also to my Daughter who was an infant when you last saw her. Mrs. Davis you know was always your particular friend.

We have all rejoiced when we have heard of your honorable prosperity & have felt that it was what was due to your integrity & fidelity. The many years which have come & gone since we parted have in no wise diminished my regard for you and interest in your welfare. On Xmas day I mailed to you the last photograph taken of me in order that you might see me as I now am. With the best wishes of myself, Mrs. Davis and all my household I am

TRULY YOUR FRIEND
JEFFERSON DAVIS

To A. J. Halbert (JDC)†

BEAUVOIR, MISSISSIPPI, JUNE 8, 1889
MY DEAR SIR.

Please accept my thanks for your kind attention in sending to me the Columbus Dispatch containing the history of the Prairie Guards Co. 11th Missi. C.S.A.

It is very desirable that such full record of the services of every company should be made & preserved for the use of the future historian & I am grateful to Mr. Love for the performance of this task in the case of the Prairie Guards. The paragraph with which he closes his historical sketch is beautiful & peculiarly gratifying. Mississippi never

An African-American who was a freeman before 1861 and became a wartime servant of JD. He had a successful business and political career in Raleigh, North Carolina, in the 1870s and 1880s. Jones had written JD a warm letter detailing his career for the previous decade and a half.
† Mississippian and Confederate veteran.

failed in the hour of trial to do her full duty and has not received the deserved recognition. The services of our people were illustrious at Fredericksburg at Gettysburg at Petersburg & elsewhere. In the east as well as many places in the west. It is only by such exact accounts as may be given by the survivors of each organization, that the future historian will be able to do justice to those who staked all & lost all save honor in defence of their inherited unalienable rights. Much has been written to cast unjust censure upon the South for the treatment of prisoners. Our people are not generally writers but brave & generous & such men never illtreat the helpless. It would be a desirable service if your historian would add, from the testimony of survivors the "dark page" to which he refers.

Again thanking you for your kind attention I am

YOURS FAITHFULLY,
JEFFERSON DAVIS.

To the North Carolina Centennial Invitation Committee (JDC)

BEAUVOIR, OCTOBER 30, 1889

GENTLEMEN:

Your letter inviting me to attend North Carolina's Centennial, to be held at Fayetteville on the 21st of November next, was duly received; but this acknowledgement has been delayed under the hope that an improvement in my health would enable me to be present as invited. As the time approaches I find that cherished hope unrealized, and that I must regretfully confess my ability to join you in the commemorative celebration.

. . .

It is to be remembered that the articles of Confederation for the "United States of America" declared that "the union shall be perpetual," and that no alteration should be made in the said articles unless it should be "confirmed by the legislature of every State." True to her creed of State sovereignty, North Carolina recognized the power of such States as chose to do so to withdraw from the Union, and, by the same token, her own unqualified right to decide whether or not she would subscribe to the proposed compact for a more perfect union, and from which, it is to be observed, the declaration for perpetuity was omitted. In the hard school of experience she had learned the danger to popular liberty from a government which could claim to be the final judge of its own powers.

She had fought a long and devastating war for State independence, and was not willing to put in jeopardy the priceless jewel she had gained. After a careful examination, it was concluded that the proposed Constitution did not sufficiently guard against usurpation by the usual resort to implication of powers not expressly granted, and she declined to act upon the general assurance that the deficiency would soon be supplied by the needful amendments. In the meantime, State after State had acceded to the new Union, until the requisite number had been obtained for the establishment of the "Constitution between the States so ratifying the same."

With characteristic self reliance North Carolina confronted the prospect of isolation, and calmly resolved, if so it must be, to stand alone rather than subject to hazard her most prized possession, *Community Independence.*

Confiding in the security offered by the first ten Amendments to the Constitution, especially the 9th and 10th of the series, North Carolina voluntarily acceded to the new Union. The 10th Amendment restricted the functions of the Federal Government to the exercise of the powers delegated to it by the States, all of which were especially stipulated.

Beyond that limit nothing could be done rightfully. If covertly done, under color of law, or by reckless usurpation of an extraneous majority, which, feeling power, should disregard right, had the State no peaceful remedy? Could she, as a State in a Confederation the bedrock of which is the consent of its members, be bound by a compact which others broke to her injury? Had her reserved rights no other than a paper barrier to protect them against invasion?

Surely the heroic patriots and wise statesmen of North Carolina, by their sacrifices, utterances and deeds, have shown what, their answer would have been to these questions, if they had been asked on the day when in convention they ratified the amended Constitution of the

United States. Her exceptional delay in ratification marks her vigilant care for rights she had so early asserted and so steadily maintained. Of her it may be said, as it was of Sir Walter Scott in his youth, that she was "always the first in a row and the last out of it."

...

Devotion to principle, self-reliance and inflexible adherence to resolution when adopted, accompanied by conservative caution, were the characteristics displayed by North Carolina in both her colonial and State history. All these qualities were exemplified in her action on the day of the anniversary which you commemorate. If there be any, not likely to be found with you, but possibly elsewhere, who shall ask: "How, then, could North Carolina consistently enact her ordinance of secession in 1861?" he is referred to the Declaration of Independence of 1776; to the Articles of Confederation of 1777, for a perpetual union of the States, and a secession of States from the union so established: to the treaty of 1783, recognizing the independence of the States severally and distinctively; to the Constitution of the United States, with its first ten amendments: to the time-honored resolutions of 1798–'99:——that from these, one and all, he may learn that the State, having won her independence by heavy sacrifices, had never surrendered it, nor had ever attempted to delegate the inalienable rights of the people.

How gallantly her sons bore themselves in the War Between The States the lists of the killed and wounded testify. She gave them, a sacrificial offering on the altar of the liberties their fathers had won and left as an inheritance to their posterity. Many sleep far from the land of their nativity. Peace to their ashes. Honor to their memory and the mother who bore them.

FAITHFULLY,
JEFFERSON DAVIS

To Alice Evelyn Desmaris (JDC)[*]

BRIERFIELD, MISSISSIPPI, NOVEMBER 13, 1889

May all your paths be peaceful and pleasant, charged with the best fruit, the doing good to others.

FAITHFULLY,
JEFFERSON DAVIS

[*] Daughter of an overseer at Brierfield; these are the last words JD ever wrote.

INDEX

"Created equal" explained, 193

— unconquerable heart, 365 (title of Felicity Allen's biography 1999)

A Note on the Type

The principal text of this Modern Library edition
was set in a digitized version of Janson, a typeface that
dates from about 1690 and was cut by Nicholas Kis,
a Hungarian working in Amsterdam. The original matrices have
survived and are held by the Stempel foundry in Germany.
Hermann Zapf redesigned some of the weights and sizes for
Stempel, basing his revisions on the original design.

MODERN LIBRARY IS ONLINE AT
WWW.MODERNLIBRARY.COM

MODERN LIBRARY ONLINE IS YOUR GUIDE
TO CLASSIC LITERATURE ON THE WEB

THE MODERN LIBRARY E-NEWSLETTER

Our free e-mail newsletter is sent to subscribers, and features sample chapters, interviews with and essays by our authors, upcoming books, special promotions, announcements, and news.

To subscribe to the Modern Library e-newsletter, send a blank e-mail to: **sub_modernlibrary@info.randomhouse.com** or visit **www.modernlibrary.com**

THE MODERN LIBRARY WEBSITE

Check out the Modern Library website at
www.modernlibrary.com for:

- The Modern Library e-newsletter
- A list of our current and upcoming titles and series
- Reading Group Guides and exclusive author spotlights
- Special features with information on the classics and other paperback series
- Excerpts from new releases and other titles
- A list of our e-books and information on where to buy them
- The Modern Library Editorial Board's 100 Best Novels and 100 Best Nonfiction Books of the Twentieth Century written in the English language
- News and announcements

Questions? E-mail us at **modernlibrary@randomhouse.com**
For questions about examination or desk copies, please visit
the Random House Academic Resources site at
www.randomhouse.com/academic